FUNDAMENTAL EXISTENTIALISM

(the emotional blackmail of existence.)

4 collections in one volume.

1/ VIEWED WITH SUSPICION.

2/ DOWN IN ONE.

3/THE MEANING OF LIFE.

4/EXISTENTIALISM.

VIEWED WITH SUSPICION.

(Or: THE NEED TO BE SEEN TO BE DOING SOMTHING IN BETWEEN BEING BORN AND DYING.)

A collection of recently typed up work from the infamously obscure 'poet' and observer of life as he knows it, and whose catchphrase is: 'EACH DAY I DIE A THOUSAND TIMES BECAUSE OF THE FUTILITY OF EVERYTHING'. I'm only joking really, life's a gas, methane mostly in my case).

This collection is dedicated to me, for keeping myself alive against massive provocation not too.

Not for the overly squeamish, or slavishly politically correct.

KING OF THE PARANOIDS.

Sometimes, inside myself, I feel like a King, or a living God. I hold these feelings in check by telling myself I'm suffering from delusions of grandeur, a typical paranoid symptom, and I'm symptomatically paranoid. Not too severely, but enough for it to cause me problems in my personal life. I think delusions of grandeur are the only saving grace of this debilitating illness. It intrigues me to ponder on what type of ' monarch' I would make, after all, the reincarnated, reconstituted King Arthur Pen Dragon hasn't cut much of a dash or swathe outside of Somerset or wherever it is he's based. I might be totally corrupted by absolute power, and end up like Vlad the Impaler, or Gille de Rais, ('The most evil man in history'…or one of them), or some of the more lurid of the ancient roman emperors; it seems that all tyrants and dictators are predisposed to madness.
At my worse I could be on a par with Hitler, at the other extreme, I could envisage myself as a first generation hippy version of King Arthur, a sort of psychedelic (with magic powers) messiah and womaniser, and legitimise hallucinogenic drugs, light shows, and acid rock. But the Arthurian version is just a desire to relive my long - dead youth more successfully than I did the first time round. There are days now when I feel almost insane from the pressures of too much failure, and attendant emotional distress. The blackness of death seeps into the brain like an infusion of tarry black ink, or at least I perceive it will one day.
I can't think of a better way to die than in an alcoholic stupor, it has to be a thousand times more preferable to waking up from one and having to nurse your sanity back to health. Excessive alcohol intake is a depressant, and I am a depressive; yet when I drink, I drink to excess to get drunk, I must be a masochist as well. The fragrance of incense and the mind expanding effects of hashish would be a lot less toxic to the mind and body than ethynol alcohol, and in the right circumstances, a lot more rewarding too.
'Lame Barbara Cartwheel', and the plots of her 723 'novels' went round and round as limply as the records she made; one billion pulp fiction-buying punters CAN be wrong, very, very wrong! Enid Blyton? I've had a shiner or two in my time, but the fabled '69er' has always eluded me, and that hurts really deeply, even steeply, 'I wondered lonely as a bad smell in a HELL of society's making', is how I feel now, on the rare occasions when I go out. The isolation clings round me like a cold clammy shroud; and travelling on awful,

5

depressing buses really emphasises my total aloneness. It's not quite as bad on trains, but there's not much in it. As Samuel Beckett said in one of his horrible books: 'I can't go on I must go on'.

....

15/6/00.
ITV, 9.45 pm, 'PLEASURE ISLAND'. 'More unsavoury prancing about at the Jamaican beach resort, where rebels without a clue go to stare nervously at each other's privates'. (THE SUN TV guide). Now that's what I call good descriptive 'blurb' writing, I doubt if I could ever put it so succinctly.
19/6/00. A couple of 'lonely hearts' ads out of the local paper this week, I think they're mildly amusing and intriguing: 'Single? Lonely? Join hundreds in White Rose Singles Directory, West York's largest agency'. And: 'Alone? Join Perfect Harmony, large list, local people'.
Blessedly fortunate are those who meet a shagging partner at work, or on a night out. I hate the whole 'singles' rat race, with its £1.00 a minute phone calls or £3.00 to reply to a box number. I'm better off remaining as I am until I become too psychotic to function, I'm past caring whether I end up in a loony bin; 'I shouldn't be here you know, I've done nothing wrong, they were too provocatively dressed...' Only the facially challenged know the way I feel tonight as I spend another night in on my own, attended by bad guts and a twinge in my right testicle.
Ban the bomb? Ban the 'bummers' I say. Human madness is killing the world, as well as me. There's no more poignant pain than when your ripped and torn emotions bleed into your stomach and set off a chain reaction of sadness; this happens to me when I think too much about the last woman I loved, who casually left me to die alone. I seem to think I'm having a more abysmal life than Vincent van Gogh, and am being groomed for posthumous fame and celebrity; to be used and abused by the same cynical system that he hated, and so do I. One way to rob my accursed fate of what it might be expecting, would be to destroy all my writings before I die, to have a ceremonial bonfire over a few brandies and a good cigar. Of course, I'll have to be diagnosed with a terminal illness first so I can nerve myself up to do it; if I die suddenly it will be a non-starter, and my stuff will never see the light of day anyway.

25/6/00. THE ONE-EYED KING is someone to be reckoned with, in this country of the largely spiritually blind...Well, he should be, but he's not really, (it is a miserable Monday). It's occurred to me lately that I'm only a King inside my own castle, outside I'm totally at the mercy of any clod who wants to take a pop at me, i.e., a snide remark, actual violence, or the hideous roar of the traffic; outside of my house I am the stumbling blind man.

I read something in THE SUN the other day about the very transient Liverpool girl group: 'ATOMIC KITTEN', having all their knickers stolen (presumably not the ones they were wearing, but the pairs lying about in their hotel rooms) while they were on tour in Japan, the 'Japs' have a thing abut buying adolescent girls used pants, so I've come up with this potential headline, NIFTY NIPONESE KNICKER SNIFFING NICKERS, NICK MINOR POP SENSATIONS, ATOMIC KITTEN'S NIFFY KNICKS FOR KICKS!!! (It's better than glue sniffing man, tho' the smell's similar to the glue from melted down horse and fish bones, or so I've been led to believe, never actually having smelt any of these prized garments). (Atomic Kitten have gone on to have a number one hit this year, 2001, it stayed there for 4 weeks, I didn't like it.)

THE NEW MORALITY.

The new morality is: that there's no morality anymore, only sexual hypocrisy and total sexual irresponsibility, and mind warping sexual inadequacy, and repression. A mass-murdering maniac slaughtered his wife and four children in South Wales last week, and then sent his soul back to Hell by hanging his physical self. It's claimed he was experiencing ' business difficulties'; the dirty, demented piece of scum must have assumed that his family were his to dispose of as liabilities. If it was down to me he'd be put in the ground in a vertical position with the head pointing downwards, in an unmarked grave in an unmarked spot somewhere out in the wilds; he should be classified as a mass murdering monster.

'Spider' Nugent, the almost-nearly-really man, the boring old hippy, has been deleted from 'Coronation Street'; he'll be missed for about 5 minutes. Poor old Sada, (pronounced as in 'fuckerarder'), the boring, new age poser, has been the first to be publicly voted out of the 'BIG BROTHER' TV survival 'game show'; she should be walking over the exit bridge of, 'Why have the bastards got it in for me and not Caroline?' (A brummy slapper), right now. But hey, she's a writer, so now she'll have something to write about. (The 2001 version of 'BB' has just got under way, 26/5/01. The cynical bastards have put the cost of calls to vote people out up to 25p; it was only 10p

last year. I'm sticking with 'SURVUVOR' on ITV, there's no viewer required input needed, the contestants eliminate each other).
The violent onrush of death, as all too vividly displayed in this week's Concorde crash; the absolute terror experienced by the doomed passengers would be a psycho's ultimate orgasm, all those innocent souls getting instantly 'French fried'. (A similar horrific incident happened at the weekend, 24/5/01, at a Jewish wedding in Jerusalem; over a hundred guests were celebrating and dancing on the top floor of a recently constructed building, when the floor gave way beneath them, sending them plummeting 30 feet below. 24 were killed. The amazing thing was, the whole incident was videoed by a guest, and they showed it us on the news, it was a real shock to see the faces disappearing in front of you, followed shortly afterwards by a huge cloud of dust, and when that cleared a huge hole in the floor where only moments earlier a party had been going on. I reckon that short piece of video death footage will become as famous as the image of blood spurting out of the back of J.F.K.'s head when he was assassinated 38 years ago).

13 Bengal tigers, (practically the whole global population), have died recently in a 'zoo' in India, from a mysterious illness, Herons are also mysteriously dying in this country, and even the humble water vole is facing extinction here, under threat from escaped mink, among other threats.

I've just watched THE REBEL again, starring Tony Hancock, prophetic, man, prophetic.

There's a 'man' on the radio talking about the 'bender agenda', (copyright: Phil Fletcher). Giving them equal status to us heterosexuals, (I'm 95% certain I am normal, just vastly out of practice). My 'agender' for them would be that they 'SHUT THE FUCK UP OR ELSE', and that they keep out of public shithouses; they're bad enough as it is.
(Unless Alzheimer's, or schizophrenia seeps in), a snog in a bog! (I don't understand myself here, PLF, 20/4/06). When you've cum, you feel like scum; ultra violet, ultra violence. (I'm not talking from personal experience here). The brain remains the same, even when the rest of the body is deteriorating at a rapid rate; well mine does anyway.
In the year 2000ad, in England, we have a situation where the Prime Minister's 16-year-old son can be found lying drunk and incapable, in Leicester Square, and even more recently, a world famous classical

pianist was faced with a life threatening confrontation with muggers, only hours after entertaining 'royalty'.

As it was, he almost had his fingers ruined in a knife attack. It took the Tories 18 years to really piss the populace off, it's looking more and more like Tony Blair's 'new' Labour will achieve this odious honour in the relatively short space of 4.5 years. I hope they get one more term in office, even if with a much reduced majority. 29/5/01,

With 8 days to go before this year's general election it's looking likely that Labour will win, there could be a last minute swing to the 'gargoyle's party over Europe, (William Hague), and that would mean, 'hang 'em high', vertically challenged, Anne Widdicombe taking over from 'man of straw' Jack . Here endeth this particular chapter inspired by events that took place last year (2000AD).

....

FRIVOLITY (A 'fromage' to The Hourglass Writers Group, which disappeared up its own fundament a long time ago.)

We disappear, then reappear, once a fortnight, to fight the good literary fight with our literary chums.

Bums on hard seats for a 2-hour stint is no deterrent, I'm the knight Errant from Todmorden, the place that time and progress have forgotten.

Sometimes the atmosphere is strained, pained expressions go around if someone has overstepped the mark of 'good taste', and laid waste to values someone else held dear. I often quake with fear at the prospect of reading out loud, a cloud of foreboding hovering above my head.

But then I'll let rip, wishing everyone else was dead who had more luck than me, in the least nice literary way I can think of.

Chekhov would know what I mean, I'm a SPLEEN MACHINE! A grumpy old tiger on heat, hampered by boxing gloves on his feet, preventing him from reaching his goal. On the whole, I'd like to pull it off, a spectacular artistic success that is, and become the ageing whiz kid of the poetic world, blowing all the opposition away, including John Cooper Clarke.

Earning large wads of pay every time I parked my arse on a stool, looking down the cleavage of cool young chicks who're gazing up with adulation at me. Which one will I choose for breakfast, dinner and tea, to lock away in my Bluebeard's aviary of literary S&M?

I'll pull the wings off them and then send them to work in 'WOOLWORTHS' to gain some real life experience of working for me.

HIGH PLAINS DRIFTER.

(Or 'TUMESENCE', or 'A LONGED FOR END TO MEPHITIS'.)

Tumescence is the essence of life in my book, you can't beat a good fuck within a loving relationship.
It's finding the loving relationship that's so hard to do, I'd love to find it with you.
But no doubt you'll say 'No!' and I'll have to go on existing in this pointless hell, the first level of much deeper ones still to come.
Who says you can only die once? I've died a thousand times because of rejection, each time resurrection is harder to achieve. I believe that loving should be fun and for mutual benefit; I've experienced little of either in my blighted life. With you as my 'wife', things might change,I could stop going round singing: 'PEOPLE ARE STRANGE' all the time, with emphasis on the line, 'Woman seem wicked when you're unwanted', (or should that be: 'look ugly'?), and " When you're strange, faces come out of the rain."
You have the power to end my pain, one whispered or shouted word from you and I could start to live again. It's as corny as blueberry pie and cream, but I don't care, I'm sick of looking in anger everywhere.
Alas, I don't hold out much hope, I think you might think I'm some kind of demon sent to haunt and taunt you, I'm just a big pussy cat really, I long to love you dearly.
The toothless old Mephistopheles.   Phil Fletcher.

....

THE ASCENDENCY OF THE ID.
OR 'ARE YOU LOOKING AT MY PINT YOU FUCKING BENDER?'

Every time I walk down the road, death on wheels hurtles past, within inches of my head, morons in murdering, high-powered wheelchairs, for the most part, spiritually dead.
Even on the pavement you need eyes in your arse or behind your ears; I almost got mowed down today by a self obsessed cretin on a bike, who had no right of way, on the wrong side of the thoroughfare. This all adds to my fears that the Id is in the ascendant; it's in the air. As more and more people cease to care about themselves, and anyone,
 or anything else, turning really ugly from the inside out, with voracious appetites to match; insatiable hunger for soulless sex on the Costa del Sol, with their genitalia lolling out of their thongs and bikini briefs. It gives me the same kind of grief that George Harrison felt when he wrote: 'WHILE MY GUITAR GENTLY WEEPS', 33 years ago.
Ah, but so what? Why should I care or give a damn? I never figured very highly in the great global plan, I'm the 21st century's totally unreconstructed man. I should try and get my kicks before everything runs out, and then, when I'm finally burnt out, and sick and tired of this old, bloated show, I'll destroy by fire these last vestiges of my existence, encountering some resistance from the Ego no doubt. Well, no need to worry, my self-destructive Id will win out.

From, A LIFE GONE UP IN SMOKE.

....

I DIED WITH A DREAM OF HAPPINESS ON MY MIND
FOR THE ONE I LOVE.

I died with a dream of happiness on my mind, perhaps it's just as well that I died before the dream had a chance to turn sour. She was a goddess, and I a mere mortal, badly flawed; though I loved her with a god-like intensity; she was heaven sent to me.
A harvest moon gets swallowed up by black clouds, leaving the cornfields and the reapers covered in a shroud of melancholy. They'll leave and return at dawn, still tired and aching, bolstered up by their

communal suffering, but the corn must be got in before the rain can flatten it or ergot get into it, and cause people to die insane.

When I was young, I was told by someone I wanted to love that I was only in love with love. I think this was said to confuse me and put me off my quest, it succeeded.

But now I know I'm in love with beauty, being convinced that I never had any. But I also know now that I can only be in love with quality and beauty, beauty is only skin deep on the coarse and the vulgar, they're only fit for shagging and leaving.

The moon's come back out now, and the reapers have gone home, but she's on the wane, already half eaten away, she'd only throw a very pale glow on the land, a poor sighted worker could cut someone's leg off scything in such poor light.

His looks veered from the depressingly plain to the decidedly ugly, depending on how the light was reflected off his magnified glasses lenses, he relied on a forceful personality to get by, it quite often wasn't enough.

He had no idea of how she saw him, I mean actually saw him. The only view he had of himself was his mirror image, which never tallied with any photos he had taken, especially passport ones; the price you had to pay for horror pic's!

....

LIGHT MY FARTS

'I know that it would be untrue, I know I would be a liar, if I was to say to you, you couldn't set my farts on fire, and make the room smell like a burning tyre'.

....

TAME BARBERER CARTLOAD

'Don't mention the word'fuck' in books; she swallowed a pile of bullshit before sitting down to compose, now she's decomposing slowly.

....

ANOTHER SATURDAY NIGHT AND I AINT WON THE LOTTERY (To the tune of Sam Cooke's 'ANOTHER SATURDAY NIGHT', also covered by Cat Stevens).

'Another Saturday night and I ain't won the lottery, another week and my fortune's not been made, how I wish I could just win the jackpot, then the tiger can be saved', (my brain's too numb to think of any other verses).
The ascetic principle that should be one for me: a long and unhappy life of controlled misery and austerity. I'd love to be in permanent control of my emotions, instead of the other way round. The pound in your pocket is worth a lot more than your heart ruling your head, I'm sick of waking up feeling worthless, and that I'd be better off dead. (28/8/00. Another blank, Bank holiday Monday, and I ain't got nobody' etc, etc.   Phil Fletcher.)
....
A homage to the unreconstructed male, long may he impale himself on his bluff and bluster, and long may his unwashed socks and 'undies' remain in a cluster.

....

THERES A SNAKE IN MY TOILET AND I NEED A POO!

There's a snake in my toilet and I need a poo!, Rather badly now I've just seen It's head swaying above the bowl, with it's long black tongue darting in and out.
I'd scream and shout but there's no one to hear, this hideous reptile has awoken my deepest fear. How did it get here? Leering at me over the rim; I've heard about this sort of thing happening, they come up

through the drains, searching for heat and light. Thank fuck I wasn't having a shite when it poked it's ugly head around the u bend, it might have gulped it down thinking it was a nice juicy frog. Once it tasted it was a 'chocolate log', it probably would have felt rally upset, and more determined to get me.

Let me tell you now, the urge to go is becoming extremely intense, overriding all sense and sensibility. I'm going to have to squat over the sink, my God! What a stink! Luckily it's mostly turned to liquid now, I can't get near the toilet paper, it's too near the snake that's starting to shake violently from side to side, a bit like a clubber in a dance trance. I think the smell's really turning it on, as if it's scented some putrid, decaying meat.

Oh no! That things launching itself off the toilet seat, and heading straight for the sink, landing with a horrid squishy splash!

I can get to the toilet paper now. Somehow I've got to get out past it's awful deaf head; hello! I think it's dead! Looks like my toxic waste droppings were too much for it's refined palate, nobody will believe this tale when I tell it.

'Snake Eyes' Phil Fletcher.

....
....
.

....

....

Lyplaurodon: a 150-ton, biological factory ship of flesh-eating death, moving without conscious thought.

PRE-METEORIC-HISTORY
('Meteoric' as in the theory that a huge meteor crashing into the Earth's surface, wiped out the dinosaurs).

You were some dark deity's most evil creation, dreamed up in the subterranean depths of nightmare, a mindless killing and eating machine, 150 tons of ferocious intent, the largest carnivore this planet has ever seen.

You could have devoured a whole Tyrannosaurus Rex for breakfast, and still have had enough room left for another.

You were an immense biological factory ship of death, hoovering everything up in your path, a diabolical creature without conscious thought; (how can anything function without conscious thought?). Lyplaurodon, you may have gone but your primal instincts live on in the human race; a species that far outranks you in its capacity for mindless slaughter. What we lack in size, we make up for with cunning and ferocity, and most of our actions are atrocities against nature.

Did this colossal monster become too successful a predator and exhaust its available food supply? And did it sink mindlessly back into the deep from whence it came? Or was it a victim of the meteor theory that is reckoned to have wiped out the dinosaur as a whole? We'll never truly know.

We are becoming too rapacious for the planet to sustain our ever-increasing numbers, ripping, tearing, plundering, blundering about with our assumption of supremacy over the powers of sustainable reproduction. Ultimate destruction will be the price of ignorance and superstition.

The sometimes, unnervingly prophetic Phil Fletcher.

....

PERNOD, LSD, AND ME.

As the plot reached it's climax in the film 'THE MISFITS', I was down on the desert floor with the tethered horses slowly being choked to death, and mentally screaming in sympathy with Marilyn Monroe, at the hypocrisy of these men she'd trusted. Her finest screen moment as far as I'm concerned; it burned a hole into my heightened state of consciousness. Thanks to the 'acid' I'd taken several hours earlier, I had 'surround sound' TV, years before it became widely available. Also that weird and enhanced night, Joe Orton's 'VISITOR ON THE STAIR' was on the TV as well; it made perfect sense to me. The only thing that filled me with a sense of unreality was the main evening news bulletin; I couldn't get my head round man's inhumanity to man, at all.

Thankfully, the acid wore off around midnight, the same time as the TV in those days, so I took myself off, in a purple haze, to bed. I don't remember much about the 'trip' I started off writing about, it wasn't the one where I thought I'd spat it out before it had time to take hold, and I had such a bad time 'going up', I thought I was dying, and set out on foot to the nearest casualty department, arriving at the hospital gates just as dawn was breaking; feeling so relieved to have got there that all my worries faded away. I went on to have quite a decent day, LSD-wise. And the best colours I ever had were on my first full trip in Manchester on a Saturday night, around 1969 or '70; the follies of youth! It could have been the death of me. All that I remember about the trip that inspired this piece's title, is being mesmerised by the glowing tip of a roll-up cigarette as I arced it from side to side in front of me. I seemed to see it in freeze frame time; a trail of orange red light like the tail of a comet. And I had some Pernod from somewhere, a quarter of a bottle left, turned milky white with water. I must have had some suitable music on low in my council bed-sit: 'DARK STAR' by the Grateful Dead perhaps, I always got off on that. And a scrambled line from a song on the first Leonard Cohen LP comes back to me, about a highway curling up like smoke above his shoulder, and 'I told you when I came I was a stranger'; which reminds me of the line : 'There's danger on the edge of town", from the immortal 'THE END' by 'THE DOORS'. And just like Bob Dylan's 'MR Tambourine Man', the last 30 years of my life have disappeared through the smoke-rings of my mind, leaving only the foggy ruins of time behind, but the essence of some beautiful learning curves linger on...and on.   The iridescent Phil Fletcher.

....

PERNOD, LSD, AND ME. (2)

I can't remember at what point in the evening I dropped the acid, it was 30 years ago when I was young and free.

It was probably on a Friday night at the art college disco, which I used to 'blag' my way into every week; me not being a bona fide student; indeed, me having a downer on students! (Like Steve Coogan's 'Paul Calfe'.)

It's a rash act to make an unplanned 'trip' on LSD, but that never hindered me back then.

Heaven or Hell? Which one will it be this time? I mostly chose to 'trip out' alone, it was less confusing that way, I wasn't one of the beautiful people, inside or out; and 'beautiful people' have a nasty habit of screwing you up, just when you have begun to trust them. My own mind could conjure up beautiful images and fantasies, and with plenty of 'trippy' music swirling round my brain I didn't have too much time to notice the pain of unreality.

I tripped out on a Sunday afternoon once, there was nothing else to do, it was my favourite, 'microdot'. I really lost the plot 'going up', it felt like the crescendo of Pink Floyd's 'SET THE CONTROLS FOR THE HEART OF THE SUN'. At one point, a wintry, pale sun acted like a spotlight coming into my living room. When I levelled out a bit I smoked a joint of 'bush', and drank the last mouthfuls of the martini I had in the fridge; I wanted to slow my mind down a bit. Id never felt so cosmically aware, I solved all life's mysteries at one time, but time had lost it's meaning anyway. I wrote it all down but none of it made any sense the following day.

Having taken a quick trip round the universe and back, I found myself watching TV, an old black and white set. A film called 'THE MISFITS' came on, starring Clarke Gable and Marilyn Monroe. It was the last film both of them were to make, death for one, and a slow destruction for the other, ending their careers. (It was a quick death in Gable's case, shortly after the film was made, of a heart attack). The plot was centred on rounding up wild mustang horses for the pet meat trade. It was to be their last roundup owing to the fact that they'd already decimated the herds; the movie was made in black and white in 1958.

(This piece now seems to feel unfinished, but if you take the two versions as a whole, I think you'll catch my drift, I hope so. Phil Fletcher. 21/4/06.)

BAD SMELL. (Or: I am 'THE LONER', as in the track by the same name, off Neil young's first solo LP)

I wandered lonely as a bad smell in a hell of society's making. Everywhere I went I didn't fit in, I felt so goddamn lonely it was a cardinal sin against me. In the end I opted for staying in as much as possible,
it was a lot less painful, interfacing with characters and actions on the TV, a lust for life was reawakened in me. A psychological profiler would probably label me as a 'serious 'saddo'. But ogling top totty on the telly couldn't satisfy my appetite for sex, and you can only do it with yourself so often before the novelty wears off completely. So I bought myself a pet sheep and goat, they would have only gone for slaughter anyway, at three months old. So 'DEEP THROAT' here I'd come, once I'd trained them up and bonded with them. Why didn't I settle for a blow up doll you may well ask? I didn't want to mask my love of the female form and psyche in such a hollow sham. Better to ram it in to the interior of an innocent ewe, or slip it into the fanny of an acquiescent nanny, than sully my proud penis in the ever open mouth of some permanently pouting patsy; life's taken me for enough of a cunt already.
'Steady now Gertie', (that's the goat acting up, I'll have to grab her by the ears till she is ready to calm down and learns to bleat appreciatively). Too much coital pleasure can have an unpleasant side effect; post coital depression has caused me to neglect my home. The unsavoury aroma of uncleared up goat and sheep shit permeates every room, the flies have moved in, in ever increasing numbers, disturbing my slumbers between bouts of ever more demanding sex. The 'girls' have sensed the level of my weakness and make me chase them round the house before they'll let me satisfy it. Sometimes, when I'm seeing to the sheep, the goat will come up behind me and give me a playful butt up the backside once or twice. That's very nice for Emily the ewe; she gets an extra inch or two inside her. I've decided I can't go on, I'm going to do a runner, I'll phone the RSPCA when I'm a hundred miles away, saying there are a couple of debauched animals at No.33. Let them clean the mess up and find

new homes, and counselling, for two abused and disturbed adolescents.

I'm going to take holy orders where nobody knows who I am, an ashram where I can shave my head and sleep on a bed of snail's shells in a sweaty sack, and eat boiled cack for breakfast, dinner and tea, (organic of course). The resulting wind problem should be atrocious in my lonely monks cell, a sulphurous prelude to a well-deserved hell still to come. (He said 'come', heh, heh, heh!)

....

Life's very oppressive to me, being disabled; this is a reaction to that oppression.

I'M FOREVER BLOWING IT OUT OF MY ARSE.

Optimism that is, I've got so much to spare it has to come out somewhere. The baseball bat would be my weapon of choice, lightweight but lethal, then if anyone tried to bring my optimism down, I'd crown them with a single thwack of my bat. And as they were dropping cork legged, to the ground, I'd say, "Depress me again and you're dead you twat!" I know this title sounds a lot like the old haunting song: 'I'M FOREVER BLOWING BUBBLES', about fortune always hiding; well it's always giving me the slip too. I'm feeling cornered by adversity and I'm blaming this lamentable state of affairs entirely on you. So what are you going to do about it, start smiling in my direction, or what? If not, I'll shatter your kneecaps and then your chin, this is the big league of disaffection you're meddling in. I'll shatter your nose and then your hands, if you mess too much with my optimistic plans. I mean, my motto is, 'It's nice to be nice' and if you can't be nice shut the fuck up and keep your vitriolic bile to yourself; if I have to cope with living in a world without love, so can you. Just in case you think this is aimed at you, it'll prove that you're paranoid and fucked up too. I mean, would I do that to you?
Well not to your face anyway.

The poet with the psychotic brain.   Phil Fletcher.

···

FRUSTRATION.

Frustration is when everything you want remains stubbornly out of reach, year in and year out.

Some people decide to do something about it, like robbing banks or stealing tanks. I make do with having boring wanks instead of mind blowing shags; it looks like DIY till I die, or until my wanking hand becomes too arthritic to perform its wifely duty. Having, effectively, only one partially sighted eye, in a predominantly able-bodied society, is very frustrating. Maybe I should always have looked for a partner with a similar complaint, but I set my sights too high, no compromises for me, and no 'nooky' either. It's like playing a board game and never being able to pass GO! The others are nudging ahead, while every time you throw the dice, it's a 3 or a 5, and not the required 6; so you end up prematurely retired, with hurt feelings and wounded pride; but still refusing to admit that realistically, your life ended a long time ago. Another of my mottos is: 'Take what existence throws at you as beat you can'. If, at the 33rd or 55th time you don't succeed, then try another plan to escape your fate. Nobody ever said that life was going to be a plate of rose petals and a jug of mead, it's more like a feeding frenzy of piranhas and lice. Life's travails have left me mentally crippled and physically broken, who was it that said, 'Life is but a joke'? And a really nasty one at that.

The jaundiced Phil Fletcher.

···

Title thought up on 8/9/00. THE FAT LAZY BITCH? A PORTRAIT OF AN OVERWEIGHT DOG. (And that's as far as it got)

All he asked of her was a little gift of time, and for her to whisper three little words, "Please be mine."
'Gimme, gimme,gimme, a lover after midnight, failing that the shopping channels will have to do'.

('a little gift of time', it's a good title that).
A LITTLE GIFT OF TIME.

All he asked of her was a little gift of time, and for her to whisper three little words, "Please be mine."
But she wouldn't give him either, so he had his head sliced off on a railway line. Microscopic traces of his unrequited slime are still smeared along the track.

....

WASPS NEST.

A fifteen-year-old girl was murdered in America, and her body dumped in woods. By the time she was found, her remains were skeletal. Her head had decomposed into a skull, into which wasps had built a nest. Forensic scientists with specialised knowledge were able to decipher how long she'd been there by studying the behaviour of the insects. She was identified as a missing girl. You'd never think while you're alive that your head could end up as a home to a nest of wasps would you?

....

MOVE OUT OF THE WAY JESUS, THERE'S NO PROFIT MARGIN LEFT IN YOU FOR THE 'NEW DEAL' MEANING OF 'CRIMBO'.

I don't know, any more, who are the biggest turkeys, us humans, or the other two-legged variety they fatten up for the festering season? Either way, we're both being stuffed rotten. I saw my first TV ad for Xmas on October 5th, a personal best for commercialism I think. For the next two months it's overkill on the long suffering Great British public, and their seemingly bottomless pockets.
I still love the Victorian concept of Christmas, as depicted on greetings cards; but in 'A CHRISTMAS CAROL', the story didn't begin till Christmas Eve, with Bob Cratchet working his frozen fingers to the bone in stonyhearted Scrooge's back office.
That's how it used to be, the season would creep up (in the nicest possible way) on you; that magic feeling. I can remember when I was about sixteen, bringing a tall Christmas tree home on the bus from

21

Manchester town centre, to Wythenshawe, at my mother's request. I think it was tied up but nowadays they probably wouldn't let me on a bus with one; or else charge me extra for it.

The worst Christmas dinner I ever had, (apart from the tuna and oven chips I now make do with), was some years ago when I went to stay with an alcoholic friend in Brighton. We ended up having some rather burnt vegetable curry, while the skeletal remains of a huge bird that he'd devoured over the previous week, acted as the spectre at the feast; 1 can safely say that was the worst Xmas I've ever had, and I've had some terrible ones; the last 25 to be exact. Nowadays, my attitude is: 'I've been roasted, and I don't want to go there again'; and I'm quite happy to buy a t-shirt with Santa's face on it, two sizes too small, for someone I don't really like. Goodwill to all men? Where's the mileage in that? I'm off to Tunisia this yuletide to avoid my fellow man, and woman, and their smug, extended family 'Crimbo'; there's no room at the inn for this tortured soul, so they can all fuck off and get salmonella on Boxing day, and take up a whole hospital ward.

Unlike Scrooge, I don't think there's any hope for me, I think I might out-depress the ghost of Xmas yet to come. The ghost of my pas**
****
****
****
****
****
****
****
***for the January sales to start on Boxing Day. (I'm always in the mood for a good punch-up after the 'festive' holiday's over.)

The unreformed, and unrepentant, Scrooge-like, Phil Fletcher.

....

DARK SIDE OF THE MIND.

One of the most hideous atrocity stories I've ever heard happened quite recently, this year sometime, in Belfast. I heard it on a BBC TV newscast. An Irish mafia death squad, burst into a man's home, and shot him dead; and they then pistol-whipped his wife; all this while there were three children in the house. These inhuman monsters were masquerading behind a so-called 'Orange Order' feud, to carry out this fiendish act of murder and terror. This evil filth, like the Omagh bombers, can seemingly live with what they've done; even justify it in the name of their perverted ideals. If this was Belfast, and I was writing this for publication there, there's a good chance I'd receive a visit from ski-mask-wearing, baseball bat, or pistol wielding terrorists, bent on teaching me the error of my ways. Once you've become a dehumanised brute, you can commit any act of violence; you enjoy your victim's screams of pain, or cries for mercy, it enhances your feelings of power and control over them.

You've become, for the most part, man that was not born of woman, a creature without compassion, a hate-filled thing, a fiend to be feared above all others, because YOU JUST DON'T CARE! I have my own cold-blooded outsider to keep securely chained up, that loathsome aspect of myself which regards certain other individuals as potential prey. But enough of my dark side, I've been its gaoler for nearly 54 years now. Last night I heard an item of news on one of the local TV bullettins, 'CALENDAR' I think. 2 raiders wearing ski masks, terrifying for anyone to come across, forced their way into an old lady's bungalow; she's 88, and physically assaulted her in order to find out if she had any money and valuables in her home. What kind of creatures are these? The Devil's own boot-boys?

The hooded terrorist is the most frightening in aspect, it could be anyone. I also wonder if the sale of ski masks and baseball bats has really spiralled in the last few years? And have they been put on the official list of torture instruments, like electric shock stunners perhaps? I also wonder which piece of human slime first thought that the innocent ski mask could become a symbol of international terror? Was it a terrorist on a skiing holiday, of the Bader Meinov gang? Or a bank robber, mugger, rapist, stalker, or psycho killer???

Hate is the easiest human emotion to feel, it thrives on itself. The more you hate, the happier it is; like a cancerous tumour feeding on its host victim. And if your hate becomes all consuming, then it may well kill you; just like the cancer tumour. Though, unlike the tumour, which has to die along with its host victim, hate can move on and spread like a deadly virus. A case in point is the current conflict between the Israelis and the Palestinians, even though basically they're the same ethnicity, their different religions set them at each other's throats. I'm afraid if I were a Palestinian right now, I'd be thinking, 'Let's make bigger bombs and kill more jews, what have we got to lose'?

(Which of course, is precisely what's happening on that front, 5 years on; but on the home front, I heard a terrifying story yesterday. A man (down south) asked a couple of men to keep their dogs under control; their response was to attack him with a meat cleaver. I did hear that he's lost 3 fingers, as well as other serious injuries, and the police are treating this as a case of attempted murder. I can only sympathise with the state of terror and shock he must be in; I always think of getting out of this country pronto, when I hear stories like that, but nowhere's that safe anymore.   Phil Fletcher.   22/4/06.)

....

MISERY DOESN'T ALWAYS NEED COMPANY

People who live on their own are supposed to be miserable and self-effacing, especially those who live in flats. In exceptional circumstances they're allowed to keep dogs or cats, or even budgerigars. Some also own cars, which are kept parked outside, sometimes they go for a ride at night, looking for excitement in the red light districts; which is what I would do if I couldn't be bothered looking for 'love' on the internet, or LOOT.
There aren't many prostitutes who'll turn down a meaningless root for twenty quid, or a hand job for even less. A quick, "Yes, yes, yes!, and you're on your own again, ready to go back to your flat to lavish your love on the bird or the cat, and the fond memory of some stranger's twat or soft warm hand, and the pair of used panties you paid her an extra fiver for.

SCUM KULCHER

If you're of a fairly low I.Q, this may well apply to you. Within your reasoning, you can justify what you do. Nobody cares about you, so you're sure as hell going to make them pay; it's good fun anyway, burn down your school and you won't have to go there the next day. Drop a concrete block off a motorway bridge, and watch the stricken motorist swerve and sway, and possibly crash, then run away. Mindless anarchy in the UK, and if you can derail a train on a busy line, that's a '9' on the Richter scale of mindless and moronic acts of urban terrorism. The facts are clear, society's too wrapped up in its own selfish pursuits to clearly see what a threat to its basic fabric this evil cancer is; maybe it deserves everything it gets for its smug complacency. If it was down to me, I'd put the culprits up against a wall, after all, they're worth fuck-all, and I'd make them dig their own graves...small and squat.

(And it's still going on, just over a week ago it was reported that a 'group of youths' threw a concrete block off a bridge in Rochdale, which went through the windscreen of an oncoming train, seriously injuring the driver; one of the culprits was described as being as young as four. I'm sure this tot didn't know what it was there for, but the older one's did. If it was down to me, they'd get a minimum of 20 years for a crime like that; after all, you're not allowed to instantly eliminate these worthless lumps of human garbage are you? (I wouldn't lump a 4-year-old in under this heading, there's still time for him to be rehabilitated...isn't there?   Phil Fletcher. 24/4/06.)

....

TERRIFYING IN ITS AWFULNESS. (A cross between the Ricki Lake Show, and severe diarrhoea.)

I never realised till last weekend, how awful severe diarrhoea can be. i reckon, that in a two-day bout of the worst stomach bug I've ever had, I passed enough foul-smelling liquid to fill a gallon bucket. The cramps and spasms were the most painful I've ever experienced as well; on a par with labour pains perhaps, as I evacuated 'Rosemary's' dead and badly decomposed baby.
It also occurred to me that, given the atrocious weather conditions we've been having, that if the drains overflowed, some of this toxic waste might well find its way back into my old house in central Todmorden; a truly horrifying prospect. Which brings me to Ricki Lake, a woman I've seen described as a 'once celebrated porker' .She

certainly has enough 20-stone-plus porker's on her show; they even have lard for brains. Some are gargantuan in proportion, how their hearts support their bulk is a mystery. They have to take the roof off the studio to crane lift them in, and then they sit there wobbling, and blubbering on, about how they've tried to lose weight, but the first sign of stress 'y'all', and they greedily reach out for a still live and kicking cow to eat between two concrete-like slabs of pastry, made with the melted down fat of other dead obesities.

Within this turbulent reality of modern day living, I try and hide myself away. I can exist at times in a space no bigger than six feet by two feet; not a coffin, but a comfy settee. And with my personal stereo headphones clamped firmly over my ears, listening to late night Radio 2, with the infectious Janice Long, I'm in virtual heaven.

(That catalogue of woe relates to the worst six months sojourn I've ever had to endure, in my 20-year sojourn in Calderdale. It was in a place called Walsden; 'World's End' would have been more appropriate. The floor material was so porous, that I could hear everything that was going on in the flat below, and most of the time those goings on weren't very pleasant. It was while I was besieged in that god-forsaken hole that I was inspired to write: 'PLEBISHITE'. Phil Fletcher. 24/4/06…………………………………………………………..)

IMPINGEMENT.

I was enduring a tedious bus journey to Halifax yesterday from Todmorden, of about 12 miles; there was the usual stink of stale tobacco, whittering passengers, one of them with a persistent cough, and an equally persistent child. We seemed to stop at every stop. By the time we got to Mytholmroyd, (any similarity to the opening line of 'WOODSTOCK' is purely intentional), my mind was almost as numb as my feet. I had loads of clothes on but I was still cold; I'd got on at Todmorden bus station, I was looking disinterestedly out the window, when my male instinct forced me to turn round in time to see a woman in a white short skirt, and short leather jacket, with fantastic legs, clad only in flimsy tights or stockings, getting on the bus. She sat down two seats in front of me, her immaculate behind staring me full in the face for all too brief a moment as she did so; the whittering dropped to a whisper.

The incongruousness of her attire on such a cold day almost caused me to laugh out loud, I don't think I took my good eye off her till she got off at Bull Green in Halifax, impervious to the stir she'd caused. I ogled as much of her curvaceous legs, and bottom, as my limited eyesight would allow. It did cross my mind that she might have been a recovering prostitute on her way to the Ebenezer Day Centre, for people with mental health problems, on St. James road; she must have been mad to dress like that on such a cold day.

(This was also while I was 'living' in Walsden, and I caught a nasty cold off the woman who'd been openly coughing on the bus. A few years later, I caught a near terminal dose of flu (just after I'd had my flu jab), off some character who was again, openly coughing, on a long bus journey I was on; his germs made a bee-line straight for my nose. Phil Fletcher. 24/4/06.)

....

TEMPORARILY BACK FROM THE DEAD

At 54, I still feel guilty about liking what I like and pursuing what I want to pursue. It's not cost effective, which is a pity, unless I can land a job in radio city, writing plays for the hard of hearing or creating quiz shows for the mentally challenged, and panel games for the socially unhinged.
I still remember how they cringed when I offered them MACBETH in Braille for an experimental production on tactile radio; I wasn't to know it wouldn't all fit on the cover of a Bakelite set. Better yet, I could devise a signing version of 'THE COUNTRY OF THE BLIND' for late night broadcast Radio 3; I bet there'd only be me listening, as usual.

....

THERES DOG SHIT, AND CHEWING GUM, ON MY SHOE.
(IT'S ALL ABOUT OPPRESSION.)

Every time I walk on the pavement, my shoe sticks from this goo, and every time I sit down, an awful smell of dog shit rises up to greet me. This muck's ingrained in the indentations on the soles, they cost me 60 quid. Why couldn't the brain dead chewer have thrown it's used gum down a grid, or the moronic dog owner force it to shit in the gutter?

But they throw their used wads of gum down on the pavement because they think its their right to do so, and they're so disaffected from any sense of social responsibility, that they want some unsuspecting, mug to step in it or sit on it, (even worse), and the more laws there are brought out against dog fouling, the more it encourages certain anti social elements to flaunt them; walking their innocent four-legged offenders at 3 a.m, if necessary, to avoid cleaning up after it. Scoop it up with a plastic bag and bin it? "FUCK OFF PAL...EUGH!!!"

But I've got a control freak's instincts when it comes to downright anti social behaviour, I'd adopt a policy of zero tolerance towards those free spirits who think graffiti art is cool; it's not their property they're defacing. The mark of the 'mong', as displayed by fag ends squashed out just where you want to sit, or stand, in bus stations, or railway platforms, and the bright sparks who think it's funny to leave their empty coke cans, and bottles, and chip papers and trays, on top of, or near, receptacles for this kind of rubbish. Nowhere's safe from this self-centred, sullen, over-aggressive type of (usually) surly youth. Not the pavement, with its plethora of, 'Out of my way, cunt!' cyclists, skateboarders, roller-skaters, and latterly, motorised 'silver surfer' scooter riders.

People like me with a severe visual handicap, are living dangerously every time we go out. I was brought down by a tow-rope, stretched between two crappy old cars, while crossing a side road earlier this year in Todmorden; a horrendous experience, with none of the occupants of the two vehicles getting out to see if I was okay, they were probably too busy pissing themselves laughing to move.

Even the lovely countryside isn't safe from these aesthetically brain dead monsters; the slopes of the Himalayas are covered in all kinds of crap, including human shit, dead bodies, and parts of dead bodies

I**
****
****
****
****
****
****
****
************************************** because we have
insufficient cash or assets, to become members of its exclusive club.
But, as I've written elsewhere, you can't make a silk purse out of an
ignorant cunt's pissflaps, the lumpen proletariat is just that; full of
low IQ lumps of humanity, who it would make sound genetic sense to
breed out of the species. We've moved on a lot from the stone age,
haven't we?   Phil Fletcher.

....

At the start of this year, (2001), the BBC Radio Drama Department
were putting out feelers for new disabled writers to submit potential
material; they suggested a scenario on the theme of 'ADRENALIN'. I
impetuously decided to have a go, and sent in the following piece,
along with a covering letter. I've decided to print the letter first, as
my prediction came horribly, predictably true.

7 HENRY PLACE,

WALSDEN,

TODMORDEN.

*8/1/01. Dear Zoe Marchant, your communication was sent to my other address in
Todmorden, from which I was hounded out by hostile locals, it's currently up for sale.*

I get an adrenalin rush from reaching out to 'real' people. One of the
setbacks of disability for some of us, is the awful social isolation it can
have. I spend long periods of time on my own, watching TV, and not
listening to as much radio drama as I did when I was a lot younger.
I've written the enclosed piece for you, I dare say it will be far too
politically incorrect for current tastes, but you could very easily go
mad trying to perch perfectly still, on the fence, hoping not to offend
anybody. My C.V. (track record) isn't very impressive I'm afraid,
only one published poem to my name so far. I've done an ARVON

5-day writing course at Lumb Bank, West Yorks. I regularly attend a Creative Writers group in Hebden Bridge, West Yorks, at the Hourglass Studio. I'm nearly 54 years old, and registered as partially sighted, (it's getting worse). I suffer from circumstantial depression and physical 'wear and tear'. I've written a lot of 'poetry' over the past five years.

It's difficult to write about disability without falling into the trap of self-pity and self-patronisation, or offending your potential audience; a real can of worms.

I can type; I'm not willing to pay for any advice that might be on offer. I'd love to be able to get off State benefits, and allow my fertile imagination to take flight and flourish.

No doubt you won't be able to use me.

Yours dejectedly. Phil Fletcher.

(I was right of course, I received my rejection letter on Valentine's day, no valentines, just that letter.)

I've just typed-up 'ADRENALIN RUSh', it's not as bad as I'd led myself to believe it was; it's probably more suited to Radio 3, if it could ever have been developed, which is highly unlikely; I run out of steam after a few minutes. (No allusions to my non-existent sex life, please.)

ADRENALIN RUSH.

First actor: 'Like 1 was saying, before you so rudely interrupted me, if I was a dictator somewhere, I could have you shot for that.'.
Second actor, 'Sorry, man'.
1st A. 'There! You're doing it again. I get this feeling of power and grandeur welling up inside me at times, as if I could rule the world and everyone in it. If I didn't hold it in check, I don't know what would happen, or where it would take me; it's a real good buzz though'.
2nd A. 'It's called megalomania; your real life's a pile of crap, so a part of your metabolism tries to 'over compensate'. You're a prime example really, only you're not charismatic enough to convincingly pull it off, you could never be a Hitler or a Napoleon'.
1st A. 'For someone who wasn't given permission to speak, you've got a lot to say. I'm better looking than Hitler, and taller than Napoleon; I'm a tortured artist, like Vincent van Gogh. I'm probably not meant to be discovered till I've met a tragic end.'

2nd A. 'It's tragic how you can't get your end away, you've been rejected more times than Vincent, and you can't paint, except unintentionally badly. At least he used prostitutes, all you use is Mrs Palmer and her five lovely daughters, and feel sorry for yourself afterwards'.

1st A. 'I can never find any tarts, the country's supposed to be heaving with them, and I can't locate one. If I could see well enough to drive I could go looking for them, but I can't even ride a bike; at least you can't catch a dose of anything from wanking, and it's cost effective too. And you get to sleep after a good 'fifty off the wrist', no-one to moan, 'What about me'?

2nd A. 'We always end up going down that road when we have this argument, you're just a tight-fisted old git with a persecution complex. You make me sick!'

1st A. 'But it's going to be different this time'.

2nd A. 'Why? How?'

1st A. 'Because, I'm going to kill you, that's why. How? With this extra-sharp bread knife that I bought for 3Op from a charity shop, years ago. I always knew it would come in handy someday; I'll be able to cut your head off with it, after I've bashed it in'.

2nd A. 'You fucking maniac!'

1st A. 'No, I'm a partially sighted megalomaniac, remember? I'm God! I'll say you were the anti-Christ sent to torment me, and I snapped. I'm going to take your head, on a plate, to the cop shop, and say the voices of Joan of Arc, and John Lennon told me to do it. Imagine that in your headless limbo'.

2nd A. 'Come anywhere near me with that blade, and I'll kick your knackers in, you blind bastard; you know I can run rings round you. I mean it you nutter! You nearly had my eye out then. Right, you've asked for it, you wanker!

1st A. 'OOOHHH! ME NUTS, YOU'VE CRUSHED 'EM! I'M GOING TO BE SICK! BLEURRGGHH! OOH! Get me some frozen peas now! You rotter! Not 'BIRDSEYE', I don't like their stuff. Can't you take a joke? You've destroyed my manhood, oh God! No, that's me isn't it? The pain's terrible, my pee will feel like red hot fish hooks coming out'.

2nd A. "You'll be okay, Hitler was impotent'.

(Now if I was any good at writing scripts, I might have been able to develop that into a '2-man' dialogue play for radio, but I'm not, so....
Phil Fletcher.   24/4/06.)

....

Egyptian cobra, black rat, vagina, mouth, stomach, dungeon,
bands of live electric wire current holding you down.

THE FIRST ASPECT OF YOUR PERSONAL HELL (AN ACCOUNT ALMOST TOO TERRIFYING TO RELATE? MAYBE I WON'T).

Dappled streetlight on the pavement after midnight, with the full
moon overhead, and the soft sighing of leaves in the summer breeze;
these things I wanted to share with you. You were young and easily
led, or so I thought, you soon aborted those romantic notions in me,
making me your unrequited slave instead. You never invited me, but
I longed to take you to your bed and teach you tricks you probably
knew already, behind your beautiful look of innocence.
Fucking you was an immense pleasure I used to fantasise about,
dragging the masturbation out for as long as my cock could stand it,
I debauched you in every way I could think of, then I'd wipe the
spunk off my belly or my chest, and rest exhausted, feeling a little less
depressed for a while. I wanted to share your quiet mystery, as you
became a woman full blown, but all that was ancient history to you,
some nameless tutor had got to you and claimed your innocence for
his own. Leaving you with a cunt like a bucket, that half the town has
thrown one up; the mouthier ones say your a fantastic tup, especially
when you're really on heat, while I just 'beat my meat' and bide my
time.
I know you'll get round to me eventually, and ridicule my poor and
brief performance, and destroy my remaining flimsy sexual
confidence. Maybe I'll kidnap you and handcuff your hands and feet
to a brass-framed, double bed, at least you'll be in a receptive
position then, whenever I want you. Or else I'll relinquish all
thoughts of you, and get myself into a monastery, where the first
things I'll be handed will be a pair of boxing gloves and a penis ring
to stop any blood flow to my cock while I'm asleep; with a bit of luck
it will drop off like a shrivelled and withered finger. Perhaps I should
concentrate on food and drink to take my mind off you, especially the
latter. Absinthe with its high wormwood content, but maybe it will
fill my mind with the green worms of envy, as I imagine you
preferring every other man to me; as if I was the one too many in the
'Annabel Chong' saga, (she had sex with 251 men in a little over ten
hours to prove a point that she later regretted). Lager could rot my
insides if I drank enough of it, and strong white cider might give me
permanent, smelly diarrhoea.

Good English beer by the gallon should cause me to pile on the pounds, then I could sit there in my mounds of flesh, and seeping gas, and drool at every beautiful piece of ass that entered my gaze, a tear running down each cheek, in my permanently drunken haze of self pity.
Best option yet, I'm going to leave this city that you infest, and walk this whole world over, a stranger in an insane asylum with no walls, roof's, or doors. If the lunatics offer to help me when I pass by, all well and good; if my luck runs out I'll gladly slip down in the mud of some inviting swamp.

(My original handwritten sheet tells me I wrote this potent poem between the 5th and 6th of January this year, 2001, I might have taken time out to wank about you, oh! I've embarrassed you now, sorry.)

....

MORE LIFE IN A TRAMP'S VEST.

There's more life in a tramp's vest right now, than there is in mine; life that is, not vest. I'm much too macho to wear one, except on really cold days. All I want to do is have some fun, not the kind that Cheryl Crowe sang about a few years ago in her hit song, where some inane twat got his kicks from peeling the labels off Budweiser beer bottles, and lighting matches and holding them till they burnt down to his fingertips, in some godforsaken bar in L.A.
Or the kind where you jump off into space, and pray that the rope holding you won't snap or tangle; or jet ski, or snowboard, paraglide, abseil, cross Niagara Falls on a tight-rope while riding a bike, or be a knife thrower's assistant, or dive fifty feet into a small circular pool from the top of a ladder. Or be a stripper with a large python, snakes, as well as worms, can turn rather nasty.
Like the late Sir John Betcheman, I haven't had enough sex; some cruel spirits might say that with a face like mine, what else can I expect? Although I've seen plenty of gargoyles with beautiful women on their arms, William Hague is a case in point. The only athleticism that interests me, apart from wrestling, is sexual prowess; it's what a full-blooded male was made for, to have women lusting after him, just like in the natural world, until he's too old or knackered to keep up the good work. If I weren't too old and knackered, I'd opt to be a

gigolo, not just for the rampant sex that might be on offer, but also because I'm fascinated by the mental and physical makeup of women, from sixteen to sixty. I love it when you break down their icy reserve, and even get them lavishing presents on you, (wishful thinking there on my part).

What I would also find interesting, would be steering a diplomatic course round their fiercely monogamous natures, as I floated effortlessly from one to another in my chosen harem; I really envy those Mormons who have enough wives for each day of the week, seven that is, not 365. What I would draw the line at is pimping, I think this lowest form of life, if convicted, should be castrated and made to eat its lightly grilled tackle. I don't believe in violence or coercion, but if I could persuade some willing victim to do all my typing and promote my lifeless career, I'm sure I could show her my gratitude in several different positions, sorry, I mean ways. Oh, to end my book of empty days, and even more boring nights.

Well, it's 6/6/01, and I'm still 'pulling my pud', when I can be bothered. The only attentions I get are from unsavoury freaks of nature, my mind stalkers, abominations and obscenities in the eyes of the Great Spirit; I think they're also known as sex vampires.

....

NO LUCK ON THE LOTTERY (To the tune of : 'ANOTHER SATURDAY NIGHT', sung either by Sam Cooke or Cat Stevens, take your pick.)

NO LUCK ON THE LOTTERY.

It's another Saturday night and I ain't won
The lottery, I bought some tickets 'cos' I just
Got paid by the D.S.S., how I wish I could
Win me a fortune, I'm in an awful mess.

I've got these rat-bags for neighbours,
They're really giving' me a hard time,
I'm always afraid they're gonna kick
My head in, and cover me in regurgitated

Green slime.

I really deserve to win it, it really should
Be me, with a good few bob in my pocket,
I could fuel my trouser rocket by buying
Some female company.

If I carry on like this for much longer,
I'll be too old to have any fun,
All my joints will cease up,
My sex drive will
     ****
     ****
     ****
     ****
     ****
     ****
     ****
     ****
     **e
  m in a state of constant fright,
My hair's turning nearly white,
My prospects are history.

(Repeat the first verse to finish; not bad ay?)

....

Very loosely based on 'I AM THE WALRUS' by 'THE BEATLES', to the tune of I AM THE WALRUS; not that it will ever be performed.)

I AM THE MANDRILL.

I am he, I live in a tree, I'm a thing of rare beauty, I am the Mandrill. I'm flying round the jungle like a red, white, and blue-faced baboon, to this tune, (with a full stretch of the imagination). I'm crying… with ecstasy, at the envy felt for me by the uglier apes in our community. They can't hold a candle to me when it comes to facial hair colour, I'm on a par with a New Guinea head hunter, in full plumage; I am the red and blue-faced ape-man, I am the ape-man…I AM THE MANDRILL!! GOO-GO-KA-CHOO!!
Tarragon flavoured mustard in a hedgehog pie, hornomatic, blow-up doll living in a pig sty, man you've been a naughty manikin, you let the zip on your crotchless knickers down, to the first pork sworder to give you the eye; I'm a cheese and pickle man myself, I AM THE MANDRILL!
Sitting in an English garden, wondering why the hell I'm here, when I should be preening myself in a massive tree, it's a mystery, when I should be getting a tan far away from the English rain. Oh! The pain of being a captive creature in a zoo, watching you watching me in my artificial tree. I was dreaming, silly me, of how things used to be before I became an endangered species; soon only my faeces will be left to carry traces of my DNA. Hey! I WAS THE MANDRILL!

....

PLEBISHITE.

I'm waging constant war against the pleb's next door, or rather, underneath me in the flat below. There isn't a day goes by when I don't fantasise about doing an 'Arnie' on them, in his terminator mode; kicking down their first line of defence, and emptying a fully loaded Ouzi automatic into their thick skulls. Small recompense for the damage they've done to my nerves and peace of mind.

Every time I start to unwind, their warped sixth sense alerts them, and a door gets slammed, or a loud argument breaks out. I'd move out but it's not long since I moved in, little knowing that they were lying in wait, looking for a new victim to hate, out of warped principle I think. Anyone who lives above them, must think they're better than them, according to their twisted way of reasoning. Of course, in my case, they would be politically correct; I'm as far above them in intellect as it's possible to be. They hammer away on their play station while I wave an imaginary baton listening to Radio 3, when the mood takes me; at other times I 'veg' out' to 'CROSSROADS' in the afternoon, having just put down 'DARKNESS AT NOON', Arthur Koestler's seminal masterwork, (I hope I've got his name right?), while the pleb' below, noisily calls his downtrodden consort a stupid jerk. I think I was meant to go insane, possibly even homicidally so, my spleen says yes, my mind says no. You see, I like tranquillity, and lots of it, but there's always legions of the undead only too willing to rob me of it. There is no shortage of vampire slayers to be found, on TV at any rate, I'd like to be able to mete out a similar fate to all unnecessary noise polluters, using a pair of golden shooters that would emit jets of high frequency noise, as sharp and concentrated as a laser beam, that would go in one ear and out the other of these damned souls, leaving massive holes in their spongy brains, so they'd stagger about shouting, 'Who pulled my ear plugs out?', before dropping down dead by the side of their pneumatic drills, motor bikes, or chainsaws.
The only thing I can stand in loud abundance, is music, it blots a lot of this hideously evil noise out that the mentally deficient, insensitive plebeian moron loves to make. Sweet music is the only safety brake between me and that insanity that I don't want to oblige. Also, the sound of birdsong in a peaceful setting can act as a salve to my tortured nerves, though nowadays you have to be up very early on a summer's morning to hear it in all its glory, life in a beautiful idyll is a life I'll never know.

....

ONE NIGHT WITH OLGA

Olga is a beautiful Russian princess, forced into becoming a courtesan because her title alone can't keep her in the lifestyle she aspires to. I saw her in a recent TV programme about the vice trade, she was captivating. She's 28, and speaks English with that deeply sexy accent that only Russian women have. Olga has her own website, she charges her clients £1000 a night, and dare I say, I'm sure she's worth every penny; the client she was expecting to meet in Paris, had booked her services for three days. One night with Olga would make my dreams come true. Unless of course, I could afford to acquire an Olga-lookalike, Russian bride, out of the thriving international marriage market. Russia, and Eastern Europe in general, is full of beautiful and accomplished women, who are desperate to get to the West, via marriage.

I answered an ad in LOOT once, from a Russian lady, never expecting a reply, and just when I'd forgotten all about her, I received an introductory letter from a lecturer at Moscow University. I even phoned her once in Moscow, she was very surprised to hear from me. Alas, it all went downhill rather rapidly from there on in; me not being able to offer her anything more than a holiday visit. I think sending her a passport-type photo of my rather individual features, was a big mistake as well.

....

IT'S A LOT EASIER, AND CHEAPER, STAYING IN.
Or, THE PARTHIAN SHOT CUTS THE DEEPEST.

(First paragraph of a play review I finished on my manual typewriter, and which I gave to J.S. to read; I still haven't got the finished article back, she's been too preoccupied with her own world to spare me much thought; I can't remember the name of the play I went to see at the Todmorden Hippodrome on 28/2/01.

'I'll give them nine out of ten for trying, no, they didn't go the full distance for me. E is for energy and efficiency, but Chekhov it was not; mind you, it had all the underlying pathos of a Chekhov plot, meaningless and empty lives, with a faint glimmer of hope at the end.

(I remember that it was freezing in the theatre when the curtain came up, the temperature outside was well below freezing, on a clear, bitterly cold winter's night, and that cold came right into the auditorium; it marred what limited enjoyment there was to be had from the play. How the players coped with the icy blast, is a mystery;

but of course, they were moving about, weren't they? Phil Fletcher. 25/4/06.)

....

THE FROZEN NORTH, FANTASY FANNY.

How's this for an Anne Robinson, 'WEAKEST LINK'-type put-
down, 'You count for nothing, you are nothing. FUCK OFF!'
Plebs stink! Plebs are scum....with attitude!
DEJA VU REVISITED. I have a feeling that I've been here before.
(man, my head's cabbaged).
The rabid rat nipping at my left ear, and the demented filth blowing
horrible heat at my right ear, are awful bi-products of life in this
claustrophobic (ESP-wise) valley of Calderdale.
I've been judged too harshly, too often, and too soon; mainly by
women.
If you want to move from a feeling of vapidity to a state of élan, in
three easy stages, just take a HOP, SKIP,....AND JUMP!
Her love heat fills my cock. (That's a fucking, wishful thinking
scenario.)

....

SNAPE'S LAST CRAP.

High anxiety will be the death of me, the epicentre of my debility is in
my head and the base of my skull; sending little shock waves, and an
undercurrent of trembling, down into my upper limbs and body. I
think I have a condition called 'Prostatodynia', which I discovered in
a book about the prostate gland, several years ago. I seem to have all
the symptoms: ultra sensitivity, an inability to urinate easily, even if
only slightly stressed out, (and I'm usually stressed out to the
maximum.) I even took some prescribed medication for it once, but it
didn't seem to alleviate the symptoms in any way. I've been exposed
to exceptional levels of stress for most of my life, especially the last 15
years here in Calderdale; you'd have to read my diaries to
understand my agony. 'Prostatodynia' isn't as well known as

prostate cancer is, it might even be more discomforting; I'm surprised I'm still alive. (I've now discovered that it's akin to 'Prostatitis', I take a pollen extract tablet every day to help my urine flow. PLF, 25/4/06.)

There's a stink like boiled sweat coming up from the flat below, it could be a chicken being roasted. It's turning my stomach, and setting off the painful pricking sensations in the skin of my upper arms. In the Christian faith, Jesus is enduring his annual crucifixion, I think it's supposed to last till 5pm, when he says: 'It is done," or something like it, and they can take him down off the cross. For a lot of us now, it's just another day; (Good Friday? Why do they call it 'Good Friday' if their saviour, Jesus, is being horribly put to death?). Those who can, are escaping to sunnier climes for the Easter holiday. Those of us who can't, because they haven't got anyone to go with, or can't afford to, (like me), are stuck here with our own Easter misery. It's a form of crucifixion, and it doesn't end at 5pm; more like 7pm, when my three favourite soaps are on TV.

I hope to feel resurrected enough on Eater Sunday, to venture out for a few hours, on my own.

Sat. 14/4/01. The weather has got worse as the day wears on, it's truly demoralising, unless you like staying in with the wind whistling round your wonky window frames, and the gas fire on, and your stomach feeling bloated, trying to make you expel clouds of putrid-smelling gas. You can't afford to have too many allergies when you're poor; for instance, I'd like to find out why my insides are rotten, more often than not. Maybe I'm allergic to wheat, a staple food source for me; nearly everything I eat produces a toxic result. I'd like to be able to book myself into a private clinic and have tests done, far too prohibitively expensive, unless I become a lottery millionaire. I've been trying to wade through the mire of self-pity that I'm constantly in, due to my loveless state. I've realised that I've had most things I've wanted, except what all 'normal' humans crave the most, love and affection in regular doses. I think I'm the most unloved man in Britain; and I can never get all the lost, loveless years back, the last 26 to be exact. No wonder I've got myriad health problems. Even if I find someone now it will be virtually too late to reverse this process of mental and physical deterioration.

SNAPE'S LAST CRAP. (2)

Women, we now indelibly know, suffer from PMT, I defy any potential reader not to know what that means. Less well publicised, is PE, and BB syndrome, mystified? 'Premature ejaculation', and 'Bad Back' syndrome. I mean, I'd like to be able to go at it all night, with my favourite lady, in lots of risqué positions, but the odds are against it. For a start, I don't have the lady on hand, I only have my hand; and this train of thought can cause me to feel so disaffected with life, that death seems a soft option. And we all know that this is not so. DEATH IS FOREVER! Some of the icons of my youth are already sleeping the big sleep, only last Thursday, I heard that Nirie Dawn Porter has died; I was really keen on her in the'70s, in an unobtainable kind of way; and Julie London, singer of the haunting 'CRY ME A RIVER', as featured in the classic '50s Rock 'n' Roll movie: 'THE GIRL CAN'T HELP IT'. 'Neddy Seagoon', the Welsh warbler (Harry Secombe), also 'kicked-off' on Thursday; that only leaves Spike Milligan to go, he's really old and frail now, the last of the GOONS. (He went in 2002 or 2003, or even 2004, I can't remember. PLF, 25/4/06)

Another aspect of my weird condition is self-torture. Right now, at II.55pm, it's shit that's making me feel nauseous, not mine. It was something I heard on that annoying homo's, 'The Graham Norton Show, a couple of weeks ago, concerning Jane Macdonald and her shit. (Beads of it to be precise), and it was Jane herself who elaborated on the subject; which I won't do any further here.

15/4/01. It's Easter Sunday, 'Christians awake, rejoice the happy throng', etc. I wasn't allowed to sleep till past 3.30am, because of the plebs below. They were yapping until nearly 2am, then when I did lay me down to sleep, one of them had a radio on, or something. I think I had about five hours solid slumber; that's enough in itself, but I still needed another two hours dozing before I could face today. I had a letter to post, I'm sending off for a topaz and diamond ring, at a reduced price of £100. The ideal scenario would be that I could get down on one arthritic knee to J.S., and she would accept my proposal of a shagging relationship; the reality will probably be much harsher. It's under a 10-day, no obligation, home trial, so if I'm certain she won't accept it, I can send it back, along with a tear jerking note, along the lines that I've been rejected...again. I also thought I might be able to buy some daffodils to mark my mother's 77th birthday, (she's dead of course), for tomorrow. I could have bought a bunch yesterday for 60p, but I was too mean, someone I know said they got five bunches for a pound last week at Hebden Bridge market. Because of trading laws, the local garden centre isn**

41

****
****
****
****
****
****
****
*** Moments later,
after shouting these exultant remarks, he was a ball of flames in a
blazing inferno.

SNAPE'S LAST CRAP. (3)

15/4/01. 5.45 pm. A horrible incident happened here about 30
minutes ago, I had to kill some kind of large insect. The odds of it
coming into my living room the way it did must be fairly long; I had
a side window opened about 3 or 4 inches, (about 30 feet above
ground level). This thing could have been blown in on an up draught
gust of wind. I tried getting it on some paper so I could tip it out of
the, by now, fully opened window, but it was too stupid to co-operate.
Instead, it kept getting more and more angry. Me being partially
sighted, meant I couldn't see it in any great detail, it might have been
a bee, a hornet, or a horsefly; it was disrupting my enjoyment of
Coronation Street, and I didn't want it in my flat any longer than I
had to.
I gave it one last chance to escape, and when it wouldn't, I whacked it
with a rolled-up copy of yesterday's SUN newspaper a few times,
only then would it do my bidding. As far as I'm concerned it was an
embodiment of evil. This, combined with a harrowing 70-minute slice
of social drama, has left me feeling shaky and bilious. Just think,
there are men out there killing hundreds of harmless sheep, cows,
and pigs every day, due to the 'foot and mouth' epidemic; I wonder if
they ever wake up in the middle of the night screaming? 1 think i
would.
I phoned the one remaining sister I have who isn't feuding with me,
earlier; I (mainly) spoke for about forty minutes. She has a weird
condition; it's a cross between learning difficulties and autism, that's
my diagnosis anyway. I wonder what Easter Monday will bring?
I6/4/0I. Sorry ma, no flowers; I can't face going down that lonesome

road to the garden centre again, it's a nightmare world out there, thanks to murdering, moronic motorists, and there's the noise and stench off them as well; the car is truly the Devil's invention. My mother was a remarkably strong woman, mentally and physically. (1924-1986). She had five of us children, with a little help from my (now much hated) dad. There's too much mental memorabilia to even gloss over, but like me, in her latter years, she was always on her own, apart from acquaintances. I'm only eight years younger now than she was when she died of pancreatic cancer (I'm 54, she died when she was 62). She smoked too many fags, which she used to inhale too deeply; it's a wonder they didn't find a huge block of tar in her stomach. She lived her life according to her own standards, leaving home after over a quarter of a century's marriage, to start her own life in London. I think she had at least ten years there, she seemed to love the place, I hated it; still do. 1 think she was AC/DC emotionally, and 95% lesbian in her final years; she could come across as very 'butch'. But she was a good mother to me, and that's all that counts. She was a believer in Spiritualism most of her life, (she could be one of my 'mind stalkers'), and had a Spiritualist funeral; her coffin was a waste of good wood, seeing as how she was cremated; she'd been kept in the freezer for a week beforehand. I never saw her body after she died; I've always been squeamish about that sort of thing. Oh well, I hope your spirit's still out there somewhere mum, give someone a head slap for me will you.

....
...

A SELF-PARODY. I KEEP REINVENTING MYSELF, BUT NO ONE SEEMS TO CARE.

Hey! You won't catch me out with that, 'growing old gracefully' routine, not while there's some lead left in my pencil anyway. Going as grey as the weather is not my idea of fun, I've tried it. I felt like I was a hundred and one. Now I'll colour my hair till I die, even if my face caves in, and I'm left with a toothless grin, dribbling into my dotage.
In some primitive tribes, it was the older men, or elders, who got the young girls, to ensure they'd be looked after in their feeble years.

Here, the only way a man can guarantee a similar luxurious state, is to go and procure a mate from a far eastern country.

I find it hard to believe that in eleven years time, I'll be an O.A.P. I feel so young, cool and trendy; 60-year-old Cliff Richard's got nothing on me, with his Botox injections, and wrinkle-removing surgery. I could sing 'THE YOUNG ONES' and get away with it, with the words writ in large font, in front of me, and a karaoke machine behind, tapping out a rhythm orchestrated by Jive Bunny. Of course, things might change when I'm 55, I might not want to stay alive when I'm 55, (remember David Bowie's 'ALL THE YOUNG DUDES'?) After all, I'll be officially classified as elderly, a bona fide qualifier for the 'silver surfer' and 'snowbird' clubs; and 'tinsel and turkey' breaks for my Christmas grub, wearing my kingly paper party hat, looking like a prize twat.

But wait! If I reach the ripe old age of 65, and still have some hair and teeth left, I'll be able to take 3-month winter breaks in Benidorm or Tenerife, and even Fuengirola, the Snowbird's capital. I might even be able to find an old granny or two, while I'm out there; they'll soon find out I'm no square, but totally hip…replacement that is. When it comes to twisting the night away, I'll be an absolute whiz! Unless my back goes, and my false choppers glow like Belisha beacons in the ultra violet disco light, and I have to be carried out with my prostrate gland on fire. I think I'd better give up the booze and cigars now, while I still can, and join the polyunsaturated clan, drinking calcium impregnated mineral water by the litre, if I want to be a grim reaper-cheater for as long as possible.

Nowadays, coffin-dodging's my main preoccupation, I want to be a part of our ageing nation until I'll enjoy a libation in an old folks home, clutching my telegram from Queen Sophie of Wessex, still fantasising about sex with the more agile care workers. They'd best not bend over in front of me to make my bed, the shock of what could happen might kill me. PHWOARRRRRRRR!!!!

(The ending of this piece caused a bit of a controversy between myself and the joint host of 'The Hourglass Writers', she strongly disapproved, and I wouldn't compromise, so I walked out of a performance reading evening. What year? I can't remember; but this was another nail in the coffin of the group, as I'd known it. Phil Fletcher. 27/4/06.)

....

I'm sick of the need to feel altruistic, Or: 'DESOLATION ROW'.
('ROW' pronounced as in 'HOW')

Is the end of the world really nigh? Are we all doomed because our
global population, and our wanton global destruction and pollution
are out of control? Destroying Nature's ability to recover effectively?
Or, does living in a cold and dismal climate discolour our judgement
on these thorny issues? Leaving us predisposed to a gloomy outlook
on the planet's future? There's a lot of space on this relatively small
globe of ours, two thirds of it covered in water; and as the world
heats up, maybe this will increase to four fifths, or even seven
eighth's, and we'll all be stranded on islands, with only each other to
eat...eventually.
What concerns me is, do I care any more? And the disconcerting
answer is, no I don't; I'm past caring. I'll continue to recycle my
empty wine bottles and aluminium cans, and look for bargains in
OXFAM. But apart from this rather futile attempt on my part to
save the dwindling global ecology, to quote the, by now, well-rotted
Jim Morrison of 'THE DOORS', (he's been dead for thirty years
now), 'As long as I get my kicks, the whole shit-house can go up in
flames.' And who knows, maybe something beautiful and phoenix-
like will emerge from the ashes, preferably not human, or if so, only a
strain that lacks the overriding desire to dominate the whole
universe.

....

VIEWED WITH SUSPICION.

'I look at you all', to quote a line from a famous George Harrison
song of more than 30 years ago, ('WHILE MY GUITAR GENTLY
WEEPS'). You women that is; and unless you're with your mates,
and not on your own, you always look miserable and preoccupied, as
if someone's just died, or you're wondering where your next free
night out's coming from, with some Tom, Dick, or Leroy. While my
eye's always looking to the main chance to get into your pants for as
little outlay as possible.

And yet, I feel you all viewing me with suspicion, and not a little derision. A figure of fun to be scorned by you and your mates, the type you don't make dates with; after all, you've got your reputation's to think about, haven't you? 'You wouldn't want to be seen out with him, he's minging'. You seem totally unapproachable to me, with your impossibly high expectations of your average male. I'll have to languish in my lonely gaol, with my villainous countenance, until I've learnt the art of necromancy, and can put you in a submissive trance to do my every bidding, only kidding! I prefer my women ('my women' that's a laugh) to be a bit feisty, as long as they're being nice to me. And nowadays you very rarel are social niceties; why should you? You've got the upper hand. And nowadays you very rarely are (nice, that is), there's not enough in it for you, I'm a much older, and uglier version, of guys you're dating already; and they've got all the cash and youthful zest. At best I might be able to manage it twice a night, as long as we only have a weekend relationship.

VIEWED WITH SUSPICION (2)

If I'd only ever met one of you who would have shown me some trust, instead of seeing me latterly, (for the last fifteen years or so), as nothing more than a rusty old lust bucket, you'd have had some fun; I can get things done, I can make your dreams come true, as long as it's within the law. I'd have given you more than you thought I was capable of; but now I don't think you're worth any special effort. If I saw you lying in the gutter on fire, I don't think I could be bothered to piss on you to put you out, not unless I went and had a few pints first, to quench my thirst for life and love and the stars up above. If only wine could be my mistress and not my ultimate destroyer. If I'd had as much sex as I've had intimate relations with the bottle, I might not feel like throttling the cold, callous bitch who's become the norm in the UK today; but you expect nothing from a pig but a grunt.
Oh, to meet a hot, hairy, juicy cunt, who'll be pleased to see my purple head, all swollen up; and who won't mind being shafted and bathed in spunk, and licked and sucked, and getting well fucked on a

regular basis. Such an oasis in this desert of feminine aridity is all that's left for me to find. All I have at the moment is a mirage, way off in the distance, my resistance in this waterless land is getting lower and lower, I need a 'goer' right now, or else it's the hole in the mattress again. Oh, the shame of it all, and that spring can be so vicious too.

I hope this is my literary swan song as well.

....

(But of course, it wasn't. I wonder if that last, outspoken piece was the reason why Joolz Denby never responded to me? I'll never know now, most likely; and do I even care? The answer is a resounding NO!
I have a couple of additions to add to this collection, from this year, 2006, they'll appear in the e-book version on my web site, when I get round to setting it up; after I've finished correcting my other 7 collections.

....

OPEN MAC' NIGHT.   12-14/4/06.

The bitterly cold, lifeless, greasy film of winter, is once again being melted; albeit somewhat slowly and begrudgingly. By the arrival of another Spring.
I thought that line up while I was having a crap (a noisome one), in my cold and unheated 'crapper'. Too much information? (Especially for my sultry lady readers, a non-existent following, so far). I wish I had a toilet with a solid wooden seat and lid, in a bathroom where the temperature never dropped below 65F, with a pot-pouri scent in the air, and a wooden toilet roll holder that wouldn't ever squeak, holding peach-coloured, strong, kitten soft, shite paper. I also wish my faecal matter (sometimes it has the consistency of 'matter') didn't smell so bad; is it a sign of getting old, or is it a medical complaint? If I was loaded, I'd go and have myself thoroughly checked out in a private health hospital, (even though you can get MRSA in them as well); but I'm not, so thank fuck for air freshener...not 'OUST', 'OOF!' Have you seen the price of it?
I've no need to write anymore; I've even sworn off writing, but I hate to waste a good title. I've already e-mailed 'Roger's Profanisaurus',

courtesy of VIZ, with a take on 'open mac' sounding similar to 'open mic'. I'll reproduce that e-mail after this piece, on disc, in VWS. Alogarithm has the same rearranged letters as 'logarithm', and both words essentially relate to numbers, apropos of nothing in particular. It's been about 45 years since I had to tackle logarithms, and I'm still systematically working my way through an algorithmic problem of how to get a quart's worth of life out of a pint's worth of money. I've done a couple of 'open mic' nights, and I have to say I think I would have had more enjoyment if they'd been 'open mac'.

Not that I want to see other men's stiff cocks, there's something disturbing about the erect male phallus, especially if it's thicker and longer than yours; I think it's got something to do with the origins of our species, or maybe something even more primeval than that...maybe it's just me being girlish?

The actual title piece of 'VIEWED WITH SUSPICION', is thought to be too sexually explicit for the more sensitive palate. I sent a copy of this, my first self published (and badly flawed) collection, to Jools Denby, c/o Bradford Library; I was assured she'd get it, but as I never got any response from her, I either have to assume that she never received it, or if she did, she disapproved of its misogynistic bias.

I chose Jools/z because I thought she was a kindred spirit, in that she knows all about being depressed, like me. There are two types of depression, clinical, and circumstantial. I can (again) only assume, that with Joolz, it's clinical, because she's got nothing physically wrong with her; even having dyed, bright, pillar box, red hair, hasn't got in the way of her becoming a moderately successful poet and novelist. I've heard her on Radio Leeds quite recently, and she sounded quite upbeat; I think she's selling more books these days.

Sexual explicitness in print, is a hit or miss affair; there's even a 'worst sex description in print' list now. I've had to channel all my pent-up sexual frustration into my writings; like I've said elsewhere, I could well be 69 before I get my first '69-er'; I just hope she's got a really nice cunt, whoever she may be. For me, the sex urge, is the strongest there is, and all young women should have their first sexual encounters with a much older man...like me for instance.

....

Transcript of e-mail sent to: profanisaurus@viz.co.uk recently.

'Open mac'. I went to an 'Open mic' night recently, mistaking it for 'open mac' night; I'm a compulsive flasher you know. I was first up

to the mic', I opened my mac' and stood there, proudly erect, expecting to win 1st prize. It came as a nasty surprise when I was bundled out by the cops, with a helmet over my 'helmet'; the next 'open mac' night I'm going to will be in Wormwood Scrubs.
Mac the flasher.

....

I sent another one about 'biz', along the lines of, 'Instead of saying: 'I'm going for a biz', say, 'I'm going for a viz', that way, people who hold you in high esteem, won't associate you with the rest of us mere mortals and our unpleasant toilet habits. Of course, if you get a galloping dose of the squits, your cover could be blown, along with the pristine state of the white porcelain where you've pebble-dashed it.

....

And that's it, I hope the next time this collection reappears it will be in cyber space; I want to remain as anonymous as possible, like B. Traven (no one remembers him now anyway), it would be great if I was well known but nobody knew my face; it hasn't made my fortune so far.   Phil Fletcher.

....

As part of my policy of burying new work amongst the old, this is what I'm doing right now on 25/9/07. I hope I'll soon be nearer to setting up my E-book site, when all my collections will be for sale, ha ha ha !

THE NEW GODS.

I watched a programme last Tuesday night called 'TRIBE'; this guy called Bruce Parry goes to remote parts of the world where tribes of people still live Spartan lives compared to ours. I think he's mad for the most part, as are the people he goes and stays with, with their bizarre and macabre customs; the worst thing I've seen him do is drink warm blood drained from a cow's neck, the very thought of it makes me want to gag; last week he ate a piece of still steaming liver from a freshly slain Kudu deer, gruesome.
On Tuesday night he was up in the mountains of Tibet where, for once, he was able to keep his clothes on. He stayed with some

pleasant tribes people who are Buddhists, and one of them said that if you've behaved really badly in a past life you'll return to this one either as an animal, a demon, or a hungry ghost; I've been a hungry (for love) ghost most of my life, under the control of a demon.
The Buddhist man also said that the main teaching of the Buddha was/is: 'The root of all our suffering is desire,' (Bruce took this on board after he failed to make it over a snowed-up mountain pass to his next destination; he and his team tried for about 5 days but had to give up when his yaks refused to go any further. He adopted a philosophical viewpoint from then on and contented himself with spending more time at his first village.)
I reckon that the root of all my suffering is down to UNFULFILLED desire, 'it's a killer, man.' (I'm experiencing some unfulfillable desire right now, ha ha ha!)

THE NEW GODS.

The new gods interests are at odds
With the welfare of the planet, they're
Siphoning off its lifeblood, no good can
Come of it. What will be the use of
Personal wealth when the health of the
World is beyond repair?
They're in league with the Devil, these new gods;
If they ever had souls they've sold them long since.
The only quest for a 'golden fleece' today is the
So-called 'golden handshake for taking as much
Out of the communal pot as you can, while putting
Nothing back in but a belch and a fart of fetid air.
I'm not making a moral statement here, I'm no
Buddha-like saint, I'm tainted with enough greed lust
As the next wannabe capitalist.

Errol Finn, down-at-heel socialist.

....

Anal sex and double penetration are Britain's most popular porn on film right now, apparently.

A LIMERICK TOO FAR MOST LIKELY IN THIS ANALLY RETENTIVE AGE OF FALSE MORALITY. 17/9/07.

There was a young lady from Kent,
Who knew what Reggie meant when
He asked for a bit of what she'd vowed
To give up for Lent.

He said he spent a fair amount on scent
(from the 99p shop actually), which he
wanted her to spray around her fundament
so he could stick his tongue where a tongue
doesn't naturally belong, but she said no,
so he went before he came.

Determined to seek pleasure wherever he
Could, he got 'wood' just by looking at
Scantily clad models in a shop window display;
He ended up pulling his pud just before daybreak
In front of the erotically clad manikin of his
Choice, panickin' lest a cop car went cruisin'
Past. He was pumpin' hard and fast in the pre
Dawn light, fighting the good fight against flaccidity
At the futility of his wrist action.

There was no real interaction between himself
And this stoney-faced wench, she continued to stare
Blindly out in front of her, not seeing his features
Blur momentarily in an orgasmic wrench; a really
Discerning eye would have caught her smirking
Slyly as he bent to pull back up his dropped pants.

Phil Fletcher-Stokes.

....

THE FEAR OF IMPENDING DEATH IS AN OBSTACLE TO MY
MATERIAL HAPPINESS.   18/9/07.

I've 'dissed' you, so in order to make me pay, you're going to
Have to spray my splattered brains around my shattered skull
With a few well aimed wallops from a baseball bat, you
Educationally subnormal twat…unless I get you first.

At worst I could only come off second best, done in

51

By a pestilential threat to society; the only thought
You ever had was, 'If I act hard enuf they'll be
Shit-scared o' me,' which is patently true. Who,
In their right mind wouldn't be terrified of a
Knuckle dragger along the pavement like you?

This short piece has been inspired by another oafish neighbour of
mine, everywhere I go there's always at least one bullying brute to
mar my joy. Oh well, I'm 60 now so inevitably my sufferings can't go
on for ever…not unless I get consigned to the confines of Hell after I
die.

Phil, 'I'd rather take flight than fight', Fletcher.

•••

DOWN IN ONE.

(THE FOLLOW UP TO

'VIEWED WITH SUSPICION')

BY

PHIL FLETCHER

A BLACK SUN PRODUCTION   2001AD (THIS IS MY

MILLENNIUM COLLECTION, IT WILL LAST FOR A

THOUSAND YEARS.)

This collection contains some very sexually and harrowing material,

so if you're easily offended or nauseous, don't read it…JUST BUY

IT!!!.

I HATE ALL INSECTS EXCEPT BUTTERFLIES. (The torture of prolonged social isolation & exclusion.)

A few weeks ago, I saw two examples of real death on TV; a man hanging from a set of goal posts, and a woman shot in the back of the head; but you couldn't see her face, she was covered from head to foot in one of those blue tent-l[ke garments that Afghan women are now compelled to wear; she just keeled over silently after the bullet had killed her; at any rate she didn't appear to be moving very much, as she lay on the ground.

This harrowing scene was filmed surreptitiously by a Western female journalist of Afghan origin, who was risking her own life and liberty, to alert us to the excessive horrors of the seemingly, criminally insane, Taliban regime; destroyers of people they don't like, and huge Buddhist statues of World Heritage, historical importance. Oh yes, there was another atrocity picture I saw before I switched over in apathetic disinterest, thinking, 'Well what the fuck can I do about it?' (I was in Amnesty International once, it didn't work out, I was too judgmental in my letter writing to tyrants and despots.) It was a colour photo of a young Afghan man whose head had allegedly been skinned, his eyes were still in his head, and his teeth were clenched together; it looked as if he'd been roasted from the neck up.

When I was much younger, the sight of such images would have left me feeling horrified. I can still remember the feeling of absolute terror and despair I experienced when, at the age of fourteen, some forty years ago, I opened, and looked through, a library book my mother had specifically told me not too. It was called 'KNIGHTS OF THE BUSHIDO', it dealt with Japanese atrocities against POWs during the last World War.

There were black and white photographs of mutilations and mass executions; but what upset me the most was some hand drawn depictions of torture. Two in particular were totally diabolical. The victim was held down, and a hose pipe was forced into his mouth, and his body filled with water; the next crude drawing showed a guard jumping on his stomach, and the man's head exploding, at least that's the way it looked to me. I remember feeling, for the first time,

absolutely helpless against a cruel, and evil world, and rushing out
into the open so I could gulp in some clean air.

A couple of years ago, on another Saturday night in on my own, there was
a programme on C4, about people still being burnt as witches in rural
South Africa; up to 200 a year. There were a couple of colour photos of
burnt heads, one skull still had the flesh on it, but its mouth was wide
open in a pain, and horror-driven, death scream. It's another way of
pointing the bones at someone; if you don't like an individual, or family,
in your village, or you're jealous of their success, you accuse them of
witchcraft, and unless they do a runner, they're dead meat.
All these recollections of crimes against humanity, was brought on
because I was trying to think of something to write for 'ROUTE'
magazine's crime anthology, well this is one area where fact is much
more unbelievable than fiction.
14/7/01.

....
......

STRANGLEHOLD.

'You can't go against your fate', is an expression I've always hated,
especially now that mine's been signed, sealed and delivered.
And do you know what it says? 'YOU'RE FUCKED!!! Physical and
mental pain's gonna getcha!' Which is a pity, because if it wasn't for
this awful decision, (which I'm trying to treat with derision), I'd still
feel I had a lot of living to do.
But I fear this tiding of ill omen is true, the physical pain is on the
increase, urged on by a persecution complex, depression, and an
over-riding sense of inadequacy too,
It's a 'chicken and egg' situation about what's happening to me, I've
had a long and fairly unrelenting history of emotional turmoil, now
I'm paying for it physically. My body's racked with pain, from my
lower back to the skull casing housing my brain.
I've classified myself as Britain's most unloved man, I am. But if it
wasn't for my marked physical decline, I'd still feel I had plenty of
time to put this right, provided a massive injection of cash could
come my way; well heeled older men are in demand today. Broken
down old farts need not apply, they, like me, can wait to die in any
way they choose; booze would be my favoured option, slurring, 'Fuck
'em all!' with my final conscious breath.
9/8/01

....

......

SYRUP.

On syrup of figs and figurines, I have nothing to say, on stirrups and stirrup pumps, I could write a play; Mumps and Rubella aren't as common as they used to be today. 'I'm feeling gay in a melancholy way', is a line from an old 'torch' song that I'd play at two in the morning, while reflecting on days gone by, with a tear in my eye, and a large bottle of wine close by, and a good cigar.
I'd be praying for the promised land of eternal sleep, as my set of false teeth looked on at me from their glass at the side of my bed, at my ever increasing state of decay; no one would miss me much anyway.

Night and day would come and go in their eternal cycle, my St Micheal underpants would fill up with brown ooze, my 'snooze' pillow would absorb my rotting scalp; it's nature's way of breaking physical matter down.
Maggots would materialise out of nowhere, wriggling around under the duvet and inside my nose and eyes; flies might lay eggs in the crevice between my thighs, my back passage becoming their larva's front door. No more loneliness and despair for me, my soul won't hang around. I'll be free to roam over sea and foam; evening sunsets a speciality. Full golden moon's on the oceans, lapping against the shore, mine forever more if I want them. And inbetween? Haunting holiday-makers in a most unpleasant way, by enveloping them in a grey, depressing smog.
11/8/01

....

....

DOWN IN ONE.

It's already done and dusted, I'm already up and gone, 'Aspro aparto!'. I've got it down in one.

I'm writing up a storm, having spent a night in one on a hillside in the pitch black; storm water thudding off my back, and only an old tarpaulin groundsheet between me and the rain. That was at a washed-out rock festival at Barkisland, near Halifax, 30 years ago. How I made it back to Manchester without catching double pneumonia I'll never know.

A similar thing happened six years later in Crete, just outside a little village called Fournes, we got flooded out of our tent by torrential sheets of rain. Finding a big ruined house to shelter in, was heaven sent for me, it allowed me to break away from the crowd I'd come out of England with, and hit rock bottom on my own, alcoholically.

I really abused my body while I was out there, it took it in its stride; I never really felt any pain no matter how hard I tried to destroy myself, nearly 24 years ago. I'm paying for it now though, 'Aspro aparto', (loosely translated as) 'Down in one!' Glasses of Greek red wine, in my 'Zorba the Greek' days. The atmosphere was right for it, I had an Afghan coat and a Gandalf staff, which some spiteful local broke in half one night, when I stumbled drunkenly back to our squat without it. Even that couldn't ruin the magic that I felt, I still had a leather belt that could take the full weight of my upper body if I leaned back on it, buckled tightly round my waist.

And there was a celtic cross hung around my neck, to which I was able to attach weird little pierced Cretan coins, the size of old sixpences. They used to make a pleasant little jangling sound when I walked; later, in Amsterdam,, a Dutch cop found this free-spirited adornment, something he didn't like, ripping it off my neck and warning me to get out of Amsterdam before I was deported.

Actually, it's the last 15 years spent here in Calderdale, that I believe have really broken my health; there's an atmosphere of cunning and stealth here that isn't always perceptible to the untrained psychic eye. Some of the local populace have their own hidden agenda's, dating back centuries. A bit like those, left alone together too long, cretins; sorry, I meant to say Cretans, who snapped my sturdy walking stave in half.

I don't think they'll be happy here, till they've put me in my grave, but I won't go down without a monumental fight, I'll not go quietly into that last unwelcome goodnight.
Or maybe it's just the drab grey weather here that makes me feel so oppressed, plus the fact that I can't get arrested when it comes to finding a halfway decent-looking soul mate.

11/8/01.

....

......

TONGUE ON THE COUNTER.

I'm 'in love' with a young woman who works on the liquor counter at 'SUPABUYS'. If you've got only a small amount of groceries, you can take them to her counter too. I think she's really fit, in a classy sort of way; I'd like to be able to say 'I'm writing a poem about you', but she'd probably laugh in my face, or turn really frosty, the way most females do if they sense I'm interested in them…the cheeky cunts!!!
When I look at a woman appreciatively, and she looks back at me as if I'm some sort of pond life, I feel like saying, 'A frog can look at a princess can't he'? But most of them are so self-centred and vain, they still wouldn't come across with a mercy shag; like Jimi Hendrix said: 'Loneliness is such a drag', in his song: ' THE BURNING OF THE MIDNIGHT LAMP'.

I reckon my 'SUPABUYS' girl could be a real vamp, she could place her stilleto heel on my chest anytime she liked, as long as the spiked heel wouldn't pierce my heart, unless she was into total sadistic cruelty; pissing on me while I writhed in agony, lapping up her warm rain; helplessly erect in my pain and ecstasy. I wonder if she'd go down on me before I died? And I could wedge my nose in her bum crack and lick her fanny out.

Of course, she might be a thoroughly nice young lady, and if she ever found out the real nature of this work, go completely berserk; and any remote chance I might have had of winning her affections would be blown out of the water big style!!!

I'll most likely continue to ogle her furtively through my squinty eye, whenever I take my basket up to her, and fantasise about having oral sex with her on the counter, by her sitting on the said counter with her legs up and open, and her love juice dribbling cunt, perched just over the edge, so I could slide my tongue in and up, (excuse me for a moment while I relieve my frustration).
This behaviour might hold up the tutting queue behind, which is what I'll be doing,, holding her behind while she fucks my tongue.
In reality, there are too many hidden boundary lines I mustn't cross; not unless I wish to risk losing a complete loss of face, and being barred out of 'SUPABUYS' in abject disgrace; never to be allowed back in again to buy spaghetti at 7 pence a tin, or Irish Stew at 32. Both of my favourites, with a dash of pepper and a pinch of dried herbs. There's no flavour in the herbs unfortunately, but I've got to use them up.
Sadly, I'll have to continue feigning stolidity each time I see her lovely face, like a Cigar Store Indian, and who knows, just maybe, one day she'll throw her knickers in my face and say, 'Sniff those you old perv', and I can pass away in ecstasy.   14/8/01.

JOEY THE BUDGIE.

When I was a kid we had a succession of pet budgies, one of them was called Joey. We also used to live in a cobbled back street in Rusholme, Manchester, where I can still remember the gas filament lighting in our living room/kitchen, it gave off a yellow light. There was also an old fashioned kitchen range in the house, and a room on the landing which me and my sisters treated with dread, it was probably just a store room but to us it held unnamed terrors, we called it 'the dark room'.
We also had fly papers in our old house, because back in the early 1950s, summer was really summer and flies were a nuisance, at least they were to my parents I presume, I can't say I was unduly aware of their presence at the tender age of six.
I think Joey was one of our more sociable budgies, always chirping and knocking seven bells out of a little bell in his cage, clamouring to be let out.

Obviously, I don't remember every aspect of the unfortunate event clearly, it happened roughly 48 years ago, but one evening during one of his frequent exercise periods, Joey flew straight into a fly paper and got stuck. All I really remember was his frantic squawking (or was it screaming?) and a flurry of green and yellow feathers, before being shooed off into the rarely used back living room (sorry, 'parlour'.)

Joey never got over the shock of what happened to him, and ceased to be the perky little bird we'd all been so fond of; in fact, very shortly afterwards he just ceased to be, and was given the ceremonial cardboard shoe box burial in our seldomly cultivated, or productive, back garden plot. I want a cardboard coffin myself, to be buried in a field with a Fever Tree planted on top of me, very appropriate seeing as how I've lived most of my adult life in a fever of numb terror, due to making the wrong decisions most of the time.

When I was ten or eleven I had a 'pet' rabbit foisted on to me, called Patch, he was kept in a hutch outside the back door of our recently acquired three-

bedroomed, council house in Wythenshawe, South Manchester; a palace compared with our Rusholme abode. I never really bonded with Patch, I don't know who was more depressed, me or him? I did occasionally try to give him some of the love I felt I was being deprived of, even at that early age, but he'd always wriggle out of my grasp and hop off down the garden in a bid for freedom.

On the odd occasion that another rabbit was put in with him to try and cheer him up, all hell would break loose, and the interloper would be pulled out missing bits of fur. Eventually Patch did us all a favour and disappeared, the only trace left of him was a hole burrowed beneath the wire netting my dad had put up at the bottom of the garden to try and keep him from escaping. There was a little area of woodland not far away, maybe he made it across to it, and lived on in lonely splendour for a time, before old age or a vicious dog got to him.

14/8/01.

....
....

THE HALIFAX PIPE SMOKERS CLUB.

The Halifax pipe smokers club doesn't meet in Halifax, they meet at The Ram's Head in Sowerby Bridge, on the first Monday of each month at 8pm, contact Margret on tel no……. I must admit that I laughed uproariously when I saw this club's name listed in an inventory of groups and clubs in Calderdale. I never see anyone smoking a pipe any more, I wonder if Margret smokes one? And does this disappearing breed all wear tweed jackets with leather patches at the elbows, and have a worn leather pouch of 'CONDOR READY RUBBED' pipe tobacco in their jacket pocket, along with their favourite pipe, and a box of 'SWAN VESTAS' matches (no longer made I fear, why do I fear? I always hated the stink of matches, a horrible sulphurous reek!), and pipe cleaners just in case the stem had got bunged up with thick tarry spittle?

I'm as fascinated with this, by today's standards anyway, eccentric club, as the late Frankie Vaughn was with what went on behind 'the green door' in the classic 'rock'n'roll' song (called 'GREEN DOOR') of forty-odd years ago; here's a slight adaptation, "There's a thick blue haze because they smoke a lot behind the brown door, wish they'd let me in so I could smoke a pipe of CONDOR, and they'd all chorus: 'Ah! It's that ready rubbed moment' in the back room of THE RAM'S HEAD.

I only ever tried pipe smoking once, that was 30 years ago after I'd retrieved a couple of old pipes that had been thrown out in a box of junk, when I was a 'refuse disposal operative', or 'dust bin man' to you. I was living in a dingy bedsit in Withington, South Manchester, experimenting with hallucinogenic drugs at the weekend, and doing this gruelling job during the week. I remember boiling the pipes to sterilise them, I don't remember what tobacco I used, it might well have been 'Old Holburn' cigarette rolling tobacco, I smoked roll ups back then in those halcyon days when I could abuse my lungs and get away with it. Obviously pipe smoking was not my forte, except if you include inhaling cannabis smoke through a chillum, something else I couldn't do now, unless I had an oxygen mask handy, and I'm paranoid enough already.

I experienced my first bout of severe clinical depression while I was staying in that awful house of thin walls, and a shared toilet and bathroom. It was one of those Bed-sit dumps where the various occupants crept about, desperately trying to avoid each other. I had to nerve myself up to go down to the toilet, clutching my toilet roll and sneaking out again hoping it didn't smell too bad, I probably ended up peeing in the sink in my room, I don't think I ever sang in the bath while I was there.

I had to return to my parent's house after three months, which didn't please my dad very much. I don't remember how long I was back there before I was offered a council bed-sit flat not too far away. The best thing that could be said for that council hovel was that I didn't have to share a toilet with strangers, I lived there for the next fourteen years.

16/8/01.

....
....

I GUESS I'LL JUST STOLIDIFY, TILL I DIE OF BOREDOM.
(A catalogue of woe from a thoroughly modern middle-aged man).

It isn't the sex act itself that's 'God's' ultimate joke against mankind, (especially if you do it in the dark, much more exciting and primal, or so my long distance memory tells me); it's being male, seemingly not very desirable, but primed and ready for sexual action, with only the slightest encouragement from a pair of flashing female thighs, eyes, and a set of glistening white teeth.
It's been an unnaturally long time since I last had sex, it's all part of the curse of being a gargoyle among the 'normals'. The sex act itself can be little more than a short, sharp, shock to the senses of the inexperienced male; you're no sooner in, than you're out, having possibly taken hours to get the female 'in the mood'; they being a lot slower to sexual arousal (or so we're led to believe), except when they get to around thirty six, when they're supposed to become as rampant as the average eighteen-year-old spotty youth. That seems like an immaculate misconception to me; as society still frowns on older women parading 'toy boys' around town for sex on demand in public places. I was quite shocked earlier this year to read of a couple having really noisy sex in the gent's toilet in The British Library, they were thrown out of course; talk about lack of self control and chronic attention seeking! Apparently, they were still stuck together like dogs while they were being ejected from that august building.
I think the same degraded couple, were later spotted fornicating against one of the pillars of The British Museum, or was it the Tate Modern? I'm only going off memory, not accurate information. Primarily, sex is for procreative purposes, I think we're the only primate species, apart from Bonobo Chimpanzees, (who use sex as a form of greeting and communicating), who indulge in recreational sex. Most other species operate within strict social parameters, such as males coming in and killing the offspring of other males, so the

females will become sexually receptive and accept their seed; we'd call that infanticide, though whenever I hear some brat throwing a tantrum in a supermarket, I know exactly how those other male animals feel.

Women are pre programmed to be judgemental in their quest to find their perfect mate, although quite often their idea of perfection falls far short of any logic that I can understand; even more so nowadays. I'd say this country's breeding stock is going straight to HELL!, in its own 'couldn't-care-less way'. All that will be left, in fifty, or a hundred years time, will be a small nucleus of established 'British', the rest will be a hotch-potch of hybrid dysfunctionals, issuing out of one parent baby farms, in a feeding frenzy of Caligula-like sadism, greed, and lust; if the chilling line I picked out from a reality TV programme about London clubbers is anything to go by, from an otherwise intelligent young man: 'She's not my girl friend, I just fuck her'.

Tues. 28/8/01. And also, if SKY TV's 'SUMMER UNCOVERED' (which I've watched purely in the context of 'research') is anything to go by, young men and women now definitely seem to have reached soulless, sexual parity. I observed very few signs of romance, just a relentless quest for sex on both sides. I can imagine that I'd have been deeply humiliated if I'd been young now and had gone to Ibiza with my mates; it was bad enough when I went to Butlin's Holiday Camp aged 16, 38 years ago, and was given the 'minger' treatment by a party of pleb bitches, who used me unmercifully to lure my mates into their chalet; and I haven't really fared much better since. But I still don't hate women enough to go down the 'Yorkshire' Ripper's road of murdering 13 of them; my 'soft nature' has spared me that ultimate expression of misogyny. Though from what I saw on TV recently, Peter Sutcliffe has got a constant stream of female admirers, who even want to marry him, and who he plays off one against the other, through a relentless barrage of letter writing from his safe haven in Broadmoor Prison for the Criminally Insane; even a poke in the eye with a felt tip pen last year(?) hasn't slowed him down. One disgruntled ex admirer has had over 500 letters from him!!! I suppose a man with that level of mental energy, probably a megalomaniac, would desperately need to find releases for his overwhelming feelings of superiority and contempt.

Going back to 'SUMMER UNCOVERED', there was one instance where a drunken young woman singled out an older man in a nightclub in Ibiza, to ridicule; I admit his fashion sense left something to be desired, but when she first draped herself around

him, he thought he'd pulled, he was all smiles. But then she shouted to her cronies: 'He's minging!;, and flounced off. The camera panned back to his face, and the look on it said that if a look could kill, that girl would be dead. It is a dangerous world out there, (by 'there' I mean everywhere). I feel so strongly on this issue of women's judgement values, or rather, the lack of them, that's nearly destroyed me on numerous occasions, and left my physical and emotional health in tatters, that I wish I could write a treatise on it. But I lack the clinical air of detachment necessary for such a project, (as well as the intellectual capability). Suffice it to say that I trust a woman's judgement on virtually nothing when it comes to affairs of the mind and body, namely the heart; and this in an age where harsh judgemental views are frowned upon, in any but the lowest human society. (I mean plebs' who can't help being thick, but you're not supposed to say it any more are you? Not in their hearing anyway, they might hit you once, or several times.) (And just to show my own ignorance, I always thought 'plebeian' was spelt 'plebian', until the 'spellchecker' on this miraculous machine pointed out my error.)
I love writing, but I've run out of things to say; as far as I'm concerned, the human race is a lost cause, it deserves a severe chastisement. One from which it will learn indelibly, that it isn't invincible, and that the planet which it now infests and infects, isn't inexhaustible. I'm now not too far off becoming 55-years-old, and I'm still waiting to get a life; a bit like the cheesy grin I wore out waiting, 25 years ago.

....
....

THE MOON.   28/8/01.

The moon, that old rock up in the sky that draws my eye to it like a magnet.
Some nights it's clear and bright, on others it's just a luminous grey smudge on a black backdrop.
I like it best when it's big and bold like youth, and lights up the clouds with a silver glow, or shining down on wheat fields far below, as harvest time draws near.
Perhaps moonlight influences the flavour of the wine, as the grapes ripen on the vine, and the summer breeze caresses the leaves, making the fruit of Bachus such a heady brew.

I wish I could dive into a vat of you, and re-emerge, purged and cleansed of all my ills that require so many pills to keep the worst of the pain away.

I understand nothing of astronomy, though I've dutifully watched ;THE SKY AT NIGHT' on TV on numerous occasions. The universe seems to be full of negative energy, highlighted by billions of points of starlight in the night sky. If you can see even a fraction of them, then you're a lot luckier than I am; I've given up trying to spot their glow, unless I go abroad.
It's all dead light anyway, the star you have named after you today, has probably been dead for millions of light-years. Maybe 'black holes' are just black suns, absorbing, rather than giving off power; an impenetrable flower of evil, where all positive force is swallowed up and devoured, with no point of egress for its waste matter.

....
....

THE WWF, (AND WE'RE NOT TALKING 'WORLD WILDLIFE FUND' HERE EITHER.)   9/9/01.

Quite often, a ref' at the WWF, is superfluous; they're always getting floored or beaten up anyway, or even whacked with a steel chair if they can't get out the way fast enough; it's the 'right stuff' of sports entertainment for me.
When you're watching it on TV, the action doesn't always seem that real, you can't feel the bodies bouncing off the boards or the concrete floor. I used to think some of them concealed fake blood capsules inside their hair, but now I've seen bald headed 'STONE COLD' Steve Austin with his face turned bloody red, I don't think so any more.
Channel 4 (here in the UK), used to screen the World Wrestling Federation at 4pm on a Sunday afternoon, it was great, but then it came under scrutiny from the self appointed, very vociferous moral minority, who insisted that it's merely mindless violence; now it's not on till late at night, sometimes too late even for me to stay up and watch it.
If these arid killjoys have their way, Channel 4 will ditch it in favour of another series of 'QUEER AS FOLK', or something similar.
Thank fuck for SKY TV, which doesn't seem to be infected with 'PC'

(Pusillanimous Cack-spouting); I can watch five hours of All American Action Wrestling each weekend, with lots of repeats during the school holidays. And if I subscribe to 'pay per view' I can watch uncensored hardcore, where the bodies get dragged out along the floor.

(3/5/02, I've since got bored with the WWF, even mindless violence can lose its appeal, if you've an IQ bigger than that of the average moron; though it's really taken off here in the UK now. I still appreciate skilled wrestling, but most of the WWF is merely knockabout.)

....
....

DEATH.   10/9/01.

It's a thin line between life and death, you can be here one minute and gone the next, if you're lucky, and not being burnt alive in a car fire for instance; how horrific must that pain be, especially if your family's in there with you?
Or, like me, in a slow lingering decline, due to an evil fate which seems to be closing in for the kill, but never quite will, leaving me in limbo between physical and mental torture, suffering beyond all understanding, a stranger in a hostile world.
I've heard a Spiritualist say that, 'Your spirit passes over to the other side whether you'e a believer or not'; that's a great relief, because no matter how hard I've tried, I just can't buy it. If I could, I'd have gone over already, with a little help from my physical death; generously induced by a binge of booze and pills, none of that violent exiting for me. I'd want to savour the flavour of cursing all the bastards and cunts who've made my life such a misery, especially the cunts. (The only thing worth believing in is luck, if I'd had as much good luck as I've had bad, I'd no doubt be a wealthy and successful man today.)
Still, what the hell, you're only put here to procreate, and if you can't do that because you've been denied a mate, you have to circumnavigate that primary urge, and splurge your spunk up against the wall; mine's worth fuck all anyway. I'll never know if I could have fathered a 'normal' child.

Whenever I show an interest in a woman, she disappears, presumably in a state of wild alarm that she might risk falling for my manly charm, and cop for a pregnancy she'd want to abort.
Anyone who's ever had a general anaesthetic, shouldn't fear death; I don't see how much deeper you can go into the blackness than that, and still wake up. Indeed, quite a few don't, which is why we fear 'going under'. I can remember the bad old days, when a mask was placed over your nose and mouth; and me trying to resist the gas with my arms flailing about, and attempting to shout: 'NOOO!!!'
Now it's only a prick on the back of the hand, and you're out before you can count to ten. The coming round again can be fraught with difficulty. The last time it happened to me, my teeth were chattering uncontrollably and I couldn't breathe; an oxygen mask saved my bacon, and once I'd gotten over the shock, I lay on my hospital bed feeling more dead than alive, with no visitors to look forward to depressing.
I want this to be the end of my literary bent, I'm sick of the muse haunting me, using my ennui as a means of conductivity; you can only get so much mileage out of misery surely? I think Samuel Beckett was about 60 before he began to receive the adulation from women he so richly didn't deserve; (apart from his rugged good looks). He was dubbed: 'The writer of nothingness and despair'. I think he was taking the piss out of a gullible, intellectual elite; it was a form of death of the soul to wade through page after page of his endless, unintelligible guff.

....
....

THE EXPENDABLE ONE.   20/9/01.

I am the expendable one, the kind (mainly women, it has to be admitted) that people find it easy to dump on; if I wasn't prepared to put up a spirited defence, I'd already be buried six feet deep in their stinking SHIT! I've had enough of it. but what can I do, except complain to you, my long suffering pen.
In the case of good versus evil in my life, evil against me has won hands down; causing me endless strife, (for the rhyming effect). And I'm not just talking about localised evil here, it's much more orchestrated than that. Hell on Earth isn't confined to the bottom of the ocean, five miles down, with its black smoking chimneys and

incomprehensible life forms, it's right here in my living room, with its sulphur and rotting corpse fumes.

I still haven't found a one hundred percent cure for the 'evil wind'; Orientals believe that powdered rhino horn can do the trick, but the world's running out of rhino's, and it's been scientifically proven that the rhino horn's consistency is no more than hard skin; equivalent to that of human finger nails.

The good aspect in all this, is my refusal to be broken mentally and spiritually; not completely anyway, by this constant onslaught of perversity. I can't say the same physically; it could be the death of me, and everything I've fought for, the right to choose who I want to love, and to ignore the really poor, and the attendant problems they cause.

There's been a 24-hour pause in my creative flow, this piece has got nowhere else to go, unless I ask you, how would you feel if you'd endured 54 years of being told you weren't good enough to invest any love in? Could you have stood it? Have you any idea what it feels like to face each new day feeling like a reject from life? That you are totally alone, apart from the hideous, and unwanted attentions, of some unnatural, mind-stalking, malevolent creature, who's out there masquerading as a human being; unless it's a Satanic coven of 'chutney ferrets', and the king of the chutney eaters is determined to make me bow down to his encrusted phallus.

I've always hated wasting space, even if keeping up the pace in this case, is proving difficult and depressing; I'd much rather be confessing my horrendously long sexual starvation to a 'Sister of the mercy shag', who was going to excuse my first dismal attempt to please her, as dipping it in to tease her, before I shoot my load before she can get hold of it between her slippery wet thighs, and ride it like a bucking bronco.

She'd have to be really rough, to put me off getting it up again; even in the midst of my emotional pain, my penis has steadfastly stuck to its resolve of 'standing tall', even if it's poking fuck all but the hole made by my curled fingers; only the distant memory lingers of what it feels like to be making love. Maybe when I go above, I'll get my end away again, and again, and again, and my aching right testicle won't complain.

....
....

SELF DISCIPLINE.

I suppose it's a sin when you keep giving in to temptation, because you don't feel enough compunction not to. By 'you', I mean me, I initially lacked the mental self discipline of thinking things through, before I began to write. 'Shite! Fuck! Damn and Blast!' are swear words I'm fond of using; as well as 'cunt' and 'bollocks', which are words for abusing our genitalia, (I do it all the time). I wish I possessed the fortitude never to think of myself as a failure, because I can't compete in a viciously competitive world; only LOADS OF MONEY could cure that particular ill; if I ever win it big on the lottery, I can procure my fill of oriental beauties, whose duties will include, trying to breathe some life back into my sorely depleted sense of well being.

I would also like enough self-discipline, never to feel so lonely again that I want to drink myself into oblivion and never wake up; alcohol's no good for me any more, even in moderate doses. Drinking should be for pleasure, not a no win attempt to cure painful emotions. I spend countless hours engulfed in feelings of deep despair and guilt; it must be in my genes. I've got nothing to feel guilty about, except that I sometimes (quite often actually), speak before I think, and create a social stink amongst the few friends I have, and for which I castigate myself unmercifully, until I'm ready to come out of purgatory, and go and do it all over again; I guess they'll have to take me or leave me, I'm used to spending acres of time alone.

The world might be going to hell on a handcart, with a chemical, biological, or nuclear device on it, but as long as my living room smells nice, courtesy of my 'plug in air freshener', I couldn't give a bad case of Anthrax for it. It's the pleasure without pain principle for me from now on, who cares about gain? You can't take it with you when you go, and why leave it for some other parasite to leach off? If you can't be with the ones you want to be with, you might as well be on your own; that's what I say. (My words come back to haunt me in the echoing silence).

And if I was sat here in my chemical warfare suit and gas mask, (just in case), of which there's been a lot of panic-buying lately, (post Sept. 11.), and those words of self assurance were steaming up the inside of my goggles, as I repeated them to myself over and over; I could get the wrong impression that I was the only one left alive, and go running out into the street; my lead-lined boots causing my feet to drag; and some horny hooker shouted, 'Hi handsome, fancy a shag?', I'd know things were on the up. I fancy organising a rave for all us germ, and chemical warfare suit-wearing types, anyone who hadn't taken precautions wouldn't be let in, we'll be a whole new nation; the only survivors if it all goes horribly shit-faced.

....
....

The cold winds of death, ennui.)

PUBLIC DISPLAY.   6-8/10/01.

They've never liked me round here anyway, so I'm thinking of putting on a public display as a final act of defiance, a spectacular end to a life lived in fear and obscurity.
My face doesn't fit, they treat me like shit, if they'd ever smelt mine, I could understand why; they'll get the chance when I die. It's karaoke night tonight, over at the plebs' local watering hole; the booming bass sound is coming intrusively through the uninsulated stone walls of my house. I'm sure that if I walked in there, I'd kill the atmosphere stone dead; right in the middle of someone's rendition of 'Viva Espania'. An icy blast following me in, accompanying me and my ennui, and a double absinthe and angostura bitters, to a table in the far corner, shrouded in cancerous tobacco fumes; thank fuck I'm a part of the new breed, who believe that staying in is the new going out.
I like to get pissed late at night, the downside is I wake up with my nerves in a fright, and the debacle that's been my life, screaming in my head to end it once and for all; I can usually still this hellish din once the valerian capsules have kicked in; but there's the physical torture too. I sometimes wake up after a good drink in less than an hour or two, with my insides on fire and acid bile burning its way through my gullet; if I was connected to a plug, I'd pull it.
It's a fantasy, rather than reality, what I have in mind; I'm sure that if life would treat me kind for once, I'd forget all about it. After all, hope, like an optimistic phallus, springs eternal, or should do, unless it's gone into a terminal decline, that only Viagra, (Prozac for the knob), can cure.
My fantasy is to hang myself publicly. Naked. A variation on the two bed sheet's knotted together theme. I've read in William Burough's work, that when you hang you ejaculate at the same time; I would hope that when I was dangling against the outside wall of my house, suspended from the knotted bed sheets tied round the base of the

open window frame, that my penis would remain erect and my bowels evacuate, (for added effect). I think it's technically viable for me to achieve this aim, I've got a sturdy UPVC window frame, my knot making expertise is a bit lame though. I might jump out of my bedroom window, hoping my homemade noose will break my neck, only to hit the pavement some 20 feet below, a jibbering wreck with both legs broken.

It's the thought of hanging there for all to see that appeals to me; my final protest against being treated like a social leper; the modern pariah, a bloke on his own!!! People round here don't know that I like nothing better than reading good English literature, (even if only 'English' in translation), and listening to vintage Chuck Berry; not searching for kiddie porn on a computer I don't possess.

....
......

DOES RUST EAT DUST?   9-10/10/01.

I don't need to use words like 'simulacrum' and 'nadir' to prove I've got a brain, believe you me I wish I hadn't; I view too much directionless intelligence with disdain now, it's a burdensome pain.. How many esoteric poets does it take to change a light bulb? The answer is none, they're far too preoccupied with life's mysteries, and being visionaries, to notice it's even gone out; they need someone much more worldly than them to sort such a simple problem out. Maybe they'll spout about it esoterically in one of their inscrutable poems: 'The light has gone out of the world, and who are we to complain? We'll sit here in life's darkness, till some astral deity comes down to earth, and switches it on again'.

A man who was uxoriously devoted to his wife, had her buried in a coffin made of 'polyvinyl chloride', better known as PVC, after she died of Pyemia, not to be confused with piella; I wonder if I'm being guilty of literary cozenage? After all, there's more to the word 'Corrie' than just an abbreviation for 'CORONATION STREET'; check it out.

His voice sounded old and weary at times, usually during prolonged phone conversations with obtuse public servants; too much of this dreariness had flowed beneath his particular bridge; he felt unrequitedly deservant of life's rich tapestry, like the unrestrained love that could gush from a young woman's heart if you can find a way to get her to 'pop her cork!' Leading her to crave a portion of 'pork' to quench her thirst of love-ust. I'd like to drink out of her furry loving cup before I put my weapon in, and watch the flesh-scented steam pour forth as we both orgasmicly shout, 'Eureka! This is the real thing, happiness at last!' (Has this fool never heard of post coital depression?)

I feel penned in by an all pervasive, oppressive, aggressive ignorance-led, 'local' male culture; I can't react against this oppression in a physical way, for various reasons; there's also another form of human tick that's burrowed its way deep into my psyche. I can feel it squirming and moving about beneath the dome of my skull; it feeds off my emotions. If I try resisting, it squeezes my brain in a most unpleasant way. I'd need to employ the services of a top psychic medium to lure it out, and heal the hideous wound it's put inside my head, in its attempt to fill it with its own black magic soul.

But if it succeeds in sucking me dry, what will it do when I die? Crawl out through my mouth, ears, or nose, eating a few crusty morsels on its way? I know in the cosmic scheme of things, I'll never attract the attention of those oriental kings (the three wise men), and I feel my time's running out; and the way things are going I'm likely to be the only one at my own funeral; I want to have '96 TEARS' by 'QUESTION MARK AND THE MYSTERIONS' played at least twice, as my funeral music of choice, (they'll be lucky to find a copy, I've not been able to; I used to have it on a compilation LP but I got rid of my collection in a moment of madness, [I got 80 quid for the lot], which is just as well, I'd have no room for it in the poky little council 'bungalow' I,ve ended up in 14/6/02). And if there's still any time left, 'THE LARK ASCENDING' by Vaughn Williams, and when that bird has reached its zenith, my ghost will shit on you all, from a great height!

,,,
,,,,,,,,,,,

ETERNITY.   10-11/10/01.

Scientists informedly tell us that this, our blue planet, still has around four billion years of life left in it, before the death of our sun will kill it. Scientists also tell us that the secret of eternal life, or at least, a lot longer span than we can hope to enjoy now, is just round the corner; and I don't think we're talking criogenics here. I don't think they've figured out yet where they're going to get the bodies to stick all those severed heads back onto; maybe they'll have developed headless androids by then. I hope mine will have a big dick, and they can give me a new face; I couldn't bear the thought of all eternity wearing this one, otherwise I'll be wanking my enormous synthetic member forever, (I wonder what my semen will be composed of, snot?!)

There's no great mystery to the meaning of life, if you're a bloke like me, you only ever want to be seen in the company of fit-looking women. It's taking an eternity in my case to get to first base with one,; they're much too mercenary. They'll put up with a gargoyle, if he's got money and power, alas, I lack both vital commodities in sufficient quantities to please them, anyway.
We all get world-weary at times, and in this age of mass communication, who can blame us? If I hear of tragic events thousands of miles away, at best I can only pay lip service to them; at other, more depressed times, I can only shrug my shoulders in care-worn indifference.

I don't think I ever get life weary, there's so much natural beauty around to keep reinvigorating the life force; my only regret is, it looks as though I'm never going to achieve my ideals. A couple of weeks ago, I saw a programme on C4 called 'LOCATION, LOCATION, LOCATION'. A young bohemian, (but practical with it), couple, (they were involved in the media, photography or something), had bought a flat in London and were spending time and money renovating it, with a view to letting it out at a rent where they could pay the mortgage, and have a bit left over.
This enterprising pair had also bought a really dilapidated cottage in a fairly remote part of Scotland, for £12,000, which was going to be their rural idyll once they'd done it up; I can see the cannabis plants growing in the back garden even as I write.

Of course, with, lap-tops, PCs, and the internet, they need never feel isolated, or cut off from the world, if they don't want to be; or their work. I do envy this like-minded couple of young people, they can be in tune with the whole universe in their remote hideaway, and always have practical considerations to worry about, to stop them from becoming jaded.

When I was young (23), I used to say the best kind of existence would be a 'peasant' (rural) one, in an enlightened and well equipped world; it looks like it's coming true for one couple at least

....
....

IT'S A NON-NEGOTIABLE, INELUCTABLE FATE. (YOU GET NO TIME ADDED ON FOR GOOD BEHAVIOUR.) 14-16/10/01.

Apropos of nothing in particular, I like nothing better than lying curled up in bed, in a fair copy of a foetal ball, preferably with the radio on; it's one of the few times I feel secure. Another similar experience, is when I'm snug and warm watching TV, with my feet up on the TV table in front of me, and my arms folded across my chest, leaning back in my rocking chair...luxury, unashamed luxury. Judging by the amount of rampant promiscuity that seems to be rife throughout our species, (it's passed me by...), I think we might be descended from the Bonobo chimpanzees, who use sex as a greeting; anyone with a pulse within the group doesn't get left out, there are no barriers about age or gender, and no hang-ups about their incestuous, orgiastic natures either; it's not so long ago that the average human was rather short in stature...hmmm?

The only sane thing to come out of the feminist movement, is the way the modern young woman has cast off the image of being the 'weaker' sex; they're not only up for it, they're mad for it! This new aggressive approach sends out very confusing signals to men in general, whose basic instinct towards women is possessive and predatory; over protective in a lot of cases, and downright territorial and possessive in others. And unless a woman wants to be possessed, short of killing her, or locking her up, he's on a hiding to nothing, which is usually what he ends up with.

In general, they're still the fairer sex, there are some women's looks who I'd sell my soul (what's left of it) to be with. Not just from the trophy aspect, but simply because every time you look at them, you get a good feeling, and that's worth its weight in the 'feel good' factor, as opposed to gold, which is a lifeless metal; it's nice when it glitters but it won't purr when you stroke it, or moan in ecstasy when you poke it; oh dear, how sexistly crude of me.

Even in our enlightened times, I'd call them debauched and depraved actually; we could give Sodom and Gomorah a good run for their money, but then I'm not getting any am I? It's still frowned on for men of my age, (I won't see 54 again) to ogle young women with lascivious intent; though I could have sex with teenage prostitutes, ranging from street tarts, to high class escorts, if I was determined enough. But no, I'll continue in my vain hope that one day I'll get lucky, and attract a substantially younger female, with looks and a brain, even though I have very little to offer in return, compared to more well-heeled men of my age.

I used to have the same sneering British attitude towards Joan Collins and Peter Stringfellow, as your average sniping, media type; but not any more, they've become my role models for how not to age pathetically. Joan Collins at 68, (so I've just heard), still looks beddable; if the rest of her is as unwrinkled as her face, (the snipers claim that's due to a layer of make-up.) I don't know if Peter Stringfellow needs cranking up to get him started in the mornings, I know I do, I feel all heavy and groggy, like I'm on my last legs; maybe I am. No more worries, thank fuck for that.

....
....

THE DRIP, DRIP, DRIP OF CONSTERNATION!!!   17-8/10/01.

Everyone's heard of the Chinese water torture, but does anyone, outside of a qualified torturer, know how it was administered? Was the victim held down securely beneath a dripping tap, unable to move their head from left to right, up or down, so that the icy cold droplets could land on their forehead right between the eyes? I wonder how long it took before the poor unfortunate one was begging for mercy? Offering to tell everything, he or she knew, if only they'd make it stop! And could it drive you to screaming insanity, if the torturers were feeling excessively sadistic, and had a cerebral orgasm every time you screamed, and wanted to prolong your agony?

Maybe the concept behind George Orwell's 'ROOM 101' is more terrifying, where you're made to confront your worst fear, and if you can't face being tortured by it, you scream for it to be done to someone you love the most instead. I think being burnt alive is my worst fear, even a brief encounter with too much heat, like boiling water, causes horrendous pain; and severe burns cause horrible disfigurement, requiring lots of skin grafts.

There's one well known survivor from the Falklands war, whose face is so awful as a result of his injuries, I can only bear to look at him for a short while when he's on TV, He was on the Gloria Hunniford 'Open House' show a couple of weeks ago, I had to flick over while he was on; yet I understand he's married with children. I'm certain I'm not as deformed-looking as him, but all I've ever had from the women I've fallen in love with is rejection. If I was in 'ROOM 101', I'd have difficulty in finding anyone I cared about enough, (I've recently been rejected again), to scream, 'Do it to so-and-so, not me!' I might well have to burn, feeling nothing but resentment (in between my screams), against such a cruel world.

On an equal par with being burnt alive, is my fear of a masked gang (wearing ski masks obviously) of thugs, bursting into my house on some flimsy vigilante excuse. A few years ago, I saw a victim of a 'punishment beating' in Belfast, speaking from his hospital bed on TV. He said the pain of the beating was like nothing he'd ever experienced, despite his screams for mercy, and he looked, and sounded, like a hard man; to add horror to terror, they trashed his house as well. I couldn't live in that atmosphere of fear and loathing that predominates in that blighted province, I'd rather be homeless on the streets of London.
And the fear of such attacks, isn't so far-fetched over here, there's a very uneasy atmosphere on the mainland streets after dark, it's when the monsters come out to play, and there aren't enough good guys on hand to be everywhere at once, even if they wanted to be; which doesn't seem to be the case any more. Despite having a good solid front door, (the only way in), I still feel vulnerable. They could smash my ground floor kitchen window in, and come in that way. I doubt if anyone would help me, by dialing 999; if it was late at night, anyone hearing the crash of broken glass would conveniently assume it was just some yob breaking a beer bottle on the pavement, and turn over, I know I would.

It's still mainly males, mostly young ones, who perpetrate acts of mindless evil; and their actions stem from malformed intellects. A very recent motiveless murder happened at a petrol station, two males beat to death a young man, using only their fists; they then allegedly jumped back into their car, that had other people in it, laughing. They probably weren't aware they'd killed the guy till the following day, if they heard it on the local news; they're facing a charge of murder now. Their actions were caught on CCTV, they might be identifiable; I sincerely hope so.

Quite possibly, they'll feel some remorse for their actions, and when, or if, they're caught, they're asked, 'Why did you do it?', they may well reply 'I don't know what came over me, I wish I hadn't done it', especially as they'll be looking at a minimum of ten years in gaol. (They were caught on 19/10/01.)

Better to mow down a few pedestrians in your car, to assuage your blood lust, you'll most likely get let off with a fine and a temporary ban; or a derisory custodial prison sentence. Or why not go 'big game hunting'? It's still allowed under licence. If you murder a huge bull elephant, you'll get a slap on the back from the licencers, and have your exultant photograph taken next to it, proudly holding your rifle; and for all I know, you still may be able to keep its tusks, feet and ears.

I've just heard, literally a few minutes ago, again courtesy of Gloria Hunniford's 'OPEN HOUSE', a bereathed mother trying to come to terms with the fact that her lovely daughter's body was cut up by a Japanese psycho, using a chainsaw. I hope the girl was already dead before he started. How do you come to terms with such horror? I think you can only absorb so much, before a safety valve in your head clicks on, and the mind shuts itself off. Either that, or you put yourself out of the misery of other people's making, by ending it all in any way you choose; or just avoid the news.

There's a substantial amount of money to be won on tonight's midweek, 'roll over' lottery; if anyone deserves to win it it's me. I could do a lot of good with eleven or twelve million quid, but no doubt some undeserving, rapacious clod will scoop the lot up, and squander it all on conspicuous consumption. I mean, obviously, I'd splash out on some of it as well, but I'd still have loads left over to devote to 'good causes' of my own choosing, and there's only one member of my so-called family, who'd receive any financial help from me, my eldest sister, who has learning difficulties. My father's self sufficient, and the rest can FUCK OFF! They wouldn't get a bean, only a "BET YOU WANT TO KNOW ME NOW" card, sent without a stamp, so they'd have to pay the postage if they wanted to read what was on it, inside it's gold leaf-covered envelope.

Well, that's another two quid wasted, not even three numbers up; but two people netted over £6 million each, where else can you gain such a high reward for a one pound stake? Okay, you might buy loads of tickets, but it's only one set of six numbers that wins the jackpot. Six million pounds would have made me rich beyond the dreams of avarice, and more importantly, set me free from the grinding treadmill of being poor in a comparatively rich society; free to choose where I want to live; free to choose a bride from Russia or the Far East. Even free to eat out if I want to, and not feel guilty for spending money on CDs. Having said, that I got 15 CDs for 20 quid! Four boxed sets of Jazz, Blues, and '60s guitar heroes, that works out at around £1.33p per CD, and they're all over an hour in playing time; so next time you're out paying £15 for a chart CD, think of me and weep.

A couple of months ago, I almost reached rock bottom, (my personal nadir), in my physical and mental health. (I feel as though I'm heading that way again with the lousy summer we're having, 25/7/02). The few writer friends I know were likening me to Vincent van Gogh, and the similarities in our circumstances are quite remarkable; both suffering prolonged isolation and rejection, both living in small towns with small-minded locals, both being befriended by postal workers, (the manager of Todmorden's central post office has always been very cordial to me, at least till last Friday morning; maybe he'd read my letter in the local paper and misunderstood its real meaning?), and both of us not having much success in getting discovered. I think, overall, I'm in a far better position to survive than him. Vincent didn't have television, or long term Incapacity benefit, to keep him going.
What nearly did me in, was unacceptable levels of intrusion into my private space, (I'm not talking about mind stalkers here, that's still an ongoing curse); I mean noise pollution in my house deliberately caused by nasty neighbours. In the six years that I've lived in my, quite pleasant, little house, (I've had 3 social calls in that time) (it's got lots of potential for anyone into DIY), I've had to put up with hostility and nuisance from the people who own the property that my house backs on to. We share a so-called joint water supply, they draw their water through a pipe in my cellar, from a mains stop tap set outside my house.

From day one, they were antagonistic, it was as if they'd heard, through the local grapevine, that I'm allergic to mechanical noise. They ran a butcher's shop. The main source of nuisance was a fairly constant banging noise, this was eventually identified as 'water hammer', caused every time the not-so jolly butcher, turned his cold water tap on and off, up to a hundred times a day, (or so it seemed). BANG, BANG, BANG! I also had noise from a pastry mixing machine, a throbbing and humming freezer up against our 'party' wall, horrid cooking smells coming in, causing a stink like boiled sweat in the early mornings; even his sink was right up against our mutual wall, and they used that as an excuse to bang and clatter trays and pans and what ever else about. All this was far worse than the Chinese water torture, and lasted much longer.

I did get embroiled in a county court case with the obnoxious butcher, but because I've been cast in the role of scapegoat and whipping boy, in this life, I got whipped! And now there's a £2000 county court charging order hanging over me, which can't be paid till I sell this house, and my share in it. Even when his shop closed three years ago, the nuisance didn't stop, there was endless 'do it themselves' building work carried out, to make part of their property domestically habitable. Being disabled, and stuck at home most of the time, I had to endure all the hammering and drilling that went on over a 3 month period; my nerves were in a constant crisis.
This tale of woe and anguish could go on and on, there's been a lull in the torment for the past three weeks, since the last evil-minded swine vacated the maisonette (hell hole more like) next door; and the people who've received planning permission to turn the empty shop into a hot food takeaway outlet, haven't started work on converting it yet. Hopefully, they've realised they'll be wasting their money, as there are already ample food outlets here for a very limited market. If the vitriolic butcher/owner had any sense, he'd turn the whole property into a house with double glazing. The living accomodation is right over a mind bendingly noisy traffic artery, known as the A646 Halifax Road, and try and rent it out, or sell it to some poor mug unluckier than me. Perhaps the odious butcher was my Gaugin? He and his evil family's antics have nearly driven me mad, and the strange thing is, that due to my severe visual handicap, I probably wouldn't recognise him in the street. I only saw him a few times in the shop, and he always sent his solicitor to the county court.

And here in Calderdale, it's not the mistral that affects the inhabitants mental faculties, it seems to be a combined sense of greed and one-upmanship that causes the indigenous males to behave so aggressively. I've no interest in their 'culture', as far as I'm concerned, 'they ain't got no culture'!

I have no real reason to keep myself alive, other than the fact that I LIKE LIFE! It's got to be better than death, my physical health has suffered greatly because of all the accumulated adversity, that being a scapegoat and whipping boy carries. I avoid people as much as possible now, if they can't be of any use to me, they're not worth the bother. Like I said earlier, unlike Vincent, I've got radio and TV, and CDs to keep me company; mind you, he had the brothel and cheap liquor to keep him amused at night time, yeah, on balance,, I think he had the better deal.

There's no outlet for your sexual frustration in this town, unless you're prepared to go chasing sheep on 'the tops' (the hills), (you could do it on a quad bike nowadays). I just stay in, and go out once a fortnight to a writers group in Hebden Bridge. Even going there has become a pain, since the joint proprietor became ultra-precious and 'politically correct'; last time out, one of the readers used the word 'penis', and she, seemingly shocked, said, "Oh, can we use the 'p' word?"

(Author's note. The group has now crumbled into dust due to this overbearing attitude. 1/8/02.)

....
....

YOU CAN KISS MY RING ANYTIME DUCKY. (A RIGHT ROYAL COCK-UP YOUR ANUS; NOW THAT'S GOT TO HURT! AND I'M NOT TALKING FROM PERSONAL EXPERIENCE HERE EITHER, EXCEPT WHEN I STUCK MY FINGER IN MY BROWN EYE BY MISTAKE, THINKING I WAS PICKING MY NOSE. I WAS APPALLED AT WHAT CAME OUT ON THE END OF THAT FINGER, I STILL ATE IT THO'; OLD HABITS DIE HARD.) 26/10/01.

A deeper sleep has no more meaning than the voice of reason, to a chimpanzee, but both might have a soothing and beneficial effect on each other.

Life's just a race against death, let the Devil take the hindmost by the hindquarters, (now I bet that's REALLY got to hurt!). Only the truly lonely can observe that there's no real cohesiveness in a crowd, it's merely a multitudinous throng milling about willy-nilly, with an eye to rumpy- pumpy; well I do anyway when I'm wandering lonely as a bad smell.

I'm at the stage now, of galloping middle age, where I'd gladly pay to have my way with a half decent-looking, and humane hooker. I only want to fuck her in positions of my choosing, without degrading or abusing; I'd promise that if we did 'the wheelbarrow', not to push her past her mum's house. I've said goodbye to any hope of finding love, there are too many dark forces aimed against me. The incongruous prying, spying evil eye is constantly plotting against me, blinking furiously every time I avoid destruction by the skin of my teeth; it really is beneath contempt.

....
....

'CRIMBO' CRACKERS. 27/10/01.

The dirty rotten, cold-blooded, mercenary bastards, are doing it again, hitting on us ten weeks before the great non event, cynically manipulating our good intent; I hope they rot in Hell for it. One thing's for certain, they'll never relent in their pre Christmas onslaught, unless they're forced to stop. I'm not advocating direct action against their one-stop, bargain shop, I'm advocating tough legislation here; no sanitised, sentimental, phoney Yuletide cheer to be rammed down our ever open gullets till Dec, 24. And then only for an hour or two, to remind me and you, that 'A CHRISTMAS CAROL' time is here again, with all its attendant pleasure and pain; only the latter for me. I've got a long, unbroken history of waking up alone on 'Christmas morn', with only a raging hangover for company, and a sprig of mistletoe wedged firmly up my crack.
There's no going back now, the damage has been done, 31 lonely and unhappy holidays lie under my artificial Christmas tree.
I wish I could arrange for a svelte young 'call girl' to be there for me on 'Crimbo' day, wearing little more than a mini Santa suit; she'd look real cute with her 'crotchless panties' on. ready for some steamy action. I think I'd pull them down over her belly and thighs with my teeth, hoping that what lay underneath would be piping hot, and ready for me to go pushing my enormous manhood into, singing, "Jingle balls, jingle balls, jingle all the way up...'

....
....

FRENZIED LIFE ATTACK.   8/11/01
(Irritable Bowel Syndrome, here I come.)

I change my clothes about as often as I speak, usually once a week;
unless I have occasion to pass a word or two with a checkout
operative during my shopping trips. Sometimes I make witty quips as
I'm making my escape, well they make me laugh when I replay them
back in my head later on, while sitting in my smelly old rocking
chair, staring at the TV, night after night; penny for penny, and
pound for pound, it's the best value entertainment around; and it
never answers back when you hurl abuse at it, and where else would
I get to see tits, fanny, (all too rarely) and arse, for free!?…Especially
if I don't pay my licence fee.
If I was into sleazy, sordid sex, I could subscribe to Television X, or
one of the other channels that cater for the sexual voyeur; but they're
a slur on my manhood, unless they ever invent a telly with a jelly-like
screen, and I can have interactive sex with one of these queens of
porn, by sticking my full-on horn into the flexible plastic screen, right
between her ever open thighs.
One of my doctor's reckons my stress level's spiralling out of control,
after I said I felt like smashing a chair over the head of an alcohol-fed
nuisance in the waiting area; she thought I was scarier than any
threat a harmless drunk might have posed; I interposed that he
might have been carrying a knife, putting my life in jeopardy, she
just looked at me oddly.

All I've wanted to be for a long time now, is a male escort, in the
traditional sense of the term; I don't mean I want to escort gay men,
wearing perms or wigs, who might have nasty germs to pass on. No, I
want to be on the arm's of women of quality and substance, who
could find themselves stuck for a partner of the opposite sex for a
particular event, like a dinner party, or a soiree with an invitation
meant for two. I've got the height and the hue, if viewed in a soft
diffused light, and I improve as the night wears on, unless I've gone
too far on the free food and booze; then I lose my cultural edge and
am liable to dredge up all my tales of woe; a no-no in the escort game.
When you're with a dame, she does all the talking, even if you're

82

balking at her tainted breath, in which case you keep proffering her the after eight mints.

If she squints, or is as fat as a house, I wouldn't be a louse and say,"She's not with me"; I'd be too busy thinking of the hundred quid I was going to collect at the end of our engagement, and I wouldn't react with enragement if some lonely old maid with a face that could stop a truck, asked me to stay and fuck her till the cold light of dawn. I'd say, 'Well, as long as you put a bag over your head, and remain sworn to secrecy that it was me who pleasured you into a state of double time (after midnight) ecstasy, I'll see what I can do. Mind you, I'm not promising anything; they don't call me the King of the 'short time' for nothing'.

Alas, it looks like nothing is what I'm going to get.

....
....

NEW AGE STONE AGE.   8-9/11/01.

By the mystic runes of Loony Tunes, and the occult powers of that pile of old stones at Stonehenge, I hereby state that I want to take my literary revenge on 20th century 'hippy culture'...man.

I detest 'new age' travellers as much as I detest the so-called 'real' IRA; both think they are elite groups, and both are determined to have their own way; the former by boring you to death, the latter by blowing you away, at least the second option could be quicker.

It was great when I was young, having long hair and smoking dope, the Isle of Wight Rock Festival in '69, my bedroll tied up with rope. It's a pity my face didn't match my hair and flairs; though I couldn't see it then, that I wasn't really a 'beautiful' person, except from the back, or side profile perhaps. But youthful optimism sprang eternal from my loins, and I never quite gave up hope that I'd get lucky with a really groovy hippy chick; Austin Powers is a slick pile of shite, he's a 'shagadelic' fright. (Maybe it's part of his appeal in an age where 'wikkid' means 'good?)

Still, I did have my standards, and anyone who stank of patchouli oil was out; I'd prefer the odour of liniment rub to that, most of the twats who wore it are now termagants, burrowed deep into the hide of social services, and/or the lesbian parade; to think I used to be afraid of their disapproval.

It wasn't so much a counter culture as it was a cannabis culture, tune in, turn on, drop LSD. Even now, Ashrams all over the world are filled with those on the brink of serious mental illness; largely, adoring female sycophants with a burning need to abase themselves to somebody; the bagwan swami gets first pick of all the fresh young virgins, even if he stinks like an old goat wearing patchouli oil.

Somebody said: 'Freedom is a state of mind', that's apropos of nothing really, I just thought I'd throw it in; except that when your head's clogged up with half-baked doctrines, interspersed with hash fumes and incense, and you can't get up each day till three pm to brew a pot of organic 'erbal tea, to induce a non-genetically modified pee, and odourless crap, wiping your arse on unbleached, recycled shite paper, the lot falling into your composting earth closet, where all the methane is turned into fuel for your generator, which powers your information technology machine. Whereby you contact others in the anti capitalism brigade, and advocate cancelling third world debt relief, in the naïve belief that this will solve the overcrowded planet's problems.

You're doing your bit for humanity after all, and if the fallout from your demo's really hits the fan, you can drop back out of sight in your dingbat Dingley Dell, reeking of home grown weed, leaving the seeds of your discontent to blow up in the faces of those with more actual intent.

....
....

SEEPAGE. (OLD UNDERPANTS, FOR INSTANCE.)   10/11/01

There's no place like bed when you wish you were dead, unless you can't get your feet warm, which makes your chances of recovery take a lot longer. I hate feeling depressed and/or discontent, but I still fall foul of both complaints far too often. I never set out to be a professional depressive writer, like Samuel Beckett; but then I never set out to endure my fairly uniquely lonely, and isolated adult life either. But, like I've said elsewhere, (in 'VIEWED WITH SUSPICION' actually), if you're not prepared to take desperate measures to try and alter your fate, you've got to take what's thrown at you in this life; knowing my luck, desperate measures, like buying £100's worth of lottery tickets, wouldn't even win me a tenner back.

Let consistency be your watchword (and mine). I'm a big fan of American wrestling, as it is now; it's violent and seemingly anarchic, the more extreme it gets the more the crowd loves it. It's a high-risk profession, with big rewards for the more determinedly aggressive. Yet they're on a treadmill, they have to keep up the momentum each week, to keep their baying fans keen, feuds have to be established and grudges settled, and it certainly isn't all faked. On today's 'SMACKDOWN', 'Stone Cold' Steve Austin was fighting with seventeen stitches in a cut over his left eye, 2 weeks ago he had 12 staples in the back of his head. Other fighters disappear off the scene, and are never mentioned again, even if they enjoyed great popularity while they were in the limelight. I can think of five who've vanished without trace.

That vastly overrated 'laughing gnome', David Bowie, had a line in one of his songs, I can't remember which one, I'm not his biggest fan: 'I don't want to live with someone else's depression'; that's okay, I'd feel the same way if I was a loaded super poser like him; mind you, if I'd been responsible for creating Ziggy Stardust's looks, I'd still be in intensive psychotherapy, moaning, 'Why, why, why?'

I feel like I've just fought off an encroaching attack of depression, I resisted the urge to slope off to bed this evening, (it was too cold), and I've done some grooming. My idea of a manicure is to bite, and then file my finger- nails with my teeth; and to cut my own hair, seeing as how the average cost round here is £5.50p for a 'trim'.
I began with a pair of scissors, and then got my clippers out; I've been too demoralised to use them for the last twelve months, and you know, the end result isn't half bad; it took me over an hour, but what else would I be doing at 8.30pm on a Saturday night? Either 'vegging-out' in front of the TV, like tonight, or lying in bed, curled up in my favourite pre natal position, with the radio on.
My new haircut makes me look 'hard', all grizzled silver white at the sides, with a dark thatch on top, thanks to hair colour. I think I have enough testosterone to make me want to look hard to attract women; I'm not interested in competing with other males, I find the whole male thing very tedious and boring, always having to prove yourself; it's potentially very dangerous too.

I've been trying all my life, obviously unsuccessfully, to prove myself to the opposite sex; mainly for sex. I had a flurry of successes in my mid-twenties, maybe because I had a lot of hair on my head and face, but when it comes to attracting a mate…ZERO! ZILCH! I can make women laugh, but I can't impress the ones I fall in love with to love me back enough to trust me. It's very soul destroying to be pre judged, it turns some men into homicidal maniacs, it turns me into myself; harbouring homicidal thoughts against women in general, till I've got over the latest disappointment.

After all, I don't want to end up in an all-male environment, worrying if I'm going to get my arse shagged, or beaten to death because of my bad guts. I'm probably one of the few men who could live in 'solitary', quite happily in the nick; having spent most of my adulthood enduring it. I could lie in my cell, if you're allowed to, fantasising about the women who've rejected me over the past few years; I wonder if you're allowed to wank openly on 'Section 41', or whether you have to do it furtively under your prison blanket, wiping your spunk off on your prison vest?

At least I'd get some new underpants in the 'slammer', the ones I'm wearing now are an absolute disgrace; they're so old they're only hanging together by a thread, one massive fart and they'll be round my ankles in tatters. If I ever get knocked down, and end up on the slab, and they strip me down to my threadbare underwear, they'll put my carcass in quarantine, and the offending keks (it's an offensive word isn't it 'keks'?) in the incinerator.

I think my idea of perfect bliss, would've been to have copped for a really groovy and tasty-looking hippy chick, with long black hair, tall, shapely, practical and intelligent, and with mutual zeal and endeavour, acquire a smallholding together; quite possibly in Wales somewhere. We certainly wouldn't have flopped around like a couple of limp, dippy dope fiends, in a commune, having endless arguments about whose turn it was to wash up, or replace the patchouli oil stock.

We'd have been like 'Tom and Barbara' from 'THE GOOD LIFE', without the infuriating neighbours. And 'FAMILY's, 'THE WEAVER'S ANSWER' played religiously on our annual anniversary.

It should have been our fifth by now, but the hippy chick I met five years ago, a young throwback to the late '60s, wouldn't ditch her leaden lover for me. I saw him once, he was old, I should have……….!!!!!!!

....
....

KILLED BEYOND ALL REASONABLE DOUBT.   22/11/01.
(Or, HYPERCRITICAL SENSITIVITY.)

My enthusiasm for 'the game' that is, has been killed off beyond all
reasonable doubt; I mean, this is me, the 'ROB VAN DAM' (laid
back American wrestler) of the dating world: 'ABOVE THE
WAISTLINE ESCORT'. 'HI LADIES, ARE YOU LOOKING FOR
A MALE COMPANION FOR A PARTICULAR OCCASION? IF
SO, LOOK NO FURTHER, I'M YOUR MAN. I GIVE REALLY
GOOD CONVERSATION, (I TALK ABOUT MYSELF ALL THE
TIME), AND SERVICE. YOUR SENSORY SATISFACTION
GARUNTEED, NOT THAT YOU'LL EVER FEEL THE NEED TO
COMPLAIN. REASONABLE HOURLY RATES.
And this is the attitude I'm up against: 'VERY ATTRACTIVE,
VERY INTELLIGENT, VERY CHOOSY LADY SEEKS A 40 to 50
YEAR OLD, VERY HONEST, VERY TALL GUY WHO'S VERY
CHOOSY TOO'.
I hope she has to keep wanking herself to sleep for a long time to
come, (they do you know, vibrators, dildos, hairbrush handles).
I've also just come across a much more scathing attitude towards my
beleagured sex, penned by Julie Birchill in her 1989 novel:
'AMBITION', I'm sure Julie won't mind me quoting her;
incidentally, the piece of totty on the front cover of this lurid
paperback is a real stunner; sex on legs, maybe even Julie's alter-ego.
Here goes then: 'Ingrid Irving had a theory that there had been a
war that no-one had told them about, in which all the heterosexual
men under forty, over six foot and earning over 50k a year had been
wiped out. They used this weapon which was sort of a very
sophisticated version of the neutron bomb', explained Ingrid. 'You
know—that left buildings standing but wiped out people. Well this
bomb, the talent taker, wiped out all the hunks and left the jerks
standing. The sort of men that used to be called 4F: Fags, failures,
fatsos and freaks." (Unfortunately I could qualify for 2 of those F-
categories, through no fault of my own, and if I didn't control my
comfort eating, it would probably be 3; as to the other one...'I was
never confused, well not enough to give me a sore arse anyway).
'Women, unlike men, were raised on the pornography of perfection,
first pop stars, then romantic fiction heroes. The higher they climbed,
and the more they were told they could have it all, the less inclined to
compromise they became.' An inferior man would cast doubts on

their hard won status. Sexually speaking, successful women had become fussy eaters. (AMBITION, JULIE BIRCHILL, 1989, Corgi books.)

And since then, we've had to put up with 'GIRL POWER', courtesy of The Spice Girls; I wonder if this has got anything to do with so many single mums looking for someone to end their lonely nights, on the sexploitation singles circuit? One pound a minute phone calls at all times! Here's an ad that I should check out: 'Blue eyed blonde, slightly disabled, looking for someone who's loving, caring and honest, likes to read'.
But I'm thinking, 'What's her disability? If it's a speech impediment or cerebral palsy, there's no chance; and I've no idea where she lives. It could be too far away. £1 a minute, plus vat, is a lot to risk to satisfy my curiosity. No, I'll do what she does, read a book instead.

....
....

ROUGH AND SMOOTH, SILVER GREY HOPE.   31/11/01

Disturbing the sulphur laden, still air that surrounds me in my rocking chair, clouds of onion scented gas keep pumping out my ass; enough to inflate a weather balloon, if the length and strength of my farts is anything to go by; or ignite me and my old rocking chair if I dared to light a match.
What's wrong with my insides? I repeatedly ask myself amid the fug, I know I don't live a smug, self satisfied life, chance would be a fine thing.
Wholistically speaking, it's been a god-awful mess, maybe that's why my guts behave like a fermenting cess pit, a vat of bubbling, reeking shit.

My overriding loyalty now is to the earth and sky, I hope when I die I can be buried in a woodland setting, in a biodegradable coffin, with a young oak tree planted on top of me. I hope that from my rotting remains a fair sized oak will grow, and my spirit self may sit beneath its shade on a hot sunny day; why people think that a soul, even with only an ounce of intellect, would want to hang around your average dreary cemetery, in the forlorn hope that a loved one (none in my

case) will come and talk to it, is a mystery to me. I'd be back at their place watching TV, or behaving lewdly in blissful anonymity.
On certain nights I might choose to 'sleep' among the leaves and branches of my namesake tree, a summer breeze caressing me, or a winter's storm blowing my bare branches about; after all, ghosts aren't supposed to feel the cold or grow old…are they?
In 'Earth time', I'll have to wait a good number of years for my oak to take on some height and weight, I wonder how I'll wait out the time? Listen to the gurgle of my slime being sucked up through its sturdy roots? Or chase wood nymphs about the glade, hoping they don't discriminate against rough trade corpse shagging.
Perhaps there will be a thriving colony of practicing pagan undead, where I want to be laid to rest, dressed in woven clothes of mossy green, and a Queen of The May crowning it all off; magic mushrooms for breakfast, and oak sap mixed with morning dew, to ease a chesty cough.
I hope I would live as long as my tree, and when they cut it down, that would be the end of me; except for the part of me that would continue to exist in its timber. Ideally, we'd be used to make some quality items, which might turn up on 'THE ANTIQUES ROADSHOW', three hundred years from now, with grateful owners going, 'Wow! I had no idea my old rocking chair could be worth as much as that, there's always been a bit of a whiff from it, but you don't want to know that do you?

....
....

PORKED! ('GEDDIT?')   1/12/01.
(A HOMILY FOR A COCOONED COMMUNITY.)

I wonder if Vincent van Gogh's very last painting is still on view? And did any blood spill on it when he shot himself through the stomach on that ill-fated day? He didn't die straightaway, he lingered on for a night or two, I can't think why. Perhaps it's on display in that permanent exhibition of his work in Amsterdam? From what I remember of the excellent film: 'A LUST FOR LIFE', starring the equally excellent Kirk Douglas, it was a canvas depicting wheeling black crows in a stormy blue sky, in a field of golden yellow wheat; any blood spatters would look like bright red poppies.

Vincent has suffered the worst ignominy an artist of his extremely sensitive nature could suffer, he's been turned into a public property for the stinking rich, He's become 'Vince inc'. The bitter irony is, that Vincent loathed the art market establishment for the vultures and parasites he perceived them to be, he was a pauper dependent on his brother's patronage. He lived with a prostitute for a year, (not off her), he went with prostitutes; he acted as an unordained priest to impoverished and exploited French (or was it Belgian?) miners in the Borinage. He was a man of the people, the peasantry; the same ignorant types who persecuted him after he became mentally ill in Arles.

I think it's safe to say he despised 'preciousness', except in his appreciation of great art and craftsmanship; in what I remember gleaning from reading all three volumes of his letters, some years ago, mainly to his brother Theo, he had little time for pretentious people.

His biggest stumbling block seems to have been the type of woman he set his heart and hopes on, I think he was always looking for a meeting of minds, as well as bodies, but his over intense manner, or misreading of potential romantic situations, probably, as well as his erratic lifestyle, caused him to come an almighty cropper. This is where another remarkable similarity in our existences is worth noting, the type of women I tend to fall for, are all rather precious or else think they're biologically too good for me, and are terrified that with me, they might give birth to deformed offspring. As much as I like infants, (once they reach puberty they turn into sullen strangers), I've no particular desire to father any; I'd be quite happy to be a surrogate dad...but it's not going to happen.

Also in polite society today, it's not done to talk about too much ugly reality, in a world where we have suicide bombers pureeing themselves over innocent bystanders, victim's plunging to certain death from burning buildings where thousands are being fried and crushed; it doesn't do to dwell on it here in our sheltered little backwater in the Pennines; after all, another snug and cosy Xmas is almost upon us.

(A painting by Vincent van Gogh was sold in New York this week [3/5/06] for £40 million, the second highest price ever paid for a painting; excelled only by that paid for a Picasso. I'm sure Vincent would be the first to agree with me, that this is a sick waste of money!!!)

FUCK FOOTBALL, RUGBY, CRICKET, GOLF, AND TENNIS TOo.   16/1/02.

I just don't get what all the hype is about, 22 blokes kicking a ball from one end of a football pitch to the other. Well, it's 20 men really isn't it, the goalies don't necessarily see that much action; (sorry ladies, I know you play football too, much more interesting from my point of view.) Okay there are skills involved, but not in comparison with the rewards top players receive, nowhere near, 'Honest ref'!'.

It's the fans I feel sorry for, how do they do it, standing or sitting, out there on cold winter nights, cheering their teams on; maybe they have to cheer and stamp their feet to keep hypothermia at bay. There aren't too many discomforts to compare with cold feet and a cold head, I get a band of prickly pain round my scalp now if I'm out in the cold for any length of time, even though I've still got a full head of hair, (' I'm 55 me now, you know, don't look it do I? What do you mean, I look more like 65, you cheeky cunt!"), and a woolly hat, which I regard now as a permanent fixture; unlike my eyes, which are a bit 'home and away', if you know what I mean.

I've just read about an unlikely named invention called 'THE GATOR GRIP',   to allow ref's to have better control over their whistles in freezing conditions; I think it's supposed to stop the cold steel sticking to their lips in icy temperatures; I'd like to suggest that a St Bernard dog with a brandy barrel round its neck, be kept on hand to rescue fans trapped in snowdrifts in the Scottish league.

Wimbledon fortnight is another hallowed event in the sporting calendar, that I loathe with a keen vengeance; how can anyone get excited about two people whacking a little ball back and forth over a net!?!? Unless it's two young women wearing short flimsy tennis skirts and skimpy white briefs...(excuse me for a couple of minutes.)
Golf is terminally tedious too, how can so many clods with absolutely no dress sense whatsoever, be allowed to earn so much money? Snooker and Darts are two more examples of club sports being elevated to unrealistic heights, nice work if you can get it though, from the players point of view.

Rugby and Cricket are two more dangerous contact sports that do nothing for me, they're on a par with mountain, and rock climbing, for people who don't know fear, or think too far ahead about the possible consequences of their risky actions; I wouldn't do anything that would put my life or health on the line.
Having said that, I've recently flown at a height of 39,000ft above sea level without any qualms, it was just like looking down on a vast snow field, 10,000ft higher than Mount Everest; there might have been some nutter stood on its summit as we flew over Spain. If the plane's engines had cut out at that impressive altitude, we'd have hit the ground faster than the speed of light, re-emerging on the other side of the world.

....
...

WHAT DOES POETRY MAKE?   20/1/02.
(A HOMAGE TO CHRISTOPHER MARLOWE'S CREED, HE DIED IN A PUB BRAWL FROM A STABBING.)

Poetry makes cash prizes and a passable living for the chosen few, 'Recommended for inclusion in our next anthology', just won't do.
They say the road to Hell is paved with good intent, when I listen to 'POETRY PLEASE' on Radio 4, my attention invariably wanders, though I meant to listen to every word. I suppose I'm being absurd really, because it's only my own brand of poetry that in the long run counts; not too much right now I must admit, in the big bad world of literary philistinism and anal retention, oh yes, and poseur pretensions.
I can't stand classic, flowery poetry, it doesn't say a thing to me, I'd rather be hit right between the eyes, or the thighs, porno poetry appeals to me.
Ted, and Sylvia Plath-Hughes, and T.S. Eliot, were giant intellects, you need to be a black belt in MENSA to comprehensively get to grips with them. I prefer more down to earth observations of the human zoo, as penned by John Hegley, or the Liverpool poets of the late 1960s, and John Cooper Clarke too.

I don't like wasting space on paper, once I've started, I don't like to stop till I've filled both sides of a sheet of narrow margined, wide ruled A4; I pride myself on not being a bore; anyone who disagrees with this assumption can meet me outside for a couple more insights into my poetic prowess.

Lucrative public performance readings, and lecture tours elude me; Dylan Thomas enjoyed his jaunts in America so much, he drank himself to death; "I've just drunk 18 double scotches," are reputedly the last words the Welsh Bard muttered, before he went comatose into that last goodnight; a man after my own heart; though I'm afraid I'd merely wake up with a frightful hangover, either in Heaven or in Hell, with the smell of whisky vomit on my chin and breath.

I'd rather eschew trying to be too esoteric from now on, my capacity to recreate mystic visions has gone downhill, I've had my fill of 'Rimbaud' and 'Starry Nights', now I've got more in common with Baudelaire. I even know someone who looks like the hatchet-faced French necromancer, he even claimed to have Satanic powers; I think he's regretting that now, holed up in a hovel in Cornholme. I go out of my way to avoid any contact with this former friend.

'THE END' by 'THE DOORS', and 'ATMOSPHERE' by 'JOY DIVISION', are modern poetry in a rock music setting, and speak volumes to me. Jim Morrrison, was the last real bohemian; the Byronically beautiful young man, running to fat through too much excess, he should have headed for the Betty Ford clinic instead of Paris, along with Jimi and Janice, along with the whole drink and drugs inspired, psychedelic crew.

Morrisey is also a damned good poet, another who couches his words in music; I thank my good fortune that I have an ear for it.

(Some might say that the awful, baby-faced looking Pete Doherty is following in Jim Morrison's footsteps; but I find his looks repulsive, he looks like one of those silent movie characters, [more female than male], with his Charlie Chaplin-like eyes and expression. If he's lucky, he'll OD, and then he'll become more infamous dead, than he ever was while alive. 6/5/06.)

....
......

TRAPPED   WIND.
24/1/02

We all have to eat to live, you'd think the gut would be grateful for whatever we throw down our necks to keep it mollified.

It's not as if our stomach's have a mind and voice of their own, and can shout back up at us, 'If you think I'm going to let that load of chewed up rubbish, you've just sent down the grub tunncl, pass through me smoothly and easily, you've got another think coming.' Instead, it blows itself up like a balloon (it does in my case), and fills you full of trapped wind, preferably in an intimate situation; leaving you dying to fart, but you daren't because it's liable to be full of methane and sulphur (also in my case.)

I wonder if chimps, our nearest primate relatives, have the same problem after they've devoured a nice fresh, still warm Colobus monkey? Or even one of their own kind, who's inadvertently strayed into their territory? Of course, if you're a chimp, you can drop a bad fart with impunity, there's a lot of vegetable decay in a forest, stinking the place out.
I saw an ad today for stainless steel kitchen knives, I was prompted to make up a jingle along the lines of, 'Dismember a family member with ease, with these razor sharp blades', and if we were chimps, it would save on all that rending and tearing of our still-living prey, limb from limb.

I'm a mass of physical and mental imperfections, who'd have thought that the melding of one sperm and one egg, could result in such depressingly complicated DNA? I think I've always had what you could loosely term, a 'nervous' stomach, it doesn't take much to set it off, it being the wimp that it is.
The worst aspect of its contrariness is its capacity to produce excess amounts of noxious gas, enough at times to fuel a hot air balloon. Over the years, I've tried various remedies to try and pacify my raging irritable bowel; the worst was a combination of Valerian and Wormwood, which I had to brew a form of tea from. I don't know which was worse, the smell or the taste? It didn't help and I soon gave up on it; recently, I've found that avoiding onion products can help; it turns up in a lot of manufactured sauces,

avoiding these has helped to ease the discomfort, and lessen the malodorous stench.

A prime example of my stomach's perverseness, happened well over a quarter of a century ago; it was when I still had the audacity to wear flared, (28-inch bottoms), purple 'Loon' pants, and a green, velvet-type, waisted blazer; plus long fuzzy hair and prominent 'mutton chop' whiskers. I'd become friends with a very attractive young woman, a teacher with an 'open' relationship, her partner had recently fucked off to India to 'find himself', the WANKER!
One night she invited me round to her place to listen to Eno's 'HERE COME THE WARM JETS', I think we smoked a bit of hash. But my stomach decided to fill up with the 'evil wind', it was as painful as labour contractions, trying to hold it in. I did let one go in her toilet, but it created this awful stench, I was mortified and panic stricken, a bad smell can very quickly kill a 'friendship'. I stuck it for as long as I could, then said I had to go. She seemed disappointed, perhaps a shag was on the cards? I hit the street and let out a massive sulphurous fart. (I should have unceremoniously disembowelled myself there and then, but I didn't have my ceremonial disembowelling knife with me.)

....
...

VINCENT'S GUN.   11/1/02.

Where did Vincent van Gogh get his gun? The one he shot himself with on that last lonely day, and did he only have one bullet for emergency action to be taken? Perhaps saying to himself beforehand, 'One more fit and that's it, I'm going to blow my insides away'. And why not aim for the brain, the originator of all his pain? After all, if his mind hadn't kept on telling him he was unlovable and unfulfilled, thus torturing his stomach and his heart, he might not have emotionally fallen apart.

Did the revolver feel like a reassuring weight against his hip, as he went with quivering lip into his very last cornfield? Had he become epileptic from his turbulent life style, or was he suffering from an undiagnosed venereal disease? Women of easy virtue were the only ones he ever got near, and if he'd had the gun when he cut off his ear lobe, he might have shot it off instead; a bit like when Clint Eastwood winged that outlaw in the legendary film 'HIGH PLAINS DRIFTER': "He's shot my damned ear near clean off!" BRILLIANT!

And what about the bedrock of Vincent's artistic existence, his long suffering and much put upon younger brother, Theo, who only outlasted the tortured artist by a mentally, and physically deteriorating six months? He gets very little credit for Vincent's interesting, but by no means brilliant, works; the Arles ones brilliant in concept and colour perhaps; especially the 'STARRY NIGHT'; and coming at the point in history when they did. But I don't think his work was worth the sacrifice of two lives.

"I wish I were far away from everything, I am the cause of all, and bring only sorrow to everybody, I alone have brought all this misery on myself and others," wrote Theo in a letter to Vincent when he was 23. It looks like depression and low self esteem ran in the family.

Those same sentiments quite often apply to me, it's just as well I don't have a pistol handy...I'm a booze and pills man anyway, and if ever the day comes when I feel I simply can't go on anymore, then the dreaded paracetomol and brandy will have to do the job; and I hope this lethal combination would kill me quite quickly, I don't fancy bleeding to death from every orifice.

Emotional rejection, and an intense personality, don't mix very well either; they broke Vincent's spirit and have almost destroyed me. I've no Zuave brothel to seek solace in, sipping absinthe between tearful shags, I have to make do with radio and TV. I've finally given up on humanity, I won't let the bitches grind me down anymore; whatever loyalties I have left belong to the planet and its sorely threatened flora and fauna. Unlike Vincent, I'm not quite a pauper, I can withdraw from my introspective torpor long enough to get my act together, to bequeathe my worldly wealth to an organisation devoted to animal welfare; a shout rather than a whisper (WSPA: World Society for the Protection of Animals) will lead you to their name...on the internet.

(I've made my shop bought [£1.50p] Will out in favour of WSPA, leaving them copyright of all my work after I'm dead, if I get discovered. That way, no human parasite can come crawling out of the woodwork, to leech off my tortured output. Hopefully, the posthumous millions, my genius will generate, will benefit the planet,and single-handedly, stem global warming.

....
...

'A BLOKE ON HIS OWN',, sung to the tune of 'I AM A WOMAN IN LOVE', by 'THE BEEGEES'; performed by Barbara ' The Snozzle' Striesand. 27/1/02.

'I am a bloke on his own, it's a fate I bemoan, over and over again, and I'll do anything, (short of paying for a short, sharp, nasty shag up a dark alley off a tart who's too pally with a heroin habit, and her minder; and who might need a reminder that personal hygiene should play an important part in her non tax-paying line of business); invest in a ring, (to put through her nose), out-sing the 'Snozz' when it comes to the high notes, to put my case across'. (Of course, I've completely lost track of the original song now, I could do with a karaoke machine, with the words on a large screen, and those high-pitched shrieks in the background).
'It's a plight I don't recommend, Mrs Palmer and her five lovely daughters are my only friends; it's no wonder so many men are turning turtle, with our women expecting nothing less than physical perfection, in their ideal man; very few can live up to their impossible plan. I wouldn't even try to any more, if they don't like what they see, they can fuck off and leave me alone. The only real drawback to being a bloke on his own, is the lack of regular raunchy sex for free. Okay, you have to keep them happy by coughing up a bob or two for their upkeep, but they're so useless nowadays (in the home), I might as well shag a sheep!!!

....
....

FATIGUE, MENTAL AND PHYSICAL. (I've earned mine.)
29/1/02.

At fifty, bull elephants are usually ready for the elephants graveyard, biblically, we're told we can look forward to 'three score years and ten', I'm coming up to 55 now, and I feel knackered; I'm full of aches and pains and neuroses. I put a lot of my condition down to the fact that despite all my efforts I've never had a 'normal' adult heterosexual, long term relationship; or nothing even approaching one. Just eons of lonely isolation.
I've had a harder life emotionally than Vincent van Gogh, I've been rejected four times by 'women of my dreams'; once or twice is usually enough for most people. I've also kept myself alive for 18 years longer than he could bear to do, he was 37 when he killed himself. I've driven my body as hard as he did, and I've tasted insanity and depression regularly.

If at any time in the future, either before or after my death, I get 'discovered', as a writer of very short fiction, and modern poetry, and become a best seller, I'm granting ultimate copyright of my work to WSPA, (World Society for the Protection of Animals), so that any royalties that might accrue, (ha,ha,ha!), will go to helping save defenceless animals. Maybe even fund a sanctuary or two. Anything, rather than suffer the fate of Vincent and his brother Theo, who, if you look at their situations cynically, went through all their deprivations and mental tortures, merely to benefit the parasites in the art world; I mean, 54 million dollars for a painting of sunflowers!!! There's no logic to it; if anything of mine sold for even a fraction of that sum, I could help a lot of animals; preferably in the wild where they belong.

....
....

'WHAT BECOMES OF THE TOO MANY TIMES REJECTED, THE PHYSICALLY, AND EMOTIONALLY NEGLECTED?' 10/2/02.
(Inspired by the 'Motown' classic: 'WHAT BECOMES OF THE BROKEN HEARTED'.)

'All our advances spurned, our stomachs churned up a thousand times at the pain of it all, no trophy brides on our arms to make the heads turn.
'Male, unsuitable for breeding purposes, has fairly big knob, suitable for shagging with a condom on: 'HAVE KNOB WILL TRAVEL, HETEROSEXUAL WORK ONLY CONSIDERED, NO KINKS OR PERV'S PLEASE, I'M EMOTIONALLY DAMAGED ENOUGH ALREADY'.
'Women seem wicked when you're unwanted', never a truer word was sung by a long dead Rock God; nowadays they're a bunch of dildo-toting dykes, shagging gay men (queer fuckers), up the arse. The rest of us heterosexual males, ('I was never confused', Al Murray, 'the pub landlord') don't get a look in, we're much too confrontational for their 'front bottoms'; I'm not argumentative, I'd prefer girls on top most of the time so I could pull their arse cheeks apart and shag them up the bum with my middle finger while I'm knobbing them with my indefatiguable ramrod of a penis. I've decided to call him 'Old Sparky', because he'll deliver wave after wave of orgasmic pleasure to the ladies; Mrs Palmer and her five lovely daughters.

ESTRANGED FROM THE NORM. When you're deprived of normal, healthy, sexual activity for an inordinate length of time, you can develop an antipathy to normal healthy displays of affection.

....
....

I'D RATHER HAVE A MISS BETWEEN MY KNEES, THAN A BAD CASE OF MISOGYNY, 13/15/2/02.

Women hating is something I obsess a lot about, I never set out to dislike and mistrust them iintensely. In fact, it isn't women that I hate, but the modern, now more-than-ever-before, atmosphere of hostility and distrust created by the female sex, towards men in general; they have some deadly weapons in their armoury, namely, rape and child abuse accusations, and equally deadly effective, insulting the size and effectiveness of a man's manhood.

At just 3 weeks away from my 55th birthday, I've acquired my very own double bed, I've only ever slept on single beds, except when on holidays. The mattress on my new double bed is rather hard, it's a bog-standard double divan, I don't know if it would stand up to much heavy-duty sex action, the base might break, as well as my knees and back. I wonder if I'll be able to do the business in Thailand? I hope I don't end up with a lady boy, and if I do, I hope I don't like it, or feel so despondent I'll be past caring?

I think I lack the aggressive level of testosterone that a lot of women reputedly respond to, in the sack; but I also hope that I'm coming into my sexual prowess at an age where a lot of men have become emotionally, as well as sexually, impotent. I won't need viagra if I'm feeling inspired, and if I expired after my first fuck with a real vagina in twenty years, no-one will shed any tears over my demise, or any expense to bring me back to this dump of a country..

....
....

COACH RIDERS IN THE SKY.   16/2/02,
(Will we become ghost riders if we die in a plane crash?)

There's no doubt that air travel is the best thing since the invention of the steam locomotive engine, nearly 200 years ago; although until three years ago, I thought nothing would induce me to get on a plane, unlike the train, I took to that like a duck to water.

What got me on a plane the first time was, I wanted to go to Portugal; 2 days travel overland. I had a female friend who said she'd go with me, (at my expense), so I thought, 'If she can get on a plane, so can I'. On the strength of which, I booked us two weeks self catering on the Algarve. It was like 'BLIND DATE' really, especially as I'm severely visually handicapped; we had some conflicts, but at least I had my evening meals made for me for a fortnight.

The deal was that I paid for all the food and drink, and did the washing up; and as I pointed out to her later on in a letter, after she'd severed all connections with me: flight aversion therapy would have cost a lot more than our out-of-season holiday did. She has now joined the swelling ranks of hobgoblins in my life, which is made up of family, and former friends. I can get dumped at the drop of a hat, it seems that people don't have much of a crisis of conscience in leaving me out of their social circle. Potential partners feel the same way too, as one said to me some years ago, after she'd sacrificed me for the favours of someone more facially acceptable: "I threw you to the sharks."

So, apart from the fear of the plane crashing, or being hijacked and blown up, flying is as exciting as sitting on a coach. I do like the exhilarating feel of takeoff, it's an adrenalin rush. A year after Portugal, I went to Tunisia with COSMOS, it was a decent holiday; I chummed up with a 68-year-old Scottish gay man, a real character. No arse-shagging took place, thankfully, well not between me and him anyway.

On the return flight (from Tunisia), I had the misfortune to have a Scotch queer of a different calibre sat behind me; he was sat next to two off duty air hostesses, or holiday reps, (at least I think they were), and he had a South African, or New Zealand mate sitting adjacent to him, on the other side of the aisle.

I reclined my seat to make myself more comfortable, the journey began okay, he was whittering away to the two women about his little cat jumping on his bed, etc, etc; the next thing is, he's asking me to put my seat forward because he didn't have much leg room. I pointed out that the seat in front of me was reclined. I'm nearly six feet tall, and it wasn't bothering me, so I declined; an impasse ensued for another hour or so. I know now that what was really bothering him, was a fear of 'Economy Class Syndrome' or DVT: 'deep vein thrombosis'; because eventually, he manually forced my seat forward saying, "Right! That's it, my legs are really hurting me now". Which, at the time, meant nothing to me. Shortly afterwards, DVT hit the headlines, to give us one more thing to be afraid of.

If I'd have been as insecure as him, I'd have turned round and cracked him one, thus landing myself in hot water and unwanted publicity. I contented myself by calling him an idiot. He continued to snipe at me till we came into land, in the face of a high wind, causing turbulence. I was the only one laughing hysterically; it must have been my death wish kicking in.

....
....

UPPERS   AND   DOWNERS.
24/2/02.

I wish I could banish the nasty, spiteful side of my mind that rejoices in the misfortunes of others; for instance, did you know that the 'king of 'Rock 'n'Roll', Elvis 'the pelvis' Presley, was literally full of shit when he died? 15 pounds of backed-up faecal matter to be exact; it couldn't pass through his intestines because they were blocked up with a clay-like substance. Can you imagine if the 'great one' had exploded all over the first few rows at the Las Vegas nightclub where he was performing? Say, in the middle of, 'IT'S NOW OR NEVER', ("my guts won't wait"); they'd still be fumigating the place now, 25 years on.

25/2/02. As I lay in my loveless pit this morning, my mind and body all racked with pain, it occurred to me that my personal life is, and always has been, a crime against my own sense of humanity; and my life is a hell of other people's making.

Prone rhymes with crone, can you imagine shagging a prone crone? Well, technically, she'd be lying face down, so you could pull her up from her bony hips, and slip it to her doggy style. That way, you wouldn't have to see her withered old face and wasted dugs; but the vagina is supposed to be able to get moist no matter how old its owner may be. It's not for me, I must hasten to add, I could never be that sad. I'd prefer my desires to be fulfilled under the banner of, 'If they're big enough, they're old enough', (I suppose this statement will put me in line for a lynch mob, or vigilante group, wielding baseball bats and wearing ski masks), but you can't say that anymore can you? Even though I just have. (I am talking 16 and older here, if that will help my case any?)

But in 'primitive' tribes, I think this policy is the norm; among the girls anyway.

I think boys develop more slowly, just as they do in our paranoid schizophrenic society.

The best type of woman to have, is the girl/woman; women who are in their twenties and thirties, but retain certain characteristics of adolescent girls; like 'Connie' in the current series of 'TIME GENTLEMEN PLEASE' (SKY 1). She's the student/barmaid who says things like, "I'm going to have to issue a flood warning in my knickers," looking as foxy as a 14-year-old Lolita; I hope I cop for one like her in Pattaya, PPHHWWOOAARR!!!

26/2/02. BILLOWING SMOKE. Like all sensible people, I don't smoke cigarettes anymore, though I reckon I've absorbed enough tar to fill a tar barrel, from all the roll ups and 'tailor made' cancer sticks I've smoked over 30 years of my life. Judging by the number of health problems I now have, lumped under the common heading of 'wear and tear', (I forgot to list all the joints I smoked as well, sucking the smoke deep down into my stomach), I quit just in time.

I still find it hard to resist a drink on a Saturday night in the comfort of my own home, watching late night WWF/E on SKY TV; when I've reached the 'right level', to quote a character from a Graham Greene novel, (Britain's answer to John Steinbeck), I like to smoke a cheap cigar, (by Havana standards anyway). I enjoy it most when I'm nearly down to the butt, when it's almost too hot to hold, and the last two pulls on it are great; for some reason the smoke just billows out of my mouth; occasionally, when I've drunk too much and I'm nearly out of it, I'll smoke a second one, and you know, it never tastes as good. It's always too harsh on my throat, and tastes like burning rubber, and the next day my living room really stinks; only a stick of incense can shift the depressing odour. The same can be said for my guts, when I've blown off too much of the evil smelling wind, only a stick of incense can shift that sulphurous reek as well.

27/2/02. NOT A BAD NIGHT ON THE BOX, de Sade da Satanist. There was a programme on C4 last night about the Marquis de Sade, he ballooned up to 300 pounds in weight during his 16 years in prison; the man who the sultry pop singer'Sade', (pronounced 'sarday' for some peculiar reason) shares her name with; I wonder if she's aware of the comparison? It was in the C4 TV series: 'MASTERS OF DARKNESS', last week, it featured Alistair Crowley, 'the beast 666'; I don't know if they'll feature Gilles de Rais, 'the most evil man in history'? There are probably worst violators of human rights than him, the Nazis for instance. What is so chilling about these characters for me is, how they embraced EVIL!!! Dehumanising themselves and their victims. I believe that unless you're criminally insane, you have the conscious choice which path to choose; I don't believe anyone is born wholly intrinsically bad, (though I'm not so sure anymore after 17 years in Calderdale). Quite possibly, I could have chosen a dark path to follow; I've had enough provocation, but my human spirit is not for sale.

28/2/02. PANTS. I was inspired to use this title by a nice comfortable feeling I had the other night around my nether regions; in other words, my arse and bollocks. I'd had my weekly shower and change of clothes, as well as rubbing myself all over with moisturising cream; in the winter months the skin on my body from the waist down always feels dry and rough. I think it's as much neurological as it is a vitamin E deficiency, because I've been taking a vitamin E supplement (600ius) for quite some time now.

I know some people have a bath or a shower every day, as well as changing their underwear; I change my underpants, loose fitting cotton boxers, twice a week, though if I'm feeling at a low ebb psychologically, this simple rule of hygiene isn't always easy to obey. I don't enjoy showering in my pokey little shower room, there's hardly room to turn round in it, and if I didn't have a little radiator in there, the cold would cling like a second skin. There's also an economic reason for my not showering every day, the increased use in gas and electricity, and added wear and tear on my washer/drying machine, as well as towels, clothes and moisturisers. Living on a fixed income, precludes these fairly simple luxuries.

Due to a particularly virulent strain of Irritable Bowel Syndrome, I have far more than my fair share of the 'evil wind'; I've elaborated on this ever present problem elsewhere. If I ever come into a substantial amount of cash, I'll have my insides thoroughly fumigated; I'll have daily colonic irrigation and pickle onions with the residue.

28/2/02. 'YOU'D BE SO NICE TO WAKE UP NEXT TO', is a variation on the old standard song title: 'YOU'D BE SO NICE TO COME HOME TO'. (I heard it on Radio 2 only last Sunday). All my tortured life, I've longed for a nice-looking female partner, and all I've ever got for my longings, is to be tortured by a whole procession of them; I've not had penetrative, or any other kind of sex, for over 20 years. I'm so unlucky in lust and love that my last two brief encounters with a pair of cunts, (the early eighties), left me with a basketful of STDs; I've been paying for my cheap and nasty thrills ever since.

If there is a 'god', and I've no real reason to believe there is, it's ultimate joke against us, (it has to be unisex in these enlightened times), is creating ugly people like me and a whole lot of others; same sex sex, is a close second in my top 2 of 'god's ultimate jokeS against humanity. A pretty, attractive, or beautiful woman can give me a good feeling every time I look at her, how much has that got to be worth? I don't know if they resent you being able to access this gift from the gods for free, unless they can reciprocate the emotion? Especially now our roles are reversing, and 'girls' are upfront and 'mad for it', taking on all comers, while on holiday in Ibiza or

Magalouf. I'd hate to be me now as I was when I was young then, in that environment; I had it hard enough 35 years ago. Nowadays, I'd just get written off as a 'REAL MINGER!'

3/3/02. NUTS. I bought a 454 gram bag (1lb) of Brazil nuts from 'SAFEWAYS', earlier this week; (16 doesn't go evenly into 454 by the way, it's just that we've been led to believe that 454 grams is equal to one pound, it amounts to 6 grams over); (some schools of weights and measures reckon that 25 grams is equal to one ounce, usually applicable to cigarette rolling tobacco packs, but that would make one pound equal to 480 grams, why did I ever start this?).
These nuts were being sold off cheap, that's why I bought them, (best before 28/2/02), they were still in their outer hard shells; no problem, I've got a nut cracker, which I bought some years ago to open hazel nuts. My favourite-tasting nuts. Getting the brazils out of their shells has posed a tougher job, tor the most part, than I expected; quite often they've been stuck to the inside of their casing with congealed nut oil, it's been a test of patience not to give up and throw them away; how I'd go on, on a desert island, with only coconuts to eat and only a stone to bash them open with, I'll never know...I hope.
I'd always been sceptical of nut allergy, till one night last year while I was living in exile in Walsden; I'd bought a load of mixed nuts (shelled), enough to fill two one pound jars. One night, out of sheer boredom, I pigged out on these nuts and raisins. A few hours later, rumblings and gurglings of discontent began occurring in my stomach, nothing out of the ordinary there then. As the night wore on, these sensations were accompanied by an increasing sense of nausea; eventually I felt compelled to go and stick my fingers down my throat over the toilet bowl. It didn't take much prompting before an arc of semi liquid matter came gushing out of my throat, I literally felt like I was spewing my guts up. That incident's taught me to only consume nuts in moderation; I wasn't going to waste the rest of those nuts I'd bought.

Watt Tyler, Jack Straw, John Ball? All leaders of the peasants revolt of 1381, the original general strike with ATTITUDE! 'WHEN ADAM DELVED AND EVE SPAN, WHO WAS THEN THE GENTLEMAN?' Ours is the only planet teeming with life, in a turbulent universe in a massive solar system; and yet, since we learned to stand upright, the rich have been screwing and oppressing the poor. I think it's part of our genetic makeup to have acquisitive natures; every other species on the planet follows a set pattern when it comes to dominance and procreation, The strongest and the fittest do the procreating and dominating, the less able and agile just hang about on the sidelines, hoping to nip in and catch a female full of heat and lust while the top dog's tearing around shagging everything he can get his phallus into; and woe betide the unwary interloper if he catches him at it, fur and semen will be flying everywhere.

Humans seem to be the exception to the rule, otherwise why would we see really tasty-looking women with hideous gargoyles? Do they want to inflict horribly ugly brats onto an already deeply depressed populace? And if so, why? I've remained celibate for the last 20 years, in order to spare the world of 2 or3 more facially challenged 'sprogs', (it's got nothing to do with the fact that I can't get a shag for love nor money); the ancient and revered family name will die out with me, and I've opted for cremation, and for my ashes to be scattered over the moors at Haworth, so the adoring millions won't be able to make a pilgrimage to my grave site; I just hope they don't clog up the moors at Haworth.

I've developed a theory, at a time when it's unfashionable to have firm beliefs, to call a spade a spade. It's to do with intellectual evolution, a bit like it's depicted in Aldous Huxley's futuristic novel: 'BRAVE NEW WORLD', I alienated a group of writer acquaintances, (one of them was a social work team leader), by saying that 'plebs' were only one rung up on the evolutionary ladder from people with learning difficulties; shock, horror! Very un-PC! I wonder if you get really thick chimps and gorillas, who don't know their arses from their elbows?

Which other species would sycophantically allow a privileged minority to own a large proportion of the nation's wealth, while at the same time allow grinding poverty to persist? In London, people can be destitute in close proximity to 'Buck House', and the so-called duke of Westminster, (who keeps a very low profile), is a billionaire 3 times over, thanks to inherited wealth. There's no logic to this level of avarice being left to prevail, yet if a chancellor of the exchequor had the guts to tax these parasites out of existence, the howls of protest would reverberate right across the septic isle that is Britain today. (It's always been this way.)

A few centuries ago, such sentiments would have had me burnt at the stake for treason, a young Henry V had a part-burnt heretic pulled out of the flames, to see if he would repent; when he refused to, he was shoved back in. (This snippet courtesy of 'THE HUNDRED YEARS WAR' by ROBIN NEILLANDS).

Nowadays you're just marginalized if your views don't tow the 'party line', as long as you're harmless you're tolerated.

SING IF YOU'RE GLAD TO BE HOMOPHOBIC '.   March '02.

'We're a couple of queers, we've got rather strange ideas about sex, we're wired up the wrong way but that's okay today, we're as gay as coots. It's a hoot being a bender today, the British sense of fair play says it's okay to be as bent as a nine-bob-note; the horned goat rules in 'Batty man Babylon'.

I wonder if same sex, sex, includes self-satisfying masturbation, as well as mutual cock sucking, and arse fucking? The latter anal pursuit leaving a pain in the rectum and a shit stained duvet...so I'm told.

Women love manageable men, they can hen peck them without too much fear of getting a fat lip, the ones that can slip them a length and fuck off the next morning, no questions asked, are their ideal task masters.

Some find it through heroin, an ever increasing number of Satan's slaves; others at the end of a bottle, myself included; but The Jimi Hendrix Experience at full throttle, can hit that perfect spot for me, stone cold sober and drug free; no crack cocaine all in my brain, I can speed naturally. The electric blue raw power of Jimi Hendrix, is as far above the current crop of 'pop idols' as say, the music of Beethoven is to George Formby. No offence George, I hope your offspring won't sue me.

There's no paradise in C4 TV's 'EDEN' either, a more fucked up group of young flounderers couldn't be found to regenerate the human race, this side of Bedlam.

Undead arse-shagging filth, breathing in carbon dioxide and exhaling carbon monoxide, plaguing me from afar; this psychic vermin is rarely off my case, malevolent creatures from inner space.

As long as I live, I'll never understand it, if there ever was a 'god', he couldn't have planned it, not even in his worse nightmare; (I'm sure militant lesbians think 'god' was/is one of them); 'it's Adam and Eve, not Adam and Steve, bottom explorers'.

When I'm assailed too unjustly by the evil eyed spy, nipping at my ears in its negative way; (in the real world it's 'left' for love, and 'right' for hate, this unholy horror uses it the other way round), I cry out, 'Let the evil that you do be sent straight back to you, and envelop you in a cold, wet, black, blanket of fear, despair, and ultimate destruction; and I hope the words of this curse are ringing in your skull the day you get sucked back down into HELL!!!'

Satan is conspicuous by his omnipresence today, maybe he's 'god's' representative on Earth? A statement like that would be considered blasphemy by the people who issued a death sentence on Salman Rushdie, aliens in a red mist of pseudo religious fervour. If I was Allah, (more 'blaspheny'), I'd incinerate them with a single scowl. Instead I'll have to prowl round like a thief in the night, avoiding the light, for fear they'll crucify me again, (more blasphemy, which would result in my feeling the worst possible pain, that of having my head sawn off by an Alqaeda fanatic, [this statement is an update from when I wrote the original piece, 13/5/06]), oh the pain.

....
....

WHEN THE MIND TURNS, A BIT LIKE THE WORM REALLY.
March '02.

I know now that I'm emotionally damaged beyond repair, too many years of having my nose pushed out of joint, (it's physically that way too), has left me feeling like a cornered animal, snapping and snarling. I'm suffering from circumcisional repression, or circumstantial depression; or is it the other way round? Too much seratonin and not enough aggressive testosterone, I never act out my violent fantasies against plebeian transgressors, I'm too afraid of thr consequences.

As more and more layers of my humanity are ripped away from me, I'm learning to survive alone; it's just as well I like who I am, or else I could turn really hostile; like a rabid dog.

I saw a man recently who I was once unflatteringly likened to; (I think so anyway), (I was called 'the old' 'Eddie 'The eagle' Edwards'), on TV the other day. He was looking for love in the lonely hearts section; in the tradition of 'getting it in first', he described himself as having: 'Fallen out of the ugly tree, hitting every branch on the way down'. He omitted to say who he was; at 37, he's still facially challenged, even after cosmetic surgery; he's got less of a prominent chin now though, unlike me.

My features have also been likened to those of Hank Marvin, a man who, if he didn't play electric guitar really well, though like Eric Clapton, he lost his cutting edge years ago; now it's 'SINGALONGAHANK', which is hardly APACHE or MAN OF

MYSTERY is it?, might possibly have ended up like me, a back street nobody; or like 'Curly Watts' out of Coronation Street.

I love watching endurance programmes on TV; I call these adventurers 'THE CRAZY MEN'. I recently watched a programme where these two British men tracked down the last practicing tribe of cannibals in New Guinea, they had a narrow escape, and then went on to scale an almost unclimbable mountain, some 15,000ft high; mad or what? The latest series of half hour films is called 'ICE DOGS' on BBC 2. This intrepid English explorer is pitting himself against the icy wastes, with not much more than a pack of husky dogs for company. It makes me feel really snug and secure, watching this madman, from the comfort of my old rocking chair, with the heating on and the light off.

Manchester Airport is an endurance test for me, in fact any airport bigger than a small hangar is; me not being able to read information screens, and helpful staff being thin on the ground. I've been in three airports now, Manchester, Faro and Monastir. Soon, I expect to get that sinking feeling in Dubai and Bangkok. The highlight of a recent disappointing holiday in Portugal's, Praia da Rocha, (I came home a week early, missing 'Crimbo' over there), was a walk along a nearly deserted beach in the late afternoon, with the Atlantic ocean (was it the Atlantic or the Mediterranean? I don't know), and the setting sun on my right hand side, and a bracing wind in my face. I suddenly felt carefree, (after a depressing week) and started whistling Cliff Richard's 'D IN LOVE'. I wanted to walk as far as the end of the stone pier where the beacon stands, I reverted to my usual insecure self when I began to pass more 'crazy men' with fishing rods, darting about on the massive stone slabs each side of the main walkway; I paid a lot for that carefree moment.

....
....

THE MADNESS GENE, OR, THE INSANITY BUG?   May 02.

I'm psychically stalked by a fat bloated obscenity, a totally insane mind marauder, a blind idiot anti Christ, a creature that is able to insinuate itself ESP-wise, directly into my innermost private space; and living room.

A psycotherapist said to me, (over the phone), 'Believe me Philip, no one can read your thoughts', and to think, I was going to pay him £15 an hour so he could emphasise this to me; whereas in reality, like I said to him, 'I'm looking for an exorcist really, a psychic with extraordinary powers of perception, who can detect and expel an evil presence'; actually, I only said, 'I'm looking for an exorcist'.

You've heard people say, 'My ears are burning', that's how this thing lets me know it's there; I call it 'hideous heat', I hate it worse when it violates my right ear with varying degrees of sickly warmth, in a parody of affection. I always shrug it off as quickly as I can with a torrent of abuse, and at times, I feel it transferring to my left ear with a reproachful burning sensation; and yet in the real world, I understand it's 'left' for love, and 'right' for hate. If I'm being targeted by Satanists, this reversing of the norm would figure, to them bad is good, good is bad: 'Do what thou wilt shall be the whole of the law'.
Some years ago, in a programme about 'black magic', a man who'd managed to escape from the clutches of a satanic coven said, symptoms of schizophrenia were induced by them, such as 'hearing voices'. But what about irrecoverable schizophrenics who are permanently mad, and even their facial features change almost beyond recognition? Can they be being controlled by a dark force? And if so, 'WHY'? But then what is EVIL, other than madness?

Monomania, megalomania, bad guts (sulphurous reeks), social isolation and exclusion, are all aspects of evil. The human caste and class system; fancy being born an 'untouchable'! Microbes are agents of 'the devil', they can kill, maim and disfigure in myriads of ways. Having failure, and thwarted ambition forced upon you, are two more instances of insidious dark forces at work. By the time your 'loser' status has really sunk in, it's too late to do anything but lament about it. On my next passport, where it says 'Occupation', I'm going to put, 'Undiscovered literary genius, denied recognition and reward by invidious circumstances.'
And perhaps money is the root of all evil? Or rather, the lack of sufficient amounts of it to allow you financial freedom; I've just blown a fiver on the 'rollover' lottery draw tonight, and because I have various vultures circling,, waiting to pick my bones clean for small amounts of cash owing, I had a real struggle with my inbuilt sense of guilt, to afford myself this luxury. Now I've got five chances to win the big one, 'TEN MILL'! A couple of years ago it would have been more, but people have become disillusioned to some extent with the long odds. I think if I was comfortably off, I wouldn't touch it; a

lot of winners have been down on their luck until BINGO! Or words to that effect, 'I'VE FUCKIN' WON, FUCK ME!'

In the 14.5 million to one chance that I win the big one tonight, what will I do? I'll still go to Thailand with that added security behind me, checking out Pattaya for the chance to buy a disco bar; with ten mill' on board, it won't matter if it makes a loss; maybe Diane will go with me when I go back again, portentious or what? (Not, as it subsequently turned out.)

....
....

OUT AND ABOUT.   28-9/4/02.

Out and about, being buffeted by the wind, caught in squalls of rain, sorely irritated by anyone who gets in my way; wishing I was at home with some form of acceptable drug, even if it's only the TV to deaden the pain.

Why do I bother going out you may well ask? Finding fodder to feed my face is a task I can't delegate, alas. I can be trapped in doors for days because of our '4 seasons in one day' English weather, panicking in case I run out of food, confined to bed for long periods to keep heating costs down, brooding on the awfulness of my existence, knowing that if I died, I could be lying here for weeks, rotting down nicely, except on really cold days.

Radio 4 can ease the boredom sometimes, last night there was an interesting insight into Spiritual Intelligence; I drew the conclusion that it was another expression for stoicism, that you have to learn to accept your lot in life with a brave face and a stout heart. I thought, 'Fuck that!' before I dropped off to sleep; waking up 3 hours later in urgent need of a piss. Serves me right I suppose, as my feet froze on the lino of the bathroom floor.

'No more!', I hear you inwardly moan, 'leave us alone, take your misery elsewhere, frankly we don't give a damn, we've got our own crosses to bear.' But I'm drinking in the Last Chance Saloon, soon I'll be too grey and non descript to merit even the slightest glance, except maybe of pity perhaps; pretty galling when you feel as young at heart as me.

114

English society is so riddled with fears, phobias, and hidden boundary lines that 'mustn't' be crossed; a person could go 'boss eyed' trying to keep up with the 'do's and don'ts', it's no wonder we turn out psycho killers by the score; women are such bitches I'm surprised there aren't many more…myself included.

Excluded from love as I am, unless I settle for some creature that should have a label on it, and I'm beginning to doubt that even one so facially challenged would think me good enough to share her trough, I've no choice but to put on my travelling bonnet (poetic licence), and head out to the Far East, where I'll enjoy a feast of slanty-eyed delights; a different one for each of the eight nights of my stay. With a bit of luck, I'll be able to bring one away with me, not the inflatable kind I hasten to add. A taste of oriental spice might leave me gagging for more, once I've returned to this septic shore and its crippling Northern climate, for those of us who can't ride around in cars.

Well, if I like it so much I'll save up and go back again…and again! I'd like to have my own disco bar out there where it's always hot, (and that's only the weather I'm talking about), but I'd need a lot more money than the bit I've got stashed; if only to transport my large music collection. Right now I'm enjoyng a selection of '50s rock 'n' roll, it will have to do to save my doggone soul, for now.

A. Note. This piece should have preceded THE MADNESS GENE, in fact I typed it in before it, but for some mysterious reason both pieces were deleted while I was having a coffee break with a very charming, and attractive library assistant called Susan. Could it be a case of gremlins in the machine? 1/10/02.

SNOUTS IN THE 8-MILE-HIGH CLUB.   Late may, 02.

When you fly, you don't feel the distance, 6,000 miles in 13 hours might as well be 6 miles for all the effect it has; maybe that's why we suffer jet lag and culture shock? Also, when you're at an altitude of 41,000 feet, flying at almost 600 miles an hour, with an outside temperature of minus 80 degrees centigrade, and the jumbo jet starts wobbling and losing height, your nerves are apt to suffer as you contemplate your imminent end. I am at times almost clinically paranoid, as well as partially sighted, not the best combination for travelling alone.

I've just got back from my first visit to Thailand; negotiating three major airports with a little help from people who weren't too self obsessed to spare some humanity. Pattaya's a 2-hour drive from Bangkok Airport, though my travel itinerary had said it was only an hour's drive away. I was about an hour over schedule, coming through immigration at Bangkok. A Tour East Thailand rep was waiting for me, and hustled me off to a waiting taxi, I was almost a walking basket case by this time. Fortunately, the driver spoke only basic English so I was able to slump onto the back seat and make myself as inconspicuous as possible, hoping he couldn't detect my harassed state of mind through his rear view mirror.

The part of Pattaya I saw on the way to my hotel looked very haphazard, half up, half down, a weird combination of ancient and modern buildings; but nothing could have prepared me for my first visit to Walking Street. Admittedly I was drunk, dazed, and confused, and not able to see very well. Suffice it to say, that if I'd been a sharp-eyed sex addict with a bulging wallet, I'd have been in paradise.

Incidentally, (I forgot to mention it earlier), if you've ever flown at 41,000 feet and experiencing some turbulence, and suddenly thought, 'Oh no! I've left the gas fire on, and I'm not due back for ten days, if we don't crash first!', you'll understand how my stomach felt at that precise moment. I fairly quickly resigned myself to whatever fate awaited me, and carried on following our flight path and altitude on the hand set in front of me.

It's amazing how much emotional pain the body can take, at times it feels to me like my intestines are being pulled out without an anaesthetic; a bit like in the old hanging, drawing, and quartering days. For the first four days of my holiday, I felt like Marlon Brando in 'APOCALYPSE NOW', a dark soul in a dark place (my head). It was the bottomless pit of self loathing and despair; thank fuck for other people, who can't see as deeply into your psyche as you can. Two strangers helped pull me through, one reckoned to be dying of cancer, the other was a Thai escort (bar girl), who loved me way beyond the call of her job description.

I can only put my deep depression down to the accumulated pressure that much of my writing is about, loneliness and social isolation; I hope to go back to Pattaya around Yule time, and stay in the town and rekindle my relationship with the Thai who loved me. If not, there are plenty more exotic fish in the golden bowl that is 'The Honey Bar', Walking Street, Pattaya. Thailand. (It's no longer there, unless my rheumy old eyes deceive me.)

Modern airports are huge sprawling complexes, I suppose they have to be, given the volume of human traffic they're dealing with 24-7. Dubai airport was like a little air-conditioned city, as was Bangkok. There must have been literally miles of carpet in the latter, a kind of soft focus grey. Dubai was more a tile effect, with palm trees lining the aisles; it also had baggage and people carrying buggies, fast moving and silent, apart from an almost missable warning buzzer; I had to jump out the way on two occasions to avoid being flattened.

I don't think air travel is a problem for me, I've never felt terrified whilst flying; apprehensive at times, yes. Even when I hear about plane crashes, like the one that's happened today (25/5/02) off the coast of Taiwan, with the suspected loss of some 225 lives, I don't think, 'That's it, you won't catch me on a plane again'. If I was on one that was going down, I've vowed with myself not to do the headless chicken routine, running up and down the aisles screaming, knocking other screamers out the way, no, I'm going to remain seated, clutching an air hostess.

Speaking of which, a lot of them are like super model look-alikes, with dazzling smiles and perfect figures; they're a lot brighter than the average super model; they have to be to cope with the varying degrees of human temperament they have to cope with on flights, especially long haul. 'Economy Class Syndrome' isn't only about fears of deep vein thrombosis, for me at least, it's about putting up with the irritability it can engender in certain types of passenger; I've almost been involved in two instances of air rage due to unstable male passengers, projecting their insecurities on to me. The latest incident was on the flight back from Dubai, with a fat Welsh bastard sat behind me making snide remarks. I wanted to kill him, but I managed to restrain my temper, wishing him dead in my head instead.

Dubai to Manchester is an 8 hour journey. More or less as soon as we'd taken off, breakfast was served to us on trays; my stomach was churning, and it wasn't that long since I'd last eaten (Bangkok to Dubai), so I handed it back to the 'trolley dolly'; an expression I'm certain must cause feelings of air rage amongst the highly competent cabin crew.

There then seemed to be a fairly constant procession of trolleys, offering drinks to the already well fed and watered 'hogs'. I dubbed the majority of passengers thus because once their abundant liquid intake started passing through them, they had to get up and queue for the toilet. The couple in front of me were a case in point, they were too greedy to refuse anything, and with poor bladder control; I was determined not to use that over-used toilet, partly because my own bladder can refuse to work under stress, and the thought of a line of porkers waiting to get in would certainly have inhibited my flow.

I likened the situation on our plane to super model look-alike air hostesses, promenading up and down the 'catwalk' of our cabin, feeding and watering the hogs. It was totally unnecessary, one meal would have been sufficient, which is what I had, about five hours into the flight; very acceptable and more environmentally friendly than the waste being piled up from too much indulgence. Economy flying is the pits, it's business class for me from now on....Har, har, har!!!

....
....

HEAD SWEAT ON MY PILLOW, AND EAR WAX ON MY TEETH.
(FEELING LIKE SHIT, INSIDE AND OUT, LOOKING WASHED UP, FEELING WASHED OUT.)   1-2/8/02.

Why are more murderers dismembering their victims nowadays? Is it because, in their warped minds, they want to be certain the object of their rage and hate is truly dead? It's a really messy business cutting someone up, there's eight pints of blood for a start, then there's the intestines and other squishy bits, and the head! Do you avoid looking at a face you're used to see words coming out of? Eyes that may have gazed into yours? Lips you might have kissed? I'll never understand the depths the human psyche can plummet too. If I was going to do this dastardly deed, and I can think of a few people who qualify, I'd opt for a long bladed, sharks teeth hacksaw, as opposed to a chainsaw, which I imagine could throw up rather a lot of spray. A hacksaw's got to be cheaper as well; And unlike that teenage zealot who, some years ago, chopped his corpse up into 172 pieces, I'd only go for five easy to manage (relatively speaking) portions, I'd sever the legs, arms, and head, leaving the torso intact.

I read a book by Ian McKewan once where they cut the torso in half, that's just asking for problems, guts everywhere, as well as the smell to contend with. After cutting the limbs off, I'd fold them up before rigor mortis could set in, to make them easier to put into green garden waste plastic sacks, with a view to dumping them in a landfill site.

I know of one notorious wife murderer and dismemberer (through the media), who claims he put her head out with the domestic refuse for the bin men to take; suitably bagged I presume? The problem I'd have with taking mortal remains down to the tip is, I can't see well enough to drive. You'd also need a disguise, and false number plates to avoid recognition; there are supposed to be plagues of voracious rats about, who'd soon make short work of the human meat. Can you imagine, sneaking onto the tip in the dead of night, to check on decomposition with a torch, only to come upon a seething mass of brown and grey fur, and swishing pink tails; all shrieking, gnawing, and scratching, and if you didn't hop it fairly sharply they'd turn their attentions to you.

All in all, I'd say it was only the truly criminally insane who go in for such excessive measures. A youth is on trial at the moment for allegedly killing a very old lady, cutting her heart out, boiling it, and drinking the blood because he thought he was a vampire, (he's denying that now). If that isn't mad, I don't know what is; and that's here in this country, not some developing nation where superstition and voodoo are still rife.

My preferred method of despatching a thorn in my side, like some floozy who was doing me wrong, wouldn't be like Tom Jones, the Welsh warbler, did with Delilah, by stabbing her; no, I'd plump for a doorstep assassination attempt, using a gun with a silencer on it, or a crossbow pistol; one good shot and she'll be dead before she hits the deck; all crumpled and rumpled up, her nightie up around her hips, with no knickers on. There might even be time for one last……..No, no! What am I saying? (But still, if no one's about, it would seem a shame to let it go to waste while it was still warm and juicy, and no resistance would be forthcoming. After all, it would only be going to rot away from that moment on…)

....
......

HAPPY BEING FIFTY.   3/8/02.

As far as the title of this piece is concerned that is, it's the fiftieth sheet of handwritten A4 to be used in my 'DOWN IN ONE' collection, making it one hundred handwritten sides of paper, at approximately 250 words a side, making an estimated total of around 25,000 words. Some of us writers are very concerned about length and thickness of our product, and it is definitely the very last entry in this, my last unsung collection; (76 words so far).

Even at 55, I still have a burning desire to be 'discovered'; and that most of my work is good, original, and has something relevant to say; but the publishing market, skittish at the best of times, is harder to crack than a winning formula for the national LOTTO. And there's also the problem of coping with what the British deem to be good and bad taste; even Virginia Woolfe found herself on the receiving end of a morality case in the courts. I think it was 'TOO THE LIGHTHOUSE', that incurred the judge's wrath, and a whole print run was ordered to be destroyed. I haven't read any of her works, I came across a copy of 'ORLANDO' once, (not literally), but the print was so small and cramped, I soon gave it up; it seemed overly intellectual and arid to me. I wonder if she waved this cruel world goodbye while she was drowning herself? (waving and drowning at the same time.

I've just read a collection by Britain's first 'gay, socialist, transvestite poet', Chloe Poems, a bitter and twisted old queen, who writes pieces like'THE QUEEN SUCKS NAZI COCK', and gets away with it. I'm no lover of 'the monarchy', but I'd have him up for subversion just for the hell of it.

I've written to Mr/Ms Poems publishers, 'ROUTE PUBLICATIONS', (they've always ignored work I've sent them), expressing my concerns; I also threw the offending, and offensive book, along with the unplayed 14 track CD accompanying it, in the bin; it's not the sort of material I'd want the thought police to find on my bookshelf; and these people ('ROUTE'), get funding from Yorkshire Arts, which is itself funded by the Arts Council of England. Serves the fuckers right if you ask me, if they can't be bothered to monitor more carefully, what they're funding, or perhaps they even approve...?

I'd love to be able to host my own Writers Club, with acoustic music thrown in, Jazz, singer/songwriters, even the dreaded folkies, but no acclaccatura, (I've just spotted this word in a dictionary), (PLF, I don't know which one, because I've not been able to find it since, 15/5/06), in the shape of harsh, strident Indie bands, with the same misguided chip on their shoulders as Chloe Poems, only electric.

Traditional R&B groups and 'rock 'n' roll' outfits could play at my club; if I'm going to end up with an advanced case of Tinitus, (I've already got a moderate one), I'd want to have had some enjoyment getting it. But Hebden Bridge is a tight-arsed little town, full of 'right on' fascists in the guise of the 'muffia'; it is after all, the 'lesbian capital of the north west'. There's also a glaring lack of cash to start up such a venture, when I'm feeling low and dispirited, (when am I not?) I have a fantasy of sitting with a bottle of 5 star French brandy and a six-cylinder pistol, with one cartridge in it, at a table in the dead of night, playing Russian roulette, spinning the cylinders till I eventually lose, hopefully after I've drunk all the booze.

40-DEGREE   WASH.
26/8/02.

I mark the passage of time elapsing, by watching cloud formations passing by in the sky overhead; there's a shed in my back garden, I keep a bed in there and a rocking chair, and there's a double skylight in the shed roof, someone who owned the place before me must have been into astronomy. The same time will still be passing when I'm dead and gone, it's on a 24-hour cycle till eternity.

There's a sense of sadness gnawing at my insides, it's my body's way of telling me my life's wasting away, a pointless exercise really; I've done everything I can to make myself a successful man, but have failed miserably in the material, as well as the personal world. Is such candour healthy I ask myself? It helps to alleviate the pain, I equally candidly reply.

At 68, Benny Hill died alone while watching TV, his death wasn't discovered till other residents noticed the unmistakable odour of decay wafting their way. He was a multi millionaire, living as cheaply as possible, carrying his shopping home from TESCO'S in two carrier bags; no longer wanted on British TV. Some of his entourage thought they were in for a share of his dough, he certainly indicated so. One who thought she was in for a pretty penny, used to perform oral sex on 'Uncle Benny', even tho' it made her want to puke. In the end she didn't get anything, a wedding ring would have stood her in much stronger stead; ironically, his wealth went to relatives he'd never seen, and she was left with a bad taste in her mouth. The smutty comedian used to put Eau de Cologne on his wedding tackle before he'd let her start sucking him off, a smart move that, I bet Uncle Benny's cackling his cock off at the discomfiture of that tart with no heart, if he's out there driving Earnies milk cart.

What do you have to do to make the breakthrough in life, you feel you so richly deserve? There's no worse fate than becoming famous after you're dead and rotting in the ground, or your ashes have been scattered. I don't want to become the 'Nick Drake' or 'Eva Cassidy' of the modern poetry scene, a biographer's dream; likening my morbid existence to that of a latter day Vincent van Gogh; summarising that I'm better off out of it with a face like mine; the important thing being that I've left my work behind.

Unlike Benny Hill, I've left a comprehensive will, leaving copyright on all my written work to WSPA: (WORLD SOCIETY FOR THE PROTECTION OF ANIMALS.) That way, if my work ever takes off, proceeds would go towards doing something useful in the world, rather than feathering the nests of relations I've never met. I sincerely hope they will take my posthumous offer seriously, and market my work fearlessly in this duplicitous age, where it's all the rage to say the opposite of what you think and feel, and squeal like a pig being slaughtered if you get caught out.

....
....

SEX   VAMPIRE,   THE   FEEDER.
15/9/02.
(LIKE A BLOATED, PULSATING WHITE GRUB.)

I've heard it said that sex in the head is the best, by that I don't mean someone boring a hole in your skull and fucking your brains out; though there are some inhuman monsters who are so depraved, I wouldn't put it past them to contemplate, or even doing it. Can you visualise it? Of course, they could gouge your eyes out and go in through the sockets, AAARRRGGGHHH!!!

Imagine that you're lying on your deathbed and someone says, 'Hey! They've just discovered the secret of eternal life, it will soon be available in capsule form; it's too late to help you tho'; and as you gasp your last agitated breath, with an aghast look on your face, they say, 'It says so right here in the DAILY PHUN paper'. Well, that's how frustrating and damning it feels, when you know you've been selected by a sex vampire to be 'milked' as often as possible

How would you like to be 'dogged' by something you can't see or touch, but which is dug in so deep into your psyche, it can see through your eyes, (eye in my case), and hear through your ears?

And tries to control and censure you by inflicting burning sensations in your ears; left for hate and disapproval, and an arid blast of heat in the right ear for 'love'? Because it is a satanic force, black magic ESP, an incubus/succubus, it sees everything in a negative way, I believe in the real world, it's left for love and right for hate; but it's like red or pink for one sex, and blue for the other, I can never remember which is which, and where did red for a boy and blue for a girl, originate from? Or is it the other way round? (Or is it just me being paranoid schizpphrenic?)

18/9/02. I believe this thing is lodged in the top part of the back of my skull, over the bone that juts out (the occipitul bone); I say this because sometimes when I scratch the back of my head at this spot, I get a blast of cold fire in my left ear, as if I'm being rebuked for disturbing it. I wish I could locate a top class exorcist, who could detect this evil 'take worm', (it's a play on tape worm), and draw it out and destroy it, once and for all.

Some time last year, in sheer desperation, I contacted a psycotherapist over the phone, explaining that really I was looking for an exorcist. I explained to him what my problem was, and at one point he said to me, 'Believe me Philip, no-one can read your thoughts'; my mind stalker loved this. I almost signed up for a course of intensive therapy, ('Tell me about your childhood, do you have any sexual problems'?), at £15 an hour; quite cheap by today's standards.

Years ago I read something by Jean Genet, (spelling of 'Jean' uncertain), about a monster he kept caged inside his head; it's a common and popular theme, exemplified in 'DR JECKYL AND MR HYDE', by Robert Louis Stephenson. The best definition of this split personality, is to read the book, or watch the film version with Spencer Tracey in it; his transformation from Dr Jeckyl to Mr Hyde is chilling.

 But I swear that this incubus/succubus is not of my own making, it is an evil presence, which I dearly want rid of; it's a putrid pollutant, a devil spawn, slap bang in the 21st century AD! I won't let it beat me, but it does sap my energy with its persistence.

....
....

I WANT TO BE A DJ IN OLD POMPEII ON THE DAY THE CITY DIED. (DELIBERATE GRAMMATICAL ERROR.)
(IT'S ALRIGHT MA, IT'S ONLY WORDS THAT I'M DREAMWEAVING.)   30/9/02.

I want to be a DJ, and play the kind of music I think the punters will want to hear; I've built up an impressive collection of CDs, none of that scratchy vinyl for me, but how could I line up tracks in the dark? I can't see much at the best of times.

I know what I could do; I could make compilation CDs on my re-recordable CD machine, if I could learn to use it properly. Of course, the really smart people use MP3s and download for free off the internet. Better yet, you can have your own internet station, broadcasting to a small section of the global nation, before legislation tries to close most of them down.

It's cost me a small fortune, building up my back catalogue from vinyl onto CD, money I can ill afford; me being poor. I know if I was well heeled, I'd have spent a lot more. Life should be all about sensuality; for me, sex and music hold the key; well I've had to make up for the lack of sex by overdosing on that which soothes the savage breast, and saves the sanity. Modern rock and pop does it for me. From Jimi Hendrix, to The Carpenters, to the new dance music technology, The Beatles and The Stones, and Captain Beefheart's psychedelic drones; safe as milk laced with LSD, for you and me.

Well, not me any more, I'd rather have a cup of tea spiked with whisky, if I've got to indulge at all; small faces looking out at me from plane windows eight miles high, is a 'high' I can do without. it would make me twist and shout in a psychiatric ward, and I'd have to come together with the other loonies, as we beat our meat while dancing in the street with no name.

Shame, shame, shame, would be our feeling, as we walked on by, not daring to look each other in the eye ever again; our tears falling like rain on that midnight train to Skaville.

Now, I hear there are 2 million more women than men, in this shark-infested country of ours; are they tough old broilers or tasty young hens, twisting the nights away from Ibiza to the Norfolk Broads? A few drinks and the right sounds, and they're all over you like a rash. When they sober up, they get a bashful attack of amnesia, except when they're talking to their best friend about what they got up to with their knees behind their ears.

The tears of a clown is how I hide my emotions, I've cried an ocean in my beer, the best years of my life spent on the dark end of lonely street, with my nose pressed up against the green door with envy, that's why it's a bit bent. There's always something there to remind me of the empty void inside my bed, if you send me the pillow that you dream on, I'll 'cream' on it while I'm sniffing your purloined underwear. (The things I'll write just to keep the rhyming theme going.)

....
....

This collection is dedicated to Diane and Gail for whom the word 'fail' has no meaning, except in my case, I'm possibly the world's worst CLAIT (Computer Literacy and Internet Technology, ex student that ever passed through their hands; I soon gave up trying to learn, and spent my college time working on my manuscript. 4/10/02.

(PLF. I do as little creative writing as possible now, in fact the piece I'm going to type in here is the only piece I've written this year; there's no point in creating work, if virtually nobody's going to see it. I'm still trying to get some recognition as a writer via my web page, I recently sent nine postcards out to UK publishers, saying: 'Hi, if you're wondering where the next big thing in modern poetry is going to come from, please check out my web page at www.newauthors.org.uk, nothing ventured, nothing gained, as my dear departed mother used to say. I say nothing ventured, nothing sprained; especially the ego, when all you get back is a big fat zero.)

THE GRASS CUTTERS COMETH.   6/3/03.

One of the joys of being a council tenant, is that for around six months of the year, the Council come and cut the grass every other week; or so it seems, and the noise is HORRENDOUS! I think it ties in with the macho mentality that prevails around here; if you can't take it you're queer.
Unless you've experienced this extreme noise terror, you'll probably think I'm exaggerating, but as far as I'm concerned it's as terrifying as air force fighter jets flying low overhead, and it goes on for much longer. I don't know if It's my persecution complex, but they seem to single me out for special attention; these rugged sons of the soil, appearing as early as their job description allows. Bringing the roar of their industrial strength, grass cutting machines with them. How they can stand the din without wearing ear protectors is beyond me, let alone the vibrations these machines must make. Anyone who's tried using a pneumatic drill will know what I mean; I only

attempted to use one once, 30 years ago, it almost jolted my spine up through the back of my neck, and seemed to loosen my teeth.

I haven't even got round to trying to describe the racket that their hedge trimmers make, they make my window and door frames shake, rattle and roll, and my whole nervous system recoils in agony; they sound like an electric saw mill inside my head; all my privets look dead since their last torturing 5 months ago. A pair of garden shears would keep them trim, I could do it myself, 2 or 3 times a year, and cut my grass with a 'fly mow' (which I'd have to buy of course); then I wouldn't need them to come onto my 'property' no mo', (It rhymes with 'mow'). But I don't know if my lower back could take the strain, I have a lot of muscular pain in that region, and then there's the arthritis in my hands...

This periodic extreme noise pollution only adds to the constant battering my sensitive nature receives, because I can't afford to choose where I want to live. I maintain that there's a truly unwholesome, even satanic undercurrent round here, belying the 'on-the-surface' nature of the neighbourhood. I regard the indigenous males, as nothing less than evil, dead-heads; inbred and inverted telepaths, and downright shag nasty bastards. In the 12 months I've lived on this 'quiet' estate, on the outskirts of Todmorden, I've been subjected to excessive nuisance from car alarms going off, and an endemic culture of fat-arsed, lard-brained turkey necks, beeping their car horns at every available opportunity; quite often when I've just got up and dared to open a top window, to get rid of the smell of last night's sulphurous emissions; or if I open the front or back door to scent the air. It's eerily uncanny how one of them always manages to be near just at that precise moment, to say nothing of the 'display strength' fireworks that are in plentiful supply for numerous weeks of the year; a lesser personality than mine would have cracked before now, and been led away whimpering and trembling. But I retaliate by wishing death and destruction on these persistent offenders, who seem to be horribly healthy and resilient to the vehemence of my curses.

Last night, (5th March, my birthday,) I watched a programme called 'GRAND DESIGNS', on Channel 4, where a 'manifest destiny-type' couple invested £450,000 in modernising a 150 year old Victorian barn, into their idea of a 'des res'. A 'castle' for them and their two lovely baby daughters; I thought they were mad, spending their money this way, I'd have been up, up and away to Thailand for the rest of my natural existence, with that kind of dough; living a life of luxury and enjoying lots of loving.

....
....

IT'S FREEZIN' IN MY PARTS.   10/1/03.

Freezin' hands and freezin' feet,
I'm lyin' in bed tryin' to get some heat
Back into my digits.

I'm curled up into a tight little ball,
Backside to the window, face to the wall,
In my feet I can't feel f-f-f—nuthin'.

If I had a wife I could put them on her rump,
Unless she was lyin' there like a frozen lump,
It's too darn cold even to h-h-h---snuggle.

It's too darn cold, it's too darn cold, my hands are too numb
To hold the only warm part of my bod',
Two peas either side of an empty pod.

Will this cold weather never end? Will I ever be able
To phone a friend? Will my ice cold heart ever warm up enough
To send some blood back into my fingers and toes,
Let alone my nose.?

(PLF. I'd like to be able to adapt this number to the tune of
RAINING IN MY HEART by BUDDY HOLLY, if Paul 'Macca'
MacCartney wouldn't object; I think he owns the rights to Buddy
Holly's songs, the Scouse bastard. [He'd sue me for that wouldn't
he? And I'd lose; so to pay his libel costs I'd have to sell him the
rights to all my written work, then he'll own me won't he? I'm not
kidding; if he'd been on that space shuttle that recently blew up with
loss of all life on board, he somehow would have survived, he's that
jammy; as well as indestructible. I've not finished execrating this
execrable character yet, his reviled name crops up a little later on.])

....
....

NIGHTS THAT I'VE SAT IN. 4/1/03.
(Any resemblance to that incredibly tedious song, 'KNIGHTS IN WHITE SATIN', is purely intentional; and if Justin Heyward doesn't like it, I'LL SUE!!!)

'The nights that I've sat in, too numerous to mention,
I want to go out but I'm too near my pension.
(CHORUS. 'But I'd love to, I'd really love to, OH HOW I'D REALLY LOVE TO', Followed by that wailing bit at the end.)
'Night after night, I sit in on my own, no-one to talk to,
No-one to phone'. (CHORUS. 'But I'd love to, I'd really love to,
OH HOW I'D REALLY LOVE TO. (Followed by that wailing bit at the end.)

And now for the best part of this mind numbing 'rock classic', the instrumental part in the middle, with the great bass riff and flute solo.
(Go on, enjoy hearing it in your head.)

'Sometimes, I have to take myself in hand, a quick fifty off the wrist
Will make it stand down'. (CHORUS. 'But I don't want to, no I don't really want to, I'D RATHER SHOVE IT UP YOUR FLUE, YOUR FURRY FLUE'. (Followed by me wailing at the end.)

'Rat's eyes and a rat's brain, inside a human frame; eat or be eaten,
Is the name of the game. Nail their arses to the wall, let them feel what it's like to be fuck all; it makes sense too, do it to them before they can do it to you, if you have to, really have to, REALLY HAVE TO'.
(Big non lottery winners wailing finale to finish.)

(PLF. I wanted to put the boot into 'STAIRWAY TO HEAVEN', but the nearest I got to inspiration was, "And she's taking on the whole of the rugby team's first eleven," which is a pity really, because apart from Rolf Harris's version, this pretentious pile of hippy drivel needs taking down a step or two. [Get the pun on stairs or what? Am I insulting your intelligence by even pointing this out? Am I being patronising? Am I floundering waist deep in shit?])

....
....
THE MAN WHO REMEMBERED EVERYTHING HE SO PAINFULLY WISHED TO FORGET, LIKE HIS LIFE FOR

INSTANCE.   (INSTANT   IRRITABILITY.)
13/3/03.

I sometimes try to erase so much from my memory store, I fear I might do my brain some permanent damage, and be left a catatonic vegetable, staring emptily into space; at just turned 56, doors of opportunity are slamming shut in my face as rapidly as a shithouse door, banging in a force ten gale; an outdoor shithouse obviously.

I've very recently unearthed a little thing I wrote some 25 to 30 years ago, I think, my undiscovered readership. It compares favourably with something I wrote last weekend, the first piece is called:

CANDY FLOSS.

'The holes in your face give access to it all, the sperms on the carpet let it die before it lived. Peace of mind, and simplicity of existence, are its essence, death is its master.

Beat out its rhythms in darkened avenues, pluck out its lullaby for the eternal sleepers with your heartstrings'.

And KILLER WIND. 8/3/03.

'I watched the back of your head as it cut me dead, I thought I had a friend, turned out to be 'killer wind''.

Quite possibly, globally, billions of people have worse lives than mine; their hopes of a better life dashed at a very early age. And all that's left for them is a short, brutal existence; I've hung on by the skin of my teeth for the past twenty years or more, in a country which I detest, and which refuses to give me the artistic break I deserve. My physical and mental health have been greatly eroded as a result, but I have a tenacious streak that won't let me give up hope. If I make it to Thailand and back again this year, and have a good holiday as well, that'll be a huge poke in the eye to 'the system' in this country, that forces so many of us to live in abject 'poverty'; and fawns and grovels to the obscenely rich. The miniscule minority who have most of the nation's wealth tied up in their own favour.

Their greed and luck are the ideals we're all supposed to aspire to, in the spirit of free enterprise; an impossible task for most of us. And why should we want to be like Sir 'Super Macca' Paul McCartney? With a personal fortune of at least £120,000,000? And that, I'm sure, is a very conservative estimate. 'Macca' is lucky by nature, he's a sort of an all round nice guy, but in my estimation, quite ruthless. Have you seen the price of BEATLES CDs? They're still the most expensive, apart from THE ROLLING STONES back catalogue, which are a pound dearer in the shop that I've seen them in; I'd like to know why? Is it because McCartney and Mick Jagger are two ancient monuments, revered for their past output? Of the two, Jagger has retained the harder edge, Macca's new stuff is mostly cringe-making; one lyric I heard about a year ago went, "One, Two, Three, Four, Five, let's go for a drive. Six, Seven, Eight, Nine, Ten, let's go and do it again…" Anyone else would have rightly been 'slaughtered' for that abomination, but he gets away with it. Now, thanks to the rejuvenating effect of his new young wife, (she's young compared to him), he's out on the road again. I heard him on the radio this morning, accompanying himself on a ukulele singing, 'SOMETHING IN THE WAY SHE MOVES', a George Harrison song by the way; Sir super Macca; I hope you're paying royalties for abusing it, you wrinkly old twat. (He'd sue me for that if he ever knew I existed, it's highly unlikely he ever will.)

(PLF. And that's it people, the final additions added. I was tinkering with the idea of writing something to go with the title: 'UNREQUITED LUST IN A COLD CLIMATE', but what's the point? I must have worked the lonely and isolated theme to death in all my other work; even I can only take so much emotional agony before I develop compassion fatigue. 18/3/03.)

....
....

Well, that was then and this is now (19/6/06); a lot of crap's floated under my bridge since then, along with 6 more collections, which I now hope to make available, to a non-existent public, online; for sale as e-books. I've already got a blog, though that could be closed down by GOOGLE at any time for containing sexually explicit material (pornography or erotica of the solipsist/onanistic variety.) I even have a laptop now, which I've not attempted to use yet, I bought it a couple of months ago because it seemed like a good bargain. Last year I bought a new computer for 600 quid, I sold it this year for £165, all I used on it was the 'my computer' facility to put all my work on 'memory stick', but I've only re-edited my collections on floppy disc, a medium that is rapidly becoming extinct.
The only people who've shown any interest in publishing me is a subsidy publisher in America called Dorrance Publishing; I've just e-mailed them to say I realistically can't afford to go with them, I'd be looking at forking out over £1200 to have this collection featured as a 'print on demand' and e-book item featured on their online

catalogue, which is no doubt full of lists of people who've published mainly for 'vanity' reasons, (don't we all?)

I've even organised a poetry 'slam' for tomorrow night at a pub in Halifax: THE OLD COCK; an advert in the local paper cost me 30 quid, and judging by the resounding lack of response I've had, it looks as if I could be facing a loss (it's £1 in); but at least I will have tried, and you can't say fairer than that. If this venture fails dismally I wouldn't mind trying a rock 'n' roll disco there…

....

I want to include all the work I've put on my blog here now in order to really flesh this vulume out, and bring it completely up to date; incidentally, since the piece I finished on previously was a scathing attack on 'Macca', anyone who's not got their head firmly wedged up their arse, can't have failed to notice that his marriage has hit the skids, and he could be going to be taken for quite a few million pounds of his ill-gotten gains; I'd love to see him end up penniless and mad, still plunking his ukulele as a busker, singing: 'Buddy can you spare a dime'?

....

I want to reproduce my 'blog' (web log) from the optimistic note on which I began it, up to the apology I've attached to it after my last entry on it: 'EROTIC SENSUALITY'. If it was my own private web site I wouldn't have done so, even though you can get your head chopped off by Islamic militants if they think you've uttered one wrong word against their medieval belief system; they're more deranged than even the IRA (who now thankfully have packed violence in.)

My blog name is errolfinn at blogger.com, (I'm a swashbuckler with the pen and a saucy old pirate.), here goes:

11/8/06. THE BLACK SUN PRESS.

Hi, I'm the creator of 'THE BLACK SUN PRESS'. My aim is to become an 'online publisher' of 'e-books', including my own collections of modern poetry and acerbic observations on life from the viewpoint of a disadvantaged, disabled person, living in a world dedicated to youth, beauty, and the worship of money. I would like to be able to buy into all 3 idolatries, but I might only qualify for the last one of them, not being young or beautiful.

There's a huge market out there for people's misfortune, misery, and madness; what other excuse could there be for the likes of RADIOHEAD,

MORRISSEY, COLDPLAY, KEENE, EMBRACE, and all the other gratuitously miserable purveyors of meaningless despair? And I'd like some of that hardcore, hot, money-changing-hands action. So, if you're IT-curious, check out my blog and post some comments on it. (Thankfully, nobody has.)
(I don't understand this new technology very much, I could use an online assistant; so if you're young, beautiful, loaded and female, and know how to post your picture on this particular format, you've more or less got the job. Errol Finn.)
(I'd like to use AdSense on this site as well so GOOGLE please take note.)

....

Mon, 14/8/06. When I originally created the title: THE BLACK SUN PRESS, some 7 or 8 years ago, I thought it was unique to me; I did check out some press titles on the web some years ago but I didn't see it listed, I wonder if I'm in breach of someone's copyright? OO-ER!
Even my definition of 'black sun' as another term for a 'black hole', absorbing rather than radiating energy, isn't unique to me except in the respect that I created the analogy in my own mind without being aware that anyone else had done so; and it has depressed me to find out otherwise. My only other alternative collective title would be 'COPING WITH MADNESS', which is I hope, unique to me.
As for 'Errol Finn'? Well I do have sensations of wanting to be a swashbuckler, whipping out my rapier at a moment's notice to redress the imbalances in this world. But I've had to settle for the pen being mightier than the sword; also now, I'm a bit long in the tooth for swashbuckling, my arthritic fingers would have difficulty unbending if I gripped my rapier for too long, and as for my back and my knees and neck...let's not even go there!
I do have the intention of putting my latest creation on this site: 'MARILYN MONROE'S BRAIN', plus a few other bits to show that I am a creative person in my own right...but not right now. Seeya, Errol.

....

Tues, 15/8/06. 'MARILYN MONROE'S BRAIN.'

This is a copy of only the second piece I've written this year, I've given up composing for composing's sake, if there's no money to be made out of my creativity then I don't want to be bothered anymore. Here goes:

MARILYN MONROE'S BRAIN. 5/8/06.

Marilyn Monroe's brain weighed 1440 grams when it was
Removed and weighed at her autopsy, shortly after untimely death,
All her other vital organs were treated in this way too, in the report
It even mentions the state of her 'poo' as 'light brown and formed'.

She's reported to have said on the night of her death, 'It's Saturday night
And here am I, the most beautiful woman in the world, and I haven't
Got a date,' fate had other ideas about that, it sent a couple of murderers
Round to meet her, (according to a book I've just read.)

The world's greatest cinematic sex goddess never had an orgasm
According to Marilyn's 'secret tapes', made not long before her mysterious
Death in 1962, and aged 36, she wanted to become a leading Shakespearian
Actress too; and being of an intellectual bent, she knew what tautology
meant,
Do you?

Like me, Norma Jean desperately wanted her own family, but sadly it
wasn't
Meant to be; history needs its icons and infamously, Marilyn's been singled
out
To be one of them, I don't know if I can say the same for me...yet.

Errol Finn, the swashbuckling writer.

....

NERVE ENDINGS.

I always feel, after one of our prolonged cold, dark winter's, that it's left a
greasy film over everything, including me.

The new 'plebistocracy' (my own word...I hope), like 'Jordan' and Jade
Goody for instance. 'Ere, you're 'avin' a larf int-cha? Wanna see me tits
'n' minge'?

'OPEN MAC' night as opposed to 'OPEN MIC', (flashers of the world
unite.)

He gazed into her very soul. 'How very dare you!' she said.

I regard myself as being a couple of steps higher up on the social scale to Robinsin Crusoe; I have marginal, painful contact with the outside world...but I wouldn't settle for a 'Man Friday' up my 'Gary Glitter'.

The nearest I get to anything hot and wet anymore is a nice cup of tea.

The sky has all the time in the world to keep reinventing itself, day after day throughout all eternity; another anticipated 4 billion years before our Sun finally dies is enough eternity for anyone, don't you think? If you're not hoodwinked by some extreme religion, that is.

I've been targeted long and hard by a 'dark force', but I've never been enslaved by it, unlike the devil spawn, sicko, schizo scumbugs who psychically stalk and attack me. Only devil spawn could know such perverted tricks of spying and prying in this totally inhuman manner of using their warped ESP to torment me.

And lastly, as a 'severely visually handicapped person', I have a fear of losing what sight I've got; I've summed this fear up in 3 lines:

'I wouldn't want to live if I couldn't see,
But the thought of death frightens me,
Maybe I could shoot myself in the head while I wasn't listening to my psyche?

Black Sun. I've absorbed so much pain and heartache, it's left a huge black hole in my soul.

....

PRESTIDIGITATION NATION. 18/8/06.

What sleight of hand could I use in this promised land of get rich quick Britain,
To push some of that easy money my way?
I can't afford to pay up to £100 an hour to have some 'legal eagle' fight my cause,
And I can't afford to buy a thousand lottery tickets in the faint hope of winning
It big on the National Lotto.

I can 'afford' to get blotto on cheap and nasty booze, and lose my marbles

And self esteem, as I sank deeper and deeper into the mire of hopeless alcoholism;
If I can't find the discipline and self control not to.
There aren't too many options open to me as I rapidly approach 60, with only
Limited vision in one eye to see through.

Maybe I could go round collecting pigeon poo to sell as fertiliser for people's
Roses and try selling it door-to-door?

....

CARNAGE. 18/8/06.

It's hard to believe that only a few hours plane ride away, all hell has broken loose, I watch as much of it as I can stand on the news.
Israel, Lebanon, Afghanistan, Iraq, will the sanity ever come back instead of
ATTACK! ATTACK! ATTACK!
It must take a special breed to go in and clean up after a suicide bomber's gone off; like mopping up in an abattoir after a really busy killing day, clearing all the blood, guts, and shit away.

....

SASTRUGI BOOGIE 21/8/06.
('Sastrugi' is wave-like, hard packed snow created by arctic winds; making 'man-hauling' heavily laden sleds virtually impossible. Maybe the title should be SASTRUGI SHUFFLE instead.)

The highlight of Channel 4's coverage of this year's V Festival, (I don't know what the V stands for or where it was held), was the finale of Morrissey's set, culminating with 'HOW SOON IS NOW'. Morrissey threw his top into the crowd. (what are the chances of it appearing on Ebay today?)
I think Morrissey is an eccentric anachronism, the modern musical equivalent to Samuel Beckett (who he has a striking resemblance to), another purveyor of 'nothingness and despair'; I wonder how much 'Mozzer' got paid for last night's performance?
And I wonder, overall, just how healthy his bank balance is? I bet it's a damn sight healthier than mine, a basically happy human being (that's me) who's had misery forced upon him, anf has reacted accordingly by writing

loads of miserable stuff. My favourite Morrissey song, outside of the brilliant work he did with THE SMITHS, WAY BACK IN THE 80S! is 'EVERY DAY IS LIKE SUNDAY', I love it and can really relate to it, apart from going for a dip in an icy sea and coming back to find your clothes have been nicked! You wouldn't catch me going into the ocean for a paddle for anything less than £20,000, (which is ideally how much I need to escape my awful fate of a living death in the UK.) I mean, everything that we discard gets flung into the sea doesn't it? EEUURRGGHH!!!

....

RADIO(SMEG)HEAD. 20/8/06.

I watched (on TV) a huge throng (about 75000) of worshippers, worshipping at the dark 'church' of RADIO(SMEG)HEAD; they knew all the words to all the death wish 'hymns' of this life-negating band of aficionados of meaningless misery...WHY?
Rarely, if ever, apart from some beyond the grave, out of a hellish mausoleum, minimalist modern classical music, and 'death metal', have I heard such pointlessly depressing dirges.
I'm sure last night's audience was made up of young, physically healthy people of both sexes; what have they got to be miserable about? Or is it all an elaborate joke that I'm too old and disabled to see the funny side of? I don't think so.
This world's too full of stupid people bringing the planet to its knees, over-indulged young people like these should be part of the solution, not adding to the problem by idolising what I can only describe at best as professional depressives, and at worse as DEVIL SPAWN!

....

JOHN BETJEMAN, THE LAST REAL POET...LAUREATE. 22/8/06.

I'm not intellectual enough to ramble on forever about the merits of Sir John Betjeman as a man and a poet. To me he represents a quintessential English quality that is rapidly disappearing from our culture; a bit like Captain Mainwearing out of 'DADS ARMY'. As far as his poetry goes from what I've heard him perform on TV and radio (I've never read any of his work), I've always found him accessible and uncomplicated, which might account for his huge popularity with the public; and I don't think he ever swore in his work either, unlike me. (Though he did famously say he hadn't had enough sex no long before his death.) I wonder what he would have made of my efforts in the 'poetic field'? A lot more perhaps than the anally retentive shower who've re-imposed their stranglehold on anything other than 'street' poetry and John Hegley.

I find most highbrow poetry unutterably dull and depressing, and lifeless; hence my entry for this year's Bridport Arts Prize Poetry contest: 'POETRY IS DEAD!' which cost me £6 to enter, and I don't even think it stands a chance of making it into the winners anthology, let alone bagging the 1st prize of £5000. I should have compromised on the strong language in it that I felt was necessary for the authenticity of the piece, make your own judgement on it as long as your name isn't Lavinia Greenlaw, (the official judge), who probably already has:

POETRY IS DEAD! 3/2/06.

'Poetry is dead' he said, as he sank deeper into his own grey decline,
'A lot like the world, I've been out in it and used it, but it's been
no friend of mine'.

Conventional poetry gives off a horrid reek of camphor and sulphur
Combined; can you imagine that insufferable odour seeping up your nostrils
As you lay entwined in the arms of Death?

With this level of unfocused anger inside me I should be out 'rapping'
On the street, outside Sainsbury's or M&S, spitting volleys of hatred
At the well heeled, the indifferent, and the effete.

'FUCK OFF YOU FUCKING NUTTER!' some irked, wobbly wheeled, trolley-pushing shopper might feel stung enough to reply, as he or she wrestled their overloaded cart back to their car; to be followed by my poisonously barbed retort of, 'Fuck off and die you cholesterol-guzzling arsehole.'

But of course, one doesn't go round behaving in such an anti social
Manner, if one did one would soon find one's self on the receiving end
Of an ASBO or a blow or two to the head; or emotionally dead as the
Effects of the 'chemical cosh' neutralised and de-activated one's
Tortured psyche.

'Crikey! Leggo! Yaroo! Gerroff!' were my favourite words when I
was a boy, as uttered by the redoubtable Billy Bunter; 'I say you fellows'
he'd shriek as he was booted round the dorm' for stealing their tuck.
Nowadays he'd be politely shown the error of his ways and encouraged
To follow a low fat diet.

Express any politically incorrect views in the West today, and you'll be Pilloried with wrong-headed righteous indignation, or even worse….
My parting shot is: 'She was only the poet's daughter but she said she Wasn't averse'. PPHHWWOOAARR!!!

Errol Finn, the man still willing to whip out his rapier at a moment's notice, even at the ripe old age of nearly 60.

....

THE TITLE WITH NO NAME. 31/8/06.

For the very few of you who've accessed my blog, thanks, that makes about 10 if the number of hits on my personal profile is anything to go by; I've now just updated it to show what an interesting person I really am (errolfinn: blogger.com)…check me out.
Being a frustrated wannabe success, without any success, is emotionally very draining; that's why I get depressed a lot and suffer with ennui and lassitude. Both of these debilitating conditions are worse when the weather is grey and dull, thus making me SAD (Seasonal Affective Disorder), here in the north of England, we get a lot of grey and dull weather…Doh!
I don't like to have to make compromises in my work or in the language that I use; I can't call myself 'a swashbuckler with the pen' and not attempt to inflict pain and misery on my readers rather few and far between right now.) Writing is the only legitimate way I can express my feelings and frankly, I don't give a damn if what I have to say offends or upsets those 'sensitive souls' among us; they're only hypocrites anyway, and on 'Judgement Day' will be found sorely wanting on the plus side of 'What did you do to try and save the world? Oh I see, you walked round with your head firmly jammed up your own arsehole, and hoped all the problems would miraculously go away. You're going down to roast in HELL! NEXT!'
My latest attempt to find an outlet for my work is 'THE PARIS REVIEW', a literary magazine that I've never read or seen, its publishers are based in New York; it felt good yesterday to take my bulging envelope to the post office and send it on its way (at a cost of £1.51p and I think they've rejected me). I'm not very optimistic of a positive outcome, but hey, I don't care. I've still got my blog, and when I've learnt how to transfer work on to it from my 8 collections (edited on the now nearly defunct floppy disc), I'll make them available on my site…for sale. ERROLFINN the elder statesman of my dying generation, still showing veneration for all the great ones who've already broken on through to the other side of the great divide

of life after death…if it truly exists; if it doesn't we're all fucked! (Are you allowed to swear on your own blog owned by Google?)

....

I'M DODGING DEATH AS LONG AS THERE'S ANY BREATH LEFT INSIDE ME 2/9/06.

I'M DODGING DEATH… is in part a tribute to those young military personnel who are dying in Afghanistan and Iraq, so that we in the West can continue to enjoy the freedoms we largely take for granted; it's also meant to be my literary 'swan song' because my health is deteriorating at an alarming rate:

I'M DODGING DEATH AS LONG AS THERE'S ANY BREATH LEFT INSIDE ME.

At nearly 60, ill health is really kicking in,
It's a sin how I'm paying for the excesses of my youth;
Truth to be told, I'm feeling old and worn out before my time.
A whole array of vitamins and mineral supplements has
Failed to keep physical atrophy at bay.

As far as I'm concerned, it's not only me who's in terminal decline,
It's the whole of Western civilisation as well, all its values
Are shot to hell. We've got largely ignored or forgotten armies in
Afghanistan and Iraq, laying down their lives to hold the tide of
Islamic fundamentalist insurgents back from installing
Their murderous regimes.

And here in the UK we have a potential alien uprising in our
Midst, and all we can do is prevaricate and procrastinate;
If it wasn't for the actions of a dedicated few we'd be well and truly
In the shit; we're harbouring a viper in our bosom and we won't
Admit to it.

When you're living in violent it isn't so much death that you have
To fear, it's the thought of being horribly maimed in a bomb blast
That terrifies me. Something that's happening on a daily basis
In parts of the Middle East; the Devil's feasting on an excess of
Torn flesh and bloody gore, the end results of a 'dirty' war.

The world's never moved on at such a hectic pace, the same could be

Said for the human race; how many more billions will it take before we
Bleed the planet completely dry, and then have to die in ever increasing
Numbers?

It's not my world anymore, I'm heading for the exit door, and the
Human race in general doesn't interest me enough to care about
Its ultimate future; though no one knows what that's going to be.
Will 'we' become a homogeneous mass of 'gay' islamofascists,
Living in a hedonistic, fun-loving, totalitarian state, where 'we'll'
Love to hate each other, and Big Brother is 'our' Mother?

Money is the root of all freedom, not an idealistic socialist state,
We'd have to be like a massive ant colony to achieve that.
When I was young and physically strong, I never took this maxim
About money on board, I was too busy pursuing a bohemian truth
Through the end of innumerable bottles of booze, mind altering
Substances, tobacco smoke, and the bright elusive (for me anyway)
Surfeited requitement of love and lust; all my hopes have crumbled
To dust, floating about in great empty mausoleums inside my mind.

This is my literary swan song; I've lingered on here for far too long,
If I could have my time over again. and knowing what I know now,
I'd make money my 'god' and not the pain of having a soul to
Worry about.

This is Errol Finn, a swashbuckler with the pen, saying 'Over and out.'
....
A BUSKER FILLED ME WITH UNEASE.   7/9/06.

To anyone who read my last entry: I'M DODGING DEATH etc (if
anyone's read it which I strongly doubt), I'm feeling a bit less 'on my way
out' than I was then, mainly due to discovering the healing benefits of Aloe
Vera juice; which I learned about after typing irritable bowel syndrome
into Google's search engine; it came up with 4,890,000 pages! Luckily I
found what I was looking for on page 1, and I was able to find what I
wanted a lot cheaper than it was being advertised on line.
This latest piece is based loosely on reality, there's a busker who plays in
Halifax town centre from time to time who has an unsettling effect on me:

A BUSKER FILLED ME WITH UNEASE.

He was playing acoustic guitar and singing Bob Dylan's 'MR
TAMBOURINE

MAN, his guitar case open at his feet, in the street.
I slunk past him, inwardly sneering and snarling; how dare he
Remind me of a free-spirited freedom that I'd buried deep
Inside myself, and stir up emotional turmoil inside my heart,
And expect me to part with a coin or two to help him on his dizzy dancing
Way to the nearest pub, after an hour or two.

If I'd been a noise monitoring officer in my bright yellow tabard,
Sweating under the heat, I'd have loomed large at his feet and asked him
If he had a licence to play and sing music in the street, and was he paying
Bob Dylan royalties for using his material in order to extort money
From gullible members of the public? Heh, heh, heh!

'Hey man, you're blowin' my cool, get out of my face you silly old fool,
you're ruinin' my big number; this one always has 'em diggin' deep,
especially when I put some 'harp' on it. Get out of the way and let me
play, okay.'

But I wouldn't be having any of that, I'd be looking into his 'hat'
To see how much he'd made, with a view to confiscating it. 'I'm sorry
Sir, but if you haven't got a licence yoy can't play here, and I'll have to
Take your illegal earnings away to be used in evidence; I'll give you
A receipt. Now have it away on your feet before I call a police officer
To arrest you.'

'£11 42p, not bad for an hour's work, with no tax or insurance to pay;
I wish I could play a musical instrument, I've always had a hankering
For a barrel organ you know, with: 'WHEN YOU'RE IN LOVE'
 Ringing out to steal the show, and 'DOWN AT THE OLD BULL AND
BUSH; plus loads of other music hall and fairground favourites,
They knew how to write a good tune in those days'.

I'd have been so long in my reflective haze that when I came out of it
He would have slipped quietly away; not to worry, I'd catch him
Another day, hopefully when he had 15 or 20 quid in his 'tray'.
Saturday afternoon's usually the best time to catch the punters
In a generous mood, they think he needs the money for food,
Not drink and drugs.

He's probably signing on anyway, he should be made to play
In front of a group of OAPs, trapped inside their easy chairs
In the day room of their nursing home, with their false teeth
Nestling in their laps to give their aching gums some ease.

Try rousing them with the urge to roam like a freewheelin'
Gipsy rover, bowling young ladies over with your
Smouldering charms, melting like butter in your arms for nights
Of passion.

But no, the harsh reality is I'm just a sad old git, an unwilling
Member of the invisible, white-haired brigade; invisible or
Derisible to the laughing young women who approach you in
Groups, expecting you to shuffle out of their way. If they ever
Bothered to look round as they passed me, they'd see me spitting
Contemptuously on the ground.
You can get done for that as well these days.

Errol Finn, back on swashbuckling form. 7/9/06.

....
....

A LETTER TO TONY BLAIR, PRIME MINISTER.   8/9/06.

I'm posting a letter to Tony Blair, our prime minister for the time being;
I've written to him quite a lot over the past 9 years to air my views on his
giovernment; I'm going to miss him when he's finally hounded out of
office.

Dear Mr Blair,   7/9/06

Now that the knive that have been out to get you have finally got you, (and
I can't see Gordon Brown doing a better job than you), I'd like to enclose a
photocopy of a photocopy of what was to be my literary swan song on my
blog, just over a week ago (errolfinn at blogger.com)(I'm a swashbuckler
with the pen): 'I'M DODGING DEATH AS LONG AS THERE'S ANY
BREATH LEFT INSIDE ME'.
This piece was meant to be in part, a tribute to the military personnel
who've laid down their lives in Afghanistan and Iraq (both American and
British soldiers), to safeguard the freedoms that we take for granted in the
West; you can find a typed-up version of this piece on my blog.
Quite frankly, if I was in your position, I'd be thinking, 'Okay, if that's the
way they want it, let them have it. I've sacrificed 10 years of my life (if you
go in 2007 it will be 10 years) for this nation of turncoats and backstabbers,
let someone else take the flak.'
I stand by your policy on the war against terror, maybe 'we ain't seen
nothin' yet' if it kicks off with Syria and Iran; and I don't understand why

George W. Bush is always portrayed as a bumbling fool in the media,, we need strong leaders more than ever now.
Even though I'm on long term Incapacity Benefit, and don't like the way you've targeted the poor and most vulnerable in our greedy and hostile society, I'll still miss you (when you've gone) as a strong leader of our country.

Yours sincerely. Phil (errolfinn) Fletcher. Unsung poet and writer.

....

And now, as they used to say in Monty Python's Flying Circus, for something completely different. I did try submitting this piece for the poetry comp' that's featured as an ad' at the top of my blog page, but an electronic monitor kept saying that one of my lines was too long, even though I couldn't see how or why, so I gave it up. I think I've had dealings with The International Library of Poetry before...

WOMEN WITH PENISES.   7/9/06.

There's nothing quite so annoying as 'Ladyboys', sex toys for adventurous
Sex tourists to the far east.
If I was drinking in a bar in Bangkok and my eyes locked onto a beautiful
Face, and I didn't know the score, and the more I drank, the more
Beautiful this ravishing vision became, I'd become fair game for
Sexploitation, thinking I'd pulled me a real peach.
When I got her/he back to my hotel room, there'd be a loud screech
Screech of anguish as I uncovered the awful truth, as this lass became
A he/she youth; not that there's anything wrong with this of course,
If you're up for it, which I know I'm not, I like a lady to be a lady,
Not an inter-gender lookalike.
Not that some of them don't look totally convincing; if I were of the
'Gay' persuasion I'd think all my dreams had come true at once.

The 'I was never confused' errolfinn, swashbuckler with the pen, and saucy old pirate.

....

Sat, 30/9/06. The next 3 items are the only material I've deleted from my blog; I thought they might conflict with Google's pornography policy, I posted the apology a couple of days after I'd originally posted 'EROTIC SENSUALITY' and 'SPUNK'.

....

12/9/06. AN APOLOGY.

I've been experiencing some anxiety about the content of some of my work on this blog, mainly because it's not my own private and personal web site; I'm effectively renting this space from Google; so if anyone who reads my work feels offended, they should report me to Google and get my site closed down.

As a writer in the 'free' world, I find it nearly impossible to censor myself and what I have to say; I believe that my work has artistic merit, if at times expressed somewhat crudely.

If the 'medievalists' get their way, and by that word I mean Muslim fundamentalists and extreme Christian sects, we'll all be too afraid to write or say what we think for fear of punishments of one kind or another. If I was threatened with physical torture (I've heard they're using 'acid bath's in Iraq, do they use diluted acid to take the skin off? Undiluted acid would dissolve you while you were still alive...wouldn't it?) I'd cave in very quickly, I can't stand prolonged physical agony; and what gaineth a man if he stands by his principles and has his tongue and fingers cut off so he can't communicate them to anybody? If you think I'm paranoid, fair enough.

....

And now here are the two pieces I was feeling guilty about publicly displaying; I've always thought of my style of writing as a private means of communication between any potential reader/s and me. When I self published some of my collections some years ago, (most copies now languishing on a council rubbish dump somewhere, because I threw them out thinking they'd come under the category of dispensable excess weight to try and lug in my luggage to the airport when I move permanently to Thailand...this December. Collectors would never find them.) I always put a disclaimer on the cover, a bit like they do before the start of a lot of programmes on Channel 4 TV, here in the UK, like The Charlotte Church Show for instance; a few years ago she looked as though butter wouldn't melt in her mouth, as she stood warbling away like a linnet (do linnets warble? I don't know) with 'the voice of an angel', now she's got the trap of a foul-mouthed fish wife:

EROTIC SENSUALITY. (Written in the wee small hours of 9/9/06.)

144

I believe that pornography, especially hardcore, is degrading to the whole human race, let alone women; although it seems to be mainly women who are sexploited to go deeper and deeper into the murkiest areas of the human psyche, and dredge them up for 'adult entertainment'. I mean who but saddos and sickos want to watch the bestial extremes of human behaviour...and even worse? And I for one don't want to watch another man having sex, I'd much rather be doing it myself...female masturbation, yes.

I believe that pornography and soulless sex are the scurvy and blight of our age, and just as undermining as the threat of terrorism. It's hard to decide where the dividing line comes between erotic sensuality and pornography; for the chosen ones, love and a blessed union are the answer. For the outsiders like me, using paid sex could act as a stop-gap, but I don't rate that too highly, it's overpriced and leaves you feeling empty again after a while.

I believe that children are our future, but as women become more and more dominant and demanding, and decide that they only need men for sex and not telling them what to do, we're creating more and more young feral males; psychotic monsters whose only moral code is to survive at all costs, no matter what they've done. Caligula would welcome some of them as brothers in infamy as they descended into Hell, like Ian Huntley, and Ian Brady for instance.

....

See what you make of 'SPUNK' (For all the girls I've loved with my left hand,[though I can be ambidextrous when it comes to this activity of hand, mind's eye, and brain co-ordination.])   00.30 am, 9/9/06.

The moon was as big as a car's front headlight tonight, it blinded me as I walked on down the lane, and helped to deaden the pain of my aching heart; I wanted to walk away from the modern world forever. I wanted to find 'the pub at the end of the world' with a welcoming hearth, and drink Elizabethan mead from a pewter mug, and inhale clay pipe smoke deep into my lungs without coughing it up, and swallow hot juice from the hairy (unless she'd had a Brazilian) cup of thrusting love and lust as she came in my mouth.

I have contempt for people who take wild risks with their lives, always pushing the limits of their endurance and their luck to the limit, what the fuck's that all about? 'It was there so I felt I should 'conquer' it and my own fears; I could be taking years off my life but who cares? At least I'll have made it to the top of the world...ma!'

Females are biologically programmed to seek the sperm of the most suitable males, though the further down the social scale you go, the less it seems to count; I've never, due to disability, been considered worthy of fertilising any eggs, the dregs of my procreative urge splodge out onto my belly, no intimately smelly intercourse for me. Just 'brain sex', rude thoughts and desires to fan the fires of my lonely erection.

If only I could hang suspended in my orgasm indefinitely, jerking about with my tongue lolling out, like a hanged man. If women could read what goes on in the inner recesses of the mind of a man, they'd never go near them, (it's a bit one-sidedly sexist that statement, I think it applies to both sexes); it's primitive in there, and very possessive and territorial. Maybe our impulses are controlled by the pull of the full moon, as old as the Earth itself.

Errol Finn, one-time werewolf, but I'm alright nowOOOOO!!!

....

Thurs, 21/9/06.

WHAM, BAM, NO THANK YOU 'SLAM'!

I organised a poetry 'slam' a couple of weeks ago, to take place in Halifax, West Yorkshire, at a pub called 'THE OLD COCK'; I did this in an optimistic moment of madness. I even put an ad' in the local daily paper, estimated readership, 60,000, it cost me 30 quid…ouch!
Initially I had fantasies of turning people way from the venue through being over-subscribed with 'poets' wanting to enter the 'slam' with a chance of winning £10; but as the event drew nearer and nobody had contacted me about it, (the ad only gave my mobile phone number due to a misunderstanding with the person who took the details for my event; I wanted her to print both my home phone number and my mobile because I was having my home phone disconnected 3 days after the ad went out, [confused?], and people don't like phoning mobiles in the UK due to the potential cost of the call, excepting young people of course, because they don't think before they act…), I'd begun to downscale my expectations quite sharply.
So last night, once my nervous stomach had settled down, I set off for the pub, about a 10-minute walk from where I live. It was 7.45 pm, near dusk with a brisk but pleasant breeze blowing. Being severely visually handicapped I don't normally like going out after dark because it's

difficult for me to see anything along the pavements of our dimly lit streets, and I always expect to be attacked by some socially challenged psycho for the few coins in my pocket and my ancient mobile phone, which I'd left at home, or else walking into an unlit metal post set in concrete in the middle of the 'sidewalk'.

With some trepidation I entered the pub, remembering that there were five steps to negotiate down to the bar, the lighting was adequate for a normally sighted person; the place looked deserted. I announced who I was to the barmaid, who didn't seem over impressed. I ordered a pineapple juice with ice and went upstairs to the Oak Room to wait for people to turn up. Shortly afterwards the barmaid came up and said I wasn't allowed to wait up there on my own, I'd have to wait downstairs, I followed her down.

I hate sitting in pubs on my own, I always feel very self conscious just sitting there clutching my drink; I decided to wait for an hour to see if anyone would come and put an end to my embarrassment, I made my first drink last 30 minutes, listening to dance music and hip hop rubbish on the pub's speaker system. I decided that when I went up for my second drink of pineapple juice I'd have a double vodka put in it...THEY DIDN'T HAVE ANY VODKA!!! Which reflectively, I'm glad about, because I've virtually given up drinking alcohol, it's a crutch I don't need to lean on any more. I even found a more advantageous place to sit, nearer the entrance door; one or two people had drifted in, not for my venue alas, probably for either darts or karioki, or maybe even the two combined?

I left at 8.50 pm as inconspicuously as possible, on a par with sneaking out the back door. I got home unmolested, though I did have to pass a group of youths on a street corner; ideally I'd like to be able to bring my swashbuckling persona into play during instances like this if I was threatened, instead of having to slink past with my heart in my mouth.

When I got in I was needing some stimulation, so I put on an old WWE (World Wrestling Entertainment) video tape, and allowed the pent up frustration I felt to ease away by watching a load of gratuitous violence. I will never attempt to do anything of a cultural nature again in this intellectually arld desert, otherwise known as Halifax; and if I was going to live in Thailand at the end of this year, which I'd like to do but realistically can't afford it, (even though they've just had a bloodless military coup), a few more people would be on my nasty Xmas card list; I'll have to brood and lick my wounds for a lot longer yet, but I'll get my own back somehow....

Errol Finn, the destroyer of inflated egos, and senders of nasty Xmas cards.
....

And now for the very last 'sample' piece to appear on my blog, if people want any more of my genius, they're going to have to pay to download it when I set up my secure (hopefully) web site.

ENDING IT ALL...TENTATIVELY.   22/9/06.

There's nothing left on my social calendar for me to do
But take myself down to the railway line, and throw myself
Beneath the rapidly approaching wheels of the 11.09 to Manchester,
If it arrives on time.

If you're feeling full of bitterness and hate towards an unfeeling and
Uncaring world, it must feel really insulting if the train on which
You've sealed your fate, is due to arrive late because some other
Selfish bastard has jumped underneath it before you further up the line.

'Due to unforeseen circumstances, the 11.09 to Manchester has been held
Up at Bradford Interchange, a deranged nutter shouting 'God is great!',
Has been splattered all over the rails; it will take more than a few pails of
Warm soapy water and a scrubbing brush to clean that mess off. We wish
He'd jumped off a motorway bridge instead.'

Dead, dead, dead! I'll soon be 'brown bread'!
If you've ever stood on a Halifax Railway Station platform on a cold
Winter's night, barely able to see anything in the eerie, diffused,
Orange light, with the prospect of another gruelling journey ahead
In equally dimly lit surroundings, and an equally hostile atmosphere,
With only an empty house to go back to, the thought of jumping
Under a train to end your emotional pain doesn't seem such a bad
Idea after all.

The late Errol Finn, I missed the damn train through lateness, that's why
I'm still here, I lost 'my bottle' after that near miss.

....

And that's definitely it for this new extended version of 'DOWN IN ONE'.
If only it could be one of my eight collections that would make my fortune,
even at this relatively late stage of the game of life; (it's been 'cat and
mouse' with a very sadistic 'cat' cuffing and mauling me for the last 59
plus years. If only I could metamorphose into a super-sized black rat and
sink my incisors into the back of its neck, and then rip its throat out just to
get it off my case, allowing me to have some real good luck for a change,

and then metamorphose back into a cuddly Dormouse-type animal, I'd be content. Phil(errolfinn)Fletcher. 30/9/06.

....
....

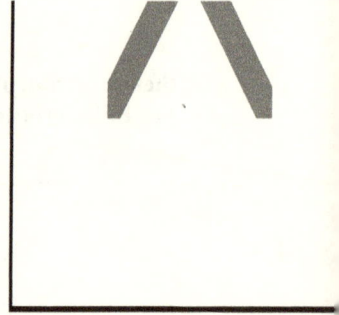

DOWN IN ONE.

(THE FOLLOW UP TO

'VIEWED WITH SUSPICION')

BY

PHIL FLETCHER

A BLACK SUN PRODUCTION   2001AD (THIS IS MY

MILLENNIUM COLLECTION, IT WILL LAST FOR A

THOUSAND YEARS.)

This collection contains some very sexually and harrowing material,
so if you're easily offended or nauseous, don't read it…JUST BUY
IT!!!.

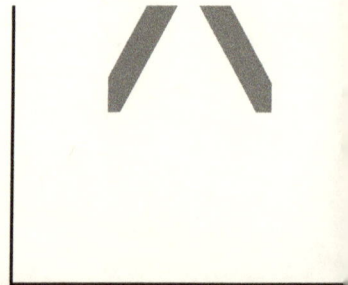

I HATE ALL INSECTS EXCEPT BUTTERFLIES. (The torture of prolonged social isolation & exclusion.)

A few weeks ago, I saw two examples of real death on TV; a man hanging from a set of goal posts, and a woman shot in the back of the head; but you couldn't see her face, she was covered from head to foot in one of those blue tent-l[ke garments that Afghan women are now compelled to wear; she just keeled over silently after the bullet had killed her; at any rate she didn't appear to be moving very much, as she lay on the ground.
This harrowing scene was filmed surreptitiously by a Western female journalist of Afghan origin, who was risking her own life and liberty, to alert us to the excessive horrors of the seemingly, criminally insane, Taliban regime; destroyers of people they don't like, and huge Buddhist statues of World Heritage, historical importance. Oh yes, there was another atrocity picture I saw before I switched over in apathetic disinterest, thinking, 'Well what the fuck can I do about it?' (I was in Amnesty International once, it didn't work out, I was too judgmental in my letter writing to tyrants and despots.) It was a colour photo of a young Afghan man whose head had allegedly been skinned, his eyes were still in his head, and his teeth were clenched together; it looked as if he'd been roasted from the neck up.
When I was much younger, the sight of such images would have left me feeling horrified. I can still remember the feeling of absolute terror and despair I experienced when, at the age of fourteen, some forty years ago, I opened, and looked through, a library book my mother had specifically told me not too. It was called 'KNIGHTS OF THE BUSHIDO', it dealt with Japanese atrocities against POWs during the last World War.
There were black and white photographs of mutilations and mass executions; but what upset me the most was some hand drawn depictions of torture. Two in particular were totally diabolical. The victim was held down, and a hose pipe was forced into his mouth, and his body filled with water; the next crude drawing showed a guard jumping on his stomach, and the man's head exploding, at least

that's the way it looked to me. I remember feeling, for the first time, absolutely helpless against a cruel, and evil world, and rushing out into the open so I could gulp in some clean air.

A couple of years ago, on another Saturday night in on my own, there was a programme on C4, about people still being burnt as witches in rural South Africa; up to 200 a year. There were a couple of colour photos of burnt heads, one skull still had the flesh on it, but its mouth was wide open in a pain, and horror-driven, death scream. It's another way of pointing the bones at someone; if you don't like an individual, or family, in your village, or you're jealous of their success, you accuse them of witchcraft, and unless they do a runner, they're dead meat.
All these recollections of crimes against humanity, was brought on because I was trying to think of something to write for 'ROUTE' magazine's crime anthology, well this is one area where fact is much more unbelievable than fiction.
14/7/01.

....
....

STRANGLEHOLD.

'You can't go against your fate', is an expression I've always hated, especially now that mine's been signed, sealed and delivered.
And do you know what it says? 'YOU'RE FUCKED!!! Physical and mental pain's gonna getcha!' Which is a pity, because if it wasn't for this awful decision, (which I'm trying to treat with derision), I'd still feel I had a lot of living to do.
But I fear this tiding of ill omen is true, the physical pain is on the increase, urged on by a persecution complex, depression, and an over-riding sense of inadequacy too,
It's a 'chicken and egg' situation about what's happening to me, I've had a long and fairly unrelenting history of emotional turmoil, now I'm paying for it physically. My body's racked with pain, from my lower back to the skull casing housing my brain.
I've classified myself as Britain's most unloved man, I am. But if it wasn't for my marked physical decline, I'd still feel I had plenty of time to put this right, provided a massive injection of cash could come my way; well heeled older men are in demand today. Broken down old farts need not apply, they, like me, can wait to die in any way they choose; booze would be my favoured option, slurring, 'Fuck 'em all!' with my final conscious breath.

9/8/01

....

......

SYRUP.

On syrup of figs and figurines, I have nothing to say, on stirrups and stirrup pumps, I could write a play; Mumps and Rubella aren't as common as they used to be today. 'I'm feeling gay in a melancholy way', is a line from an old 'torch' song that I'd play at two in the morning, while reflecting on days gone by, with a tear in my eye, and a large bottle of wine close by, and a good cigar.
I'd be praying for the promised land of eternal sleep, as my set of false teeth looked on at me from their glass at the side of my bed, at my ever increasing state of decay; no one would miss me much anyway.

Night and day would come and go in their eternal cycle, my St Micheal underpants would fill up with brown ooze, my 'snooze' pillow would absorb my rotting scalp; it's nature's way of breaking physical matter down.
Maggots would materialise out of nowhere, wriggling around under the duvet and inside my nose and eyes; flies might lay eggs in the crevice between my thighs, my back passage becoming their larva's front door. No more loneliness and despair for me, my soul won't hang around. I'll be free to roam over sea and foam; evening sunsets a speciality. Full golden moon's on the oceans, lapping against the shore, mine forever more if I want them. And inbetween? Haunting holiday-makers in a most unpleasant way, by enveloping them in a grey, depressing smog.
11/8/01

....
....

DOWN IN ONE.

It's already done and dusted, I'm already up and gone, 'Aspro aparto!'. I've got it down in one.
I'm writing up a storm, having spent a night in one on a hillside in the pitch black; storm water thudding off my back, and only an old tarpaulin groundsheet between me and the rain. That was at a washed-out rock festival at Barkisland, near Halifax, 30 years ago. How I made it back to Manchester without catching double pneumonia I'll never know.

A similar thing happened six years later in Crete, just outside a little village called Fournes, we got flooded out of our tent by torrential sheets of rain. Finding a big ruined house to shelter in, was heaven sent for me, it allowed me to break away from the crowd I'd come out of England with, and hit rock bottom on my own, alcoholically.
I really abused my body while I was out there, it took it in its stride; I never really felt any pain no matter how hard I tried to destroy myself, nearly 24 years ago. I'm paying for it now though, 'Aspro aparto', (loosely translated as) 'Down in one!' Glasses of Greek red wine, in my 'Zorba the Greek' days. The atmosphere was right for it, I had an Afghan coat and a Gandalf staff, which some spiteful local broke in half one night, when I stumbled drunkenly back to our squat without it. Even that couldn't ruin the magic that I felt, I still had a leather belt that could take the full weight of my upper body if I leaned back on it, buckled tightly round my waist.

And there was a celtic cross hung around my neck, to which I was able to attach weird little pierced Cretan coins, the size of old sixpences. They used to make a pleasant little jangling sound when I walked; later, in Amsterdam,, a Dutch cop found this free-spirited adornment, something he didn't like, ripping it off my neck and warning me to get out of Amsterdam before I was deported.
Actually, it's the last 15 years spent here in Calderdale, that I believe have really broken my health; there's an atmosphere of cunning and stealth here that isn't always perceptible to the untrained psychic eye. Some of the local populace have their own hidden agenda's,

dating back centuries. A bit like those, left alone together too long, cretins; sorry, I meant to say Cretans, who snapped my sturdy walking stave in half.

I don't think they'll be happy here, till they've put me in my grave, but I won't go down without a monumental fight, I'll not go quietly into that last unwelcome goodnight.
Or maybe it's just the drab grey weather here that makes me feel so oppressed, plus the fact that I can't get arrested when it comes to finding a halfway decent-looking soul mate.

11/8/01.

....

......

TONGUE ON THE COUNTER.

I'm 'in love' with a young woman who works on the liquor counter at 'SUPABUYS'. If you've got only a small amount of groceries, you can take them to her counter too. I think she's really fit, in a classy sort of way; I'd like to be able to say 'I'm writing a poem about you', but she'd probably laugh in my face, or turn really frosty, the way most females do if they sense I'm interested in them...the cheeky cunts!!!
When I look at a woman appreciatively, and she looks back at me as if I'm some sort of pond life, I feel like saying, 'A frog can look at a princess can't he'? But most of them are so self-centred and vain, they still wouldn't come across with a mercy shag; like Jimi Hendrix said: 'Loneliness is such a drag', in his song: ' THE BURNING OF THE MIDNIGHT LAMP'.

I reckon my 'SUPABUYS' girl could be a real vamp, she could place her stilleto heel on my chest anytime she liked, as long as the spiked heel wouldn't pierce my heart, unless she was into total sadistic cruelty; pissing on me while I writhed in agony, lapping up her warm rain; helplessly erect in my pain and ecstasy. I wonder if she'd go down on me before I died? And I could wedge my nose in her bum crack and lick her fanny out.

Of course, she might be a thoroughly nice young lady, and if she ever found out the real nature of this work, go completely berserk; and any remote chance I might have had of winning her affections would be blown out of the water big style!!!

I'll most likely continue to ogle her furtively through my squinty eye, whenever I take my basket up to her, and fantasise about having oral sex with her on the counter, by her sitting on the said counter with her legs up and open, and her love juice dribbling cunt, perched just over the edge, so I could slide my tongue in and up, (excuse me for a moment while I relieve my frustration).

This behaviour might hold up the tutting queue behind, which is what I'll be doing,, holding her behind while she fucks my tongue. In reality, there are too many hidden boundary lines I mustn't cross; not unless I wish to risk losing a complete loss of face, and being barred out of 'SUPABUYS' in abject disgrace; never to be allowed back in again to buy spaghetti at 7 pence a tin, or Irish Stew at 32. Both of my favourites, with a dash of pepper and a pinch of dried herbs. There's no flavour in the herbs unfortunately, but I've got to use them up.

Sadly, I'll have to continue feigning stolidity each time I see her lovely face, like a Cigar Store Indian, and who knows, just maybe, one day she'll throw her knickers in my face and say, 'Sniff those you old perv', and I can pass away in ecstasy.   14/8/01.

JOEY THE BUDGIE.

When I was a kid we had a succession of pet budgies, one of them was called Joey. We also used to live in a cobbled back street in Rusholme, Manchester, where I can still remember the gas filament lighting in our living room/kitchen, it gave off a yellow light. There was also an old fashioned kitchen range in the house, and a room on the landing which me and my sisters treated with dread, it was probably just a store room but to us it held unnamed terrors, we called it 'the dark room'.

We also had fly papers in our old house, because back in the early 1950s, summer was really summer and flies were a nuisance, at least they were to my parents I presume, I can't say I was unduly aware of their presence at the tender age of six.

I think Joey was one of our more sociable budgies, always chirping and knocking seven bells out of a little bell in his cage, clamouring to be let out.

Obviously, I don't remember every aspect of the unfortunate event clearly, it happened roughly 48 years ago, but one evening during one of his frequent exercise periods, Joey flew straight into a fly paper and got stuck. All I really remember was his frantic squawking (or was it screaming?) and a flurry of green and yellow feathers, before being shooed off into the rarely used back living room (sorry, 'parlour'.)

Joey never got over the shock of what happened to him, and ceased to be the perky little bird we'd all been so fond of; in fact, very shortly afterwards he just ceased to be, and was given the ceremonial cardboard shoe box burial in our seldomly cultivated, or productive, back garden plot. I want a cardboard coffin myself, to be buried in a field with a Fever Tree planted on top of me, very appropriate seeing as how I've lived most of my adult life in a fever of numb terror, due to making the wrong decisions most of the time.

When I was ten or eleven I had a 'pet' rabbit foisted on to me, called Patch, he was kept in a hutch outside the back door of our recently acquired three-

bedroomed, council house in Wythenshawe, South Manchester; a palace compared with our Rusholme abode. I never really bonded with Patch, I don't know who was more depressed, me or him? I did occasionally try to give him some of the love I felt I was being deprived of, even at that early age, but he'd always wriggle out of my grasp and hop off down the garden in a bid for freedom.

On the odd occasion that another rabbit was put in with him to try and cheer him up, all hell would break loose, and the interloper would be pulled out missing bits of fur. Eventually Patch did us all a favour and disappeared, the only trace left of him was a hole burrowed beneath the wire netting my dad had put up at the bottom of the garden to try and keep him from escaping. There was a little area of woodland not far away, maybe he made it across to it, and lived on in lonely splendour for a time, before old age or a vicious dog got to him.

14/8/01.

....
....

THE HALIFAX PIPE SMOKERS CLUB.

The Halifax pipe smokers club doesn't meet in Halifax, they meet at The Ram's Head in Sowerby Bridge, on the first Monday of each month at 8pm, contact Margret on tel no........ I must admit that I laughed uproariously when I saw this club's name listed in an inventory of groups and clubs in Calderdale. I never see anyone smoking a pipe any more, I wonder if Margret smokes one? And does this disappearing breed all wear tweed jackets with leather patches at the elbows, and have a worn leather pouch of 'CONDOR READY RUBBED' pipe tobacco in their jacket pocket, along with their favourite pipe, and a box of 'SWAN VESTAS' matches (no longer made I fear, why do I fear? I always hated the stink of matches, a horrible sulphurous reek!), and pipe cleaners just in case the stem had got bunged up with thick tarry spittle?

I'm as fascinated with this, by today's standards anyway, eccentric club, as the late Frankie Vaughn was with what went on behind 'the green door' in the classic 'rock'n'roll' song (called 'GREEN DOOR') of forty-odd years ago; here's a slight adaptation, "There's a thick blue haze because they smoke a lot behind the brown door, wish they'd let me in so I could smoke a pipe of CONDOR, and they'd all chorus: 'Ah! It's that ready rubbed moment' in the back room of THE RAM'S HEAD.

I only ever tried pipe smoking once, that was 30 years ago after I'd retrieved a couple of old pipes that had been thrown out in a box of junk, when I was a 'refuse disposal operative', or 'dust bin man' to you. I was living in a dingy bedsit in Withington, South Manchester, experimenting with hallucinogenic drugs at the weekend, and doing this gruelling job during the week. I remember boiling the pipes to sterilise them, I don't remember what tobacco I used, it might well have been 'Old Holburn' cigarette rolling tobacco, I smoked roll ups back then in those halcyon days when I could abuse my lungs and get away with it. Obviously pipe smoking was not my forte, except if you include inhaling cannabis smoke through a chillum, something else I couldn't do now, unless I had an oxygen mask handy, and I'm paranoid enough already.

I experienced my first bout of severe clinical depression while I was staying in that awful house of thin walls, and a shared toilet and bathroom. It was one of those Bed-sit dumps where the various occupants crept about, desperately trying to avoid each other. I had to nerve myself up to go down to the toilet, clutching my toilet roll and sneaking out again hoping it didn't smell too bad, I probably ended up peeing in the sink in my room, I don't think I ever sang in the bath while I was there.

I had to return to my parent's house after three months, which didn't please my dad very much. I don't remember how long I was back there before I was offered a council bed-sit flat not too far away. The best thing that could be said for that council hovel was that I didn't have to share a toilet with strangers, I lived there for the next fourteen years.

16/8/01.

....
....

I GUESS I'LL JUST STOLIDIFY, TILL I DIE OF BOREDOM.
(A catalogue of woe from a thoroughly modern middle-aged man).

It isn't the sex act itself that's 'God's' ultimate joke against mankind, (especially if you do it in the dark, much more exciting and primal, or so my long distance memory tells me); it's being male, seemingly not very desirable, but primed and ready for sexual action, with only the slightest encouragement from a pair of flashing female thighs, eyes, and a set of glistening white teeth.
It's been an unnaturally long time since I last had sex, it's all part of the curse of being a gargoyle among the 'normals'. The sex act itself can be little more than a short, sharp, shock to the senses of the inexperienced male; you're no sooner in, than you're out, having possibly taken hours to get the female 'in the mood'; they being a lot slower to sexual arousal (or so we're led to believe), except when they get to around thirty six, when they're supposed to become as rampant as the average eighteen-year-old spotty youth. That seems like an immaculate misconception to me; as society still frowns on older women parading 'toy boys' around town for sex on demand in public places. I was quite shocked earlier this year to read of a couple having really noisy sex in the gent's toilet in The British Library, they were thrown out of course; talk about lack of self control and chronic attention seeking! Apparently, they were still stuck together like dogs while they were being ejected from that august building.
I think the same degraded couple, were later spotted fornicating against one of the pillars of The British Museum, or was it the Tate Modern? I'm only going off memory, not accurate information. Primarily, sex is for procreative purposes, I think we're the only primate species, apart from Bonobo Chimpanzees, (who use sex as a

form of greeting and communicating), who indulge in recreational sex. Most other species operate within strict social parameters, such as males coming in and killing the offspring of other males, so the females will become sexually receptive and accept their seed; we'd call that infanticide, though whenever I hear some brat throwing a tantrum in a supermarket, I know exactly how those other male animals feel.

Women are pre programmed to be judgemental in their quest to find their perfect mate, although quite often their idea of perfection falls far short of any logic that I can understand; even more so nowadays. I'd say this country's breeding stock is going straight to HELL!, in its own 'couldn't-care-less way'. All that will be left, in fifty, or a hundred years time, will be a small nucleus of established 'British', the rest will be a hotch-potch of hybrid dysfunctionals, issuing out of one parent baby farms, in a feeding frenzy of Caligula-like sadism, greed, and lust; if the chilling line I picked out from a reality TV programme about London clubbers is anything to go by, from an otherwise intelligent young man: 'She's not my girl friend, I just fuck her'.

Tues. 28/8/01. And also, if SKY TV's 'SUMMER UNCOVERED' (which I've watched purely in the context of 'research') is anything to go by, young men and women now definitely seem to have reached soulless, sexual parity. I observed very few signs of romance, just a relentless quest for sex on both sides. I can imagine that I'd have been deeply humiliated if I'd been young now and had gone to Ibiza with my mates; it was bad enough when I went to Butlin's Holiday Camp aged 16, 38 years ago, and was given the 'minger' treatment by a party of pleb bitches, who used me unmercifully to lure my mates into their chalet; and I haven't really fared much better since. But I still don't hate women enough to go down the 'Yorkshire' Ripper's road of murdering 13 of them; my 'soft nature' has spared me that ultimate expression of misogyny. Though from what I saw on TV recently, Peter Sutcliffe has got a constant stream of female admirers, who even want to marry him, and who he plays off one against the other, through a relentless barrage of letter writing from his safe haven in Broadmoor Prison for the Criminally Insane; even a poke in the eye with a felt tip pen last year(?) hasn't slowed him down. One disgruntled ex admirer has had over 500 letters from him!!! I suppose a man with that level of mental energy, probably a megalomaniac, would desperately need to find releases for his overwhelming feelings of superiority and contempt.

Going back to 'SUMMER UNCOVERED', there was one instance
where a drunken young woman singled out an older man in a
nightclub in Ibiza, to ridicule; I admit his fashion sense left
something to be desired, but when she first draped herself around
him, he thought he'd pulled, he was all smiles. But then she shouted
to her cronies: 'He's minging!;, and flounced off. The camera panned
back to his face, and the look on it said that if a look could kill, that
girl would be dead. It is a dangerous world out there, (by 'there' I
mean everywhere). I feel so strongly on this issue of women's
judgement values, or rather, the lack of them, that's nearly destroyed
me on numerous occasions, and left my physical and emotional
health in tatters, that I wish I could write a treatise on it. But I lack
the clinical air of detachment necessary for such a project, (as well as
the intellectual capability). Suffice it to say that I trust a woman's
judgement on virtually nothing when it comes to affairs of the mind
and body, namely the heart; and this in an age where harsh
judgemental views are frowned upon, in any but the lowest human
society. (I mean plebs' who can't help being thick, but you're not
supposed to say it any more are you? Not in their hearing anyway,
they might hit you once, or several times.) (And just to show my own
ignorance, I always thought 'plebeian' was spelt 'plebian', until the
'spellchecker' on this miraculous machine pointed out my error.)
I love writing, but I've run out of things to say; as far as I'm
concerned, the human race is a lost cause, it deserves a severe
chastisement. One from which it will learn indelibly, that it isn't
invincible, and that the planet which it now infests and infects, isn't
inexhaustible. I'm now not too far off becoming 55-years-old, and
I'm still waiting to get a life; a bit like the cheesy grin I wore out
waiting, 25 years ago.

....
....

THE MOON.   28/8/01.

The moon, that old rock up in the sky that draws my eye to it like a
magnet.
Some nights it's clear and bright, on others it's just a luminous grey
smudge on a black backdrop.

I like it best when it's big and bold like youth, and lights up the clouds with a silver glow, or shining down on wheat fields far below, as harvest time draws near.

Perhaps moonlight influences the flavour of the wine, as the grapes ripen on the vine, and the summer breeze caresses the leaves, making the fruit of Bachus such a heady brew.

I wish I could dive into a vat of you, and re-emerge, purged and cleansed of all my ills that require so many pills to keep the worst of the pain away.

I understand nothing of astronomy, though I've dutifully watched ;THE SKY AT NIGHT' on TV on numerous occasions. The universe seems to be full of negative energy, highlighted by billions of points of starlight in the night sky. If you can see even a fraction of them, then you're a lot luckier than I am; I've given up trying to spot their glow, unless I go abroad.

It's all dead light anyway, the star you have named after you today, has probably been dead for millions of light-years. Maybe 'black holes' are just black suns, absorbing, rather than giving off power; an impenetrable flower of evil, where all positive force is swallowed up and devoured, with no point of egress for its waste matter.

....
....

THE WWF, (AND WE'RE NOT TALKING 'WORLD WILDLIFE FUND' HERE EITHER.)   9/9/01.

Quite often, a ref' at the WWF, is superfluous; they're always getting floored or beaten up anyway, or even whacked with a steel chair if they can't get out the way fast enough; it's the 'right stuff' of sports entertainment for me.

When you're watching it on TV, the action doesn't always seem that real, you can't feel the bodies bouncing off the boards or the concrete floor. I used to think some of them concealed fake blood capsules inside their hair, but now I've seen bald headed 'STONE COLD' Steve Austin with his face turned bloody red, I don't think so any more.

Channel 4 (here in the UK), used to screen the World Wrestling Federation at 4pm on a Sunday afternoon, it was great, but then it came under scrutiny from the self appointed, very vociferous moral minority, who insisted that it's merely mindless violence; now it's not on till late at night, sometimes too late even for me to stay up and watch it.

If these arid killjoys have their way, Channel 4 will ditch it in favour of another series of 'QUEER AS FOLK', or something similar. Thank fuck for SKY TV, which doesn't seem to be infected with 'PC' (Pusillanimous Cack-spouting); I can watch five hours of All American Action Wrestling each weekend, with lots of repeats during the school holidays. And if I subscribe to 'pay per view' I can watch uncensored hardcore, where the bodies get dragged out along the floor.

(3/5/02, I've since got bored with the WWF, even mindless violence can lose its appeal, if you've an IQ bigger than that of the average moron; though it's really taken off here in the UK now. I still appreciate skilled wrestling, but most of the WWF is merely knockabout.)

....
....

DEATH.   10/9/01.

It's a thin line between life and death, you can be here one minute and gone the next, if you're lucky, and not being burnt alive in a car fire for instance; how horrific must that pain be, especially if your family's in there with you?

Or, like me, in a slow lingering decline, due to an evil fate which seems to be closing in for the kill, but never quite will, leaving me in limbo between physical and mental torture, suffering beyond all understanding, a stranger in a hostile world.

I've heard a Spiritualist say that, 'Your spirit passes over to the other side whether you'e a believer or not'; that's a great relief, because no matter how hard I've tried, I just can't buy it. If I could, I'd have gone over already, with a little help from my physical death; generously induced by a binge of booze and pills, none of that violent exiting for me. I'd want to savour the flavour of cursing all the bastards and cunts who've made my life such a misery, especially the cunts. (The only thing worth believing in is luck, if I'd had as much good luck as I've had bad, I'd no doubt be a wealthy and successful man today.)

Still, what the hell, you're only put here to procreate, and if you can't do that because you've been denied a mate, you have to circumnavigate that primary urge, and splurge your spunk up against the wall; mine's worth fuck all anyway. I'll never know if I could have fathered a 'normal' child.

Whenever I show an interest in a woman, she disappears, presumably in a state of wild alarm that she might risk falling for my manly charm, and cop for a pregnancy she'd want to abort.

Anyone who's ever had a general anaesthetic, shouldn't fear death; I don't see how much deeper you can go into the blackness than that, and still wake up. Indeed, quite a few don't, which is why we fear 'going under'. I can remember the bad old days, when a mask was placed over your nose and mouth; and me trying to resist the gas with my arms flailing about, and attempting to shout: 'NOOO!!!' Now it's only a prick on the back of the hand, and you're out before you can count to ten. The coming round again can be fraught with difficulty. The last time it happened to me, my teeth were chattering uncontrollably and I couldn't breathe; an oxygen mask saved my bacon, and once I'd gotten over the shock, I lay on my hospital bed feeling more dead than alive, with no visitors to look forward to depressing.

I want this to be the end of my literary bent, I'm sick of the muse haunting me, using my ennui as a means of conductivity; you can only get so much mileage out of misery surely? I think Samuel Beckett was about 60 before he began to receive the adulation from women he so richly didn't deserve; (apart from his rugged good looks). He was dubbed: 'The writer of nothingness and despair'. I think he was taking the piss out of a gullible, intellectual elite; it was a form of death of the soul to wade through page after page of his endless, unintelligible guff.

....
....

THE EXPENDABLE ONE.   20/9/01.

I am the expendable one, the kind (mainly women, it has to be admitted) that people find it easy to dump on; if I wasn't prepared to put up a spirited defence, I'd already be buried six feet deep in their stinking SHIT! I've had enough of it. but what can I do, except complain to you, my long suffering pen.

In the case of good versus evil in my life, evil against me has won hands down; causing me endless strife, (for the rhyming effect). And I'm not just talking about localised evil here, it's much more orchestrated than that. Hell on Earth isn't confined to the bottom of the ocean, five miles down, with its black smoking chimneys and incomprehensible life forms, it's right here in my living room, with its sulphur and rotting corpse fumes.

I still haven't found a one hundred percent cure for the 'evil wind'; Orientals believe that powdered rhino horn can do the trick, but the world's running out of rhino's, and it's been scientifically proven that the rhino horn's consistency is no more than hard skin; equivalent to that of human finger nails.

The good aspect in all this, is my refusal to be broken mentally and spiritually; not completely anyway, by this constant onslaught of perversity. I can't say the same physically; it could be the death of me, and everything I've fought for, the right to choose who I want to love, and to ignore the really poor, and the attendant problems they cause.

There's been a 24-hour pause in my creative flow, this piece has got nowhere else to go, unless I ask you, how would you feel if you'd endured 54 years of being told you weren't good enough to invest any love in? Could you have stood it? Have you any idea what it feels like to face each new day feeling like a reject from life? That you are totally alone, apart from the hideous, and unwanted attentions, of some unnatural, mind-stalking, malevolent creature, who's out there masquerading as a human being; unless it's a Satanic coven of 'chutney ferrets', and the king of the chutney eaters is determined to make me bow down to his encrusted phallus.

I've always hated wasting space, even if keeping up the pace in this case, is proving difficult and depressing; I'd much rather be confessing my horrendously long sexual starvation to a 'Sister of the mercy shag', who was going to excuse my first dismal attempt to please her, as dipping it in to tease her, before I shoot my load before she can get hold of it between her slippery wet thighs, and ride it like a bucking bronco.

She'd have to be really rough, to put me off getting it up again; even in the midst of my emotional pain, my penis has steadfastly stuck to its resolve of 'standing tall', even if it's poking fuck all but the hole made by my curled fingers; only the distant memory lingers of what it feels like to be making love. Maybe when I go above, I'll get my end away again, and again, and again, and my aching right testicle won't complain.

....
....

SELF DISCIPLINE.

I suppose it's a sin when you keep giving in to temptation, because
you don't feel enough compunction not to. By 'you', I mean me, I
initially lacked the mental self discipline of thinking things through,
before I began to write. 'Shite! Fuck! Damn and Blast!' are swear
words I'm fond of using; as well as 'cunt' and 'bollocks', which are
words for abusing our genitalia, (I do it all the time). I wish I
possessed the fortitude never to think of myself as a failure, because I
can't compete in a viciously competitive world; only LOADS OF
MONEY could cure that particular ill; if I ever win it big on the
lottery, I can procure my fill of oriental beauties, whose duties will
include, trying to breathe some life back into my sorely depleted
sense of well being.
I would also like enough self-discipline, never to feel so lonely again
that I want to drink myself into oblivion and never wake up;
alcohol's no good for me any more, even in moderate doses. Drinking
should be for pleasure, not a no win attempt to cure painful
emotions. I spend countless hours engulfed in feelings of deep despair
and guilt; it must be in my genes. I've got nothing to feel guilty about,
except that I sometimes (quite often actually), speak before I think,
and create a social stink amongst the few friends I have, and for
which I castigate myself unmercifully, until I'm ready to come out of
purgatory, and go and do it all over again; I guess they'll have to take
me or leave me, I'm used to spending acres of time alone.
The world might be going to hell on a handcart, with a chemical,
biological, or nuclear device on it, but as long as my living room
smells nice, courtesy of my 'plug in air freshener', I couldn't give a
bad case of Anthrax for it. It's the pleasure without pain principle for
me from now on, who cares about gain? You can't take it with you
when you go, and why leave it for some other parasite to leach off? If
you can't be with the ones you want to be with, you might as well be
on your own; that's what I say. (My words come back to haunt me in
the echoing silence).
And if I was sat here in my chemical warfare suit and gas mask, (just
in case), of which there's been a lot of panic-buying lately, (post Sept.
11.), and those words of self assurance were steaming up the inside of
my goggles, as I repeated them to myself over and over; I could get

the wrong impression that I was the only one left alive, and go running out into the street; my lead-lined boots causing my feet to drag; and some horny hooker shouted, 'Hi handsome, fancy a shag?', I'd know things were on the up. I fancy organising a rave for all us germ, and chemical warfare suit-wearing types, anyone who hadn't taken precautions wouldn't be let in, we'll be a whole new nation; the only survivors if it all goes horribly shit-faced.

....
....

The cold winds of death, ennui.)

PUBLIC DISPLAY.   6-8/10/01.

They've never liked me round here anyway, so I'm thinking of putting on a public display as a final act of defiance, a spectacular end to a life lived in fear and obscurity.
My face doesn't fit, they treat me like shit, if they'd ever smelt mine, I could understand why; they'll get the chance when I die. It's karaoke night tonight, over at the plebs' local watering hole; the booming bass sound is coming intrusively through the uninsulated stone walls of my house. I'm sure that if I walked in there, I'd kill the atmosphere stone dead; right in the middle of someone's rendition of 'Viva Espania'. An icy blast following me in, accompanying me and my ennui, and a double absinthe and angostura bitters, to a table in the far corner, shrouded in cancerous tobacco fumes; thank fuck I'm a part of the new breed, who believe that staying in is the new going out.
I like to get pissed late at night, the downside is I wake up with my nerves in a fright, and the debacle that's been my life, screaming in my head to end it once and for all; I can usually still this hellish din once the valerian capsules have kicked in; but there's the physical torture too. I sometimes wake up after a good drink in less than an hour or two, with my insides on fire and acid bile burning its way through my gullet; if I was connected to a plug, I'd pull it.
It's a fantasy, rather than reality, what I have in mind; I'm sure that if life would treat me kind for once, I'd forget all about it. After all, hope, like an optimistic phallus, springs eternal, or should do, unless it's gone into a terminal decline, that only Viagra, (Prozac for the knob), can cure.

My fantasy is to hang myself publicly. Naked. A variation on the two bed sheet's knotted together theme. I've read in William Burough's work, that when you hang you ejaculate at the same time; I would hope that when I was dangling against the outside wall of my house, suspended from the knotted bed sheets tied round the base of the open window frame, that my penis would remain erect and my bowels evacuate, (for added effect). I think it's technically viable for me to achieve this aim, I've got a sturdy UPVC window frame, my knot making expertise is a bit lame though. I might jump out of my bedroom window, hoping my homemade noose will break my neck, only to hit the pavement some 20 feet below, a jibbering wreck with both legs broken.

It's the thought of hanging there for all to see that appeals to me; my final protest against being treated like a social leper; the modern pariah, a bloke on his own!!! People round here don't know that I like nothing better than reading good English literature, (even if only 'English' in translation), and listening to vintage Chuck Berry; not searching for kiddie porn on a computer I don't possess.

....
....

DOES RUST EAT DUST?   9-10/10/01.

I don't need to use words like 'simulacrum' and 'nadir' to prove I've got a brain, believe you me I wish I hadn't; I view too much directionless intelligence with disdain now, it's a burdensome pain.. How many esoteric poets does it take to change a light bulb? The answer is none, they're far too preoccupied with life's mysteries, and being visionaries, to notice it's even gone out; they need someone much more worldly than them to sort such a simple problem out. Maybe they'll spout about it esoterically in one of their inscrutable poems: 'The light has gone out of the world, and who are we to complain? We'll sit here in life's darkness, till some astral deity comes down to earth, and switches it on again'.

A man who was uxoriously devoted to his wife, had her buried in a coffin made of 'polyvinyl chloride', better known as PVC, after she died of Pyemia, not to be confused with piella; I wonder if I'm being guilty of literary cozenage? After all, there's more to the word

'Corrie' than just an abbreviation for 'CORONATION STREET';
check it out.

His voice sounded old and weary at times, usually during prolonged
phone conversations with obtuse public servants; too much of this
dreariness had flowed beneath his particular bridge; he felt
unrequitedly deservant of life's rich tapestry, like the unrestrained
love that could gush from a young woman's heart if you can find a
way to get her to 'pop her cork!' Leading her to crave a portion of
'pork' to quench her thirst of love-ust. I'd like to drink out of her
furry loving cup before I put my weapon in, and watch the flesh-
scented steam pour forth as we both orgasmicly shout, 'Eureka! This
is the real thing, happiness at last!' (Has this fool never heard of post
coital depression?)

I feel penned in by an all pervasive, oppressive, aggressive ignorance-
led, 'local' male culture; I can't react against this oppression in a
physical way, for various reasons; there's also another form of
human tick that's burrowed its way deep into my psyche. I can feel it
squirming and moving about beneath the dome of my skull; it feeds
off my emotions. If I try resisting, it squeezes my brain in a most
unpleasant way. I'd need to employ the services of a top psychic
medium to lure it out, and heal the hideous wound it's put inside my
head, in its attempt to fill it with its own black magic soul.

But if it succeeds in sucking me dry, what will it do when I die?
Crawl out through my mouth, ears, or nose, eating a few crusty
morsels on its way? I know in the cosmic scheme of things, I'll never
attract the attention of those oriental kings (the three wise men), and
I feel my time's running out; and the way things are going I'm likely
to be the only one at my own funeral; I want to have '96 TEARS' by
'QUESTION MARK AND THE MYSTERIONS' played at least
twice, as my funeral music of choice, (they'll be lucky to find a copy,
I've not been able to; I used to have it on a compilation LP but I got
rid of my collection in a moment of madness, [I got 80 quid for the
lot], which is just as well, I'd have no room for it in the poky little
council 'bungalow' I,ve ended up in 14/6/02). And if there's still any
time left, 'THE LARK ASCENDING' by Vaughn Williams, and
when that bird has reached its zenith, my ghost will shit on you all,
from a great height!

,,
,,,,,,,,,,

ETERNITY.   10-11/10/01.

Scientists informedly tell us that this, our blue planet, still has around four billion years of life left in it, before the death of our sun will kill it. Scientists also tell us that the secret of eternal life, or at least, a lot longer span than we can hope to enjoy now, is just round the corner; and I don't think we're talking criogenics here. I don't think they've figured out yet where they're going to get the bodies to stick all those severed heads back onto; maybe they'll have developed headless androids by then. I hope mine will have a big dick, and they can give me a new face; I couldn't bear the thought of all eternity wearing this one, otherwise I'll be wanking my enormous synthetic member forever, (I wonder what my semen will be composed of, snot?!)

There's no great mystery to the meaning of life, if you're a bloke like me, you only ever want to be seen in the company of fit-looking women. It's taking an eternity in my case to get to first base with one,; they're much too mercenary. They'll put up with a gargoyle, if he's got money and power, alas, I lack both vital commodities in sufficient quantities to please them, anyway.
We all get world-weary at times, and in this age of mass communication, who can blame us? If I hear of tragic events thousands of miles away, at best I can only pay lip service to them; at other, more depressed times, I can only shrug my shoulders in care-worn indifference.

I don't think I ever get life weary, there's so much natural beauty around to keep reinvigorating the life force; my only regret is, it looks as though I'm never going to achieve my ideals. A couple of weeks ago, I saw a programme on C4 called 'LOCATION, LOCATION, LOCATION'. A young bohemian, (but practical with it), couple, (they were involved in the media, photography or something), had bought a flat in London and were spending time and money renovating it, with a view to letting it out at a rent where they could pay the mortgage, and have a bit left over.
This enterprising pair had also bought a really dilapidated cottage in a fairly remote part of Scotland, for £12,000, which was going to be their rural idyll once they'd done it up; I can see the cannabis plants growing in the back garden even as I write.

Of course, with, lap-tops, PCs, and the internet, they need never feel isolated, or cut off from the world, if they don't want to be; or their work. I do envy this like-minded couple of young people, they can be in tune with the whole universe in their remote hideaway, and always have practical considerations to worry about, to stop them from becoming jaded.

When I was young (23), I used to say the best kind of existence would be a 'peasant' (rural) one, in an enlightened and well equipped world; it looks like it's coming true for one couple at least

....
....

IT'S A NON-NEGOTIABLE, INELUCTABLE FATE.
(YOU GET NO TIME ADDED ON FOR GOOD BEHAVIOUR.)
14-16/10/01.

Apropos of nothing in particular, I like nothing better than lying curled up in bed, in a fair copy of a foetal ball, preferably with the radio on; it's one of the few times I feel secure. Another similar experience, is when I'm snug and warm watching TV, with my feet up on the TV table in front of me, and my arms folded across my chest, leaning back in my rocking chair...luxury, unashamed luxury. Judging by the amount of rampant promiscuity that seems to be rife throughout our species, (it's passed me by...), I think we might be descended from the Bonobo chimpanzees, who use sex as a greeting; anyone with a pulse within the group doesn't get left out, there are no barriers about age or gender, and no hang-ups about their incestuous, orgiastic natures either; it's not so long ago that the average human was rather short in stature...hmmm?

The only sane thing to come out of the feminist movement, is the way the modern young woman has cast off the image of being the 'weaker' sex; they're not only up for it, they're mad for it! This new aggressive approach sends out very confusing signals to men in general, whose basic instinct towards women is possessive and predatory; over protective in a lot of cases, and downright territorial and possessive in others. And unless a woman wants to be possessed, short of killing her, or locking her up, he's on a hiding to nothing, which is usually what he ends up with.

171

In general, they're still the fairer sex, there are some women's looks who I'd sell my soul (what's left of it) to be with. Not just from the trophy aspect, but simply because every time you look at them, you get a good feeling, and that's worth its weight in the 'feel good' factor, as opposed to gold, which is a lifeless metal; it's nice when it glitters but it won't purr when you stroke it, or moan in ecstasy when you poke it; oh dear, how sexistly crude of me.

Even in our enlightened times, I'd call them debauched and depraved actually; we could give Sodom and Gomorah a good run for their money, but then I'm not getting any am I? It's still frowned on for men of my age, (I won't see 54 again) to ogle young women with lascivious intent; though I could have sex with teenage prostitutes, ranging from street tarts, to high class escorts, if I was determined enough. But no, I'll continue in my vain hope that one day I'll get lucky, and attract a substantially younger female, with looks and a brain, even though I have very little to offer in return, compared to more well-heeled men of my age.

I used to have the same sneering British attitude towards Joan Collins and Peter Stringfellow, as your average sniping, media type; but not any more, they've become my role models for how not to age pathetically. Joan Collins at 68, (so I've just heard), still looks beddable; if the rest of her is as unwrinkled as her face, (the snipers claim that's due to a layer of make-up.) I don't know if Peter Stringfellow needs cranking up to get him started in the mornings, I know I do, I feel all heavy and groggy, like I'm on my last legs; maybe I am. No more worries, thank fuck for that.

....
....

THE DRIP, DRIP, DRIP OF CONSTERNATION!!!   17-8/10/01.

Everyone's heard of the Chinese water torture, but does anyone, outside of a qualified torturer, know how it was administered? Was the victim held down securely beneath a dripping tap, unable to move their head from left to right, up or down, so that the icy cold droplets could land on their forehead right between the eyes? I wonder how long it took before the poor unfortunate one was begging for mercy? Offering to tell everything, he or she knew, if only they'd make it stop! And could it drive you to screaming insanity, if the torturers were feeling excessively sadistic, and had a cerebral orgasm every time you screamed, and wanted to prolong your agony?

Maybe the concept behind George Orwell's 'ROOM 101' is more terrifying, where you're made to confront your worst fear, and if you can't face being tortured by it, you scream for it to be done to someone you love the most instead. I think being burnt alive is my worst fear, even a brief encounter with too much heat, like boiling water, causes horrendous pain; and severe burns cause horrible disfigurement, requiring lots of skin grafts.

There's one well known survivor from the Falklands war, whose face is so awful as a result of his injuries, I can only bear to look at him for a short while when he's on TV, He was on the Gloria Hunniford 'Open House' show a couple of weeks ago, I had to flick over while he was on; yet I understand he's married with children. I'm certain I'm not as deformed-looking as him, but all I've ever had from the women I've fallen in love with is rejection. If I was in 'ROOM 101', I'd have difficulty in finding anyone I cared about enough, (I've recently been rejected again), to scream, 'Do it to so-and-so, not me!' I might well have to burn, feeling nothing but resentment (in between my screams), against such a cruel world.

On an equal par with being burnt alive, is my fear of a masked gang (wearing ski masks obviously) of thugs, bursting into my house on some flimsy vigilante excuse. A few years ago, I saw a victim of a 'punishment beating' in Belfast, speaking from his hospital bed on TV. He said the pain of the beating was like nothing he'd ever experienced, despite his screams for mercy, and he looked, and sounded, like a hard man; to add horror to terror, they trashed his house as well. I couldn't live in that atmosphere of fear and loathing that predominates in that blighted province, I'd rather be homeless on the streets of London.

And the fear of such attacks, isn't so far-fetched over here, there's a very uneasy atmosphere on the mainland streets after dark, it's when the monsters come out to play, and there aren't enough good guys on hand to be everywhere at once, even if they wanted to be; which doesn't seem to be the case any more. Despite having a good solid front door, (the only way in), I still feel vulnerable. They could smash my ground floor kitchen window in, and come in that way. I doubt if anyone would help me, by dialing 999; if it was late at night, anyone hearing the crash of broken glass would conveniently assume it was just some yob breaking a beer bottle on the pavement, and turn over, I know I would.

It's still mainly males, mostly young ones, who perpetrate acts of mindless evil; and their actions stem from malformed intellects. A very recent motiveless murder happened at a petrol station, two males beat to death a young man, using only their fists; they then allegedly jumped back into their car, that had other people in it, laughing. They probably weren't aware they'd killed the guy till the following day, if they heard it on the local news; they're facing a charge of murder now. Their actions were caught on CCTV, they might be identifiable; I sincerely hope so.
Quite possibly, they'll feel some remorse for their actions, and when, or if, they're caught, they're asked, 'Why did you do it?', they may well reply 'I don't know what came over me, I wish I hadn't done it', especially as they'll be looking at a minimum of ten years in gaol. (They were caught on 19/10/01.)

Better to mow down a few pedestrians in your car, to assuage your blood lust, you'll most likely get let off with a fine and a temporary ban; or a derisory custodial prison sentence. Or why not go 'big game hunting'? It's still allowed under licence. If you murder a huge bull elephant, you'll get a slap on the back from the licencers, and have your exultant photograph taken next to it, proudly holding your rifle; and for all I know, you still may be able to keep its tusks, feet and ears.
I've just heard, literally a few minutes ago, again courtesy of Gloria Hunniford's 'OPEN HOUSE', a bereathed mother trying to come to terms with the fact that her lovely daughter's body was cut up by a Japanese psycho, using a chainsaw. I hope the girl was already dead before he started. How do you come to terms with such horror? I think you can only absorb so much, before a safety valve in your head clicks on, and the mind shuts itself off. Either that, or you put yourself out of the misery of other people's making, by ending it all in any way you choose; or just avoid the news.

There's a substantial amount of money to be won on tonight's midweek, 'roll over' lottery; if anyone deserves to win it it's me. I could do a lot of good with eleven or twelve million quid, but no doubt some undeserving, rapacious clod will scoop the lot up, and squander it all on conspicuous consumption. I mean, obviously, I'd splash out on some of it as well, but I'd still have loads left over to devote to 'good causes' of my own choosing, and there's only one member of my so-called family, who'd receive any financial help from me, my eldest sister, who has learning difficulties. My father's self sufficient, and the rest can FUCK OFF! They wouldn't get a bean, only a "BET YOU WANT TO KNOW ME NOW" card, sent without a stamp, so they'd have to pay the postage if they wanted to read what was on it, inside it's gold leaf-covered envelope.

Well, that's another two quid wasted, not even three numbers up; but two people netted over £6 million each, where else can you gain such a high reward for a one pound stake? Okay, you might buy loads of tickets, but it's only one set of six numbers that wins the jackpot. Six million pounds would have made me rich beyond the dreams of avarice, and more importantly, set me free from the grinding treadmill of being poor in a comparatively rich society; free to choose where I want to live; free to choose a bride from Russia or the Far East. Even free to eat out if I want to, and not feel guilty for spending money on CDs. Having said, that I got 15 CDs for 20 quid! Four boxed sets of Jazz, Blues, and '60s guitar heroes, that works out at around £1.33p per CD, and they're all over an hour in playing time; so next time you're out paying £15 for a chart CD, think of me and weep.

A couple of months ago, I almost reached rock bottom, (my personal nadir), in my physical and mental health. (I feel as though I'm heading that way again with the lousy summer we're having, 25/7/02). The few writer friends I know were likening me to Vincent van Gogh, and the similarities in our circumstances are quite remarkable; both suffering prolonged isolation and rejection, both living in small towns with small-minded locals, both being befriended by postal workers, (the manager of Todmorden's central post office has always been very cordial to me, at least till last Friday morning; maybe he'd read my letter in the local paper and misunderstood its real meaning?), and both of us not having much success in getting discovered. I think, overall, I'm in a far better position to survive than him. Vincent didn't have television, or long term Incapacity benefit, to keep him going.
What nearly did me in, was unacceptable levels of intrusion into my private space, (I'm not talking about mind stalkers here, that's still an ongoing curse); I mean noise pollution in my house deliberately caused by nasty neighbours. In the six years that I've lived in my, quite pleasant, little house, (I've had 3 social calls in that time) (it's got lots of potential for anyone into DIY), I've had to put up with hostility and nuisance from the people who own the property that my

house backs on to. We share a so-called joint water supply, they draw their water through a pipe in my cellar, from a mains stop tap set outside my house.

From day one, they were antagonistic, it was as if they'd heard, through the local grapevine, that I'm allergic to mechanical noise. They ran a butcher's shop. The main source of nuisance was a fairly constant banging noise, this was eventually identified as 'water hammer', caused every time the not-so jolly butcher, turned his cold water tap on and off, up to a hundred times a day, (or so it seemed). BANG, BANG, BANG! I also had noise from a pastry mixing machine, a throbbing and humming freezer up against our 'party' wall, horrid cooking smells coming in, causing a stink like boiled sweat in the early mornings; even his sink was right up against our mutual wall, and they used that as an excuse to bang and clatter trays and pans and what ever else about. All this was far worse than the Chinese water torture, and lasted much longer.

I did get embroiled in a county court case with the obnoxious butcher, but because I've been cast in the role of scapegoat and whipping boy, in this life, I got whipped! And now there's a £2000 county court charging order hanging over me, which can't be paid till I sell this house, and my share in it. Even when his shop closed three years ago, the nuisance didn't stop, there was endless 'do it themselves' building work carried out, to make part of their property domestically habitable. Being disabled, and stuck at home most of the time, I had to endure all the hammering and drilling that went on over a 3 month period; my nerves were in a constant crisis.

This tale of woe and anguish could go on and on, there's been a lull in the torment for the past three weeks, since the last evil-minded swine vacated the maisonette (hell hole more like) next door; and the people who've received planning permission to turn the empty shop into a hot food takeaway outlet, haven't started work on converting it yet. Hopefully, they've realised they'll be wasting their money, as there are already ample food outlets here for a very limited market. If the vitriolic butcher/owner had any sense, he'd turn the whole property into a house with double glazing. The living accomodation is right over a mind bendingly noisy traffic artery, known as the A646 Halifax Road, and try and rent it out, or sell it to some poor mug unluckier than me. Perhaps the odious butcher was my Gaugin? He and his evil family's antics have nearly driven me mad, and the strange thing is, that due to my severe visual handicap, I probably wouldn't recognise him in the street. I only saw him a few times in the shop, and he always sent his solicitor to the county court.

And here in Calderdale, it's not the mistral that affects the inhabitants mental faculties, it seems to be a combined sense of greed and one-upmanship that causes the indigenous males to behave so aggressively. I've no interest in their 'culture', as far as I'm concerned, 'they ain't got no culture'!

I have no real reason to keep myself alive, other than the fact that I LIKE LIFE! It's got to be better than death, my physical health has suffered greatly because of all the accumulated adversity, that being a scapegoat and whipping boy carries. I avoid people as much as possible now, if they can't be of any use to me, they're not worth the bother. Like I said earlier, unlike Vincent, I've got radio and TV, and CDs to keep me company; mind you, he had the brothel and cheap liquor to keep him amused at night time, yeah, on balance,, I think he had the better deal.

There's no outlet for your sexual frustration in this town, unless you're prepared to go chasing sheep on 'the tops' (the hills), (you could do it on a quad bike nowadays). I just stay in, and go out once a fortnight to a writers group in Hebden Bridge. Even going there has become a pain, since the joint proprietor became ultra-precious and 'politically correct'; last time out, one of the readers used the word 'penis', and she, seemingly shocked, said, "Oh, can we use the 'p' word?"

(Author's note. The group has now crumbled into dust due to this overbearing attitude. 1/8/02.)

....
....

YOU CAN KISS MY RING ANYTIME DUCKY. (A RIGHT ROYAL COCK-UP YOUR ANUS; NOW THAT'S GOT TO HURT! AND I'M NOT TALKING FROM PERSONAL EXPERIENCE HERE EITHER, EXCEPT WHEN I STUCK MY FINGER IN MY BROWN EYE BY MISTAKE, THINKING I WAS PICKING MY NOSE. I WAS APPALLED AT WHAT CAME OUT ON THE END OF THAT FINGER, I STILL ATE IT THO'; OLD HABITS DIE HARD.) 26/10/01.

A deeper sleep has no more meaning than the voice of reason, to a chimpanzee, but both might have a soothing and beneficial effect on each other.

Life's just a race against death, let the Devil take the hindmost by the hindquarters, (now I bet that's REALLY got to hurt!). Only the truly lonely can observe that there's no real cohesiveness in a crowd, it's merely a multitudinous throng milling about willy-nilly, with an eye to rumpy- pumpy; well I do anyway when I'm wandering lonely as a bad smell.

I'm at the stage now, of galloping middle age, where I'd gladly pay to have my way with a half decent-looking, and humane hooker. I only want to fuck her in positions of my choosing, without degrading or abusing; I'd promise that if we did 'the wheelbarrow', not to push her past her mum's house. I've said goodbye to any hope of finding love, there are too many dark forces aimed against me. The incongruous prying, spying evil eye is constantly plotting against me, blinking furiously every time I avoid destruction by the skin of my teeth; it really is beneath contempt.

....
....

'CRIMBO' CRACKERS. 27/10/01.

The dirty rotten, cold-blooded, mercenary bastards, are doing it again, hitting on us ten weeks before the great non event, cynically manipulating our good intent; I hope they rot in Hell for it. One thing's for certain, they'll never relent in their pre Christmas onslaught, unless they're forced to stop. I'm not advocating direct action against their one-stop, bargain shop, I'm advocating tough legislation here; no sanitised, sentimental, phoney Yuletide cheer to be rammed down our ever open gullets till Dec, 24. And then only for an hour or two, to remind me and you, that 'A CHRISTMAS CAROL' time is here again, with all its attendant pleasure and pain; only the latter for me. I've got a long, unbroken history of waking up alone on 'Christmas morn', with only a raging hangover for company, and a sprig of mistletoe wedged firmly up my crack.

There's no going back now, the damage has been done, 31 lonely and unhappy holidays lie under my artificial Christmas tree.

I wish I could arrange for a svelte young 'call girl' to be there for me on 'Crimbo' day, wearing little more than a mini Santa suit; she'd look real cute with her 'crotchless panties' on. ready for some steamy action. I think I'd pull them down over her belly and thighs with my teeth, hoping that what lay underneath would be piping hot, and

ready for me to go pushing my enormous manhood into, singing,
"Jingle balls, jingle balls, jingle all the way up..."

....
....

FRENZIED LIFE ATTACK.   8/11/01
(Irritable Bowel Syndrome, here I come.)

I change my clothes about as often as I speak, usually once a week;
unless I have occasion to pass a word or two with a checkout
operative during my shopping trips. Sometimes I make witty quips as
I'm making my escape, well they make me laugh when I replay them
back in my head later on, while sitting in my smelly old rocking
chair, staring at the TV, night after night; penny for penny, and
pound for pound, it's the best value entertainment around; and it
never answers back when you hurl abuse at it, and where else would
I get to see tits, fanny, (all too rarely) and arse, for free!?...Especially
if I don't pay my licence fee.
If I was into sleazy, sordid sex, I could subscribe to Television X, or
one of the other channels that cater for the sexual voyeur; but they're
a slur on my manhood, unless they ever invent a telly with a jelly-like
screen, and I can have interactive sex with one of these queens of
porn, by sticking my full-on horn into the flexible plastic screen, right
between her ever open thighs.
One of my doctor's reckons my stress level's spiralling out of control,
after I said I felt like smashing a chair over the head of an alcohol-fed
nuisance in the waiting area; she thought I was scarier than any
threat a harmless drunk might have posed; I interposed that he
might have been carrying a knife, putting my life in jeopardy, she
just looked at me oddly.

All I've wanted to be for a long time now, is a male escort, in the
traditional sense of the term; I don't mean I want to escort gay men,
wearing perms or wigs, who might have nasty germs to pass on. No, I
want to be on the arm's of women of quality and substance, who
could find themselves stuck for a partner of the opposite sex for a
particular event, like a dinner party, or a soiree with an invitation
meant for two. I've got the height and the hue, if viewed in a soft
diffused light, and I improve as the night wears on, unless I've gone

too far on the free food and booze; then I lose my cultural edge and
am liable to dredge up all my tales of woe; a no-no in the escort game.
When you're with a dame, she does all the talking, even if you're
balking at her tainted breath, in which case you keep proffering her
the after eight mints.
If she squints, or is as fat as a house, I wouldn't be a louse and
say,"She's not with me"; I'd be too busy thinking of the hundred
quid I was going to collect at the end of our engagement, and I
wouldn't react with enragement if some lonely old maid with a face
that could stop a truck, asked me to stay and fuck her till the cold
light of dawn. I'd say, 'Well, as long as you put a bag over your head,
and remain sworn to secrecy that it was me who pleasured you into a
state of double time (after midnight) ecstasy, I'll see what I can do.
Mind you, I'm not promising anything; they don't call me the King
of the 'short time' for nothing'.
Alas, it looks like nothing is what I'm going to get.

....
....

NEW AGE STONE AGE.   8-9/11/01.

By the mystic runes of Loony Tunes, and the occult powers of that
pile of old stones at Stonehenge, I hereby state that I want to take my
literary revenge on 20th century 'hippy culture'…man.
I detest 'new age' travellers as much as I detest the so-called 'real'
IRA; both think they are elite groups, and both are determined to
have their own way; the former by boring you to death, the latter by
blowing you away, at least the second option could be quicker.
It was great when I was young, having long hair and smoking dope,
the Isle of Wight Rock Festival in '69, my bedroll tied up with rope.
It's a pity my face didn't match my hair and flairs; though I couldn't
see it then, that I wasn't really a 'beautiful' person, except from the
back, or side profile perhaps. But youthful optimism sprang eternal
from my loins, and I never quite gave up hope that I'd get lucky with
a really groovy hippy chick; Austin Powers is a slick pile of shite, he's
a 'shagadelic' fright. (Maybe it's part of his appeal in an age where
'wikkid' means 'good?)

Still, I did have my standards, and anyone who stank of patchouli oil was out; I'd prefer the odour of liniment rub to that, most of the twats who wore it are now termagants, burrowed deep into the hide of social services, and/or the lesbian parade; to think I used to be afraid of their disapproval.

It wasn't so much a counter culture as it was a cannabis culture, tune in, turn on, drop LSD. Even now, Ashrams all over the world are filled with those on the brink of serious mental illness; largely, adoring female sycophants with a burning need to abase themselves to somebody; the bagwan swami gets first pick of all the fresh young virgins, even if he stinks like an old goat wearing patchouli oil.

Somebody said: 'Freedom is a state of mind', that's apropos of nothing really, I just thought I'd throw it in; except that when your head's clogged up with half-baked doctrines, interspersed with hash fumes and incense, and you can't get up each day till three pm to brew a pot of organic 'erbal tea, to induce a non-genetically modified pee, and odourless crap, wiping your arse on unbleached, recycled shite paper, the lot falling into your composting earth closet, where all the methane is turned into fuel for your generator, which powers your information technology machine. Whereby you contact others in the anti capitalism brigade, and advocate cancelling third world debt relief, in the naïve belief that this will solve the overcrowded planet's problems.

You're doing your bit for humanity after all, and if the fallout from your demo's really hits the fan, you can drop back out of sight in your dingbat Dingley Dell, reeking of home grown weed, leaving the seeds of your discontent to blow up in the faces of those with more actual intent.

....
....

SEEPAGE. (OLD UNDERPANTS, FOR INSTANCE.) 10/11/01

There's no place like bed when you wish you were dead, unless you can't get your feet warm, which makes your chances of recovery take a lot longer. I hate feeling depressed and/or discontent, but I still fall foul of both complaints far too often. I never set out to be a professional depressive writer, like Samuel Beckett; but then I never set out to endure my fairly uniquely lonely, and isolated adult life either. But, like I've said elsewhere, (in 'VIEWED WITH SUSPICION' actually), if you're not prepared to take desperate measures to try and alter your fate, you've got to take what's thrown at you in this life; knowing my luck, desperate measures, like buying £100's worth of lottery tickets, wouldn't even win me a tenner back.

Let consistency be your watchword (and mine). I'm a big fan of American wrestling, as it is now; it's violent and seemingly anarchic, the more extreme it gets the more the crowd loves it. It's a high-risk profession, with big rewards for the more determinedly aggressive. Yet they're on a treadmill, they have to keep up the momentum each week, to keep their baying fans keen, feuds have to be established and grudges settled, and it certainly isn't all faked. On today's 'SMACKDOWN', 'Stone Cold' Steve Austin was fighting with seventeen stitches in a cut over his left eye, 2 weeks ago he had 12 staples in the back of his head. Other fighters disappear off the scene, and are never mentioned again, even if they enjoyed great popularity while they were in the limelight. I can think of five who've vanished without trace.

That vastly overrated 'laughing gnome', David Bowie, had a line in one of his songs, I can't remember which one, I'm not his biggest fan: 'I don't want to live with someone else's depression'; that's okay, I'd feel the same way if I was a loaded super poser like him; mind you, if I'd been responsible for creating Ziggy Stardust's looks, I'd still be in intensive psychotherapy, moaning, 'Why, why, why?'

I feel like I've just fought off an encroaching attack of depression, I resisted the urge to slope off to bed this evening, (it was too cold), and I've done some grooming. My idea of a manicure is to bite, and then file my finger- nails with my teeth; and to cut my own hair, seeing as how the average cost round here is £5.50p for a 'trim'.
I began with a pair of scissors, and then got my clippers out; I've been too demoralised to use them for the last twelve months, and you know, the end result isn't half bad; it took me over an hour, but what else would I be doing at 8.30pm on a Saturday night? Either 'vegging-out' in front of the TV, like tonight, or lying in bed, curled up in my favourite pre natal position, with the radio on.
My new haircut makes me look 'hard', all grizzled silver white at the sides, with a dark thatch on top, thanks to hair colour. I think I have enough testosterone to make me want to look hard to attract women; I'm not interested in competing with other males, I find the whole

male thing very tedious and boring, always having to prove yourself; it's potentially very dangerous too.

I've been trying all my life, obviously unsuccessfully, to prove myself to the opposite sex; mainly for sex. I had a flurry of successes in my mid-twenties, maybe because I had a lot of hair on my head and face, but when it comes to attracting a mate...ZERO! ZILCH! I can make women laugh, but I can't impress the ones I fall in love with to love me back enough to trust me. It's very soul destroying to be pre judged, it turns some men into homicidal maniacs, it turns me into myself; harbouring homicidal thoughts against women in general, till I've got over the latest disappointment.
After all, I don't want to end up in an all-male environment, worrying if I'm going to get my arse shagged, or beaten to death because of my bad guts. I'm probably one of the few men who could live in 'solitary', quite happily in the nick; having spent most of my adulthood enduring it. I could lie in my cell, if you're allowed to, fantasising about the women who've rejected me over the past few years; I wonder if you're allowed to wank openly on 'Section 41', or whether you have to do it furtively under your prison blanket, wiping your spunk off on your prison vest?

At least I'd get some new underpants in the 'slammer', the ones I'm wearing now are an absolute disgrace; they're so old they're only hanging together by a thread, one massive fart and they'll be round my ankles in tatters. If I ever get knocked down, and end up on the slab, and they strip me down to my threadbare underwear, they'll put my carcass in quarantine, and the offending keks (it's an offensive word isn't it 'keks'?) in the incinerator.

I think my idea of perfect bliss, would've been to have copped for a really groovy and tasty-looking hippy chick, with long black hair, tall, shapely, practical and intelligent, and with mutual zeal and endeavour, acquire a smallholding together; quite possibly in Wales somewhere. We certainly wouldn't have flopped around like a couple of limp, dippy dope fiends, in a commune, having endless arguments about whose turn it was to wash up, or replace the patchouli oil stock.
We'd have been like 'Tom and Barbara' from 'THE GOOD LIFE', without the infuriating neighbours. And 'FAMILY's, 'THE WEAVER'S ANSWER' played religiously on our annual anniversary.

It should have been our fifth by now, but the hippy chick I met five years ago, a young throwback to the late '60s, wouldn't ditch her leaden lover for me. I saw him once, he was old, I should have..........!!!!!!!

....
....

KILLED BEYOND ALL REASONABLE DOUBT.   22/11/01.
(Or, HYPERCRITICAL SENSITIVITY.)

My enthusiasm for 'the game' that is, has been killed off beyond all reasonable doubt; I mean, this is me, the 'ROB VAN DAM' (laid back American wrestler) of the dating world: 'ABOVE THE WAISTLINE ESCORT'. 'HI LADIES, ARE YOU LOOKING FOR A MALE COMPANION FOR A PARTICULAR OCCASION? IF SO, LOOK NO FURTHER, I'M YOUR MAN. I GIVE REALLY GOOD CONVERSATION, (I TALK ABOUT MYSELF ALL THE TIME), AND SERVICE. YOUR SENSORY SATISFACTION GARUNTEED, NOT THAT YOU'LL EVER FEEL THE NEED TO COMPLAIN. REASONABLE HOURLY RATES.
And this is the attitude I'm up against: 'VERY ATTRACTIVE, VERY INTELLIGENT, VERY CHOOSY LADY SEEKS A 40 to 50 YEAR OLD, VERY HONEST, VERY TALL GUY WHO'S VERY CHOOSY TOO'.
I hope she has to keep wanking herself to sleep for a long time to come, (they do you know, vibrators, dildos, hairbrush handles).
I've also just come across a much more scathing attitude towards my beleagured sex, penned by Julie Birchill in her 1989 novel: 'AMBITION', I'm sure Julie won't mind me quoting her; incidentally, the piece of totty on the front cover of this lurid paperback is a real stunner; sex on legs, maybe even Julie's alter-ego. Here goes then: 'Ingrid Irving had a theory that there had been a war that no-one had told them about, in which all the heterosexual men under forty, over six foot and earning over 50k a year had been wiped out. They used this weapon which was sort of a very sophisticated version of the neutron bomb', explained Ingrid. 'You know—that left buildings standing but wiped out people. Well this bomb, the talent taker, wiped out all the hunks and left the jerks standing. The sort of men that used to be called 4F: Fags, failures, fatsos and freaks." (Unfortunately I could qualify for 2 of those F-categories, through no fault of my own, and if I didn't control my comfort eating, it would probably be 3; as to the other one...'I was never confused, well not enough to give me a sore arse anyway).

'Women, unlike men, were raised on the pornography of perfection, first pop stars, then romantic fiction heroes. The higher they climbed, and the more they were told they could have it all, the less inclined to compromise they became.' An inferior man would cast doubts on their hard won status. Sexually speaking, successful women had become fussy eaters. (AMBITION, JULIE BIRCHILL, 1989, Corgi books.)

And since then, we've had to put up with 'GIRL POWER', courtesy of The Spice Girls; I wonder if this has got anything to do with so many single mums looking for someone to end their lonely nights, on the sexploitation singles circuit? One pound a minute phone calls at all times! Here's an ad that I should check out: 'Blue eyed blonde, slightly disabled, looking for someone who's loving, caring and honest, likes to read'.
But I'm thinking, 'What's her disability? If it's a speech impediment or cerebral palsy, there's no chance; and I've no idea where she lives. It could be too far away. £1 a minute, plus vat, is a lot to risk to satisfy my curiosity. No, I'll do what she does, read a book instead.

....
....

ROUGH AND SMOOTH, SILVER GREY HOPE.   31/11/01

Disturbing the sulphur laden, still air that surrounds me in my rocking chair, clouds of onion scented gas keep pumping out my ass; enough to inflate a weather balloon, if the length and strength of my farts is anything to go by; or ignite me and my old rocking chair if I dared to light a match.
What's wrong with my insides? I repeatedly ask myself amid the fug, I know I don't live a smug, self satisfied life, chance would be a fine thing.
Wholistically speaking, it's been a god-awful mess, maybe that's why my guts behave like a fermenting cess pit, a vat of bubbling, reeking shit.

My overriding loyalty now is to the earth and sky, I hope when I die I can be buried in a woodland setting, in a biodegradable coffin, with a young oak tree planted on top of me. I hope that from my rotting remains a fair sized oak will grow, and my spirit self may sit beneath its shade on a hot sunny day; why people think that a soul, even with only an ounce of intellect, would want to hang around your average dreary cemetery, in the forlorn hope that a loved one (none in my case) will come and talk to it, is a mystery to me. I'd be back at their place watching TV, or behaving lewdly in blissful anonymity.

On certain nights I might choose to 'sleep' among the leaves and branches of my namesake tree, a summer breeze caressing me, or a winter's storm blowing my bare branches about; after all, ghosts aren't supposed to feel the cold or grow old…are they?

In 'Earth time', I'll have to wait a good number of years for my oak to take on some height and weight, I wonder how I'll wait out the time? Listen to the gurgle of my slime being sucked up through its sturdy roots? Or chase wood nymphs about the glade, hoping they don't discriminate against rough trade corpse shagging.

Perhaps there will be a thriving colony of practicing pagan undead, where I want to be laid to rest, dressed in woven clothes of mossy green, and a Queen of The May crowning it all off; magic mushrooms for breakfast, and oak sap mixed with morning dew, to ease a chesty cough.

I hope I would live as long as my tree, and when they cut it down, that would be the end of me; except for the part of me that would continue to exist in its timber. Ideally, we'd be used to make some quality items, which might turn up on 'THE ANTIQUES ROADSHOW', three hundred years from now, with grateful owners going, 'Wow! I had no idea my old rocking chair could be worth as much as that, there's always been a bit of a whiff from it, but you don't want to know that do you?

....
....

PORKED! ('GEDDIT?')   1/12/01.
(A HOMILY FOR A COCOONED COMMUNITY.)

I wonder if Vincent van Gogh's very last painting is still on view? And did any blood spill on it when he shot himself through the stomach on that ill-fated day? He didn't die straightaway, he lingered on for a night or two, I can't think why. Perhaps it's on display in that permanent exhibition of his work in Amsterdam? From what I remember of the excellent film: 'A LUST FOR LIFE', starring the equally excellent Kirk Douglas, it was a canvas depicting wheeling black crows in a stormy blue sky, in a field of golden yellow wheat; any blood spatters would look like bright red poppies.

Vincent has suffered the worst ignominy an artist of his extremely sensitive nature could suffer, he's been turned into a public property for the stinking rich, He's become 'Vince inc'. The bitter irony is, that Vincent loathed the art market establishment for the vultures and parasites he perceived them to be, he was a pauper dependent on his brother's patronage. He lived with a prostitute for a year, (not off her), he went with prostitutes; he acted as an unordained priest to impoverished and exploited French (or was it Belgian?) miners in the Borinage. He was a man of the people, the peasantry; the same ignorant types who persecuted him after he became mentally ill in Arles.

I think it's safe to say he despised 'preciousness', except in his appreciation of great art and craftsmanship; in what I remember gleaning from reading all three volumes of his letters, some years ago, mainly to his brother Theo, he had little time for pretentious people.

His biggest stumbling block seems to have been the type of woman he set his heart and hopes on, I think he was always looking for a meeting of minds, as well as bodies, but his over intense manner, or misreading of potential romantic situations, probably, as well as his erratic lifestyle, caused him to come an almighty cropper. This is where another remarkable similarity in our existences is worth noting, the type of women I tend to fall for, are all rather precious or else think they're biologically too good for me, and are terrified that with me, they might give birth to deformed offspring. As much as I like infants, (once they reach puberty they turn into sullen strangers), I've no particular desire to father any; I'd be quite happy to be a surrogate dad...but it's not going to happen.

Also in polite society today, it's not done to talk about too much ugly reality, in a world where we have suicide bombers pureeing themselves over innocent bystanders, victim's plunging to certain death from burning buildings where thousands are being fried and crushed; it doesn't do to dwell on it here in our sheltered little backwater in the Pennines; after all, another snug and cosy Xmas is almost upon us.

(A painting by Vincent van Gogh was sold in New York this week [3/5/06] for £40 million, the second highest price ever paid for a painting; excelled only by that paid for a Picasso. I'm sure Vincent would be the first to agree with me, that this is a sick waste of money!!!)

....
....

FUCK FOOTBALL, RUGBY, CRICKET, GOLF, AND TENNIS TOo.   16/1/02.

I just don't get what all the hype is about, 22 blokes kicking a ball from one end of a football pitch to the other. Well, it's 20 men really isn't it, the goalies don't necessarily see that much action; (sorry ladies, I know you play football too, much more interesting from my point of view.) Okay there are skills involved, but not in comparison with the rewards top players receive, nowhere near, 'Honest ref'!'.
It's the fans I feel sorry for, how do they do it, standing or sitting, out there on cold winter nights, cheering their teams on; maybe they have to cheer and stamp their feet to keep hypothermia at bay. There aren't too many discomforts to compare with cold feet and a cold head, I get a band of prickly pain round my scalp now if I'm out in the cold for any length of time, even though I've still got a full head of hair, (' I'm 55 me now, you know, don't look it do I? What do you mean, I look more like 65, you cheeky cunt!"), and a woolly hat, which I regard now as a permanent fixture; unlike my eyes, which are a bit 'home and away', if you know what I mean.
I've just read about an unlikely named invention called 'THE GATOR GRIP',   to allow ref's to have better control over their whistles in freezing conditions; I think it's supposed to stop the cold steel

sticking to their lips in icy temperatures; I'd like to suggest that a St Bernard dog with a brandy barrel round its neck, be kept on hand to rescue fans trapped in snowdrifts in the Scottish league.

Wimbledon fortnight is another hallowed event in the sporting calendar, that I loathe with a keen vengeance; how can anyone get excited about two people whacking a little ball back and forth over a net!?!? Unless it's two young women wearing short flimsy tennis skirts and skimpy white briefs...(excuse me for a couple of minutes.)

Golf is terminally tedious too, how can so many clods with absolutely no dress sense whatsoever, be allowed to earn so much money? Snooker and Darts are two more examples of club sports being elevated to unrealistic heights, nice work if you can get it though, from the players point of view.

Rugby and Cricket are two more dangerous contact sports that do nothing for me, they're on a par with mountain, and rock climbing, for people who don't know fear, or think too far ahead about the possible consequences of their risky actions; I wouldn't do anything that would put my life or health on the line.

Having said that, I've recently flown at a height of 39,000ft above sea level without any qualms, it was just like looking down on a vast snow field, 10,000ft higher than Mount Everest; there might have been some nutter stood on its summit as we flew over Spain. If the plane's engines had cut out at that impressive altitude, we'd have hit the ground faster than the speed of light, re-emerging on the other side of the world.

....
...

WHAT DOES POETRY MAKE?   20/1/02.
(A HOMAGE TO CHRISTOPHER MARLOWE'S CREED, HE DIED IN A PUB BRAWL FROM A STABBING.)

Poetry makes cash prizes and a passable living for the chosen few, 'Recommended for inclusion in our next anthology', just won't do.
They say the road to Hell is paved with good intent, when I listen to 'POETRY PLEASE' on Radio 4, my attention invariably wanders, though I meant to listen to every word. I suppose I'm being absurd really, because it's only my own brand of poetry that in the long run counts; not too much right now I must admit, in the big bad world of literary philistinism and anal retention, oh yes, and poseur pretensions.
I can't stand classic, flowery poetry, it doesn't say a thing to me, I'd rather be hit right between the eyes, or the thighs, porno poetry appeals to me.
Ted, and Sylvia Plath-Hughes, and T.S. Eliot, were giant intellects, you need to be a black belt in MENSA to comprehensively get to grips with them. I prefer more down to earth observations of the human zoo, as

penned by John Hegley, or the Liverpool poets of the late 1960s, and John Cooper Clarke too.

I don't like wasting space on paper, once I've started, I don't like to stop till I've filled both sides of a sheet of narrow margined, wide ruled A4; I pride myself on not being a bore; anyone who disagrees with this assumption can meet me outside for a couple more insights into my poetic prowess.

Lucrative public performance readings, and lecture tours elude me; Dylan Thomas enjoyed his jaunts in America so much, he drank himself to death; "I've just drunk 18 double scotches," are reputedly the last words the Welsh Bard muttered, before he went comatose into that last goodnight; a man after my own heart; though I'm afraid I'd merely wake up with a frightful hangover, either in Heaven or in Hell, with the smell of whisky vomit on my chin and breath.

I'd rather eschew trying to be too esoteric from now on, my capacity to recreate mystic visions has gone downhill, I've had my fill of 'Rimbaud' and 'Starry Nights', now I've got more in common with Baudelaire. I even know someone who looks like the hatchet-faced French necromancer, he even claimed to have Satanic powers; I think he's regretting that now, holed up in a hovel in Cornholme. I go out of my way to avoid any contact with this former friend.

'THE END' by 'THE DOORS', and 'ATMOSPHERE' by 'JOY DIVISION', are modern poetry in a rock music setting, and speak volumes to me. Jim Morrrison, was the last real bohemian; the

Byronically beautiful young man, running to fat through too much excess, he should have headed for the Betty Ford clinic instead of Paris, along with Jimi and Janice, along with the whole drink and drugs inspired, psychedelic crew.

Morrisey is also a damned good poet, another who couches his words in music; I thank my good fortune that I have an ear for it.

(Some might say that the awful, baby-faced looking Pete Doherty is following in Jim Morrison's footsteps; but I find his looks repulsive, he looks like one of those silent movie characters, [more female than male], with his Charlie Chaplin-like eyes and expression. If he's lucky, he'll OD, and then he'll become more infamous dead, than he ever was while alive. 6/5/06.)

....
......

TRAPPED   WIND.
24/1/02

We all have to eat to live, you'd think the gut would be grateful for whatever we throw down our necks to keep it mollified.

It's not as if our stomach's have a mind and voice of their own, and can shout back up at us, 'If you think I'm going to let that load of chewed up rubbish, you've just sent down the grub tunnel, pass through me smoothly and easily, you've got another think coming.' Instead, it blows itself up like a balloon (it does in my case), and fills you full of trapped wind, preferably in an intimate situation; leaving you dying to fart, but you daren't because it's liable to be full of methane and sulphur (also in my case.)

I wonder if chimps, our nearest primate relatives, have the same problem after they've devoured a nice fresh, still warm Colobus monkey? Or even one of their own kind, who's inadvertently strayed into their territory? Of course, if you're a chimp, you can drop a bad fart with impunity, there's a lot of vegetable decay in a forest, stinking the place out.

I saw an ad today for stainless steel kitchen knives, I was prompted to make up a jingle along the lines of, 'Dismember a family member with ease, with these razor sharp blades', and if we were chimps, it would save on all that rending and tearing of our still-living prey, limb from limb.

I'm a mass of physical and mental imperfections, who'd have thought that the melding of one sperm and one egg, could result in such depressingly complicated DNA? I think I've always had what you could loosely term, a 'nervous' stomach, it doesn't take much to set it off, it being the wimp that it is.

The worst aspect of its contrariness is its capacity to produce excess amounts of noxious gas, enough at times to fuel a hot air balloon. Over the years, I've tried various remedies to try and pacify my raging irritable bowel; the worst was a combination of Valerian and Wormwood, which I had to brew a form of tea from. I don't know which was worse, the smell or the taste? It didn't help and I soon gave up on it; recently, I've found that avoiding onion products can help; it turns up in a lot of manufactured sauces, avoiding these has helped to ease the discomfort, and lessen the malodorous stench.

A prime example of my stomach's perverseness, happened well over a quarter of a century ago; it was when I still had the audacity to wear flared, (28-inch bottoms), purple 'Loon' pants, and a green, velvet-type, waisted blazer; plus long fuzzy hair and prominent 'mutton chop' whiskers. I'd become friends with a very attractive young woman, a teacher with an 'open' relationship, her partner had recently fucked off to India to 'find himself', the WANKER!
One night she invited me round to her place to listen to Eno's 'HERE COME THE WARM JETS', I think we smoked a bit of hash. But my stomach decided to fill up with the 'evil wind', it was as painful as labour contractions, trying to hold it in. I did let one go in her toilet, but it created this awful stench, I was mortified and panic stricken, a bad smell can very quickly kill a 'friendship'. I stuck it for as long as I could, then said I had to go. She seemed disappointed, perhaps a shag was on the cards? I hit the street and let out a massive sulphurous fart. (I should have unceremoniously disembowelled myself there and then, but I didn't have my ceremonial disembowelling knife with me.)

....
...

VINCENT'S GUN.   11/1/02.

Where did Vincent van Gogh get his gun? The one he shot himself with on that last lonely day, and did he only have one bullet for emergency action to be taken? Perhaps saying to himself beforehand, 'One more fit and that's it, I'm going to blow my insides away'. And why not aim for the brain, the originator of all his pain? After all, if his mind hadn't kept on telling him he was unlovable and unfulfilled, thus torturing his stomach and his heart, he might not have emotionally fallen apart.

Did the revolver feel like a reassuring weight against his hip, as he went with quivering lip into his very last cornfield? Had he become epileptic from his turbulent life style, or was he suffering from an undiagnosed venereal disease? Women of easy virtue were the only ones he ever got near, and if he'd had the gun when he cut off his ear lobe, he might have shot it off instead; a bit like when Clint Eastwood winged that outlaw in the legendary film 'HIGH PLAINS DRIFTER': "He's shot my damned ear near clean off!" BRILLIANT!

And what about the bedrock of Vincent's artistic existence, his long suffering and much put upon younger brother, Theo, who only outlasted the tortured artist by a mentally, and physically deteriorating six months? He gets very little credit for Vincent's interesting, but by no means brilliant, works; the Arles ones brilliant in concept and colour perhaps; especially the 'STARRY NIGHT'; and coming at the point in history when they did. But I don't think his work was worth the sacrifice of two lives.

"I wish I were far away from everything, I am the cause of all, and bring only sorrow to everybody, I alone have brought all this misery on myself and others," wrote Theo in a letter to Vincent when he was 23. It looks like depression and low self esteem ran in the family.

Those same sentiments quite often apply to me, it's just as well I don't have a pistol handy...I'm a booze and pills man anyway, and if ever the day comes when I feel I simply can't go on anymore, then the dreaded paracetomol and brandy will have to do the job; and I hope this lethal combination would kill me quite quickly, I don't fancy bleeding to death from every orifice.

Emotional rejection, and an intense personality, don't mix very well either; they broke Vincent's spirit and have almost destroyed me. I've no Zuave brothel to seek solace in, sipping absinthe between tearful shags, I have to make do with radio and TV. I've finally given up on humanity, I won't let the bitches grind me down anymore; whatever loyalties I have left belong to the planet and its sorely threatened flora and fauna. Unlike Vincent, I'm not quite a pauper, I can withdraw from my introspective torpor long enough to get my act together, to bequeathe my worldly wealth to an organisation devoted to animal welfare; a shout rather than a whisper (WSPA:

World Society for the Protection of Animals) will lead you to their name...on the internet. (I've made my shop bought [£1.50p] Will out in favour of WSPA, leaving them copyright of all my work after I'm dead, if I get discovered. That way, no human parasite can come crawling out of the woodwork, to leech off my tortured output. Hopefully, the posthumous millions, my genius will generate, will benefit the planet,and single-handedly, stem global warming.

....
...

'A BLOKE ON HIS OWN',, sung to the tune of 'I AM A WOMAN IN LOVE', by 'THE BEEGEES'; performed by Barbara ' The Snozzle' Striesand. 27/1/02.

'I am a bloke on his own, it's a fate I bemoan, over and over again, and I'll do anything, (short of paying for a short, sharp, nasty shag up a dark alley off a tart who's too pally with a heroin habit, and her minder; and who might need a reminder that personal hygiene should play an important part in her non tax-paying line of business); invest in a ring, (to put through her nose), out-sing the 'Snozz' when it comes to the high notes, to put my case across'. (Of course, I've completely lost track of the original song now, I could do with a karaoke machine, with the words on a large screen, and those high-pitched shrieks in the background).
'It's a plight I don't recommend, Mrs Palmer and her five lovely daughters are my only friends; it's no wonder so many men are turning turtle, with our women expecting nothing less than physical perfection, in their ideal man; very few can live up to their impossible plan. I wouldn't even try to any more, If they don't like what they see, they can fuck off and leave me alone. The only real drawback to being a bloke on his own, is the lack of regular raunchy sex for free. Okay, you have to keep them happy by coughing up a bob or two for their upkeep, but they're so useless nowadays (in the home), I might as well shag a sheep!!!

....
....

FATIGUE, MENTAL AND PHYSICAL. (I've earned mine.) 29/1/02.

At fifty, bull elephants are usually ready for the elephants graveyard, biblically, we're told we can look forward to 'three score years and ten', I'm coming up to 55 now, and I feel knackered; I'm full of aches and pains and neuroses. I put a lot of my condition down to the fact that despite all my efforts I've never had a 'normal' adult heterosexual, long term relationship; or nothing even approaching one. Just eons of lonely isolation.
I've had a harder life emotionally than Vincent van Gogh, I've been rejected four times by 'women of my dreams'; once or twice is usually enough for most people. I've also kept myself alive for 18 years longer than he could bear to do, he was 37 when he killed himself. I've driven my body as hard as he did, and I've tasted insanity and depression regularly.

If at any time in the future, either before or after my death, I get 'discovered', as a writer of very short fiction, and modern poetry, and become a best seller, I'm granting ultimate copyright of my work to WSPA, (World Society for the Protection of Animals), so that any royalties that might accrue, (ha,ha,ha!), will go to helping save defenceless animals. Maybe even fund a sanctuary or two. Anything, rather than suffer the fate of Vincent and his brother Theo, who, if you look at their situations cynically, went through all their deprivations and mental tortures, merely to benefit the parasites in the art world; I mean, 54 million dollars for a painting of sunflowers!!! There's no logic to it; if anything of mine sold for even a fraction of that sum, I could help a lot of animals; preferably in the wild where they belong.

....
....

'WHAT BECOMES OF THE TOO MANY TIMES REJECTED, THE PHYSICALLY, AND EMOTIONALLY NEGLECTED?' 10/2/02.
(Inspired by the 'Motown' classic: 'WHAT BECOMES OF THE BROKEN HEARTED'.)

'All our advances spurned, our stomachs churned up a thousand times at the pain of it all, no trophy brides on our arms to make the heads turn.
'Male, unsuitable for breeding purposes, has fairly big knob, suitable for shagging with a condom on: 'HAVE KNOB WILL TRAVEL, HETEROSEXUAL WORK ONLY CONSIDERED, NO KINKS OR PERV'S PLEASE, I'M EMOTIONALLY DAMAGED ENOUGH ALREADY'.
'Women seem wicked when you're unwanted', never a truer word was sung by a long dead Rock God; nowadays they're a bunch of dildo-toting dykes, shagging gay men (queer fuckers), up the arse. The rest of us heterosexual males, ('I was never confused', Al Murray, 'the pub landlord') don't get a look in, we're much too confrontational for their 'front bottoms'; I'm not argumentative, I'd prefer girls on top most of the time so I could pull their arse cheeks apart and shag them up the bum with my middle finger while I'm knobbing them with my indefatiguable ramrod of a penis. I've decided to call him 'Old Sparky', because he'll deliver wave after wave of orgasmic pleasure to the ladies; Mrs Palmer and her five lovely daughters.

ESTRANGED FROM THE NORM. When you're deprived of normal, healthy, sexual activity for an inordinate length of time, you can develop an antipathy to normal healthy displays of affection.

....
....

I'D RATHER HAVE A MISS BETWEEN MY KNEES, THAN A BAD CASE OF MISOGYNY, 13/15/2/02.

Women hating is something I obsess a lot about, I never set out to dislike and mistrust them iintensely. In fact, it isn't women that I hate, but the modern, now more-than-ever-before, atmosphere of hostility and distrust created by the female sex, towards men in general; they have some deadly weapons in their armoury, namely, rape and child abuse accusations, and equally deadly effective, insulting the size and effectiveness of a man's manhood.

At just 3 weeks away from my 55th birthday, I've acquired my very own double bed, I've only ever slept on single beds, except when on holidays. The mattress on my new double bed is rather hard, it's a bog-standard double divan, I don't know if it would stand up to much heavy-duty sex action, the base might break, as well as my knees and back. I wonder if I'll be able to do the business in Thailand? I hope I don't end up with a lady boy, and if I do, I hope I don't like it, or feel so despondent I'll be past caring?

I think I lack the aggressive level of testosterone that a lot of women reputedly respond to, in the sack; but I also hope that I'm coming into my sexual prowess at an age where a lot of men have become emotionally, as well as sexually, impotent. I won't need viagra if I'm feeling inspired, and if I expired after my first fuck with a real vagina in twenty years, no-one will shed any tears over my demise, or any expense to bring me back to this dump of a country..

....
....

COACH RIDERS IN THE SKY.   16/2/02,
(Will we become ghost riders if we die in a plane crash?)

There's no doubt that air travel is the best thing since the invention of the steam locomotive engine, nearly 200 years ago; although until three years ago, I thought nothing would induce me to get on a plane, unlike the train, I took to that like a duck to water.

What got me on a plane the first time was, I wanted to go to Portugal; 2 days travel overland. I had a female friend who said she'd go with me, (at my expense), so I thought, 'If she can get on a plane, so can I'. On the strength of which, I booked us two weeks self catering on the Algarve. It was like 'BLIND DATE' really, especially as I'm severely visually handicapped; we had some conflicts, but at least I had my evening meals made for me for a fortnight.

The deal was that I paid for all the food and drink, and did the washing up; and as I pointed out to her later on in a letter, after she'd severed all connections with me: flight aversion therapy would have cost a lot more than our out-of-season holiday did. She has now joined the swelling ranks of hobgoblins in my life, which is made up of family, and former friends. I can get dumped at the drop of a hat, it seems that people don't have much of a crisis of conscience in leaving me out of their social circle. Potential partners feel the same way too, as one said to me some years ago, after she'd sacrificed me for the favours of someone more facially acceptable: "I threw you to the sharks."

So, apart from the fear of the plane crashing, or being hijacked and blown up, flying is as exciting as sitting on a coach. I do like the exhilarating feel of takeoff, it's an adrenalin rush. A year after Portugal, I went to Tunisia with COSMOS, it was a decent holiday; I chummed up with a 68-year-old Scottish gay man, a real character. No arse-shagging took place, thankfully, well not between me and him anyway.

On the return flight (from Tunisia), I had the misfortune to have a Scotch queer of a different calibre sat behind me; he was sat next to two off duty air hostesses, or holiday reps, (at least I think they were), and he had a South African, or New Zealand mate sitting adjacent to him, on the other side of the aisle.

I reclined my seat to make myself more comfortable, the journey began okay, he was whittering away to the two women about his little cat jumping on his bed, etc, etc; the next thing is, he's asking me to put my seat forward because he didn't have much leg room. I pointed out that the seat in front of me was reclined. I'm nearly six feet tall, and it wasn't bothering me, so I declined; an impasse ensued for another hour or so. I know now that what was really bothering him, was a fear of 'Economy Class Syndrome' or DVT: 'deep vein thrombosis'; because eventually, hemanually forced my seat forward saying, "Right! That's it, my legs are really hurting me now". Which, at the time, meant nothing to me. Shortly afterwards, DVT hit the headlines, to give us one more thing to be afraid of.

If I'd have been as insecure as him, I'd have turned round and cracked him one, thus landing myself in hot water and unwanted publicity. I contented myself by calling him an idiot. He continued to snipe at me till we came into land, in the face of a high wind, causing turbulence. I was the only one laughing hysterically; it must have been my death wish kicking in.

....
....

UPPERS   AND   DOWNERS.
24/2/02.

I wish I could banish the nasty, spiteful side of my mind that rejoices in the misfortunes of others; for instance, did you know that the 'king of 'Rock 'n'Roll', Elvis 'the pelvis' Presley, was literally full of shit when he died? 15 pounds of backed-up faecal matter to be exact; it couldn't pass through his intestines because they were blocked up with a clay-like substance. Can you imagine if the 'great one' had exploded all over the first few rows at the Las Vegas nightclub where he was performing? Say, in the middle of, 'IT'S NOW OR NEVER', ("my guts won't wait"); they'd still be fumigating the place now, 25 years on.
25/2/02. As I lay in my loveless pit this morning, my mind and body all racked with pain, it occurred to me that my personal life is, and always has been, a crime against my own sense of humanity; and my life is a hell of other people's making.

Prone rhymes with crone, can you imagine shagging a prone crone? Well, technically, she'd be lying face down, so you could pull her up from her bony hips, and slip it to her doggy style. That way, you wouldn't have to see her withered old face and wasted dugs; but the vagina is supposed to be able to get moist no matter how old its owner may be. It's not for me, I must hasten to add, I could never be that sad. I'd prefer my desires to be fulfilled under the banner of, 'If they're big enough, they're old enough', (I suppose this statement will put me in line for a lynch mob, or vigilante group, wielding baseball bats and wearing ski masks), but you can't say that anymore can you? Even though I just have. (I am talking 16 and older here, if that will help my case any?)
But in 'primitive' tribes, I think this policy is the norm; among the girls anyway.
I think boys develop more slowly, just as they do in our paranoid schizophrenic society.
The best type of woman to have, is the girl/woman; women who are in their twenties and thirties, but retain certain characteristics of adolescent girls; like 'Connie' in the current series of 'TIME GENTLEMEN PLEASE' (SKY 1). She's the student/barmaid who says things like, "I'm going to have to issue a flood warning in my knickers," looking as foxy as a 14-year-old Lolita; I hope I cop for one like her in Pattaya, PPHHWWOOAARR!!!

26/2/02. BILLOWING SMOKE. Like all sensible people, I don't smoke cigarettes anymore, though I reckon I've absorbed enough tar to fill a tar barrel, from all the roll ups and 'tailor made' cancer sticks I've smoked over 30 years of my life. Judging by the number of health problems I now have, lumped under the common heading of 'wear and tear', (I forgot to list all the joints I smoked as well, sucking the smoke deep down into my stomach), I quit just in time.

I still find it hard to resist a drink on a Saturday night in the comfort of my own home, watching late night WWF/E on SKY TV; when I've reached the 'right level', to quote a character from a Graham Greene novel, (Britain's answer to John Steinbeck), I like to smoke a cheap cigar, (by Havana standards anyway). I enjoy it most when I'm nearly down to the butt, when it's almost too hot to hold, and the last two pulls on it are great; for some reason the smoke just billows out of my mouth; occasionally, when I've drunk too much and I'm nearly out of it, I'll smoke a second one, and you know, it never tastes as good. It's always too harsh on my throat, and tastes like burning rubber, and the next day my living room really stinks; only a stick of incense can shift the depressing odour. The same can be said for my guts, when I've blown off too much of the evil smelling wind, only a stick of incense can shift that sulphurous reek as well.

27/2/02. NOT A BAD NIGHT ON THE BOX, de Sade da Satanist. There was a programme on C4 last night about the Marquis de Sade, he ballooned up to 300 pounds in weight during his 16 years in prison; the man who the sultry pop singer'Sade', (pronounced 'sarday' for some peculiar reason) shares her name with; I wonder if she's aware of the comparison? It was in the C4 TV series: 'MASTERS OF DARKNESS', last week, it featured Alistair Crowley, 'the beast 666'; I don't know if they'll feature Gilles de Rais, 'the most evil man in history'? There are probably worst violators of human rights than him, the Nazis for instance. What is so chilling about these characters for me is, how they embraced EVIL!!! Dehumanising themselves and their victims. I believe that unless you're criminally insane, you have the conscious choice which path to choose; I don't believe anyone is born wholly intrinsically bad, (though I'm not so sure anymore after 17 years in Calderdale). Quite possibly, I could have chosen a dark path to follow; I've had enough provocation, but my human spirit is not for sale.

28/2/02. PANTS. I was inspired to use this title by a nice comfortable feeling I had the other night around my nether regions; in other words, my arse and bollocks. I'd had my weekly shower and change of clothes, as well as rubbing myself all over with moisturising cream; in the winter months the skin on my body from the waist down always feels dry and rough. I think it's as much neurological as it is a vitamin E deficiency, because I've been taking a vitamin E supplement (600ius) for quite some time now.

I know some people have a bath or a shower every day, as well as changing their underwear; I change my underpants, loose fitting cotton boxers, twice a week, though if I'm feeling at a low ebb psychologically, this simple rule of hygiene isn't always easy to obey. I don't enjoy showering in my pokey little shower room, there's hardly room to turn round in it, and if I didn't have a little radiator in there, the cold would cling like a second skin. There's also an economic reason for my not showering every day, the increased use in gas and electricity, and added wear and tear on my washer/drying machine, as well as towels, clothes and moisturisers. Living on a fixed income, precludes these fairly simple luxuries.

Due to a particularly virulent strain of Irritable Bowel Syndrome, I have far more than my fair share of the 'evil wind'; I've elaborated on this ever present problem elsewhere. If I ever come into a substantial amount of cash, I'll have my insides thoroughly fumigated; I'll have daily colonic irrigation and pickle onions with the residue.

28/2/02. 'YOU'D BE SO NICE TO WAKE UP NEXT TO', is a variation on the old standard song title: 'YOU'D BE SO NICE TO COME HOME TO'. (I heard it on Radio 2 only last Sunday). All my tortured life, I've longed for a nice-looking female partner, and all I've ever got for my longings, is to be tortured by a whole procession of them; I've not had penetrative, or any other kind of sex, for over 20 years. I'm so unlucky in lust and love that my last two brief encounters with a pair of cunts, (the early eighties), left me with a basketful of STDs; I've been paying for my cheap and nasty thrills ever since.

If there is a 'god', and I've no real reason to believe there is, it's ultimate joke against us, (it has to be unisex in these enlightened times), is creating ugly people like me and a whole lot of others; same sex sex, is a close second in my top 2 of 'god's ultimate jokeS against humanity. A pretty, attractive, or beautiful woman can give me a good feeling every time I look at her, how much has that got to be worth? I don't know if they resent you being able to access this gift from the gods for free, unless they can reciprocate the emotion? Especially now our roles are reversing, and 'girls' are upfront and 'mad for it', taking on all comers, while on holiday in Ibiza or Magalouf. I'd hate to be me now as I was when I was young then, in that environment; I had it hard enough 35 years ago. Nowadays, I'd just get written off as a 'REAL MINGER!'

3/3/02. NUTS. I bought a 454 gram bag (1lb) of Brazil nuts from 'SAFEWAYS', earlier this week; (16 doesn't go evenly into 454 by the way, it's just that we've been led to believe that 454 grams is equal to one pound, it amounts to 6 grams over); (some schools of weights and measures reckon that 25 grams is equal to one ounce, usually applicable to cigarette rolling tobacco packs, but that would make one pound equal to 480 grams, why did I ever start this?).
These nuts were being sold off cheap, that's why I bought them, (best before 28/2/02), they were still in their outer hard shells; no problem, I've got a nut cracker, which I bought some years ago to open hazel nuts. My favourite-tasting nuts. Getting the brazils out of their shells has posed a tougher job, tor the most part, than I expected; quite often they've been stuck to the inside of their casing with congealed nut oil, it's been a test of patience not to give up and throw them away; how I'd go on, on a desert island, with only coconuts to eat and only a stone to bash them open with, I'll never know...I hope.
I'd always been sceptical of nut allergy, till one night last year while I was living in exile in Walsden; I'd bought a load of mixed nuts (shelled), enough to fill two one pound jars. One night, out of sheer boredom, I pigged out on these nuts and raisins. A few hours later, rumblings and gurglings of discontent began occurring in my stomach, nothing out of the ordinary there then. As the night wore on, these sensations were accompanied by an increasing sense of nausea; eventually I felt compelled to go and stick my fingers down my throat over the toilet bowl. It didn't take much prompting before an arc of semi liquid matter came gushing out of my throat, I literally felt like I was spewing my guts up. That incident's taught me to only consume nuts in moderation; I wasn't going to waste the rest of those nuts I'd bought.

Watt Tyler, Jack Straw, John Ball? All leaders of the peasants revolt of 1381, the original general strike with ATTITUDE! 'WHEN ADAM DELVED AND EVE SPAN, WHO WAS THEN THE GENTLEMAN?' Ours is the only planet teeming with life, in a turbulent universe in a massive solar system; and yet, since we learned to stand upright, the rich have been screwing and oppressing the poor. I think it's part of our genetic makeup to have acquisitive natures; every other species on the planet follows a set pattern when it comes to dominance and procreation, The strongest and the fittest do the procreating and dominating, the less able and agile just hang about on the sidelines, hoping to nip in and catch a female full of heat and lust while the top dog's tearing around shagging everything he can get his phallus into; and woe betide the unwary interloper if he catches him at it, fur and semen will be flying everywhere.

Humans seem to be the exception to the rule, otherwise why would we see really tasty-looking women with hideous gargoyles? Do they want to inflict horribly ugly brats onto an already deeply depressed populace? And if so, why? I've remained celibate for the last 20 years, in order to spare the world of 2 or3 more facially challenged 'sprogs', (it's got nothing to do with the fact that I can't get a shag for love nor money); the ancient and revered family name will die out with me, and I've opted for cremation, and for my ashes to be scattered over the moors at Haworth, so the adoring millions won't be able to make a pilgrimage to my grave site; I just hope they don't clog up the moors at Haworth.

I've developed a theory, at a time when it's unfashionable to have firm beliefs, to call a spade a spade. It's to do with intellectual evolution, a bit like it's depicted in Aldous Huxley's futuristic novel: 'BRAVE NEW WORLD', I alienated a group of writer acquaintances, (one of them was a social work team leader), by saying that 'plebs' were only one rung up on the evolutionary ladder from people with learning difficulties; shock, horror! Very un-PC! I wonder if you get really thick chimps and gorillas, who don't know their arses from their elbows?

Which other species would sycophantically allow a privileged minority to own a large proportion of the nation's wealth, while at the same time allow grinding poverty to persist? In London, people can be destitute in close proximity to 'Buck House', and the so-called duke of Westminster, (who keeps a very low profile), is a billionaire 3 times over, thanks to inherited wealth. There's no logic to this level of avarice being left to prevail, yet if a chancellor of the exchequor had the guts to tax these parasites out of existence, the howls of protest would reverberate right across the septic isle that is Britain today. (It's always been this way.)

A few centuries ago, such sentiments would have had me burnt at the stake for treason, a young Henry V had a part-burnt heretic pulled out of the flames, to see if he would repent; when he refused to, he was shoved back in. (This snippet courtesy of 'THE HUNDRED YEARS WAR' by ROBIN NEILLANDS).

Nowadays you're just marginalized if your views don't tow the 'party line', as long as you're harmless you're tolerated.

....
....
'

SING IF YOU'RE GLAD TO BE HOMOPHOBIC '.   March '02.

'We're a couple of queers, we've got rather strange ideas about sex, we're wired up the wrong way but that's okay today, we're as gay as coots. It's a hoot being a bender today, the British sense of fair play says it's okay to be as bent as a nine-bob-note; the horned goat rules in 'Batty man Babylon'.
I wonder if same sex, sex, includes self-satisfying masturbation, as well as mutual cock sucking, and arse fucking? The latter anal pursuit leaving a pain in the rectum and a shit stained duvet...so I'm told.
Women love manageable men, they can hen peck them without too much fear of getting a fat lip, the ones that can slip them a length and fuck off the next morning, no questions asked, are their ideal task masters.
Some find it through heroin, an ever increasing number of Satan's slaves; others at the end of a bottle, myself included; but The Jimi Hendrix Experience at full throttle, can hit that perfect spot for me, stone cold sober and drug free; no crack cocaine all in my brain, I can speed naturally. The electric blue raw power of Jimi Hendrix, is as far above the current crop of 'pop idols' as say, the music of Beethoven is to George Formby. No offence George, I hope your offspring won't sue me.
There's no paradise in C4 TV's 'EDEN' either, a more fucked up group of young flounderers couldn't be found to regenerate the human race, this side of Bedlam.
Undead arse-shagging filth, breathing in carbon dioxide and exhaling carbon monoxide, plaguing me from afar; this psychic vermin is rarely off my case, malevolent creatures from inner space.
As long as I live, I'll never understand it, if there ever was a 'god', he couldn't have planned it, not even in his worse nightmare; (I'm sure militant lesbians think 'god' was/is one of them); 'it's Adam and Eve, not Adam and Steve, bottom explorers'.
When I'm assailed too unjustly by the evil eyed spy, nipping at my ears in its negative way; (in the real world it's 'left' for love, and

'right' for hate, this unholy horror uses it the other way round), I cry out, 'Let the evil that you do be sent straight back to you, and envelop you in a cold, wet, black, blanket of fear, despair, and ultimate destruction; and I hope the words of this curse are ringing in your skull the day you get sucked back down into HELL!!!'

Satan is conspicuous by his omnipresence today, maybe he's 'god's' representative on Earth? A statement like that would be considered blasphemy by the people who issued a death sentence on Salman Rushdie, aliens in a red mist of pseudo religious fervour. If I was Allah, (more 'blaspheny'), I'd incinerate them with a single scowl. Instead I'll have to prowl round like a thief in the night, avoiding the light, for fear they'll crucify me again, (more blasphemy, which would result in my feeling the worst possible pain, that of having my head sawn off by an Alqaeda fanatic, [this statement is an update from when I wrote the original piece, 13/5/06]), oh the pain.

....
....

WHEN THE MIND TURNS, A BIT LIKE THE WORM REALLY.
March '02.

I know now that I'm emotionally damaged beyond repair, too many years of having my nose pushed out of joint, (it's physically that way too), has left me feeling like a cornered animal, snapping and snarling. I'm suffering from circumcisional repression, or circumstantial depression; or is it the other way round? Too much seratonin and not enough aggressive testosterone, I never act out my violent fantasies against plebeian transgressors, I'm too afraid of thr consequences.

As more and more layers of my humanity are ripped away from me, I'm learning to survive alone; it's just as well I like who I am, or else I could turn really hostile; like a rabid dog.

I saw a man recently who I was once unflatteringly likened to; (I think so anyway), (I was called 'the old' 'Eddie 'The eagle' Edwards'), on TV the other day. He was looking for love in the lonely hearts section; in the tradition of 'getting it in first', he described himself as having: 'Fallen out of the ugly tree, hitting every branch on the way down'. He omitted to say who he was; at 37, he's still facially challenged, even after cosmetic surgery; he's got less of a prominent chin now though, unlike me.

My features have also been likened to those of Hank Marvin, a man who, if he didn't play electric guitar really well, though like Eric Clapton, he lost his cutting edge years ago; now it's

208

'SINGALONGAHANK', which is hardly APACHE or MAN OF MYSTERY is it?, might possibly have ended up like me, a back street nobody; or like 'Curly Watts' out of Coronation Street.

I love watching endurance programmes on TV; I call these adventurers 'THE CRAZY MEN'. I recently watched a programme where these two British men tracked down the last practicing tribe of cannibals in New Guinea, they had a narrow escape, and then went on to scale an almost unclimbable mountain, some 15,000ft high; mad or what? The latest series of half hour films is called 'ICE DOGS' on BBC 2. This intrepid English explorer is pitting himself against the icy wastes, with not much more than a pack of husky dogs for company. It makes me feel really snug and secure, watching this madman, from the comfort of my old rocking chair, with the heating on and the light off.

Manchester Airport is an endurance test for me, in fact any airport bigger than a small hangar is; me not being able to read information screens, and helpful staff being thin on the ground. I've been in three airports now, Manchester, Faro and Monastir. Soon, I expect to get that sinking feeling in Dubai and Bangkok. The highlight of a recent disappointing holiday in Portugal's, Praia da Rocha, (I came home a week early, missing 'Crimbo' over there), was a walk along a nearly deserted beach in the late afternoon, with the Atlantic ocean (was it the Atlantic or the Mediterranean? I don't know), and the setting sun on my right hand side, and a bracing wind in my face. I suddenly felt carefree, (after a depressing week) and started whistling Cliff Richard's 'D IN LOVE'. I wanted to walk as far as the end of the stone pier where the beacon stands, I reverted to my usual insecure self when I began to pass more 'crazy men' with fishing rods, darting about on the massive stone slabs each side of the main walkway; I paid a lot for that carefree moment.

....
....

THE MADNESS GENE, OR, THE INSANITY BUG?   May 02.

I'm psychically stalked by a fat bloated obscenity, a totally insane mind marauder, a blind idiot anti Christ, a creature that is able to insinuate itself ESP-wise, directly into my innermost private space; and living room.

A psycotherapist said to me, (over the phone), 'Believe me Philip, no one can read your thoughts', and to think, I was going to pay him £15 an hour so he could emphasise this to me; whereas in reality, like I said to him, 'I'm looking for an exorcist really, a psychic with extraordinary powers of perception, who can detect and expel an evil presence'; actually, I only said, 'I'm looking for an exorcist'.

You've heard people say, 'My ears are burning', that's how this thing lets me know it's there; I call it 'hideous heat', I hate it worse when it violates my right ear with varying degrees of sickly warmth, in a parody of affection. I always shrug it off as quickly as I can with a torrent of abuse, and at times, I feel it transferring to my left ear with a reproachful burning sensation; and yet in the real world, I understand it's 'left' for love, and 'right' for hate. If I'm being targeted by Satanists, this reversing of the norm would figure, to them bad is good, good is bad: 'Do what thou wilt shall be the whole of the law'.
Some years ago, in a programme about 'black magic', a man who'd managed to escape from the clutches of a satanic coven said, symptoms of schizophrenia were induced by them, such as 'hearing voices'. But what about irrecoverable schizophrenics who are permanently mad, and even their facial features change almost beyond recognition? Can they be being controlled by a dark force? And if so, 'WHY'? But then what is EVIL, other than madness?

Monomania, megalomania, bad guts (sulphurous reeks), social isolation and exclusion, are all aspects of evil. The human caste and class system; fancy being born an 'untouchable'! Microbes are agents of 'the devil', they can kill, maim and disfigure in myriads of ways. Having failure, and thwarted ambition forced upon you, are two more instances of insidious dark forces at work. By the time your 'loser' status has really sunk in, it's too late to do anything but lament about it. On my next passport, where it says 'Occupation', I'm going to put, 'Undiscovered literary genius, denied recognition and reward by invidious circumstances.'
And perhaps money is the root of all evil? Or rather, the lack of sufficient amounts of it to allow you financial freedom; I've just blown a fiver on the 'rollover' lottery draw tonight, and because I have various vultures circling,, waiting to pick my bones clean for small amounts of cash owing, I had a real struggle with my inbuilt sense of guilt, to afford myself this luxury. Now I've got five chances to win the big one, 'TEN MILL'! A couple of years ago it would have been more, but people have become disillusioned to some extent with

the long odds. I think if I was comfortably off, I wouldn't touch it; a lot of winners have been down on their luck until BINGO! Or words to that effect, 'I'VE FUCKIN' WON, FUCK ME!'

In the 14.5 million to one chance that I win the big one tonight, what will I do? I'll still go to Thailand with that added security behind me, checking out Pattaya for the chance to buy a disco bar; with ten mill' on board, it won't matter if it makes a loss; maybe Diane will go with me when I go back again, portentious or what? (Not, as it subsequently turned out.)

....
....

OUT AND ABOUT. 28-9/4/02.

Out and about, being buffeted by the wind, caught in squalls of rain, sorely irritated by anyone who gets in my way; wishing I was at home with some form of acceptable drug, even if it's only the TV to deaden the pain.

Why do I bother going out you may well ask? Finding fodder to feed my face is a task I can't delegate, alas. I can be trapped in doors for days because of our '4 seasons in one day' English weather, panicking in case I run out of food, confined to bed for long periods to keep heating costs down, brooding on the awfulness of my existence, knowing that if I died, I could be lying here for weeks, rotting down nicely, except on really cold days.

Radio 4 can ease the boredom sometimes, last night there was an interesting insight into Spiritual Intelligence; I drew the conclusion that it was another expression for stoicism, that you have to learn to accept your lot in life with a brave face and a stout heart. I thought, 'Fuck that!' before I dropped off to sleep; waking up 3 hours later in urgent need of a piss. Serves me right I suppose, as my feet froze on the lino of the bathroom floor.

'No more!', I hear you inwardly moan, 'leave us alone, take your misery elsewhere, frankly we don't give a damn, we've got our own crosses to bear.' But I'm drinking in the Last Chance Saloon, soon I'll be too grey and non descript to merit even the slightest glance, except maybe of pity perhaps; pretty galling when you feel as young at heart as me.

English society is so riddled with fears, phobias, and hidden boundary lines that 'mustn't' be crossed; a person could go 'boss eyed' trying to keep up with the 'do's and don'ts', it's no wonder we turn out psycho killers by the score; women are such bitches I'm surprised there aren't many more...myself included.

Excluded from love as I am, unless I settle for some creature that should have a label on it, and I'm beginning to doubt that even one so facially challenged would think me good enough to share her trough, I've no choice but to put on my travelling bonnet (poetic licence), and head out to the Far East, where I'll enjoy a feast of slanty-eyed delights; a different one for each of the eight nights of my stay. With a bit of luck, I'll be able to bring one away with me, not the inflatable kind I hasten to add. A taste of oriental spice might leave me gagging for more, once I've returned to this septic shore and its crippling Northern climate, for those of us who can't ride around in cars.

Well, if I like it so much I'll save up and go back again...and again! I'd like to have my own disco bar out there where it's always hot, (and that's only the weather I'm talking about), but I'd need a lot more money than the bit I've got stashed; if only to transport my large music collection. Right now I'm enjoyng a selection of '50s rock 'n' roll, it will have to do to save my doggone soul, for now.

B. Note. This piece should have preceded THE MADNESS GENE, in fact I typed it in before it, but for some mysterious reason both pieces were deleted while I was having a coffee break with a very charming, and attractive library assistant called Susan. Could it be a case of gremlins in the machine? 1/10/02.

SNOUTS IN THE 8-MILE-HIGH CLUB.   Late may, 02.

When you fly, you don't feel the distance, 6,000 miles in 13 hours might as well be 6 miles for all the effect it has; maybe that's why we suffer jet lag and culture shock? Also, when you're at an altitude of 41,000 feet, flying at almost 600 miles an hour, with an outside temperature of minus 80 degrees centigrade, and the jumbo jet starts wobbling and losing height, your nerves are apt to suffer as you contemplate your imminent end. I am at times almost clinically paranoid, as well as partially sighted, not the best combination for travelling alone.

I've just got back from my first visit to Thailand; negotiating three major airports with a little help from people who weren't too self obsessed to spare some humanity. Pattaya's a 2-hour drive from Bangkok Airport, though my travel itinerary had said it was only an hour's drive away. I was about an hour over schedule, coming through immigration at Bangkok. A Tour East Thailand rep was waiting for me, and hustled me off to a waiting taxi, I was almost a walking basket case by this time. Fortunately, the driver spoke only basic English so I was able to slump onto the back seat and make myself as inconspicuous as possible, hoping he couldn't detect my harassed state of mind through his rear view mirror.

The part of Pattaya I saw on the way to my hotel looked very haphazard, half up, half down, a weird combination of ancient and modern buildings; but nothing could have prepared me for my first visit to Walking Street. Admittedly I was drunk, dazed, and confused, and not able to see very well. Suffice it to say, that if I'd been a sharp-eyed sex addict with a bulging wallet, I'd have been in paradise.

Incidentally, (I forgot to mention it earlier), if you've ever flown at 41,000 feet and experiencing some turbulence, and suddenly thought, 'Oh no! I've left the gas fire on, and I'm not due back for ten days, if we don't crash first!', you'll understand how my stomach felt at that precise moment. I fairly quickly resigned myself to whatever fate awaited me, and carried on following our flight path and altitude on the hand set in front of me.

It's amazing how much emotional pain the body can take, at times it feels to me like my intestines are being pulled out without an anaesthetic; a bit like in the old hanging, drawing, and quartering days. For the first four days of my holiday, I felt like Marlon Brando in 'APOCALYPSE NOW', a dark soul in a dark place (my head). It was the bottomless pit of self loathing and despair; thank fuck for other people, who can't see as deeply into your psyche as you can. Two strangers helped pull me through, one reckoned to be dying of cancer, the other was a Thai escort (bar girl), who loved me way beyond the call of her job description.

I can only put my deep depression down to the accumulated pressure that much of my writing is about, loneliness and social isolation; I hope to go back to Pattaya around Yule time, and stay in the town and rekindle my relationship with the Thai who loved me. If not, there are plenty more exotic fish in the golden bowl that is 'The Honey Bar', Walking Street, Pattaya. Thailand. (It's no longer there, unless my rheumy old eyes deceive me.)

Modern airports are huge sprawling complexes, I suppose they have to be, given the volume of human traffic they're dealing with 24-7. Dubai airport was like a little air-conditioned city, as was Bangkok. There must have been literally miles of carpet in the latter, a kind of soft focus grey. Dubai was more a tile effect, with palm trees lining the aisles; it also had baggage and people carrying buggies, fast moving and silent, apart from an almost missable warning buzzer; I had to jump out the way on two occasions to avoid being flattened.

I don't think air travel is a problem for me, I've never felt terrified whilst flying; apprehensive at times, yes. Even when I hear about plane crashes, like the one that's happened today (25/5/02) off the coast of Taiwan, with the suspected loss of some 225 lives, I don't think, 'That's it, you won't catch me on a plane again'. If I was on one that was going down, I've vowed with myself not to do the headless chicken routine, running up and down the aisles screaming, knocking other screamers out the way, no, I'm going to remain seated, clutching an air hostess.

Speaking of which, a lot of them are like super model look-alikes, with dazzling smiles and perfect figures; they're a lot brighter than the average super model; they have to be to cope with the varying degrees of human temperament they have to cope with on flights, especially long haul. 'Economy Class Syndrome' isn't only about fears of deep vein thrombosis, for me at least, it's about putting up with the irritability it can engender in certain types of passenger; I've almost been involved in two instances of air rage due to unstable male passengers, projecting their insecurities on to me. The latest incident was on the flight back from Dubai, with a fat Welsh bastard sat behind me making snide remarks. I wanted to kill him, but I managed to restrain my temper, wishing him dead in my head instead.

Dubai to Manchester is an 8 hour journey. More or less as soon as we'd taken off, breakfast was served to us on trays; my stomach was churning, and it wasn't that long since I'd last eaten (Bangkok to Dubai), so I handed it back to the 'trolley dolly'; an expression I'm certain must cause feelings of air rage amongst the highly competent cabin crew.

There then seemed to be a fairly constant procession of trolleys, offering drinks to the already well fed and watered 'hogs'. I dubbed the majority of passengers thus because once their abundant liquid intake started passing through them, they had to get up and queue for the toilet. The couple in front of me were a case in point, they were too greedy to refuse anything, and with poor bladder control; I was determined not to use that over-used toilet, partly because my own bladder can refuse to work under stress, and the thought of a line of porkers waiting to get in would certainly have inhibited my flow.

I likened the situation on our plane to super model look-alike air hostesses, promenading up and down the 'catwalk' of our cabin, feeding and watering the hogs. It was totally unnecessary, one meal would have been sufficient, which is what I had, about five hours into the flight; very acceptable and more environmentally friendly than the waste being piled up from too much indulgence. Economy flying is the pits, it's business class for me from now on….Har, har, har!!!

....
....

HEAD SWEAT ON MY PILLOW, AND EAR WAX ON MY TEETH.
(FEELING LIKE SHIT, INSIDE AND OUT, LOOKING WASHED UP, FEELING WASHED OUT.)   1-2/8/02.

Why are more murderers dismembering their victims nowadays? Is it because, in their warped minds, they want to be certain the object of their rage and hate is truly dead? It's a really messy business cutting someone up, there's eight pints of blood for a start, then there's the intestines and other squishy bits, and the head! Do you avoid looking at a face you're used to see words coming out of? Eyes that may have gazed into yours? Lips you might have kissed? I'll never understand the depths the human psyche can plummet too. If I was going to do this dastardly deed, and I can think of a few people who qualify, I'd opt for a long bladed, sharks teeth hacksaw, as opposed to a chainsaw, which I imagine could throw up rather a lot of spray. A hacksaw's got to be cheaper as well; And unlike that teenage zealot who, some years ago, chopped his corpse up into 172 pieces, I'd only go for five easy to manage (relatively speaking) portions, I'd sever the legs, arms, and head, leaving the torso intact.

I read a book by Ian McKewan once where they cut the torso in half, that's just asking for problems, guts everywhere, as well as the smell to contend with. After cutting the limbs off, I'd fold them up before rigor mortis could set in, to make them easier to put into green garden waste plastic sacks, with a view to dumping them in a landfill site.

I know of one notorious wife murderer and dismemberer (through the media), who claims he put her head out with the domestic refuse for the bin men to take; suitably bagged I presume? The problem I'd have with taking mortal remains down to the tip is, I can't see well enough to drive. You'd also need a disguise, and false number plates to avoid recognition; there are supposed to be plagues of voracious rats about, who'd soon make short work of the human meat. Can you imagine, sneaking onto the tip in the dead of night, to check on decomposition with a torch, only to come upon a seething mass of brown and grey fur, and swishing pink tails; all shrieking, gnawing, and scratching, and if you didn't hop it fairly sharply they'd turn their attentions to you.

All in all, I'd say it was only the truly criminally insane who go in for such excessive measures. A youth is on trial at the moment for allegedly killing a very old lady, cutting her heart out, boiling it, and drinking the blood because he thought he was a vampire, (he's denying that now). If that isn't mad, I don't know what is; and that's here in this country, not some developing nation where superstition and voodoo are still rife.

My preferred method of despatching a thorn in my side, like some floozy who was doing me wrong, wouldn't be like Tom Jones, the Welsh warbler, did with Delilah, by stabbing her; no, I'd plump for a doorstep assassination attempt, using a gun with a silencer on it, or a crossbow pistol; one good shot and she'll be dead before she hits the deck; all crumpled and rumpled up, her nightie up around her hips, with no knickers on. There might even be time for one last……..No, no! What am I saying? (But still, if no one's about, it would seem a shame to let it go to waste while it was still warm and juicy, and no resistance would be forthcoming. After all, it would only be going to rot away from that moment on…)

....
......

HAPPY BEING FIFTY.   3/8/02.

As far as the title of this piece is concerned that is, it's the fiftieth sheet of handwritten A4 to be used in my 'DOWN IN ONE' collection, making it one hundred handwritten sides of paper, at approximately 250 words a side, making an estimated total of around 25,000 words. Some of us writers are very concerned about length and thickness of our product, and it is definitely the very last entry in this, my last unsung collection; (76 words so far).

Even at 55, I still have a burning desire to be 'discovered'; and that most of my work is good, original, and has something relevant to say; but the publishing market, skittish at the best of times, is harder to crack than a winning formula for the national LOTTO. And there's also the problem of coping with what the British deem to be good and bad taste; even Virginia Woolfe found herself on the receiving end of a morality case in the courts. I think it was 'TOO THE LIGHTHOUSE', that incurred the judge's wrath, and a whole print run was ordered to be destroyed. I haven't read any of her works, I came across a copy of 'ORLANDO' once, (not literally), but the print was so small and cramped, I soon gave it up; it seemed overly intellectual and arid to me. I wonder if she waved this cruel world goodbye while she was drowning herself? (waving and drowning at the same time.

I've just read a collection by Britain's first 'gay, socialist, transvestite poet', Chloe Poems, a bitter and twisted old queen, who writes pieces like'THE QUEEN SUCKS NAZI COCK', and gets away with it. I'm no lover of 'the monarchy', but I'd have him up for subversion just for the hell of it.

I've written to Mr/Ms Poems publishers, 'ROUTE PUBLICATIONS', (they've always ignored work I've sent them), expressing my concerns; I also threw the offending, and offensive book, along with the unplayed 14 track CD accompanying it, in the bin; it's not the sort of material I'd want the thought police to find on my bookshelf; and these people ('ROUTE'), get funding from Yorkshire Arts, which is itself funded by the Arts Council of England. Serves the fuckers right if you ask me, if they can't be bothered to monitor more carefully, what they're funding, or perhaps they even approve...?

I'd love to be able to host my own Writers Club, with acoustic music thrown in, Jazz, singer/songwriters, even the dreaded folkies, but no acclaccatura, (I've just spotted this word in a dictionary), (PLF, I don't know which one, because I've not been able to find it since, 15/5/06), in the shape of harsh, strident Indie bands, with the same misguided chip on their shoulders as Chloe Poems, only electric.

Traditional R&B groups and 'rock 'n' roll' outfits could play at my club; if I'm going to end up with an advanced case of Tinitus, (I've already got a moderate one), I'd want to have had some enjoyment getting it. But Hebden Bridge is a tight-arsed little town, full of 'right on' fascists in the guise of the 'muffia'; it is after all, the 'lesbian capital of the north west'. There's also a glaring lack of cash to start up such a venture, when I'm feeling low and dispirited, (when am I not?) I have a fantasy of sitting with a bottle of 5 star French brandy and a six-cylinder pistol, with one cartridge in it, at a table in the dead of night, playing Russian roulette, spinning the cylinders till I eventually lose, hopefully after I've drunk all the booze.

40-DEGREE　　　　　　　　　　　　　　　　　　　　　　　**WASH.**
26/8/02.

I mark the passage of time elapsing, by watching cloud formations passing by in the sky overhead; there's a shed in my back garden, I keep a bed in there and a rocking chair, and there's a double skylight in the shed roof, someone who owned the place before me must have been into astronomy. The same time will still be passing when I'm dead and gone, it's on a 24-hour cycle till eternity.
There's a sense of sadness gnawing at my insides, it's my body's way of telling me my life's wasting away, a pointless exercise really; I've done everything I can to make myself a successful man, but have failed miserably in the material, as well as the personal world. Is such candour healthy I ask myself? It helps to alleviate the pain, I equally candidly reply.

At 68, Benny Hill died alone while watching TV, his death wasn't discovered till other residents noticed the unmistakable odour of decay wafting their way. He was a multi millionaire, living as cheaply as possible, carrying his shopping home from TESCO'S in two carrier bags; no longer wanted on British TV. Some of his entourage thought they were in for a share of his dough, he certainly indicated so. One who thought she was in for a pretty penny, used to perform oral sex on 'Uncle Benny', even tho' it made her want to puke. In the end she didn't get anything, a wedding ring would have stood her in much stronger stead; ironically, his wealth went to relatives he'd never seen, and she was left with a bad taste in her mouth. The smutty comedian used to put Eau de Cologne on his wedding tackle before he'd let her start sucking him off, a smart move that, I bet Uncle Benny's cackling his cock off at the discomfiture of that tart with no heart, if he's out there driving Earnies milk cart.

What do you have to do to make the breakthrough in life, you feel you so richly deserve? There's no worse fate than becoming famous after you're dead and rotting in the ground, or your ashes have been scattered. I don't want to become the 'Nick Drake' or 'Eva Cassidy' of the modern poetry scene, a biographer's dream; likening my morbid existence to that of a latter day Vincent van Gogh; summarising that I'm better off out of it with a face like mine; the important thing being that I've left my work behind.

Unlike Benny Hill, I've left a comprehensive will, leaving copyright on all my written work to WSPA: (WORLD SOCIETY FOR THE PROTECTION OF ANIMALS.) That way, if my work ever takes off, proceeds would go towards doing something useful in the world, rather than feathering the nests of relations I've never met. I sincerely hope they will take my posthumous offer seriously, and market my work fearlessly in this duplicitous age, where it's all the rage to say the opposite of what you think and feel, and squeal like a pig being slaughtered if you get caught out.

....
....

SEX VAMPIRE, THE FEEDER.
15/9/02.
(LIKE A BLOATED, PULSATING WHITE GRUB.)

I've heard it said that sex in the head is the best, by that I don't mean someone boring a hole in your skull and fucking your brains out; though there are some inhuman monsters who are so depraved, I wouldn't put it past them to contemplate, or even doing it. Can you visualise it? Of course, they could gouge your eyes out and go in through the sockets, AAARRRGGGHHH!!!

Imagine that you're lying on your deathbed and someone says, 'Hey! They've just discovered the secret of eternal life, it will soon be available in capsule form; it's too late to help you tho'; and as you gasp your last agitated breath, with an aghast look on your face, they say, 'It says so right here in the DAILY PHUN paper'. Well, that's how frustrating and damning it feels, when you know you've been selected by a sex vampire to be 'milked' as often as possible

How would you like to be 'dogged' by something you can't see or touch, but which is dug in so deep into your psyche, it can see through your eyes, (eye in my case), and hear through your ears?

And tries to control and censure you by inflicting burning sensations in your ears; left for hate and disapproval, and an arid blast of heat in the right ear for 'love'? Because it is a satanic force, black magic ESP, an incubus/succubus, it sees everything in a negative way, I believe in the real world, it's left for love and right for hate; but it's like red or pink for one sex, and blue for the other, I can never remember which is which, and where did red for a boy and blue for a girl, originate from? Or is it the other way round? (Or is it just me being paranoid schizpphrenic?)

18/9/02. I believe this thing is lodged in the top part of the back of my skull, over the bone that juts out (the occipitul bone); I say this because sometimes when I scratch the back of my head at this spot, I get a blast of cold fire in my left ear, as if I'm being rebuked for disturbing it. I wish I could locate a top class exorcist, who could detect this evil 'take worm', (it's a play on tape worm), and draw it out and destroy it, once and for all.

Some time last year, in sheer desperation, I contacted a psycotherapist over the phone, explaining that really I was looking for an exorcist. I explained to him what my problem was, and at one point he said to me, 'Believe me Philip, no-one can read your thoughts'; my mind stalker loved this. I almost signed up for a course of intensive therapy, ('Tell me about your childhood, do you have any sexual problems'?), at £15 an hour; quite cheap by today's standards.

Years ago I read something by Jean Genet, (spelling of 'Jean' uncertain), about a monster he kept caged inside his head; it's a common and popular theme, exemplified in 'DR JECKYL AND MR HYDE', by Robert Louis Stephenson. The best definition of this split personality, is to read the book, or watch the film version with Spencer Tracey in it; his transformation from Dr Jeckyl to Mr Hyde is chilling.

 But I swear that this incubus/succubus is not of my own making, it is an evil presence, which I dearly want rid of; it's a putrid pollutant, a devil spawn, slap bang in the 21st century AD! I won't let it beat me, but it does sap my energy with its persistence.

....
....

I WANT TO BE A DJ IN OLD POMPEII ON THE DAY THE CITY DIED. (DELIBERATE GRAMMATICAL ERROR.)
(IT'S ALRIGHT MA, IT'S ONLY WORDS THAT I'M DREAMWEAVING.)   30/9/02.

I want to be a DJ, and play the kind of music I think the punters will want to hear; I've built up an impressive collection of CDs, none of that scratchy vinyl for me, but how could I line up tracks in the dark? I can't see much at the best of times.

I know what I could do; I could make compilation CDs on my re-recordable CD machine, if I could learn to use it properly. Of course, the really smart people use MP3s and download for free off the internet. Better yet, you can have your own internet station, broadcasting to a small section of the global nation, before legislation tries to close most of them down.

It's cost me a small fortune, building up my back catalogue from vinyl onto CD, money I can ill afford; me being poor. I know if I was well heeled, I'd have spent a lot more. Life should be all about sensuality; for me, sex and music hold the key; well I've had to make up for the lack of sex by overdosing on that which soothes the savage breast, and saves the sanity. Modern rock and pop does it for me. From Jimi Hendrix, to The Carpenters, to the new dance music technology, The Beatles and The Stones, and Captain Beefheart's psychedelic drones; safe as milk laced with LSD, for you and me.

Well, not me any more, I'd rather have a cup of tea spiked with whisky, if I've got to indulge at all; small faces looking out at me from plane windows eight miles high, is a 'high' I can do without. it would make me twist and shout in a psychiatric ward, and I'd have to come together with the other loonies, as we beat our meat while dancing in the street with no name.

Shame, shame, shame, would be our feeling, as we walked on by, not daring to look each other in the eye ever again; our tears falling like rain on that midnight train to Skaville.

Now, I hear there are 2 million more women than men, in this shark-infested country of ours; are they tough old broilers or tasty young hens, twisting the nights away from Ibiza to the Norfolk Broads? A few drinks and the right sounds, and they're all over you like a rash. When they sober up, they get a bashful attack of amnesia, except when they're talking to their best friend about what they got up to with their knees behind their ears.

The tears of a clown is how I hide my emotions, I've cried an ocean in my beer, the best years of my life spent on the dark end of lonely street, with my nose pressed up against the green door with envy, that's why it's a bit bent. There's always something there to remind me of the empty void inside my bed, if you send me the pillow that you dream on, I'll 'cream' on it while I'm sniffing your purloined underwear. (The things I'll write just to keep the rhyming theme going.)

....

This collection is dedicated to Diane and Gail for whom the word 'fail' has no meaning, except in my case, I'm possibly the world's worst CLAIT (Computer Literacy and Internet Technology, ex student that ever passed through their hands; I soon gave up trying to learn, and spent my college time working on my manuscript. 4/10/02.

(PLF. I do as little creative writing as possible now, in fact the piece I'm going to type in here is the only piece I've written this year; there's no point in creating work, if virtually nobody's going to see it. I'm still trying to get some recognition as a writer via my web page, I recently sent nine postcards out to UK publishers, saying: 'Hi, if you're wondering where the next big thing in modern poetry is going to come from, please check out my web page at www.newauthors.org.uk, nothing ventured, nothing gained, as my dear departed mother used to say. I say nothing ventured, nothing sprained; especially the ego, when all you get back is a big fat zero.)

THE GRASS CUTTERS COMETH.   6/3/03.

One of the joys of being a council tenant, is that for around six months of the year, the Council come and cut the grass every other week; or so it seems, and the noise is HORRENDOUS! I think it ties in with the macho mentality that prevails around here; if you can't take it you're queer.
Unless you've experienced this extreme noise terror, you'll probably think I'm exaggerating, but as far as I'm concerned it's as terrifying as air force fighter jets flying low overhead, and it goes on for much longer. I don't know if It's my persecution complex, but they seem to single me out for special attention; these rugged sons of the soil, appearing as early as their job description allows. Bringing the roar of their industrial strength, grass cutting machines with them. How they can stand the din without wearing ear protectors is beyond me, let alone the vibrations these machines must make. Anyone who's tried using a pneumatic drill will know what I mean; I only

attempted to use one once, 30 years ago, it almost jolted my spine up through the back of my neck, and seemed to loosen my teeth.

I haven't even got round to trying to describe the racket that their hedge trimmers make, they make my window and door frames shake, rattle and roll, and my whole nervous system recoils in agony; they sound like an electric saw mill inside my head; all my privets look dead since their last torturing 5 months ago. A pair of garden shears would keep them trim, I could do it myself, 2 or 3 times a year, and cut my grass with a 'fly mow' (which I'd have to buy of course); then I wouldn't need them to come onto my 'property' no mo', (It rhymes with 'mow'). But I don't know if my lower back could take the strain, I have a lot of muscular pain in that region, and then there's the arthritis in my hands...

This periodic extreme noise pollution only adds to the constant battering my sensitive nature receives, because I can't afford to choose where I want to live. I maintain that there's a truly unwholesome, even satanic undercurrent round here, belying the 'on-the-surface' nature of the neighbourhood. I regard the indigenous males, as nothing less than evil, dead-heads; inbred and inverted telepaths, and downright shag nasty bastards. In the 12 months I've lived on this 'quiet' estate, on the outskirts of Todmorden, I've been subjected to excessive nuisance from car alarms going off, and an endemic culture of fat-arsed, lard-brained turkey necks, beeping their car horns at every available opportunity; quite often when I've just got up and dared to open a top window, to get rid of the smell of last night's sulphurous emissions; or if I open the front or back door to scent the air. It's eerily uncanny how one of them always manages to be near just at that precise moment, to say nothing of the 'display strength' fireworks that are in plentiful supply for numerous weeks of the year; a lesser personality than mine would have cracked before now, and been led away whimpering and trembling. But I retaliate by wishing death and destruction on these persistent offenders, who seem to be horribly healthy and resilient to the vehemence of my curses.

Last night, (5th March, my birthday,) I watched a programme called 'GRAND DESIGNS', on Channel 4, where a 'manifest destiny-type' couple invested £450,000 in modernising a 150 year old Victorian barn, into their idea of a 'des res'. A 'castle' for them and their two lovely baby daughters; I thought they were mad, spending their money this way, I'd have been up, up and away to Thailand for the rest of my natural existence, with that kind of dough; living a life of luxury and enjoying lots of loving.

....
....

IT'S FREEZIN' IN MY PARTS.   10/1/03.

Freezin' hands and freezin' feet,
I'm lyin' in bed tryin' to get some heat
Back into my digits.

I'm curled up into a tight little ball,
Backside to the window, face to the wall,
In my feet I can't feel f-f-f—nuthin'.

If I had a wife I could put them on her rump,
Unless she was lyin' there like a frozen lump,
It's too darn cold even to h-h-h---snuggle.

It's too darn cold, it's too darn cold, my hands are too numb
To hold the only warm part of my bod',
Two peas either side of an empty pod.

Will this cold weather never end? Will I ever be able
To phone a friend? Will my ice cold heart ever warm up enough
To send some blood back into my fingers and toes,
Let alone my nose.?

(PLF. I'd like to be able to adapt this number to the tune of
RAINING IN MY HEART by BUDDY HOLLY, if Paul 'Macca'
MacCartney wouldn't object; I think he owns the rights to Buddy
Holly's songs, the Scouse bastard. [He'd sue me for that wouldn't
he? And I'd lose; so to pay his libel costs I'd have to sell him the
rights to all my written work, then he'll own me won't he? I'm not
kidding; if he'd been on that space shuttle that recently blew up with
loss of all life on board, he somehow would have survived, he's that
jammy; as well as indestructible. I've not finished execrating this
execrable character yet, his reviled name crops up a little later on.])

....
....

224

NIGHTS THAT I'VE SAT IN.   4/1/03.
(Any resemblance to that incredibly tedious song, 'KNIGHTS IN WHITE SATIN', is purely intentional; and if Justin Heyward doesn't like it, I'LL SUE!!!)

'The nights that I've sat in, too numerous to mention,
I want to go out but I'm too near my pension.
(CHORUS. 'But I'd love to, I'd really love to, OH HOW I'D REALLY LOVE TO', Followed by that wailing bit at the end.)
'Night after night, I sit in on my own, no-one to talk to,
No-one to phone'. (CHORUS. 'But I'd love to, I'd really love to,
OH HOW I'D REALLY LOVE TO. (Followed by that wailing bit at the end.)

And now for the best part of this mind numbing 'rock classic', the instrumental part in the middle, with the great bass riff and flute solo.
(Go on, enjoy hearing it in your head.)

'Sometimes, I have to take myself in hand, a quick fifty off the wrist
Will make it stand down'. (CHORUS. 'But I don't want to, no I don't really want to, I'D RATHER SHOVE IT UP YOUR FLUE, YOUR FURRY FLUE'. (Followed by me wailing at the end.)

'Rat's eyes and a rat's brain, inside a human frame; eat or be eaten,
Is the name of the game. Nail their arses to the wall, let them feel what it's like to be fuck all; it makes sense too, do it to them before they can do it to you, if you have to, really have to, REALLY HAVE TO'.
(Big non lottery winners wailing finale to finish.)

(PLF. I wanted to put the boot into 'STAIRWAY TO HEAVEN', but the nearest I got to inspiration was, "And she's taking on the whole of the rugby team's first eleven," which is a pity really, because apart from Rolf Harris's version, this pretentious pile of hippy drivel needs taking down a step or two. [Get the pun on stairs or what? Am I insulting your intelligence by even pointing this out? Am I being patronising? Am I floundering waist deep in shit?])

....
....

THE MAN WHO REMEMBERED EVERYTHING HE SO PAINFULLY WISHED TO FORGET, LIKE HIS LIFE FOR

INSTANCE.   (INSTANT   IRRITABILITY.)
13/3/03.

I sometimes try to erase so much from my memory store, I fear I
might do my brain some permanent damage, and be left a catatonic
vegetable, staring emptily into space; at just turned 56, doors of
opportunity are slamming shut in my face as rapidly as a shithouse
door, banging in a force ten gale; an outdoor shithouse obviously.
I've very recently unearthed a little thing I wrote some 25 to 30 years
ago, I think, my undiscovered readership. It compares favourably
with something I wrote last weekend, the first piece is called:
CANDY FLOSS.
'The holes in your face give access to it all, the sperms on the carpet
let it die before it lived. Peace of mind, and simplicity of existence, are
its essence, death is its master.
Beat out its rhythms in darkened avenues, pluck out its lullaby for
the eternal sleepers with your heartstrings'.
And KILLER WIND. 8/3/03.
'I watched the back of your head as it cut me dead, I thought I had a
friend, turned out to be 'killer wind''.

Quite possibly, globally, billions of people have worse lives than
mine; their hopes of a better life dashed at a very early age. And all
that's left for them is a short, brutal existence; I've hung on by the
skin of my teeth for the past twenty years or more, in a country
which I detest, and which refuses to give me the artistic break I
deserve. My physical and mental health have been greatly eroded as
a result, but I have a tenacious streak that won't let me give up hope.
If I   make it to Thailand and back again this year, and have a good
holiday as well, that'll be a huge poke in the eye to 'the system' in
this country, that forces so many of us to live in abject 'poverty'; and
fawns and grovels to the obscenely rich. The miniscule minority who
have most of the nation's wealth tied up in their own favour.
Their greed and luck are the ideals we're all supposed to aspire to, in
the spirit of free enterprise; an impossible task for most of us. And
why should we want to be like Sir 'Super Macca' Paul McCartney?
With a personal fortune of at least £120,000,000? And that, I'm sure,
is a very conservative estimate. 'Macca' is lucky by nature, he's a
sort of an all round nice guy, but in my estimation, quite ruthless.
Have you seen the price of BEATLES CDs? They're still the most
expensive, apart from THE ROLLING STONES back catalogue,
which are a pound dearer in the shop that I've seen them in; I'd like
to know why? Is it because McCartney and Mick Jagger are two

ancient monuments, revered for their past output? Of the two, Jagger has retained the harder edge, Macca's new stuff is mostly cringe-making; one lyric I heard about a year ago went, "One, Two, Three, Four, Five, let's go for a drive. Six, Seven, Eight, Nine, Ten, let's go and do it again…" Anyone else would have rightly been 'slaughtered' for that abomination, but he gets away with it. Now, thanks to the rejuvenating effect of his new young wife, (she's young compared to him), he's out on the road again. I heard him on the radio this morning, accompanying himself on a ukulele singing, 'SOMETHING IN THE WAY SHE MOVES', a George Harrison song by the way; Sir super Macca; I hope you're paying royalties for abusing it, you wrinkly old twat. (He'd sue me for that if he ever knew I existed, it's highly unlikely he ever will.)

(PLF. And that's it people, the final additions added. I was tinkering with the idea of writing something to go with the title: 'UNREQUITED LUST IN A COLD CLIMATE', but what's the point? I must have worked the lonely and isolated theme to death in all my other work; even I can only take so much emotional agony before I develop compassion fatigue. 18/3/03.)

....
....

Well, that was then and this is now (19/6/06); a lot of crap's floated under my bridge since then, along with 6 more collections, which I now hope to make available, to a non-existent public, online; for sale as e-books. I've already got a blog, though that could be closed down by GOOGLE at any time for containing sexually explicit material (pornography or erotica of the solipsist/onanistic variety.) I even have a laptop now, which I've not attempted to use yet, I bought it a couple of months ago because it seemed like a good bargain. Last year I bought a new computer for 600 quid, I sold it this year for £165, all I used on it was the 'my computer' facility to put all my work on 'memory stick', but I've only re-edited my collections on floppy disc, a medium that is rapidly becoming extinct.
The only people who've shown any interest in publishing me is a subsidy publisher in America called Dorrance Publishing; I've just e-mailed them to say I realistically can't afford to go with them, I'd be looking at forking out over £1200 to have this collection featured as a 'print on demand' and e-book item featured on their online

catalogue, which is no doubt full of lists of people who've published mainly for 'vanity' reasons, (don't we all?)

I've even organised a poetry 'slam' for tomorrow night at a pub in Halifax: THE OLD COCK; an advert in the local paper cost me 30 quid, and judging by the resounding lack of response I've had, it looks as if I could be facing a loss (it's £1 in); but at least I will have tried, and you can't say fairer than that. If this venture fails dismally I wouldn't mind trying a rock 'n' roll disco there...

....

I want to include all the work I've put on my blog here now in order to really flesh this vulume out, and bring it completely up to date; incidentally, since the piece I finished on previously was a scathing attack on 'Macca', anyone who's not got their head firmly wedged up their arse, can't have failed to notice that his marriage has hit the skids, and he could be going to be taken for quite a few million pounds of his ill-gotten gains; I'd love to see him end up penniless and mad, still plunking his ukulele as a busker, singing: 'Buddy can you spare a dime'?

....

I want to reproduce my 'blog' (web log) from the optimistic note on which I began it, up to the apology I've attached to it after my last entry on it: 'EROTIC SENSUALITY'. If it was my own private web site I wouldn't have done so, even though you can get your head chopped off by Islamic militants if they think you've uttered one wrong word against their medieval belief system; they're more deranged than even the IRA (who now thankfully have packed violence in.)

My blog name is errolfinn at blogger.com, (I'm a swashbuckler with the pen and a saucy old pirate.), here goes:

11/8/06. THE BLACK SUN PRESS.

Hi, I'm the creator of 'THE BLACK SUN PRESS'. My aim is to become an 'online publisher' of 'e-books', including my own collections of modern poetry and acerbic observations on life from the viewpoint of a disadvantaged, disabled person, living in a world dedicated to youth, beauty, and the worship of money. I would like to be able to buy into all 3 idolatries, but I might only qualify for the last one of them, not being young or beautiful.

There's a huge market out there for people's misfortune, misery, and madness; what other excuse could there be for the likes of RADIOHEAD,

MORRISSEY, COLDPLAY, KEENE, EMBRACE, and all the other gratuitously miserable purveyors of meaningless despair? And I'd like some of that hardcore, hot, money-changing-hands action. So, if you're IT-curious, check out my blog and post some comments on it. (Thankfully, nobody has.)

(I don't understand this new technology very much, I could use an online assistant; so if you're young, beautiful, loaded and female, and know how to post your picture on this particular format, you've more or less got the job. Errol Finn.)

(I'd like to use AdSense on this site as well so GOOGLE please take note.)

....

Mon, 14/8/06. When I originally created the title: THE BLACK SUN PRESS, some 7 or 8 years ago, I thought it was unique to me; I did check out some press titles on the web some years ago but I didn't see it listed, I wonder if I'm in breach of someone's copyright? OO-ER!

Even my definition of 'black sun' as another term for a 'black hole', absorbing rather than radiating energy, isn't unique to me except in the respect that I created the analogy in my own mind without being aware that anyone else had done so; and it has depressed me to find out otherwise. My only other alternative collective title would be 'COPING WITH MADNESS', which is I hope, unique to me.

As for 'Errol Finn'? Well I do have sensations of wanting to be a swashbuckler, whipping out my rapier at a moment's notice to redress the imbalances in this world. But I've had to settle for the pen being mightier than the sword; also now, I'm a bit long in the tooth for swashbuckling, my arthritic fingers would have difficulty unbending if I gripped my rapier for too long, and as for my back and my knees and neck...let's not even go there!

I do have the intention of putting my latest creation on this site: 'MARILYN MONROE'S BRAIN', plus a few other bits to show that I am a creative person in my own right...but not right now. Seeya, Errol.

....

Tues, 15/8/06. 'MARILYN MONROE'S BRAIN.'

This is a copy of only the second piece I've written this year, I've given up composing for composing's sake, if there's no money to be made out of my creativity then I don't want to be bothered anymore. Here goes:

MARILYN MONROE'S BRAIN. 5/8/06.

Marilyn Monroe's brain weighed 1440 grams when it was
Removed and weighed at her autopsy, shortly after untimely death,
All her other vital organs were treated in this way too, in the report
It even mentions the state of her 'poo' as 'light brown and formed'.

She's reported to have said on the night of her death, 'It's Saturday night
And here am I, the most beautiful woman in the world, and I haven't
Got a date,' fate had other ideas about that, it sent a couple of murderers
Round to meet her, (according to a book I've just read.)

The world's greatest cinematic sex goddess never had an orgasm
According to Marilyn's 'secret tapes', made not long before her mysterious
Death in 1962, and aged 36, she wanted to become a leading Shakespearian
Actress too; and being of an intellectual bent, she knew what tautology
meant,
Do you?

Like me, Norma Jean desperately wanted her own family, but sadly it
wasn't
Meant to be; history needs its icons and infamously, Marilyn's been singled
out
To be one of them, I don't know if I can say the same for me...yet.

Errol Finn, the swashbuckling writer.

....

NERVE ENDINGS.

I always feel, after one of our prolonged cold, dark winter's, that it's left a
greasy film over everything, including me.

The new 'plebistocracy' (my own word...I hope), like 'Jordan' and Jade
Goody for instance. 'Ere, you're 'avin' a larf int-cha? Wanna see me tits
'n' minge'?

'OPEN MAC' night as opposed to 'OPEN MIC', (flashers of the world
unite.)

He gazed into her very soul. 'How very dare you!' she said.

I regard myself as being a couple of steps higher up on the social scale to Robinsin Crusoe; I have marginal, painful contact with the outside world…but I wouldn't settle for a 'Man Friday' up my 'Gary Glitter'.

The nearest I get to anything hot and wet anymore is a nice cup of tea.

The sky has all the time in the world to keep reinventing itself, day after day throughout all eternity; another anticipated 4 billion years before our Sun finally dies is enough eternity for anyone, don't you think? If you're not hoodwinked by some extreme religion, that is.

I've been targeted long and hard by a 'dark force', but I've never been enslaved by it, unlike the devil spawn, sicko, schizo scumbugs who psychically stalk and attack me. Only devil spawn could know such perverted tricks of spying and prying in this totally inhuman manner of using their warped ESP to torment me.

And lastly, as a 'severely visually handicapped person', I have a fear of losing what sight I've got; I've summed this fear up in 3 lines:

'I wouldn't want to live if I couldn't see,
But the thought of death frightens me,
Maybe I could shoot myself in the head while I wasn't listening to my psyche?

Black Sun. I've absorbed so much pain and heartache, it's left a huge black hole in my soul.

....

PRESTIDIGITATION NATION. 18/8/06.

What sleight of hand could I use in this promised land of get rich quick Britain,
To push some of that easy money my way?
I can't afford to pay up to £100 an hour to have some 'legal eagle' fight my cause,
And I can't afford to buy a thousand lottery tickets in the faint hope of winning
It big on the National Lotto.

I can 'afford' to get blotto on cheap and nasty booze, and lose my marbles

And self esteem, as I sank deeper and deeper into the mire of hopeless alcoholism;
If I can't find the discipline and self control not to.
There aren't too many options open to me as I rapidly approach 60, with only
Limited vision in one eye to see through.

Maybe I could go round collecting pigeon poo to sell as fertiliser for people's
Roses and try selling it door-to-door?

....

CARNAGE. 18/8/06.

It's hard to believe that only a few hours plane ride away, all hell has broken loose, I watch as much of it as I can stand on the news.
Israel, Lebanon, Afghanistan, Iraq, will the sanity ever come back instead of
ATTACK! ATTACK! ATTACK!
It must take a special breed to go in and clean up after a suicuide bomber's gone off; like mopping up in an abattoir after a really busy killing day, clearing all the blood, guts, and shit away.

....

SASTRUGI BOOGIE 21/8/06.
('Sastrugi' is wave-like, hard packed snow created by arctic winds; making 'man-hauling' heavily laden sleds virtually impossible. Maybe the title should be SASTRUGI SHUFFLE instead.)

The highlight of Channel 4's coverage of this year's V Festival, (I don't know what the V stands for or where it was held), was the finale of Morrissey's set, culminating with 'HOW SOON IS NOW'. Morrissey threw his top into the crowd. (what are the chances of it appearing on Ebay today?)
I think Morrissey is an eccentric anachronism, the modern musical equivalent to Samuel Beckett (who he has a striking resemblance to), another purveyor of 'nothingness and despair'; I wonder how much 'Mozzer' got paid for last night's performance?
And I wonder, overall, just how healthy his bank balance is? I bet it's a damn sight healthier than mine, a basically happy human being (that's me) who's had misery forced upon him, anf has reacted accordingly by writing

loads of miserable stuff. My favourite Morrissey song, outside of the brilliant work he did with THE SMITHS, WAY BACK IN THE 80S! is 'EVERY DAY IS LIKE SUNDAY', I love it and can really relate to it, apart from going for a dip in an icy sea and coming back to find your clothes have been nicked! You wouldn't catch me going into the ocean for a paddle for anything less than £20,000, (which is ideally how much I need to escape my awful fate of a living death in the UK.) I mean, everything that we discard gets flung into the sea doesn't it? EEUURRGGHH!!!

....

RADIO(SMEG)HEAD. 20/8/06.

I watched (on TV) a huge throng (about 75000) of worshippers, worshipping at the dark 'church' of RADIO(SMEG)HEAD; they knew all the words to all the death wish 'hymns' of this life-negating band of aficionados of meaningless misery...WHY?
Rarely, if ever, apart from some beyond the grave, out of a hellish mausoleum, minimalist modern classical music, and 'death metal', have I heard such pointlessly depressing dirges.
I'm sure last night's audience was made up of young, physically healthy people of both sexes; what have they got to be miserable about? Or is it all an elaborate joke that I'm too old and disabled to see the funny side of? I don't think so.
This world's too full of stupid people bringing the planet to its knees, over-indulged young people like these should be part of the solution, not adding to the problem by idolising what I can only describe at best as professional depressives, and at worse as DEVIL SPAWN!

....

JOHN BETJEMAN, THE LAST REAL POET...LAUREATE. 22/8/06.

I'm not intellectual enough to ramble on forever about the merits of Sir John Betjeman as a man and a poet. To me he represents a quintessential English quality that is rapidly disappearing from our culture; a bit like Captain Mainwearing out of 'DADS ARMY'. As far as his poetry goes from what I've heard him perform on TV and radio (I've never read any of his work), I've always found him accessible and uncomplicated, which might account for his huge popularity with the public; and I don't think he ever swore in his work either, unlike me. (Though he did famously say he hadn't had enough sex no long before his death.) I wonder what he would have made of my efforts in the 'poetic field'? A lot more perhaps than the anally retentive shower who've re-imposed their stranglehold on anything other than 'street' poetry and John Hegley.

I find most highbrow poetry unutterably dull and depressing, and lifeless; hence my entry for this year's Bridport Arts Prize Poetry contest: 'POETRY IS DEAD!' which cost me £6 to enter, and I don't even think it stands a chance of making it into the winners anthology, let alone bagging the 1st prize of £5000. I should have compromised on the strong language in it that I felt was necessary for the authenticity of the piece, make your own judgement on it as long as your name isn't Lavinia Greenlaw, (the official judge), who probably already has:

POETRY IS DEAD!   3/2/06.

'Poetry is dead' he said, as he sank deeper into his own grey decline,
'A lot like the world, I've been out in it and used it, but it's been
no friend of mine'.

Conventional poetry gives off a horrid reek of camphor and sulphur
Combined; can you imagine that insufferable odour seeping up your
nostrils
As you lay entwined in the arms of Death?

With this level of unfocused anger inside me I should be out 'rapping'
On the street, outside Sainsbury's or M&S, spitting volleys of hatred
At the well heeled, the indifferent, and the effete.

'FUCK OFF YOU FUCKING NUTTER!' some irked, wobbly wheeled,
trolley-pushing shopper might feel stung enough to reply, as he or she
wrestled their overloaded cart back to their car; to be followed by my
poisonously barbed retort of, 'Fuck off and die you cholesterol-guzzling
arsehole.'

But of course, one doesn't go round behaving in such an anti social
Manner, if one did one would soon find one's self on the receiving end
Of an ASBO or a blow or two to the head; or emotionally dead as the
Effects of the 'chemical cosh' neutralised and de-activated one's
Tortured psyche.

'Crikey! Leggo! Yaroo! Gerroff!' were my favourite words when I
was a boy, as uttered by the redoubtable Billy Bunter; 'I say you fellows'
he'd shriek as he was booted round the dorm' for stealing their tuck.
Nowadays he'd be politely shown the error of his ways and encouraged
To follow a low fat diet.

Express any politically incorrect views in the West today, and you'll be
Pilloried with wrong-headed righteous indignation, or even worse....
My parting shot is: 'She was only the poet's daughter but she said she
Wasn't averse'. PPHHWWOOAARR!!!

Errol Finn, the man still willing to whip out his rapier at a moment's
notice, even at the ripe old age of nearly 60.

....

THE TITLE WITH NO NAME.   31/8/06.

For the very few of you who've accessed my blog, thanks, that makes about
10 if the number of hits on my personal profile is anything to go by; I've
now just updated it to show what an interesting person I really am
(errolfinn: blogger.com)...check me out.
Being a frustrated wannabe success, without any success, is emotionally
very draining; that's why I get depressed a lot and suffer with ennui and
lassitude. Both of these debilitating conditions are worse when the weather
is grey and dull, thus making me SAD (Seasonal Affective Disorder), here
in the north of England, we get a lot of grey and dull weather...Doh!
I don't like to have to make compromises in my work or in the language
that I use; I can't call myself 'a swashbuckler with the pen' and not
attempt to inflict pain and misery on my readers rather few and far
between right now.) Writing is the only legitimate way I can express my
feelings and frankly, I don't give a damn if what I have to say offends or
upsets those 'sensitive souls' among us; they're only hypocrites anyway,
and on 'Judgement Day' will be found sorely wanting on the plus side of
'What did you do to try and save the world? Oh I see, you walked round
with your head firmly jammed up your own arsehole, and hoped all the
problems would miraculously go away. You're going down to roast in
HELL! NEXT!'
My latest attempt to find an outlet for my work is 'THE PARIS REVIEW',
a literary magazine that I've never read or seen, its publishers are based in
New York; it felt good yesterday to take my bulging envelope to the post
office and send it on its way (at a cost of £1.51p and I think they've rejected
me). I'm not very optimistic of a positive outcome, but hey, I don't care.
I've still got my blog, and when I've learnt how to transfer work on to it
from my 8 collections (edited on the now nearly defunct floppy disc), I'll
make them available on my site...for sale. ERROLFINN the elder
statesman of my dying generation, still showing veneration for all the great
ones who've already broken on through to the other side of the great divide

of life after death…if it truly exists; if it doesn't we're all fucked! (Are you allowed to swear on your own blog owned by Google?)

....

I'M DODGING DEATH AS LONG AS THERE'S ANY BREATH LEFT INSIDE ME 2/9/06.

I'M DODGING DEATH… is in part a tribute to those young military personnel who are dying in Afghanistan and Iraq, so that we in the West can continue to enjoy the freedoms we largely take for granted; it's also meant to be my literary 'swan song' because my health is deteriorating at an alarming rate:

I'M DODGING DEATH AS LONG AS THERE'S ANY BREATH LEFT INSIDE ME.

At nearly 60, ill health is really kicking in,
It's a sin how I'm paying for the excesses of my youth;
Truth to be told, I'm feeling old and worn out before my time.
A whole array of vitamins and mineral supplements has
Failed to keep physical atrophy at bay.

As far as I'm concerned, it's not only me who's in terminal decline,
It's the whole of Western civilisation as well, all its values
Are shot to hell. We've got largely ignored or forgotten armies in
Afghanistan and Iraq, laying down their lives to hold the tide of
Islamic fundamentalist insurgents back from installing
Their murderous regimes.

And here in the UK we have a potential alien uprising in our
Midst, and all we can do is prevaricate and procrastinate;
If it wasn't for the actions of a dedicated few we'd be well and truly
In the shit; we're harbouring a viper in our bosom and we won't
Admit to it.

When you're living in violent it isn't so much death that you have
To fear, it's the thought of being horribly maimed in a bomb blast
That terrifies me. Something that's happening on a daily basis
In parts of the Middle East; the Devil's feasting on an excess of
Torn flesh and bloody gore, the end results of a 'dirty' war.

The world's never moved on at such a hectic pace, the same could be

Said for the human race; how many more billions will it take before we
Bleed the planet completely dry, and then have to die in ever increasing
Numbers?

It's not my world anymore, I'm heading for the exit door, and the
Human race in general doesn't interest me enough to care about
Its ultimate future; though no one knows what that's going to be.
Will 'we' become a homogeneous mass of 'gay' islamofascists,
Living in a hedonistic, fun-loving, totalitarian state, where 'we'll'
Love to hate each other, and Big Brother is 'our' Mother?

Money is the root of all freedom, not an idealistic socialist state,
We'd have to be like a massive ant colony to achieve that.
When I was young and physically strong, I never took this maxim
About money on board, I was too busy pursuing a bohemian truth
Through the end of innumerable bottles of booze, mind altering
Substances, tobacco smoke, and the bright elusive (for me anyway)
Surfeited requitement of love and lust; all my hopes have crumbled
To dust, floating about in great empty mausoleums inside my mind.

This is my literary swan song; I've lingered on here for far too long,
If I could have my time over again. and knowing what I know now,
I'd make money my 'god' and not the pain of having a soul to
Worry about.

This is Errol Finn, a swashbuckler with the pen, saying 'Over and out.'
....
A BUSKER FILLED ME WITH UNEASE.   7/9/06.

To anyone who read my last entry: I'M DODGING DEATH etc (if
anyone's read it which I strongly doubt), I'm feeling a bit less 'on my way
out' than I was then, mainly due to discovering the healing benefits of Aloe
Vera juice; which I learned about after typing irritable bowel syndrome
into Google's search engine; it came up with 4,890,000 pages! Luckily I
found what I was looking for on page 1, and I was able to find what I
wanted a lot cheaper than it was being advertised on line.
This latest piece is based loosely on reality, there's a busker who plays in
Halifax town centre from time to time who has an unsettling effect on me:

A BUSKER FILLED ME WITH UNEASE.

He was playing acoustic guitar and singing Bob Dylan's 'MR
TAMBOURINE

MAN, his guitar case open at his feet, in the street.
I slunk past him, inwardly sneering and snarling; how dare he
Remind me of a free-spirited freedom that I'd buried deep
Inside myself, and stir up emotional turmoil inside my heart,
And expect me to part with a coin or two to help him on his dizzy dancing
Way to the nearest pub, after an hour or two.

If I'd been a noise monitoring officer in my bright yellow tabard,
Sweating under the heat, I'd have loomed large at his feet and asked him
If he had a licence to play and sing music in the street, and was he paying
Bob Dylan royalties for using his material in order to extort money
From gullible members of the public? Heh, heh, heh!

'Hey man, you're blowin' my cool, get out of my face you silly old fool,
you're ruinin' my big number; this one always has 'em diggin' deep,
especially when I put some 'harp' on it. Get out of the way and let me
play, okay.'

But I wouldn't be having any of that, I'd be looking into his 'hat'
To see how much he'd made, with a view to confiscating it. 'I'm sorry
Sir, but if you haven't got a licence yoy can't play here, and I'll have to
Take your illegal earnings away to be used in evidence; I'll give you
A receipt. Now have it away on your feet before I call a police officer
To arrest you.'

'£11 42p, not bad for an hour's work, with no tax or insurance to pay;
I wish I could play a musical instrument, I've always had a hankering
For a barrel organ you know, with: 'WHEN YOU'RE IN LOVE'
 Ringing out to steal the show, and 'DOWN AT THE OLD BULL AND
BUSH; plus loads of other music hall and fairground favourites,
They knew how to write a good tune in those days'.

I'd have been so long in my reflective haze that when I came out of it
He would have slipped quietly away; not to worry, I'd catch him
Another day, hopefully when he had 15 or 20 quid in his 'tray'.
Saturday afternoon's usually the best time to catch the punters
In a generous mood, they think he needs the money for food,
Not drink and drugs.

He's probably signing on anyway, he should be made to play
In front of a group of OAPs, trapped inside their easy chairs
In the day room of their nursing home, with their false teeth
Nestling in their laps to give their aching gums some ease.

Try rousing them with the urge to roam like a freewheelin'
Gipsy rover, bowling young ladies over with your
Smouldering charms, melting like butter in your arms for nights
Of passion.

But no, the harsh reality is I'm just a sad old git, an unwilling
Member of the invisible, white-haired brigade; invisible or
Derisible to the laughing young women who approach you in
Groups, expecting you to shuffle out of their way. If they ever
Bothered to look round as they passed me, they'd see me spitting
Contemptuously on the ground.
You can get done for that as well these days.

Errol Finn, back on swashbuckling form. 7/9/06.

....
....

A LETTER TO TONY BLAIR, PRIME MINISTER. 8/9/06.

I'm posting a letter to Tony Blair, our prime minister for the time being;
I've written to him quite a lot over the past 9 years to air my views on his
giovernment; I'm going to miss him when he's finally hounded out of
office.

Dear Mr Blair, 7/9/06

Now that the knive that have been out to get you have finally got you, (and
I can't see Gordon Brown doing a better job than you), I'd like to enclose a
photocopy of a photocopy of what was to be my literary swan song on my
blog, just over a week ago (errolfinn at blogger.com)(I'm a swashbuckler
with the pen): 'I'M DODGING DEATH AS LONG AS THERE'S ANY
BREATH LEFT INSIDE ME'.
This piece was meant to be in part, a tribute to the military personnel
who've laid down their lives in Afghanistan and Iraq (both American and
British soldiers), to safeguard the freedoms that we take for granted in the
West; you can find a typed-up version of this piece on my blog.
Quite frankly, if I was in your position, I'd be thinking, 'Okay, if that's the
way they want it, let them have it. I've sacrificed 10 years of my life (if you
go in 2007 it will be 10 years) for this nation of turncoats and backstabbers,
let someone else take the flak.'
I stand by your policy on the war against terror, maybe 'we ain't seen
nothin' yet' if it kicks off with Syria and Iran; and I don't understand why

George W. Bush is always portrayed as a bumbling fool in the media,, we need strong leaders more than ever now.

Even though I'm on long term Incapacity Benefit, and don't like the way you've targeted the poor and most vulnerable in our greedy and hostile society, I'll still miss you (when you've gone) as a strong leader of our country.

Yours sincerely. Phil (errolfinn) Fletcher. Unsung poet and writer.

....

And now, as they used to say in Monty Python's Flying Circus, for something completely different. I did try submitting this piece for the poetry comp' that's featured as an ad' at the top of my blog page, but an electronic monitor kept saying that one of my lines was too long, even though I couldn't see how or why, so I gave it up. I think I've had dealings with The International Library of Poetry before...

WOMEN WITH PENISES.   7/9/06.

There's nothing quite so annoying as 'Ladyboys', sex toys for adventurous
Sex tourists to the far east.
If I was drinking in a bar in Bangkok and my eyes locked onto a beautiful
Face, and I didn't know the score, and the more I drank, the more
Beautiful this ravishing vision became, I'd become fair game for
Sexploitation, thinking I'd pulled me a real peach.
When I got her/he back to my hotel room, there'd be a loud screech
Screech of anguish as I uncovered the awful truth, as this lass became
A he/she youth; not that there's anything wrong with this of course,
If you're up for it, which I know I'm not, I like a lady to be a lady,
Not an inter-gender lookalike.
Not that some of them don't look totally convincing; if I were of the
'Gay' persuasion I'd think all my dreams had come true at once.

The 'I was never confused' errolfinn, swashbuckler with the pen, and saucy old pirate.

....

Sat, 30/9/06. The next 3 items are the only material I've deleted from my blog; I thought they might conflict with Google's pornography policy, I posted the apology a couple of days after I'd originally posted 'EROTIC SENSUALITY' and 'SPUNK'.

....

12/9/06. AN APOLOGY.

I've been experiencing some anxiety about the content of some of my work on this blog, mainly because it's not my own private and personal web site; I'm effectively renting this space from Google; so if anyone who reads my work feels offended, they should report me to Google and get my site closed down.

As a writer in the 'free' world, I find it nearly impossible to censor myself and what I have to say; I believe that my work has artistic merit, if at times expressed somewhat crudely.

If the 'medievalists' get their way, and by that word I mean Muslim fundamentalists and extreme Christian sects, we'll all be too afraid to write or say what we think for fear of punishments of one kind or another. If I was threatened with physical torture (I've heard they're using 'acid bath's in Iraq, do they use diluted acid to take the skin off? Undiluted acid would dissolve you while you were still alive...wouldn't it?) I'd cave in very quickly, I can't stand prolonged physical agony; and what gaineth a man if he stands by his principles and has his tongue and fingers cut off so he can't communicate them to anybody? If you think I'm paranoid, fair enough.

....

And now here are the two pieces I was feeling guilty about publicly displaying; I've always thought of my style of writing as a private means of communication between any potential reader/s and me. When I self published some of my collections some years ago, (most copies now languishing on a council rubbish dump somewhere, because I threw them out thinking they'd come under the category of dispensable excess weight to try and lug in my luggage to the airport when I move permanently to Thailand...this December. Collectors would never find them.) I always put a disclaimer on the cover, a bit like they do before the start of a lot of programmes on Channel 4 TV, here in the UK, like The Charlotte Church Show for instance; a few years ago she looked as though butter wouldn't melt in her mouth, as she stood warbling away like a linnet (do linnets warble? I don't know) with 'the voice of an angel', now she's got the trap of a foul-mouthed fish wife:

EROTIC SENSUALITY. (Written in the wee small hours of 9/9/06.)

I believe that pornography, especially hardcore, is degrading to the whole human race, let alone women; although it seems to be mainly women who are sexploited to go deeper and deeper into the murkiest areas of the human psyche, and dredge them up for 'adult entertainment'. I mean who but saddos and sickos want to watch the bestial extremes of human behaviour...and even worse? And I for one don't want to watch another man having sex, I'd much rather be doing it myself...female masturbation, yes.

I believe that pornography and soulless sex are the scurvy and blight of our age, and just as undermining as the threat of terrorism. It's hard to decide where the dividing line comes between erotic sensuality and pornography; for the chosen ones, love and a blessed union are the answer. For the outsiders like me, using paid sex could act as a stop-gap, but I don't rate that too highly, it's overpriced and leaves you feeling empty again after a while.

I believe that children are our future, but as women become more and more dominant and demanding, and decide that they only need men for sex and not telling them what to do, we're creating more and more young feral males; psychotic monsters whose only moral code is to survive at all costs, no matter what they've done. Caligula would welcome some of them as brothers in infamy as they descended into Hell, like Ian Huntley, and Ian Brady for instance.

....

See what you make of 'SPUNK' (For all the girls I've loved with my left hand,[though I can be ambidextrous when it comes to this activity of hand, mind's eye, and brain co-ordination.])   00.30 am, 9/9/06.

The moon was as big as a car's front headlight tonight, it blinded me as I walked on down the lane, and helped to deaden the pain of my aching heart; I wanted to walk away from the modern world forever. I wanted to find 'the pub at the end of the world' with a welcoming hearth, and drink Elizabethan mead from a pewter mug, and inhale clay pipe smoke deep into my lungs without coughing it up, and swallow hot juice from the hairy (unless she'd had a Brazilian) cup of thrusting love and lust as she came in my mouth.

I have contempt for people who take wild risks with their lives, always pushing the limits of their endurance and their luck to the limit, what the fuck's that all about? 'It was there so I felt I should 'conquer' it and my own fears; I could be taking years off my life but who cares? At least I'll have made it to the top of the world...ma!'

Females are biologically programmed to seek the sperm of the most suitable males, though the further down the social scale you go, the less it seems to count; I've never, due to disability, been considered worthy of fertilising any eggs, the dregs of my procreative urge splodge out onto my belly, no intimately smelly intercourse for me. Just 'brain sex', rude thoughts and desires to fan the fires of my lonely erection.

If only I could hang suspended in my orgasm indefinitely, jerking about with my tongue lolling out, like a hanged man. If women could read what goes on in the inner recesses of the mind of a man, they'd never go near them, (it's a bit one-sidedly sexist that statement, I think it applies to both sexes); it's primitive in there, and very possessive and territorial. Maybe our impulses are controlled by the pull of the full moon, as old as the Earth itself.

Errol Finn, one-time werewolf, but I'm alright nowOOOOO!!!

....

Thurs, 21/9/06.

WHAM, BAM, NO THANK YOU 'SLAM'!

I organised a poetry 'slam' a couple of weeks ago, to take place in Halifax, West Yorkshire, at a pub called 'THE OLD COCK'; I did this in an optimistic moment of madness. I even put an ad' in the local daily paper, estimated readership, 60,000, it cost me 30 quid...ouch!
Initially I had fantasies of turning people way from the venue through being over-subscribed with 'poets' wanting to enter the 'slam' with a chance of winning £10; but as the event drew nearer and nobody had contacted me about it, (the ad only gave my mobile phone number due to a misunderstanding with the person who took the details for my event; I wanted her to print both my home phone number and my mobile because I was having my home phone disconnected 3 days after the ad went out, [confused?], and people don't like phoning mobiles in the UK due to the potential cost of the call, excepting young people of course, because they don't think before they act...), I'd begun to downscale my expectations quite sharply.
So last night, once my nervous stomach had settled down, I set off for the pub, about a 10-minute walk from where I live. It was 7.45 pm, near dusk with a brisk but pleasant breeze blowing. Being severely visually handicapped I don't normally like going out after dark because it's

difficult for me to see anything along the pavements of our dimly lit streets, and I always expect to be attacked by some socially challenged psycho for the few coins in my pocket and my ancient mobile phone, which I'd left at home, or else walking into an unlit metal post set in concrete in the middle of the 'sidewalk'.

With some trepidation I entered the pub, remembering that there were five steps to negotiate down to the bar, the lighting was adequate for a normally sighted person; the place looked deserted. I announced who I was to the barmaid, who didn't seem over impressed. I ordered a pineapple juice with ice and went upstairs to the Oak Room to wait for people to turn up. Shortly afterwards the barmaid came up and said I wasn't allowed to wait up there on my own, I'd have to wait downstairs, I followed her down.

I hate sitting in pubs on my own, I always feel very self conscious just sitting there clutching my drink; I decided to wait for an hour to see if anyone would come and put an end to my embarrassment, I made my first drink last 30 minutes, listening to dance music and hip hop rubbish on the pub's speaker system. I decided that when I went up for my second drink of pineapple juice I'd have a double vodka put in it...THEY DIDN'T HAVE ANY VODKA!!! Which reflectively, I'm glad about, because I've virtually given up drinking alcohol, it's a crutch I don't need to lean on any more. I even found a more advantageous place to sit, nearer the entrance door; one or two people had drifted in, not for my venue alas, probably for either darts or karioki, or maybe even the two combined?

I left at 8.50 pm as inconspicuously as possible, on a par with sneaking out the back door. I got home unmolested, though I did have to pass a group of youths on a street corner; ideally I'd like to be able to bring my swashbuckling persona into play during instances like this if I was threatened, instead of having to slink past with my heart in my mouth.

When I got in I was needing some stimulation, so I put on an old WWE (World Wrestling Entertainment) video tape, and allowed the pent up frustration I felt to ease away by watching a load of gratuitous violence. I will never attempt to do anything of a cultural nature again in this intellectually arid desert, otherwise known as Halifax; and if I was going to live in Thailand at the end of this year, which I'd like to do but realistically can't afford it, (even though they've just had a bloodless military coup), a few more people would be on my nasty Xmas card list; I'll have to brood and lick my wounds for a lot longer yet, but I'll get my own back somehow....

Errol Finn, the destroyer of inflated egos, and senders of nasty Xmas cards.
....

And now for the very last 'sample' piece to appear on my blog, if people want any more of my genius, they're going to have to pay to download it when I set up my secure (hopefully) web site.

ENDING IT ALL...TENTATIVELY.   22/9/06.

There's nothing left on my social calendar for me to do
But take myself down to the railway line, and throw myself
Beneath the rapidly approaching wheels of the 11.09 to Manchester,
If it arrives on time.

If you're feeling full of bitterness and hate towards an unfeeling and
Uncaring world, it must feel really insulting if the train on which
You've sealed your fate, is due to arrive late because some other
Selfish bastard has jumped underneath it before you further up the line.

'Due to unforeseen circumstances, the 11.09 to Manchester has been held
Up at Bradford Interchange, a deranged nutter shouting 'God is great!',
Has been splattered all over the rails; it will take more than a few pails of
Warm soapy water and a scrubbing brush to clean that mess off. We wish
He'd jumped off a motorway bridge instead.'

Dead, dead, dead! I'll soon be 'brown bread'!
If you've ever stood on a Halifax Railway Station platform on a cold
Winter's night, barely able to see anything in the eerie, diffused,
Orange light, with the prospect of another gruelling journey ahead
In equally dimly lit surroundings, and an equally hostile atmosphere,
With only an empty house to go back to, the thought of jumping
Under a train to end your emotional pain doesn't seem such a bad
Idea after all.

The late Errol Finn, I missed the damn train through lateness, that's why
I'm still here, I lost 'my bottle' after that near miss.

....

And that's definitely it for this new extended version of 'DOWN IN ONE'.
If only it could be one of my eight collections that would make my fortune,
even at this relatively late stage of the game of life; (it's been 'cat and
mouse' with a very sadistic 'cat' cuffing and mauling me for the last 59
plus years. If only I could metamorphose into a super-sized black rat and
sink my incisors into the back of its neck, and then rip its throat out just to
get it off my case, allowing me to have some real good luck for a change,

and then metamorphose back into a cuddly Dormouse-type animal, I'd be content. Phil(errolfinn)Fletcher. 30/9/06.

....
....

THE MEANING OF LIFE (IS A FULL STOMACH.)
FOR TORTURE VICTIMS EVERYWHERE.

(TORTURE COMES IN MANY GUISES; URBAN AND PSYCHIC

TERRORISM HAS MADE A BASKET CASE OUT OF ME.)

FREE AEROBICS FOR ALL AT HALIFAX RAILWAY STATION, AND I'LL THROW IN THE MEANING OF LIFE FOR FREE. 13/6/03.

It's 7pm on a bright and breezy summer's evening, I'm waiting for the Manchester train to come and drop me off at the wild west frontier town of Todmorden, where it's every one for their self, and the Devil take the hindmost; which is usually me. Whilst on the platform I wonder whether there's such a thing as a lonely old farts, lonely hearts club that I could join online, and chat on all day? Using Halifax Central Library's Access Room for People With Disabilities free computers and electricity?

My reverie is broken into by a business-like metallic voice with an attendant echo, bouncing off a building opposite somewhere; could it be an announcement that the train has been delayed for 15 minutes at Bradford because someone more unfortunate than myself has jumped under it, and only managed to cut their legs off below the knee? A couple of bewildered Japanese tourists look anxiously at the time table screen that I can't see well enough to read, we shrug our shoulders in mute resignation. But no! This nasal twang has got nothing to do with doom, gloom, or disaster; it's the aerobics class (you can hear some of them panting), coming from a location on Huddersfield Road; and the instructor is most likely wearing one of those evil contraptions that fit over your head and have a semi circular arm that comes round to your mouth, with a mike in and it makes you look like a complete prat; like the girl drummer out of THE CORRS, who bounces up and down on her seat with every beat of her drums with her headset on, bouncing with her, and sporting black gloves as well, what a poser!

I found the aerobics instructor's exhortations rather infectious, and quite wanted to join in. I imagined myself as the old TV incarnation of WONDER WOMAN, where she'd go into a spin and come out of it in her skimpy, tight-fitting costume, that used to leave many a red-blooded adolescent sneaking off to his bedroom to relieve his tumescent frustration, or was it only me?

In my fantasy I emerged wearing a leotard over my jeans, headband and wristbands, and trainers with heels and soles about six inches thick. And I'd be there on the platform making giant leaps to the left, then the right, thrusting my arms above my head and bringing them down with my elbows jutting out, just missing knocking someone's eye out or breaking their nose, and touching my toes 20 times and straightening up again, without having a dizzy spell severe enough to leave me sprawling dangerously near the edge.

The mournful wail of the Black Diamond Train to Hell approaching, brought me out of this pleasant interlude with a jolt, harsh reality in the sombre expressions of my fellow travellers kicked in on both my shins, metaphorically; still, the pleasantly plump lady guard on the train punched my ticket with some aplomb; I think she fancied me. The meaning of life is to procreate, and if you're not in constant demand to fulfil that particular duty, be aware of your surroundings at all times, keep looking up at the sky, savour Nature in all its moods, and try to live as long as possible, just to spite death.

....

I've written this extra poem for you Elise, I hope you won't be embarrassed or offended. As a writer I can't help bearing my 'soul' to anyone who I think will be appreciative, and you have given me some positive feedback.

I LOVE WORDS AND HONEY.   27/6/03

I love words and honey and also pots of money, if one of my 'lucky dips' comes up trumps tomorrow night I'll be moving to Heptonstall myself, as Lord of The Manor, buying all my food and drink over the 'net and keeping a housekeeper as a pet.

(That's one in the eye for all you 'right on' fascist lesbian feminists out there.)

If I could perchance to win the whole £15 mill' that's up for grabs, I'd buy Lumb Bank off The Arvon Foundation and live in near splendid isolation; it's so lovely up there. I could watch and feel the seasons come and go, drinking white or rose wine on the patio, soaking up the summer sun and howling at the winter's moon.

And when I wasn't 'lording' it there, I'd be in Thailand or Rio for the carnival, always on the lookout for the elixir of eternal life. Maybe an enigmatic young wife would keep me on my toes; there's one thing for certain, if I don't win the lotto I'll never know, it'll just be the same old show of wishing and hoping...and moping.

....

EVEN KEEL.

I've never been allowed to live my life on an even keel, forces within me and without have seen to that, but I believe that the longer you live, the more you can achieve, and if I could do it with impunity, I'd drink to that.

But the stresses and strains I've endured are now taking their toll, I've suffered agonies and tortures I can't begin to describe to you, all for the sake of being a perverse fate's plaything; a loveless pauper who should have been a psychotic King. It's the physical pain that's so hard to bear, as if the roots of my hair have become vicious little barbs digging down into my brain, with my skull feeling like concrete pressing down on top. I just wish it would STOP, STOP, STOP!!!

Because I could take adversity till eternity, if it was only in my mind. Sometimes my blood feels like thick pea soup coming to the boil, with an electric current running through it; if I was immersed in a bath full of ice cubes, the room would soon be filled with steam; the initial cooling effect would turn this nightmare into a dream.

Isolation and rejection are the root cause of all my pain, if I could lay down and go to sleep and never wake up I wouldn't complain, my brain would breathe a sigh of relief; I'm a walking corpse anyway. The only time I'm content is when I'm reading a good book and listening to music on the radio or on CD; I used to have a libido but even that's deserted me.

....

THE THRILL OF IT ALL.   26/6/03.
(How to become a marauder in two easy stages.)

The unutterable boredom of keeping to the straight and narrow; as long as you (me) are observing the protocols of faceless anonymity, you are posing no threat, especially to women. Now that male superiority has ostensibly been put on the back burner, the 'fairer sex' has become more and more judgmental; anything remotely less than their idea of male perfection just won't do, and they're more and more licentious as well, as long as it's on their terms; sewing the seeds of dissension and resentment in the 'under performing male'; whose basic length of shagging duration can't compete with theirs. They can accommodate a pair of cocks at any one time if they feel so inclined.

Because of the diabolical treatment I've been subjected to by women in this country, I now have nothing left but scathing contempt and loathing towards them; while at the same time harbouring feelings of lust and longing; much less attractive propositions than me get doted on and more. If I decided to turn marauder, I would imagine myself as a lone male leopard lying in the undergrowth, on the lookout for a stray Thomson's gazelle; secure in the knowledge that sooner or later one would come along. And when she did I'd rise up at the last moment and clamp my jaws round her throat, snarling and growling for effect.

At this point she'd be expecting instant death, and not dishonour; what a shock she'd get when I was on her 'like mud on a pig', ramming my spotted dick (query?) into her goat-like orifice, and kissing the back of her neck with my slavering chops. When my orgasm had stopped I'd let her run off; I wonder what a cross between a leopard and a gazelle would look like? Or would she just abort a bloody mess?

....

ALL MY HEROES ARE NOW DEAD, APART FROM KIRK DOUGLAS, AND HE HASN'T GOT LONG TO GO. (AS WELL AS CLINT EASTWOOD, BUT…) 13/6/03

Yes, I was a young man back in the 1960s, and anyone familiar with the work of The Incredible String Band, will know where that line's coming from? That's right, one of their songs. I still considered myself to be fairly young at the end of the '70s, being a mere 33 years old when that decade came to a turbulent close, with the advent of so-called 'PUNK ROCK'.

Retrospectively, I equate the end of the hippy era with the release of Al Stewart's 'YEAR OF THE CAT', which, if my not very accurate memory is right, came out in the mid seventies; and would have had punks digging deep into the backs of their throats for thick green gobs of phlegmy spittle to aim at diehard hippy's flairs.

I still get a warm nostalgic glow every time I hear the sumptuous arrangement of this swan song of a deluded section of a generation; who ever coined the phrase, 'Never trust a hippy', was right. Even Timothy Leary spied for the FBI, (great record by 'The Shadows' that, FBI, it still sounds great after 40 years) to avoid either going to, or to get out of gaol. 'Tune in, turn on, and drop LSD' was the mantra for me, The Doors of Perception, and The Gates of Heaven and Hell, (mostly hell for me), psychedelically bursting open and releasing a confused

Kaleidoscope of many colours; some never seen before, or again since. And removing the safety net of measured time and understood meaning; at least till the effects of the acid wore off anyway. I've heard of a rock musician repeatedly taking LSD every day for a year! What a constitution! I'd have been a complete basket case after one week; needing heavy sedation to bring me down off the ceiling.

I believe that full-blown schizophrenia is akin to being on a permanent LSD trip; and one look in the suffering faces of this terrible illness's victims, can confirm this belief. No safety or surprise for them, just one continuous nightmare of being on a different and entangled wavelength to the majority; terrorising their families with their bulging eyes, and at times, unintelligible speech, and strange belief systems and nocturnal activities. Full-blown, irreversible schizophrenia is a fate worse than death; at least with AIDS you know there's a time limit on your suffering.

19/6/03. By the end of the '70s I realised I was getting too old to blag my way into the Manchester Art College disco on a Friday night; in the normal scheme of things I'd have been married with a couple of kids to worry about. But normality has never played a major role in my bizarre existence; it's been a largely unrelenting struggle to retain what limited sanity, and powers of logic, I was born with. The struggle has now become so intense that I get hypertension headaches, bands of pain around my brain, and pressure in my skull that feels like a geyser waiting to blow. I attribute these symptoms to having to eke out my existence among what I can only term as the 'local yokel mafia'.

Where I live the males announce their dominance by aggressively beeping their car horns...but I've written about this already. Maybe I shouldn't have such sensitive hearing; all the irritating nuisance noise caused by this intellectually challenged dross is peripheral to the core of my being. Even in a small and confined space like the bedroom of my council bungalow, I've got everything to hand, a double bed, comfortable armchair, TV, VCR, radio/CD player, books, videos, CDs, DVDs, and a 'nice' green view from the window. Right now, I'm seriously thinking of going to Rio for next year's carnival before I get too old to enjoy its vibrant atmosphere; though in my present circumstances I'm getting too old to enjoy anything. There's no fun to be had in 'Babylon' if you're 'poor', and forced to live in a solitary state; (I think I've written copiously enough about my sorry plight elsewhere, don't you?)

The title of this piece was inspired by the recent death of Gregory Peck at 87; when I was growing up there was a raft of film star's names that were imprinted on your brain; they were permanent as well as being memorable, and they were superb at their jobs. I can still see Kirk Douglas's tortured expression from when he played Vincent van Gogh in 'A LUST FOR LIFE'. Nowadays, when I look at the TV listings and there are films on, I never know who the people are who're starring in them, for the most part; and there seems to be a lot of them, male and female alike, (Reece Witherspoon is an exception to this new rule, although, if I didn't know differently, I'd think Reece was a boy.)

Mind you, I don't really care, I only watch TV to pass the time at night; I'd much rather be doing other things. The truly Hollywood greats will be with us for all time now if we want them, as well as the truly awful. Oh yeah, Bob Hope died on Tuesday, seven weeks after his 100th birthday, but I've not heard much of him for the last 40 years; he was good in 'PALEFACE'; at least I think it was called 'PALEFACE', it was so long ago…about 50 years to be roughly exact. (PLF, 2/6/06, it was called 'PALEFACE'; I might be losing my short-term memory, but my long distance one is okay.)

M y life has now become so awful in this, the country of my birth, that I've started fantasising about my own personal 'paradise', a hippy heaven where I'll permanently be 23, and Lord and master of my own harem of beautiful women, who spurned me in this life; having only girl children, (you can mistrust my motive as much as you like but they're lovely when they're infants). I'll eliminate everything I hate on this hellish level, which doesn't leave very much, but I can assure you if you were allowed to enter, (which is highly unlikely), you'd love it, it's going to be all my dreams come true; one long and eternal sequence of dreams in unreal time actually, so I never get bored.

My 'tag' for the remainder of my time in this life is going to be 'AK/47', which is short for Anathema Kane, born 1947. (Geddit?)

....

SURREALISTIC ENNUI. 28/6/03.

I sleep, or just lie in bed a lot, it's cost effective, and at times even
though I rack my brains, 'THERE'S BUGGER ALL ELSE TO
DO!'; drowsiness is one of my favourite feelings.
16/7/03. The moon slowly comes into view, low down on the western
(I think) horizon of the night sky; it's a summer moon of deep
burnished gold, though by the time she reaches the peak of her
trajectory she'll be a big luminous silver disc; a call to lovers and
howling wolves everywhere. But that won't be till about 2am, I'll be
asleep by then, behind my blackout curtain, snoring and farting like
an old wart hog in a hurry to get the night over with; I can sleep 7
hours in 7 minutes, it goes so fast; precious time being wasted
sleeping the sleep of the dead.
In 7 hours during the day, I can get things done, and have my lonely
fun. The other afternoon while waiting for a bus, sitting on a step, I
watched a young mum on the other side of the road pushing a
substantial baby buggy up an incline; she was wearing a pair of
shorts. I cursed my partial sight for not enabling me to see right up
her crack as she staggered on, bent forward at a fetching 45-degree
angle.
'Hey, it's me and I'm in love again, I ain't had no lovin' since I don't
know when', (a line from an old Fats Domino song). Right now I've
got romantic inclinations for someone young enough to be my
granddaughter, it's probably a complete non starter, and it's making
me suffer the old ennui in the pit of my stomach, like I want to fade
away from life in despair. Oh, the plans I could make for her, not
least a 'honeymoon' in Thailand; I've seen a good deal for two people
advertised in METRO. I know I should let go of such silly notions;
they only cause me oceans of pain and misery.
(Yes, I think that hopeless notion's been put permanently on hold,
one lesson I have painfully learnt is that if you've got the money, you
can have anything you want. There was a short film on C4 TV the
other night, about a Russian prostitute called Julia, she's a trained
doctor, or so she said, stunningly attractive in an oriental way, and
this film maker had hired her services for less than £150 a night; she
also said she liked anal sex! My point is that if you'd seen her as a

doctor in a white coat, you'd probably have thought she was an unobtainable goddess. 2/8/03.)

....

I'M LACONICALLY SARDONIC ME, YOU HAVE TO BE WHEN YOU'RE UP AGAINST STOLID ARIDITY. 6/7/03.

With a social standing not much higher than that of a pariah dog, and each day a hard slog to stay one step ahead of being dead, you wouldn't think I'd find much to laugh about would you? But I do! Not as much as I used to, I've lost my really facetious edge, I've had it brow beaten out of me by the pernicious crew. How's this for a tale to tell: 'BALLOON CHICK'S GUN HELL'? (Culled from the DAILY STAR, 28/6/03, from Paul Tetley in Los Angeles.) 'A chicken that took off after sick jokers tied it to 100 helium balloons, came back to earth with a bump...when it was shot down by police marksmen. The officers were called in to save the terrified bird as it was lifted above a fairground. The brown and white hen—since nicknamed Amelia—was only rescued after the balloons got trapped in power cables above the site in San Francisco.
The sharpshooters were then able to pick off each balloon individually until the bird floated to the ground. Last night Amelia was recovering at an animal rescue centre, where staff were trying to find her a home. "This is a friendly chicken", said deputy director Kat Brown. "It is a chicken that is ready for a relationship. But we'll be screening people carefully. She's been through a lot."
Believe you me, I know just how that traumatised bird feels; I get terrorised daily by sick jokers behind four wheels making me jump out of my skin with the raucous din they make with their honking horns. Why isn't there a rescue centre for me to go to, where some ministering angel could mop my fevered brow and cooingly say, "All your troubles are over now"?

7/7/03
Now the glim and glitter has finally fallen away from me for 'new labour', who are really just 'old tories' in well cut and expensive

254

clothing, I thought I'd try and capitalise on Tony Blair's row with the BBC by sending him this 'rap' style tirade against the licence fee; written on a plain white post card and sent in a plain brown envelope. I have identified myself on it; I like getting acknowledgements from No. 10 Downing St:

Hi there Mr B.   0.10am. 7/7/03.

Your government supports the BBC, which operates an unfair monopoly. We, the public, are being made to pay £116 for their licence fee, for which most of us on low incomes only get two terrestrial TV channels. Parliamentary panels have sanctioned this tax against the poor, anyone who's a benefits slave like me, 'unrealistically employable' due to disability, struggles to pay for the luxurious lifestyles of the self aggrandising barons of the 'corporation'; the BBC is a parasitic blight on the nation. Abolish the licence fee and free us from this usurpation. After all, they've just turned and bit the hand that's feeding them, haven't they?
You can't imagine how hated and loathed 'Aunty' really is, two terrestrial channels filled mostly with BIZ! If they had to compete fairly in the open market they'd soon 'crash and burn'; they're nothing compared to SKY as far as value for money's concerned. If I didn't have to pay for the 'Beeb', I could afford to pay for SKY.
You've got no one else to blame but yourselves for keeping this outdated institution artificially alive.
(You can get quite a lot on a postcard can't you if you use both sides? I only wish he'd listen to me and take my advice, and get rid of the viewing tax that is the licence fee.

....

IMPOTENT RAGE AGAINST THE SYSTEM   7/7/03
(The DSS want to pay me a visit...)

There's no immunity from the jejunity and stolidity of our 'welfarc' state. The state having 'your welfare in mind' couldn't be further from the truth; in its dull-witted and emotionless way it's mainly concerned with how much money you're costing it, and finding ways of harassing you into an early grave; well that's how I feel its attitude towards me is anyway.

The system would like to see you earning, no matter how disabled you are, they want one more direct tax payer on the books. There are even supposed to be carrot-tempting grants available, till you try and access them. What there is, is an abundance of able-bodied 'workers' in place to make sure the system's working properly. They can point out all the pitfalls when you try and improve your lot, and at the same time offer no helpful solutions, just act synthetically sympathetic, the two-faced shower of hypocrites.

Nowadays, if you contact the Jobcentre for any reason, like I did a few weeks ago, and you're on Incapacity benefit, they're onto the DSS as soon as you've put the phone down. 'Possible benefits fraudster here, he cried off as soon as he found out there's no easy money available for him to embezzle; get on his case NOW!' And they send you a forbidding looking buff envelope to put the fear in you.

I had a totally impractical idea to set myself up as a newsagent in one of the longstanding empty shops on our estate, to fill a gap in the market; I even checked out the interior of one property, it was the right size but in need of a complete makeover, requiring an outlay that I kind of hoped the 'system' might provide; to help a disadvantaged person like me to get off benefits...NO FUCKING CHANCE!

(Just in case you're feeling a bit stressed out by what you've read so far, there's a nice restful picture overleaf to help you get your mental strength back, so you can carry on till the next one. [Apparently not on screen, the downloaded Vincent van Gogh prints are contained in the one and only printed off copy of this collection, apart from the copy I made for Elise, and which said person never spoke to me again after reading it on a train, and never paid me the 2 quid I asked for it...{I wonder where she is now? I still miss her, 2 years down the poo shute of my life.}] 3/6/06. PLF.)

....
....
....
....
....
....
....
....

....
....
....
....
....
....
....
....
....
....
....?

NON-INTELLECTUAL INTELLECTUALS.   18/7/03.

I detest Shakespeare on principle; all that 400-year-old language
written in a back to front style, causing you to strain your brain in
order to keep track of it. I've got great respect for Dickens, if, for no
other reason, than the sheer enormity of his output; though if he'd
only ever written 'A CHRISTMAS CAROL' and 'OLIVER TWIST',
he could have sat back and put his feet up; most of his other stuff is
much too longwinded and sentimental for me to take seriously.
But all that writing churned out using just pen and ink!!! If the man
hadn't been 'drunk with the powers of his own verbosity', he could
have found something more useful to do, like being a lawyer for
instance; they go in for histrionics and pulling the wool over people's
eyes don't they? The robbing dogs!
And as far as the caterwauling that masquerades as opera goes?
Some of the shrieking that goes on, mainly from the women singers
admittedly, has such a deleterious effect on my nerves, (Lesley Garret
please take note), that I have to switch it off quick! And the ballet is
simply too effeminate for my taste; mind you, I wouldn't mind seeing
an all nude female version of Swan Lake on the box, with lots of
close-ups when the dancers were being lifted up and spreading their
legs...PHWOARRRR!!!
No, give me simplicity every time in my culture, unless it's in modern
writing like Graham Greene and Gerald Kersh, or raunchy humour
as depicted in VIZ comic. The old blues men like Muddy Waters and
Howlin' Wolf weren't intellectuals, but their music appeals to the
intelligentsia, along with the great jazz men, and I don't mean Louis
'Satchmo' Armstrong by that term either.
And two of my favourite lyric lines from pop songs are: 'I needed
money 'cos' I had none, I fought the law and the law won.' (From the
song of the same name.) And: 'I ain't never done no wrong' from

Elvis Presley's 'ONE NIGHT WITH YOU'. (I used to think that line was, 'I ain't never done nobody no wrong', till I listened more closely.)

....

A WORLD FULL OF STRANGERS   30/6/03 to 7/7/03.

Such is the nature of my popularity that I always seem to be on my own, perhaps never more so than when I'm out. After a miserable forage in 'SAFEWAY' recently, I was inspired to create these lines after holding up the queue at the checkout because a reduced to clear loaf I'd bought, wouldn't 'scan', and 'backup' had to be summoned to sort it out.
A woman behind me had unpacked her trolley in double quick time, and was looking at me stony-faced for holding her up. If you live your life at a breakneck pace you don't want anyone getting in your face, and God help him or her if they invade your personal space…you'll kill them! It's the same with this queue, you expected to be thru' it in two minutes, and now this clod has held you up; you hadn't allowed time loss for that, why doesn't he hurry up and fuck off, the stupid twat!? You've got a trolley full of shopping and a 'people carrier' to get to.
What I'm noticing is that the more impatient and self centred we all become, the more miserable we're all getting; barely retaining the tolerance not to attack or abuse each other. There was a really interesting statistical piece in today's METRO newspaper about the human cost of modern living; I'm sure they won't mind if I quote it in full: 'Traffic accidents claim four times as many lives globally as wars. According to the World Health Organisation, 1.26 million people died on the roads in 2000, while 310,000 lost their lives in wars. Suicide, murder, and drowning also kill more than armed conflict, with 815,000, 520,000 being murdered. (Hey! We really don't like each other do we?), and 450,000 dying by each mode respectively'.
(That suicide figure should really read, 815,001; I keep feeling suicidal but just manage to avoid taking the final exit out of this cruel and heartless world.)

POWDERED SKIN.   23/7/03.

'My baby left me before she ever came,
Tho' she'd never let me, she called me by some other guy's name,
And even tho' she'd never met me she said,
"You men are all the same, but I hate you anyway."'

....

STAYING POWER.   23/7/03.

I haven't got any, when the going gets tough
I've soon had enough. If my life depended on it
I couldn't work in a chicken factory for £3.70p an hour;
Getting 'showered' with their blood like that 'HULL'S ANGEL'
Described last night, (C4, 11.10pm, 22/7/03); pulling out
their innards, smelling their shite.

....

BRUTE FORCE.   23/7/03.

I'd fully endorse the use of brute force to keep illegals and asylum
seekers out. Whatever problems and terrors they're fleeing from, are
not ours. With unemployment here standing at 1.5 million, it makes
no sense to keep letting them in. It's a sin against the native born
British like me, to be stranded in a 'society' totally alien to the one I
grew up in. I reckon that in another 50 years, (luckily I'll be dead,
won't I?), Britain will have become Britanistan; these people are
fanatics when it comes to the Koran, and they're tenacious too.
They're prepared to suffer for as long as they have to in order to
create the global state of Islam.

(I suppose I'll be branded as a fascist for the above piece, but I don't care; I can't be any more alienated and isolated than I already am. Being sent to Coventry wouldn't be too much of a problem for me, as long as I've my radio and TV.)(5/8/03.)

....

METRO PEOPLE. (I'D LOVE TO BE ONE.)   23-25/7/03.

It's not called 'lonely hearts' or 'I'm too ugly to get a date in the conventional way' any more; 'METRO PEOPLE' is for people on the move; not for 'saddos' with their chins and stomachs on the floor. With calls costing £1 a minute at all times, it's not a dating game for the financially squeamish, which is what I am. Facetiously, my ad' would read: 'Realistically and financially embarrassed Todmorden man, has a plan to make you ladies happy. If you're not afraid to spend your dough, then out we go, ho, ho, ho! Me? I'm tallish, dark, thanks to hair colour and fake tan, a loser in life and love, but well blessed down below, to make up for being facially challenged above my reclaimed jaw line, by the removal of a burgeoning double chin'. Actually, this ad is far too long-winded, it would be rescinded by METRO, you're allowed 20 words to alert the 'birds' to your attractions, so here goes with no distractions: 'Interesting male available, 56, I'm not a cheesy charmer. Seeking holiday companion, 35-40, for Thailand and Rio, preferably solvent, Todmorden.' (19 words at a pinch.)
Yesterday, I came (not literally) across a full page advert in VIZ, (which the more highbrow readers regard as a pile of fizzy nonsense) for DATELINE; they're offering one free contact for 20p, the price of a second class stamp; that'll do me. And even if it's only a ruse to get you to join, I might ultimately have to part with less coin than £1 a minute phone lines. I wish I could see well enough to go trawling for tarts, they're the loneliest of lonely hearts, deluding themselves that their pimp loves them.

(Update, 7/8/03. To join 'DATELINE', it's something like a £100 online and £150 any other way. They sent me written hints of potential delights to come, in the shape of two ladies from Rochdale, both in their mid-40s; was I tempted? Was I fuck! I would have had

260

to join to get contact details, and who's to say we would have been compatible anyway? If I had some real money I could find my own idea of compatibility, and I don't think it would come from Rochdale, unless she spoke with a cultured accent; the way Lisa Stansfield speaks when she's off record, (when she sounds like an international recording star) is appalling.

....

MILDLY MANIC MANNEQUIN.   17-25/7/03.
(For chronically depressed 'dummies' everywhere.)

The delusion of grandeur comes with a persuasive and seductive voice, telling you, you are a 'god' or a 'king'; and lesser people should look up to you and serve you. All very well if you can keep it in check, but ultimate disaster if you 'let it go to your head', like Adam Ant has adamantly failed to prevent. (THE MADNESS OF PRINCE CHARMING, C4, 9pm, 17/7/03.) I would define the delusion of grandeur, as the Gods elevating to a great height those whom they wish to destroy, before they allow them to fall, minus a parachute, to hit the skids with a nasty, sickening, squelching thud. If you believe that there's no 'God', like I've been forced to; (no benevolent deity could ever sanction what's been done to me in this unfulfilled life of mine), what do you do? Some people turn to an evil deity to worship, probably a hell of a lot more of them than we could begin to suspect; believing the 'Devil' will give them all that they want. But we all know that the Devil exacts a terrible price for short-term gains, (a bit like mortgage lenders).
Namely, for your soul to be tortured in his underworld realm for all eternity. Hades is not for me on those terms, having Satan's worms sucking at your brain forever doesn't seem like a very clever move to me.
At 56, my physical health has been sorely undermined through my 'unrealistic expectations from life'; like a modicum of success, a nice house, a few kids and a lovely wife. Who do I think I am to want what a large portion of the population takes as their natural right? I'd say my plight was fairly unique in the annals of loneliness; something like 30 of my last Christmases spent waking up alone on Yuletide morn, frightfully hung over and forlorn. It's a vicious cycle; you drink to blot out the pain of social failure of being alone on Christmas and New Year's Eve, only to suffer the torments of a lonely hell for two days (on each occasion) afterwards; this kind of

pressure is enough to make anyone crack up! I've never even succeeded at that!

A nice bed in a psychiatric unit, tea and sympathy, and finding the right medication with lots of side effects; all those anti psychotic drugs are the devil's work, anti depressants and tranquillisers have nearly killed me in the past. I've painfully learnt through trial and error that there's no medical cure for a deep-rooted sense of unfulfillment and injustice. It's best to kill yourself quickly by jumping under a train if you feel you can't take it anymore; though I think having said that, a more private means of self disposal would spare train drivers needless upset; as well as the Railway Police who have to pick up the pieces (literally) that you've left behind.

Without wishing to be unkind to Adam Ant, real name Stuart Goddard, (wouldn't it be awful if I couldn't even get his name right?), I couldn't help noticing how his facial features have changed for the worse; his face is now round and podgy where it used to be long and lean; can this be attributed to an under, or over active thyroid gland, or melancholy spleen? I feel my spleen is the major cause of my depression, I get a physical sensation of lassitude and despair emanating outwards from my stomach, attempting to stifle all creativity within me; it's so much easier to do nothing except rail against an unrelenting and perverse fate. It's too late now to dwell upon the past, my future's fading fast.

....

A CACHET OF CASH FOR DR. GACHET.   24/7/03.

Last night, through the medium of TV, I learnt a little bit more about Vincent van Gogh's history; or rather, that of one of his paintings, the portrait of Dr Gachet. This picture's had an interesting life, even passing through the hands of the German Third Reich, to be sold off as a piece of 'degenerate art'; to start a new phase of its journey to New York. All the time, Dr Gachet continuing to wear his mournful and resigned expression, with his cheek resting on his hand.

He stayed in the 'promised land' till the late '80s when, due to financial straits, far and away above the kind that I endure, he was put up for auction during the most decadent and obscene selling frenzy the art market has ever seen; a bit like the so-called house price boom we're experiencing here now; benefiting only the seller's baser instincts of greed and avarice, and ultimately pricing ordinary decent people (like myself) out of the market. But would I be moaning if I had anything half decent to offload? I doubt it, greed is a gratifying feeling.

Dr Gachet was sold to the highest bidder at a New York auction, $75 million plus a 10% auctioneers commission fee, making it $82.5 million altogether; and the highest priced painting in history. It's savagely ironic that the artist, Vincent van Gogh, died in an embittered sense of personal failure and misery; apparently the self inflicted pistol shot wound wasn't necessarily fatal, but at 37 he'd had enough physical and emotional suffering.

He was one of the most altruistic artists in history, leaving behind a huge body of canvases and letters that initially were considered worthless. And he had a healthy disgust for the art market while he was alive, probably putting the dealers on a par with the moneylenders in the temple, who JC most violently expelled. I think it's the only violent act JC is reputed to have committed, and Vincent was more sinned against than sinning; taking his anger and frustration out against himself rather than others. Hence the missing right ear lobe, which he took round to his favourite harlot at the local brothel.

It's crossed my mind to wonder how would Vincent have reacted if his colourful excesses had taken off while he was visibly painting them? If his Arles output had been eagerly snapped up by collectors at the time, would a good few bob coming in have alleviated his tortured sense of failure and rejection? A man after my own heart when it comes to being unlucky in love and selling 'product'. Would some of his principles and values have gone out the window in favour of a spot of personal indulgence? Or would he have given it all to those Belgian miners he felt so sorry for? Fuck the poor; they're a shower of bastards mate. (Ask 'Father Ted'.)

To avoid a similar fate to V van G's, (because in my delusions of grandeur I feel there's an affinity between us), I've left copyright of all my written work to WSPA (World Society for the Protection of Animals) in my will; so in the unlikely event that I get 'discovered' after I'm dead, (just my bad luck), then all the bears they rescue will be able to enjoy brown bread and butter for their tea...on me.

Dr Gachet is now languishing deep within the vaults of a private collector, again in New York; having been bought back from Japan for either $19 or 90 million, (I couldn't quite make out what the narrator said); if I were Vincent I'd haunt him till he was dead, the bastard.

··

I'D RATHER HAVE A WOMAN OF QUALITY UNDERNEATH ME, THAN AN 'OLOGY' CERTIFICATE ABOVE MY BED. 26/7/03.

All the women I've set my limited sight on, have been attractive and brainy, but I never got to fuck one of them; I just got fucked up by them instead. I'd have wed each one in turn, if only for the honeymoon, but what would we have lived on? A hope and a prayer that one of them would keep me in a manner to which I could have become accustomed until my literary genius was discovered, and I could have moved on to a brand new set of lovers?
(It's only my emotionally ruptured spleen that makes me write in this jaundiced manner, I'm sure that if I ever find a regular source of 'sex on tap', I'll never stray again.)

··

PHILIP LARKIN, THE MAN WHO DID FOR POETRY WHAT REGINALD CHRISTIE DID FOR NECROPHILIA; HE KILLED WHATEVER LIFE IT HAD LEFT IN IT.   26/7/03.

He even looked like the beast of 10 Rillington Place, the bone domed skull above the bespectacled, deadpan face; and he could charm a certain type of woman into eating out of the palm of his hand, before dragging them down through the quicksand of death by gas. And Christie even let another man get hanged in his stead before he'd finished fucking the dead.
I find Philip Larkin as gloomy as Micheal Parkinson, the chat show ghost who was last seen interviewing people at bus stops on 'DEADRINGERS' on BBC2; (he's now been demoted to harassing men in a urinal). They fuck you up, these impersonators like Rory

264

Bremner; I can't tell him and Tony Blair apart, but I know which one's dearest to my heart, and I don't know why, but deep down I think he's still a regular guy.

....

ABSTRACT INTELLECTUALISM. (On the cusp of midnight, 27/7/03.)

Abstract intellectualism appeals to only a few, Virginia Woolfe, James Joyce, and the rest of that inaccessible crew. I wouldn't piss on Ulyses, or shit on Finnigan's Wake, as 'TO THE LIGHTHOUSE', a different route I'd take.
In fact I wouldn't even go there, a phallic shaped beacon on bare rocks, exposed to Nature's wear and tear? Though if I did go there I'd want to be tied to the 'cock' all night long; being driven mad by the Sirens Song of lashing rain, howling winds and crashing waves; after which I'd say to myself, "Well what was the point of that? You could have caught pneumonia and died, you silly twat!"
I've always read, mainly to improve my mind, and I've written what I've written to try and find a way out of the labyrinth of madness and despair that this life has mapped out for me. England kills you extremely slowly and painfully if your face doesn't fit, my loneliness and declining health is a proof of it.
But please don't spare any sympathy for the devil who rules my fate, I hate it with a cold vengeance, and I'll hold out against it as long as I can. I wouldn't mind so much if I was making some money out of all my toil and trouble, or gaining some much deserved recognition, instead of the perdition I'm suffering, of endless monotony and repetition.
I understand that last year Penguin Modern Poetry published only two living poets. Well this year, I've alerted them to my website, which has examples of my work on it; so far their response has been nil! Well, I've had my fill of kowtowing to snobby fuckers like them, they can keep their heads stuck up their arses...I hope they enjoy the smell.

....

GRAVE BLUE WORLD. (If the media's anything to go by.)
Title conjured up 27/7/03.

I feel fatigued before I even attempt to write this short piece, I put this down to the ennui caused by living in a barren atmosphere; hemmed in by plebs, who I loathe as a subhuman breed; they're victims of their genetic intellectual inferiority. It's not their fault they're thick and malicious, it's an accident of birth. But the unformed mind will always feel insecure, rightly so, and paranoiacally make them think that you think you're better than them, (quite true in my case, but they're the ones with loads of money, as depicted in the new 'plebistocracy'; a word I like to think I've coined), an attitude for which they'll make you pay any way they can.

If I'd never read any other writer, including the ultra depressing Bible and Shakespeare, (I'd use the paper of both obsolete and epic sets of publications as fire-lighting fodder and arse wipe, if I ever made it on to a desert island after being on 'DESERT ISLAND DISCS'), and only read Graham Greene, George Orwell, the early works of Aldous Huxley and Ian McKewan, I'd have been more than well served; Graham Greene especially, (since super ceded by Gerald Kersh). The man was a 'superman'. The ultimate in modern English (as opposed to 'modernist', although having said that I'm not so sure) writers; John Steinbeck would be his American counterpart. These five writers (six now) could supply you with all the knowledge you'd ever need to have about human nature, in an entertaining and accessible format. As opposed to psychology and sociology, which are arid, clinical, and sterile methods of observing your fellow man and woman.

The sheer physical and mental energy of writers like Graham Greene, defies my understanding; yet this prolific author still found time to read widely, as well as doing other things, like travel for instance. It's a good ego leveller for me to know that my pretensions to fame and fortune in the literary field aren't nearly as well deserved as his; and yet he wasn't listed in the recent 'best 100 novels of all time'. Which goes to show what crap taste most people have got; the day Graham Greene is forgotten, is the day the world will end…for me. (Since reading a biography that implied he was a closet homosexual, I've downgraded him; and I do think Gerald Kersh is better, and has been forgotten much more quickly than Graham Greene ever will be. PLF, 5/6/06.)

....

DEATH IS OVER-RATED. (Title spawned 28/7/03.)

I detest people who always adopt the moral high ground, like those morons who say we should admit every political refugee/asylum seeker who wants or 'needs' to come here; or take holier than thou sideswipes at the Government over the recent war in Iraq. The Americans would have gone it alone regardless, and maybe us being there with them actually saved lives, because just maybe, we're not as ruthless and indiscriminate in our bombing strategy as the Yanks seem to be.

It's estimated that 7000 Iraqis have been killed in the conflict so far; well if their saddening and unfortunate deaths have helped to free a whole nation from a merciless tyrant, they won't have died in vain will they? (I know, try telling them that.) Instant death must be vastly preferable to being maimed and disfigured; I certainly know which choice I'd opt for...the big sleep.

But the didactic (preaching as opposed to teaching) moral high grounders, can't take such simple, if ruthless logic on board. They always need to create a dichotomy, (look 'em up, I had to.) Here's a moral argument I'd like to put to them, if one of them was locked in a room with a big black plague rat, that hadn't eaten for some time, (they say some rats grow as big as cats), and it was an aggressive male with vicious teeth, who wasn't afraid to bare them, as well as screech fiercely; and just to even things up a bit, the dichotomist was offered the use of a baseball bat to be found in the room...Would the superior being try to reason with the rat about the inner satisfaction to be gained from a non violent stance, or would he or she, (and a lot of these altruistic twats are she's), edge towards the baseball bat just in case the rat made a leap for their throat, rather than wait to be bored to death? The instinct for self-preservation is a strong one, just ask any black sewer rat.

....

FOR MY HONEY PIE PRINCESS, WHOEVER AND WHEREVER SHE MAY, OR MIGHT BE. 28/7/03.

I don't know what that judge is on, the one who's just given drug dealers a licence to launder money, but I think his judgement's gone to pot! (Geddit? 'Pot', Cannabis by another name.) Because of some 'legal nicety', he's thrown 14 years of police work out the window, and cost the tax payer a minimum of £25 million; plus some of the inconvenienced drugs barons are talking of suing Scotland Yard for loss of earnings while they've been banged up. To me there's only one law, the law of right and wrong, black and white, and common sense. Take my own complicated case for instance; who can I sue for a wasted life??? Wasted in the sense that as a disabled person in a largely able bodied society, it's been a case of, as far as finding gainful employment's concerned, 'Don't bother us and we won't bother you, unless whichever political party's in power, tells us to put pressure on vulnerable people in our rapacious society'. And 'new labour' has been a stickler for keeping us disabled scroungers on our toes; if you've ever been confronted with an 18 page 'Incapacity For Work' interrogation paper, (I wonder if Gordon Brown's personally been behind this particular DSS 'booby trap'? He is Scottish after all, and they're renowned for their tight-fistedness, aren't they?), you'll have an inkling of what I'm writing about.
This government's spending billions in its attempt to tackle benefit fraud, and yet the biggest fraudsters are the super rich! Why are all governments afraid to tackle the financially obscene!?
I think I'm right when I say that the top few hundred in this country control £150 billion in private wealth; most of that wealth should be liberated for the public purse. We'd be doing them a favour, it would give the super rich their edge back; instead of wallowing around in their financially, grossly overweight, obese, corpulence; they'd come out fighting in their new fleeced, lean and mean capacity; all except the so-called duke of Westminster, who would be permanently excluded from obtaining wealth by false pretences. Oh, and J.K.Rowling as well. (So sue me J.K.)

Being a benefits scrounger's not all it's cracked up to be, no one gets their free money for nothing; take me for example. The pressures of years of lost earnings, social isolation, and an acquired sense of inadequacy, have nearly killed me. ('Dear Reader, if you've read my collected, self published work in full, do you think I've laboured my theme of social injustice too much? If you think so, and want to tell me personally, I can be found in the Access Room in Halifax Central Library, three days a week; unless my hands get too sore and stiff to use the word processor. In which case I'll be stuck at home contemplating suicide. PS, I'll sign your copies of my work if you track me down.)

But if, in our 'blame and claim' culture, I could get legal aid to fund a case against the Employment Agency, or Manpower Services, for fobbing me off over the years, and making me feel it's all my fault, and never offering any real and constructive help to get me off benefits and into lucratively paid work, (where you didn't have to do too much toiling), I'd give it a go. It would be on a par with Franz Kafka's 'THE TRIAL' and 'THE CASTLE' all rolled into one; a labyrinthine nightmare with, at the very hub of it, a lunatic Judge who'd throw my case out for lack of street credibility, and order me to do 200 hours of community work using a pneumatic drill, because he knows my arms and hands are knackered, and the strain will kill me!! I rest my case for the defence of a defenceless man; here endeth my sixth and final collection.

(That note of optimism was struck too soon, inspiration hasn't quite finished with me; though I long for it to; there's a bit more still to come, and I'm afraid that if the mood takes me, this collection will grow and grow. There's a nice relaxing VVG overleaf to brace you for the final sprint, in which there's some rather rude bits. OO-ER! [Thanks to the quirkiness of this miraculous technology, the Vincent van Gogh prints I included, aren't displaying here, I don't know why; I'm not clued-up enough with the machinations of this particular machine. PLF, 5/6/06.])

MY HIPPY HEAVEN   12.05am 1/8/03.
(No 'plebs' will be allowed within one billion light years of it.)

Because my physical health now feels under serious threat, due to too much exposure to negative stress, I'm thinking more and more of a life yet to come; if you like, my own personal hippy heaven. Once there I'll want the life I was never allowed to have here; the one I've touched upon in so much of my writings, especially my earlier work when I was in love with love, magic, and fantasy. My hippy heaven will contain the positive, rather than the negative me; that poor soul will be left behind in this Hell on Earth.

There will be no cars, or any aspect of the combustion engine; there won't be any need. It's not going to be overcrowded. In essence it will be a place of timeless time, a series of dream sequences made real and wholesome, and peopled with me and the women who spurned me in this life of my playing the part of that Frenchman with the extra long nose, Guy de Bergerak? Who had a Master's degree in the theory of love, but was denied very much practical experience because of his facial deformity. He could inspire love in women (like myself), but they preferred to seek its fulfilment with a more conventionally featured specimen of the male gender. (As has been my own painful experience.)

Also in my hippy heaven, (not 'new age', they're a bunch of imitating wankers), the poisonous filth that's been psychically stalking me for so long now, won't be able to hide in its 'long viewing', eavesdropping lair; because its will be the only black aura on my world; like the serpent in the Garden of Eden. But unlike that first serpent, which wasn't punished for its corruption of innocence, this one will be; I'll swipe its head off, (maybe there are a lot more than one) with my tungsten edged sword, and shove it down the gaping hole in its neck. Snakes are emotionless, believe me, I don't think they know fear. They may give you fair warning (unless you tread on one) before they'll attack, but they're totally cold-blooded; Satan's foot soldiers by any other name.

My sword Excalibur, will gleam and glisten when this one act of justice has been done; this black-hearted serpent's bile won't permanently stain its shining blade. The thing's carcass will be burnt, and a giant Celtic Cross will mark the place of its execution; and the Arthurian-like weapon will be sheathed, never to be needed again, unless one of my women dares to say she's bored, or that my knob isn't big enough, and has to be sent back to Hell by having her head lopped off; which I might keep in a deep freeze, (powered by

270

solar power generated by the permanently sunny climate) in case she ever signals to me that she was wrong on both counts, and is wholly repentant.

I'll need a decent-sized, and well-scattered harem, to stop me getting bored. While waiting longingly for a visit from their lord and master, they can tend to their smallholdings, like Barbara without Tom in 'THE GOOD LIFE', (have you seen it?), and make plenty of mead, and grow some 'wacky weed' because every night will be party night while I'm around. I'll have all my favourite psychedelic sounds on hand as well, on CD of course, plus lots of vintage rock 'n' roll (on the same format), and if, from the fruits of our revelling, a baby is born, it won't have to exist in a lovelorn state, like I had to, here in Hell. It can bugger off when it's old enough, and find its own fucking paradise, the little twat.

....

I THINK I'LL GO TO THE FRINGE.   5/8/03.

I'm in need of some adventure; I think I'll go to the Edinbrough 'Fringe'. You never know, I might get caught up in the late night bingeing sessions there, and cop for some minge; (it's how modern girls describe their over-ripe vaginas.)

But of course, first I've got to get there and then sort out somewhere to stay; with beds and prices at a premium, I won't be able to afford to pay for digs. There might be late night gigs I could attend, and shop doorways I could spend a couple of nights in; but I don't have a sleeping bag to sleep in, and it could blow cold after dark, even at this time of year, a bit like Heptonstall does here.

It's a long journey either by coach or by train, I don't know if I could stand the pain of going it on my own again, especially if either form of transport was packed. I'm hacked off with playing the grim-faced stranger, with the word 'danger' implied above my head; I'd rather be seen as cool and in command instead. If I can't find an en suite room at the YMCA for a fiver a day, including tea and coffee-making facilities, how am I going to do my ablutions and get a low cost drink? Let alone something to eat? All the cafes will be full of festival types, hyping up what a marvellous time they're having, and all the shows they've seen, enough to put any loner in a mean frame of mind.

I've read that the Lady Boys of Bangkok are performing at the fest', they're supposed to be the best of the bunch. Well, I look like a punch drunk boxer when I drop my guard, maybe one of these hardened, cross dressing transsexuals could take a shine to me, and 'sponsor' me during my stay, in a purely platonic way. (I don't do tongues, cock sucking, or anal fucking.)

....

THIRD TIME UNLUCKY ON THE LOTTERY.   5/8/03.

I had a stressful week last week, last Tuesday was a really bad day; so come Saturday morning I was determined to minimise my stress level by having a 'nice' day. The sun was shining, I was up just after 8am, enough time to have a good breakfast and let my bowels sort themselves out; public toilets are so awful these days.
I'd worked out my itinerary beforehand, I'd planned to be on the 10.19 train to Halifax, having first bought two tickets for that night's 'rollover' lotto draw, and the Daily Star to get my free 7-day TV guide. No problems, I made my purchases, it came to £2.35p, and I remember thinking, 'I better put this £2 lotto ticket away before I think it's a piece of litter and throw it away'. And then there was a blip on my short term memory bank...Less than 5 minutes walk away I though, 'Now where did I put that ticket?' and I went through all my pockets and the contents of my carrier bag, but it wasn't there.
I retraced my steps to the shop, looking on the ground as I went; when I was back at the counter I asked if anyone had handed in a lost lottery ticket? Only to be met with a wry smile and the comment, 'Someone's going to be lucky then'. I must have dropped it on the shop floor before I left, thinking I'd put it in an inside pocket, and some sharp-eyed rat bag had spotted it and pocketed it; the milk of human kindness can run really thin in Todmorden. Luckily, I was able to share my tale of woe with a friend at Halifax Library's Access Room; being able to laugh about my misfortune, helped to lessen my sense of gloom. And I half jokingly said, 'Well I've got a pound left to spare so I'll buy another one on the way home, you never know, it could be third time lucky'. Needless to say, it wasn't! So I was £3 down because I'm desperate to improve my lot in life...and I missed the 10.19 train as well........

The painting I've chosen to illustrate this penultimate piece is called: WHEAT FIELD WITH CROWS, Vincent was nearing the end of his tether when he did this one; he was about four days away from shooting himself. I just go and curl up in bed when I feel gutted, at 56 I don't need to fear or cheat the grim reaper, merely avoid it for as long as possible.

SUNSET ON THE MOON.   7/8/03.

It's great being dead, you can go where you want and do what you want, with no one to bother you; if you wish to avoid some wraith who's 'dead boring', you just make yourself as light and invisible as air.
Take this evening for instance, I'm sat on a rock on the moon's surface, watching the sun disappear over the rim of the beautiful blue &green planet Earth. Being ethereal I don't need to protect my gaze from the burning orb's harmful rays, it's a huge core of gold splendour surrounded by a fiery red halo.
On Earth, its radiance will have lit up the fading evening sky, burnishing the clouds with a glowing copper hue; the sort of scene that I wanted to go on forever, when I was alive. Especially when the reddish golden glow carpeted the fields on the hills at the back of where I lived. If only I'd been free then to go gliding over hill and dale with the summer breeze blowing gently in my face.
Yes, now it's doing its thing, giving the impression of a diamond ring as it goes behind the Earth; it looks resplendent in its girth, like a flaming circle around the bejewelled planet, which it gave birth to.

The afterglow has turned the moon's surface to a dusky red; this dead satellite has temporarily come to light. Something I never understood when I was alive on Earth, indeed the thought only occurred to me in my later years; if we were in darkness, how come there was moonlight up above? I knew nothing of astronomical science, and still don't, but I always loved looking up at this most luminous beacon in our night sky. Maybe it's not only the tides it has a magnetic effect on? It was literally like a ray of hope in an increasingly diseased and polluted human atmosphere.
When I was younger I always drank wine to celebrate the full moon, but ageing and failing health eventually deprived me of this solitary pleasure; like the popular Billy Fury song said: 'Last night was made for love but where were you?' It's still a cause for grief and despair that I never got to see the moon glow in my 'baby's eyes' as we made

love beneath October skies; (not in England of course, it's far too cold), on a beach next to a shining silver sea; oh woe is me till eternity. (I hope I don't end up being dubbed the world's worst poet, being more maligned by the critics' favourite whipping boy, William Magonnigal, author of 'The Silvery Tay'. If they try putting the boot into me, I'll come back and shit all over their pate de foiegras, which probably tastes like shit anyway.)

Yes, so here I am, sifting this phosphorescent moon dust through my non-existent fingers, wondering what to do next? Now I've got the whole universe to roam in, I can't be bothered; it's all negative energy anyway. Who in their right mind would want to try and watch the sunrise beneath a sea of sulphuric acid on Neptune? Not me! I'd rather nestle in the fairy hammock of some tasty young lady's pants, causing her to smile involuntarily as my tongue licks her clitoris on a train, while my fingers, mere tendrils now, are playing where they shouldn't ought to be. Aah! This is the after life for me; giving those girls an itch that they've just got to scratch as I rummage around their pubic thatch, like a sex-crazed amoeba. I only hope this fad for shaving it all off down below, doesn't catch on too widely here, otherwise I'll have nowhere to hide, and nothing to cling on to, not even a 'clinker'

Now I can safely say this collection is complete, unless I get cursed by the demands of the muse again; even tho' I seriously don't want to. The only way I'd want to write anything now is if I was being paid to order, and there doesn't seem much chance of that happening, so......GOODBYE FOREVER!!!

(10,942 WORDS IN TOTAL with the additions I've made; this was collection No. 6, there are 2 more subsequent collections, but now I definitely feel that my work is done. Let alone 'STREETLIGHT AROMA' and 'GOD IS HOPE', plus all my diaries and other stuff. PLF, 5/6/06.

....

ADDENDUM, which is not a euphemism for 'strapadicktome.'

4/2/08. I need to flesh this collection out a bit to make it worth putting a cover on it sometime; if I can employ the help of a capable IT technician I might be able to include the colour images I downloaded off the internet by Vincent van Gogh, which are not showing up on screen in this collection right now.

The only record I have of inserting them is in my original copy of this work, which is currently languishing in tropical temperatures in my room in Thailand; I hope everything's okay there till I can go and check on things in June. I hope all my CDs haven't melted.

I've taken this first chunk of work off my blog (the one that nobody's reading): errolfinn at blogger.com, it's dated 5/1/08.

Two incidents of note: I heard on the news that a 102-year-old man from the UK, and his 87-year-old wife are emigrating to New Zealand to start a new life. He's reputed to have said, 'I'd never forgive myself if I woke up one morning aged 105, regretting not having done it.' (If all Kiwis are like the nasty piece of work I had the misfortune to know in Thailand, he'll be regretting his move very soon.)

And at the other extreme, I saw a programme on TV on Thursday night about an American woman aged 29, who'd ballooned up to 64 stone in weight, which is not far short of 900 lbs (pounds.); I've no idea what the metric equivalent would be. She was confined to her bed and lying in her own liquid excrement, and she had the gall to say that contrary to popular belief, super-size people don't smell! I'm still feeling nauseated by the recollection. I wonder how bad the smell was in the room? Only the camera operator could answer that one. She was eventually given a stomach stapling operation to stop her constant craving for food (they've come up with a fancy name for this disorder, but surely it's just rampant greed when you feel you've never had enough to eat to satisfy your gargantuan appetite? It's also called gluttony.) And ironically, her heart packed up 2 weeks after her new eating regime began, she'd already lost 56 lbs of fat.

When her enormous coffin was being lowered into the ground I thought, 'That could be an offensive weapon waiting to explode with all those gases inside building up amongst the rotting flesh and fat. In nature, huge carcasses are eaten by scavengers, but we humans deserve more dignity don't we, ha ha ha!

A 73-stone man (over 9 hundredweight) has been cut out of his house in an attempt to get help; and I'm fairly sure that when I was a lot younger, I heard of an American male who'd eaten himself up to a weight of 88 stone!!! That's well over half a ton, which would be regarded as mega fauna in the wild. I don't even know how it's physically possible for a human being to reach such obscene weights

without their hearts packing up well before they reach 11 cwt (hundredweight.)
I'd advocate that anyone who gets to 25 stone in weight should be compulsorily stomach stapled for the good of society; they can't go round blaming the food companies who produce this toxic much that they dramatically over consume, it's their own weak wills that are to blame.

....

EMPTY 'GONGS' MAKE THE MOST HOLLOW NOISE.
(This is a transcript of a letter I sent to the Halifax Courier [UK] earlier this week.)

Far be it from me to rain on anyone's parade (I'd rather send a lashing storm with thunder and lightning attached), but hasn't anyone actually pointed out to the people who accept 'honours' in the New Year's 'honours' list, that Britain no longer has an empire? And it's to our great shame and regret that we ever did have one?
What's the point of being made a 'member' of the British Empire if it doesn't exist? At the very least they should rename this out-dated tradition: 'The British Commonwealth.'
If they ever offered me a 'gong' for my long suffering service and devotion to lost causes, such as my futile efforts to carve a cosy little niche for myself in the increasingly fast-paced and cut-throat literary world, (I write acerbic poetry and observations on life; I have a collection called 'COPING WITH MADNESS' available as a Sony Reader download on Lulu.com at a very reasonable price) I'd say, 'No thank you, your royal ma'amship, can I have some money instead? After all, you've got loads of dosh, ain'cha.'

PS. Did you know that the word 'royal' rearranged spells 'loyar', which sounds a lot like 'lawyer' doesn't it? And we all know what robbing bastards they are, don't we.

....

TROUSER SNAKE CHARMING RED.
(To the tune of, 'You are the sunshine of my life.' 3/1/08.)

You are the sulphur in my farts (the evil wind)
And the broken bit in my heart. (I've forgotten how the next bit of the song goes.)
You are the wind and rain that had me down

And the black cloud that brings out the tears in my clown.

You are the evil in my good and the reason I'm always
'pulling my pud' instead of 'dipping my wick'; you are
'Reggie no dick'. ('Reggie no dick' was the evil nickname that
allegedly goaded Reginald John Christie to go on to become a
murdering necrophiliac.)

You are the reason I talk to myself and for me
Still being on the shelf aged 61 (bar 2 months.)
You engineer my short term memory lapses and my relapses
Into surly depression.
Maybe you're even the reason why I hate my face, why I think
It's a big disgrace to the human race?

Are you the reason why I never got anywhere in a world
That doesn't care about me? Are you the reason why I eat 'sour
Grapes' for breakfast, dinner and tea, and pee out burning hot
Fish hooks while shitting out red hot embers from up my arse?
Are you the reason why my whole life's been a farce?

You're the poison in my blood that seeps into my brain, making
Everything look grey and of no matter; you're old fanny batter.

You've inveigled your way into my heart and into my soul,
I just hope you never worm your way up my bum hole.
Suffer the little incubi and succubae to come unto me (and live
In my guts), for with out me they would feel alone and abandoned,
Unnaturally.

Errol Finn, the anti, anti Christ.

....

COMING TOO SOON.   31/1/08-1/2/08.

Coming too soon thwarts your swoon of ecstasy,
If you want to get low down and dirty and have your girl
Gagging for more and more, your jaw's going to hit the
Floor if you're groaning 'Oh no!' after one or two pushes,
And into your condom your semen gushes.

And the older you get, that craving for sexual excess doesn't
Get any less (well not in my case anyway.)
Tho' with my sore back and sore hips, the only way I could part
Any taker's vaginal lips with my ramrod would be with her on top,
Moaning 'Don't stop, don't stop,' as she bears down on my
Thrusting shaft with her hungry clitoris; we're both going to be
Really pissed off if it's over before it's even got started.

If I tried Viagra I could have her love juice flowing like Niagara
As I stayed erect for hours, golden showers and her brown flower
Opening to excess; you only think about the mess when the passion's
Worn off.

As to the undecipherable enigma of what women want, I don't think
They know what they want from one mood swing to the next.
They can behave like a sex-crazed tramp one night and
Want to be seen in pristine white the next.
How can you trust the logic of a creature who balks at being seen
In her underwear in her home setting by 'prying eyes', and yet
Is perfectly happy to be seen on the beach almost stark naked!?
The biggest mistake men make is to trust a woman's
Instinctive judgement, it'll leave you as crazy as them if you do.

Gone are the days of 'Sugar and spice and all things nice' when it
Comes to defining what little girls are made of, all that disappears
With the onset of puberty; their looks and allure are a cunning
Device to reel you in and ultimately, turning your heart to
Stone when they throw you out, minus your underwear.

I'd love to play them at their own Machiavellian game,
Inflicting as much emotional pain as I could, even
Extracting goods to the value of the damage that's been done
To me over the last 60 years. But here's another example of
Female logic, a man can be old, ugly and rich and still be considered
'Marriage material'. The same man, if he's old, ugly and poor,
better not cast an admiring glance at any woman under 50 for fear
of being labelled a lecherous old beast.

I think at this point I'd best let the rest of my
Misogynistic thinking remain internal, not that I hate women so
Much as want to adore them and having them opening their
Legs only to me; but my pulling equipment's all wrong,
And I'm a bit long in the tooth now.

Much better for me to concentrate on music and the arts,
Leave fantasising about teenage tarts to younger and sturdier
Loins than mine; although the thought of a lovely young
Lolita still appeals to me. Such thinking is so un PC, but who
Are the thought police trying to control me and my libido?
Have they not heard of the Satyr and the Nymphet?

The Bonobo chimp, one of two strains of our closest ancestor,
Uses sex as a greeting, no-one's too old or too ugly to be left out
Of a welcoming grope; at what stage of our own evolution did we
Part company with this sound philosophy?

....

FASTER THAN THE SPEED OF LIFE
(MAELSTROM.) 8/2/08.

Faster than the speed of life lived at today's turmoil-ridden pace,
Comes the frenetic egg-and-spoon race of uncertainty.
'Will there be an eternity after I die, measurable to the one
that was here before I was born? Will Heaven come with rules
attached, or will I be better off for free speech in Hell as I roast
over an open fire being fuelled by a black imp?'
(Can you say 'black imp' anymore?)

On the grounds that if you don't say anything offensive,
Anything offensive will go away; try saying that to totalitarian
Islamist fascist scum who believe that no act of evil is too low to
Achieve their aim of murdering and maiming a population into
Submission. Two weeks ago in Bhagdad, extremist militants
Used two severely mentally handicapped women as suicide bombers,
Detonating the devices they'd strapped to them by remote control
As they mingled in crowded markets. The last death count of this
Heinous action that I heard was 99.

Perhaps a new low in human evil here, is a man on trial for
Murdering an 18-year-old girl, sexually assaulting her corpse
After it was repeatedly stabbed. And who could forget the monster
Who sexually abused a 3-month-old baby? This sack of human filth
Is currently languishing in prison when, in all sense of justice, he
Should be hung, drawn and quartered, and his monstrous remains

Fed to the pigs.
('That's a bit harsh and judgemental isn't it? It's not very nice
either.')

Phil Fletcher-Stokes.

....

OLD MAN RIVER.   8/2/08.

I've loved this old American Musical song since I was a boy
And first heard it on the radio. I especially love the lines:
'You an' me, we sweat an' strain, body's all achin' an' racked
with pain, tow that barge, lift that bail, you get a little drunk
an' you land in gaol. I get weary an' sick o' tryin', I'm tired
o' livin' but feared o' dyin', but Old Man River he just keeps
rollin' along.'

It must have been fate letting me know I was in for a rough time
Of it in my life, but I couldn't see it back then at the tender age of
Ten.
Sight, or rather a lack of enough of it, being the operative word;
If you're totally blind you know the dilemma you're in and you can
Choose to deal with it in whatever way you can. If you're 'severely
Sight impaired' (the current 'correct' terminology), you're in a
Different ball game. You can see well enough what you want,
But you're not necessarily going to get it.

In my case it's always been very attractive females with bubbly
Personalities. Ever since I was a child wearing bulbous specs and
With a rampant squint, I've loved being around them; not the best
Advert for 'marriage material' I suppose. I've paid a heavy price
For my love of the ladies, I've been cut to the quick more times
Than 'Soft Mick' (severely mentally impaired), and my physical
Health is now in ruins. But I still have a burning desire to find a
'soul mate', my fate has got to answer for.

Phil Fletcher-Stokes.

....

VALENTINE'S DAY. 8/2/08.

I think they should do away with Valentine's Day in this
Politically correct age, because it's offensive to those of us
Who've never had, or are ever likely to receive one of these
Coveted love tokens.

'Roses are red, violets are blue, your love life is deader than
a tramp's vest with no lice in it, and so will you be soon, you
sack of reeking poo.' (Now who sent me that one I wonder?)

I think I sent it to myself when I was 21, now another 40 years
Have gone by in a maelstrom, and I haven't had another one
Since. The emotional pain hurts worse than pincers being clamped
On the end of your nose, or feeling like the tendons in your toes have
Locked and won't unlock.

I've said this before, but what purpose do ugly people like me serve?
Is it to make the beautiful ones feel more secure? Quite often
Beautiful girls will go round with an ugly friend, not doing that
Friend any favours.
When I was young and really vulnerable I tagged on to a couple
(man and wife) who to me were physically stunningly good-looking.
I was staggered to learn a few years down the line from the wife,
That she'd always fancied her uncle who, the one time that I met
Him, was as plain as a male Jane, and not entirely visually unlike me.

We had the type of affair where you wouldn't want to go there,
Believe me. I got very little out of it, not even requited desire.
She became an alcoholic and I a willing drinking partner. It
Helped to case my loneliness and boosted my crippled ego to be seen
Out with a lovely-looking lady.

But she always went back to her hubby when she sobered up in the
Cold light of day, and I was left to pick up the pieces of my

Pointless life until the next time she felt like playing away from home.
I suppose I was lucky that her partner wasn't a psychotic fiend,
He was my best friend after all. We used to talk about this crappy
Situation quite candidly, and quite honestly I think I did him a
Favour; her mood swings were so severe he was glad to see the back
Of her for a day or two. He knew she'd always go crawling back
To be let into the marital home, and their reconciliation's would be
Tempestuous…he told me that as well.
That woman really unmanned me, I did say I hoped
She'd rot in Hell. But she had the looks that I love, and since her
A few look-alikes have crossed my path with similar results.
Leaving me with a broken heart and a desire to end it all.
Ten years ago there was one who loved me by proxy as it were,
Using me as a catalyst while deluding herself she loved someone
Else. When I asked her to leave him and be with me, she wouldn't,
So I had to drive her out mentally. The next time I saw her a week
Later, she looked dejected and was being comforted by the man
She now knew she wasn't in love with. Serves her right, the
Demented cow!

Phil Fletcher-Stokes.

....

3 OF A KIND.   14/2/08.
(State sponsored sadism? Human rights abuse? I'd love to watch
these on subscription TV for as long as it would take to reach a final
solution; all proceeds [after running costs have been deducted] to go
to the family's of the victims of these inhuman atrocities.)

I wonder what would happen if the Soham murderer (Ian Huntley
for any foreign readers who may one day read this) and the brute
beast who's just been caged for sexually abusing and murdering his
54-day-old daughter, as well as the monster who sexually abused a 3-
month old baby girl he was supposed to be baby-sitting, and posted
his exploits on the internet, were put into a 3 bunk cell together with
no access to the outside world: no TV, no radio, no books, no papers;
the only concession to comfort a flush toilet without seat or lid, more
for their gaolers convenience than theirs. No drawers to put anything
in and no hooks to hang anything on, especially themselves; and
being issued with the most basic harsh food and liquid (preferably
the type that would make them do smelly farts a lot), with the menu

never varying, only the times of delivery through a steel hatch in the cell door, lockable from the outside, altering so they'd never know when it was coming, they wouldn't be allowed watches. Lights would be on 24-7 along with suicide watch and obviously, CCTV.

There would be no wash basin, soap or shaving gear; thay and their cell would be hosed down once a week with a cold water jet, any resistance would be met with a jolt from an electric baton, and no ailments would be treated.

All guards dealing with them would be dressed in black with black helmets and visors, making no verbal contact whatsoever. The aim of this exercise would be for these 3 creatures to die as excruciatuingly as possible, as soon as possible.

But of course, this only my own personal perspective, I heard that the Yorkshire Ripper got paid £200,000 compensation for losing the sight of an eye after being attacked a few years ago. Who says crime doesn't pay?

Imagine how these 3 inhuman monsters (like Komodo Dragons) would fare at feeding time as the limited amount of food and liquid was pushed into their cell twice a day, never at set times? Judging by the photograph I saw of the brute beast who's just been sentenced to life imprisonment for the sexual molestation and murder of his 7-week-old daughter, I'd say he'd soon come out as top predator. No action would be taken to intervene in any fights that might break out, even if one of them bit a nose or ear off the other ones.

Obviously there would be outrage and protest at such extreme TV, along the lines of, 'What kind of society have we become to allow ourselves to wallow in such barbarity'?, etc. But these 3 monsters forfeited any claim they might have had to humane treatment when they commited their inhuman, heinous crimes. If they'd been mad dogs savaging children, they'd have been destroyed on the spot.

Such instant justice is too easy for these 3, they need to know what it feels like to really suffer. And if this scenario was actually happening, I'd bet that they'd be thinking, 'Sooner or later this is going to stop, they're going to step in and say, 'Right you scum, you've been punished enough now.' But imagine their increasing terror when they realised it wasn't going to stop until all 3 of them were dead? Possibly as a result of gangrene from wounds incurred from bitten off noses and ears? The stench would be horrendous, a foretaste of the Hell that their blasted souls were inevitably going to.

The Yorkshire Ripper has never really paid for his crimes, he's even had a string of female fans willing to marry him! (I've never inspired that level of love and loyalty from a female, maybe if I'd gone out and whacked a few of them over their turkey-brained heads I'd get the

affection I crave. Oh no! Now I'll probably get a contract-killing price put on my head by ladies who look a lot like the very mannish looking KD Lang, and other members of the Lesbian Avengers posse.)
I don't know if the Soham murderer has received any sympathetic attention? And as for the other 2 horrors…? Being burnt alive would be fitting retribution for all 4 of these monsters in human guise; I bet they would squeal like pigs about to have their throats cut, and the stink of burning pork would be enough to put you off pig products for the rest of your life.

Phil Fletcher-Stokes, the angel of death to evildoers.

....

I'VE NEVER EVEN SAID 'HELLO' TO A MEANINGFUL RELATIONSHIP, ONLY 'GOODBYE TO LOVE.'
(Did Karen Carpenter have a subconscious death wish all along?)

Did you know that Karen Carpenter, the singer whose golden voice could soothe the most savage of psyches, went from a healthy 120 pounds in weight to a skeletal 78 pounds (she was 5ft 4ins) while in the grip of anorexia nervosa? I know I didn't until a few years ago; and now I've just read a book called@ THE CARPENTERS, THE UNTOLD STORY, by Ray Coleman, Boxtree Books, 345 pages, that states she died of a heart attack after making a good recovery from this eating disorder. This because she'd abused her body for 7 years prior to her death in 1983, aged 33. She'd misused thyroid tablets for some time to increase her metabolic rate to aid weight loss, and she was also taking an incredible amount of laxatives as well, it's a miracle she ever got off the toilet.
I was aware of the Carpenters in the '70s, I picked up on 'GOODBYE TO LOVE', (the same way as I honed in on 'What Becomes Of The Broken-hearted?') because of the song's pertinent lyrics, they seemed very relevant to my own lovelorn situation.
I was still heavily into being a hippy (lots of hair and hallucinogenic drugs, as well as loads of booze and roll-up fags; that was my definition of being a hippy in the suburbs. I always wanted to join a commune but I could never find one; and I've subsequently gleaned that they're not necessarily the havens of 'free love' I thought they were at the time. More likely to involve endless prickly meetings about whose turn it was meant to be on the washing up rota, and why

were they trying to get out of it all the time? As well as who was using too much patchouli oil because it was stinking the place out.)
I remember saying to a 'friend' at the time that 'Goodbye To Love' came out that this record was meant for me, what a prophetic remark that was; 36 years later I'm still on my own.
It's only as my state of loneliness and isolation has worsened, that I've picked up on the unique quality of Karen Carpenter's voice appeal to the lost and lonely in the sad songs she sang, reflecting her own sense of spiritual despair, (she said to her therapist once, 'Quite often when the lights go out after the performance, I feel like nothing.') She was on a par with Marilyn Monroe, Marilyn was a screen icon/goddess due to her looks and sexual chemistry on screen; Karen Carpenter had a similar magnetic attraction due to her singing voice. Both of these hypnotic women endured less than fulfilling personal lives, both ending tragically when they were still comparatively young. Marilyn Monroe's death is still shrouded in conjecture, whereas Karen Carpenter's seems to have been brought about as a direct result of her eating disorder.
One of my favourite pastimes is lying in bed listening to the radio on earphones. On the coldest winter night I can snuggle under my duvet with just the top half of my head sticking out and earphones wedged into my ears. On some occasions I've actually fallen asleep while indulging myself this way. This surprises me because the sound is directly inside my head and yet my brain cuts it out completely. After the last time this happened I was prompted to write: 'If death is as painless as dreamless sleep then I have nothing to fear...except a dreamless sleep for all eternity.'
So far I've only got a DVD of the Carpenters most well known songs, 16 in all; I love 'Ticket To Ride' 'Rainy Days And Mondays' 'Superstar', etc, (the awful Amy Shitehouse with her horrible, pretentious, over-exaggerated 'singing' style could learn a lot of lessons from Karen's unaffected, heartfelt delivery.) My favourite upbeat Carpenters track is 'Calling Occupants Of Interplanetary Craft'. I'm thinking of buying a load of Carpenters CDs to listen to in bed on my earphones on my personal CD player; maybe I'll drift off into a dreamless sleep during one of Karen's particularly sad renditions...

PS. Here in Halifax, England, I've just spotted a street sign pointing to 'THE SAMARITANS', it's on King Cross Street just before you get to Bull Green roundabout.

Phil Fletcher-Stokes.

....

PERFERATIONS ON ROLLS OF KITCHEN TOWEL AND ROLLS OF TOILET PAPER THAT SEPARATE PERFECTLY EVERY TIME YOU PULL A FEW SHEETS OFF (IN THE CASE OF THE TOILET PAPER), AND DON'T RIP IN ALL THE WRONG PLACES LIKE WHAT TENDS TO HAPPEN WITH THE CHEAPER STUFF (AS WELL AS YOUR FINGERS GOING THRU' IT [AGAIN WITH THE TOILET PAPER, GUARANTEEING THAT YOU'RE GOING TO HAVE TO WASH YOUR HANDS AFTERWARDS]), IS THE BEST THING SINCE MEDIUM SLICED WHITE BREAD WHERE ALL THE SLICES ARE OF A UNIFORM THICKNESS, AND NOT WITH ONE SLICE MEDIUM THICK AND THE NEXT ONE BEING ALMOST THIN SLICED. (WHY DOES THAT HAPPEN?) 22-23/2/08.

A wielded baseball bat will cause severe damage to the human body no matter where the blows land, the blows will cause internal damage to organs and blood vessels as well as break bones and shatter skulls; a sustained attack by one or more assailants will definitely kill the unfortunate recipients/s, it's a lightweight but deadly weapon. Because I'm cursed to eke out my existence among the rougher elements of 'the common people' (like right now for instance thru' no fault of my own, [and some of these people are really rough in this block of flats I'm in, as well as the immediate neighbourhood]), I have a recurring paranoid fantasy about a bunch of these low IQ, low achiever types smashing their way into my flat, using baseball bats to smash my double glazed kitchen windows, or the slim glass panel in my front door so they can reach an arm in and unlock the door, using the key in the lock (I now remove it for safe keeping and I also keep a hammer near my bed so that if I do hear the sound of shattering glass, I can leap out of bed and break a few fingers), wearing combat jackets, ski masks and hoods, screaming at me as they demolish everything that's breakable before starting on me; and even if they don't kill me I'll be in plaster for a long time to come.
Where and how does a 16-year-old girl learn to hang herself? The latest teenage suicide in Bridgend, South Wales was just that; and

286

she didn't do it in her bedroom either, she chose to go out and hang herself from a tree. They showed a photograph of her face on the news, she was lovely-looking in that Celtic way, like Catherine Zeta Jones might have looked at that age perhaps.

She's the 17th in this extraordinary batch to take their own life in the town in a little over a year; these young people have given up on life before they've even dipped a foot into its murky waters, commiting acts of bravery and cowardice at the same time. With hanging, if you get the drop wrong you can decapitate yourself as well, more gruesome mess for others to clean up after you.

These young people probably stood a much better chance of having some real quality in their lives than I ever did, due to disability. I hope some of their organs have been donated or compulsorily taken to help others less selfish than themselves; or will they have beaten the new law coming in that presumes that unless you specifically state otherwise, at the time of your death organs can be removed for transplants (do eyes, skin and limbs count as organs?)

What is 'quality of life' in today's mucked-up world? Does grimly hanging on in the hope that something better will turn up count? Even though the odds are stacked firmly against you? It's the end of the world for me as I grew up to know it, in this country anyway; I feel like an alien in my own homeland, fighting daily ennui, lassitude and general despair at a lifetime filled with bitter disappointments, in the hope that aged 65, I'll be able to enjoy a long old age in a country far away from here on my UK state pension, plus any savings I might have.

My dream is to look for a woman with Eurasian features and long black hair, at least half my age, to share my 'wealth' and possibly halt the inevitable decline in my physical health.

Phil Fletcher-Stokes

....

Minimalism, mark 2: 'Are you feeling lucky punk?' 'No.' 'Oh!'

Nowadays we all expect to be lucky, I know a lot of my disappointments are due to this unrealistic expectation from life, but I do have a lot more to be thankful for than the majority of people on this overcrowded planet of ours, thank fuck. 26/2/08

....

PERTINACIOUS PERSPICACIOUS PERPENDICULAR
PERPETUAL PERPETRATION. (My 61st birthday ode to myself.
27/2/08.)

The earthquake we had in the UK in the early hours of this morning,
was 2 million times less strong than the 2004 tsunami; thank Christ
for that. When my bed shook violently and me as well, I thought I
was under a satanic attack.
Martin Luther was called a 'prating pig' because of his bad guts (or
at least he was in a television play I saw more years ago than I can
remember, and that crude reference to his 'evil wind' problem is all
that I remember about the play; I was christened C of E but it means
nothing to me, the only religion I believe in is freedom of the spirit;
and as for our current arch bishop, Rowan Williams [who looks like
the granddad of 'The Modern Parents' in VIZ comic], he's not even
English, he's Welsh, the beardy-wierdie old fart; now where was I?)
and he founded a whole new religion, all I want to do is sell a few
million copies of my 'product' so I can live on 'easy street.'

With violence and dumbing down becoming the norm,
I don't wish to conform to this status quo.
You never know when your time's up, when you're going to be
Forced to go, either to paradise or down below.

I watch cookery programmes with disdain,
Celebrity chefs are a pain in the brain; I wonder what they'd make
Of this as a cordon bleu breakfast suggestion:
'Put some soft margarine spread on a bed of sliced bread,
and then spread some jam or marmalade on top of it.
Have as many slices as you like, washed down with a big hot mug
Of 'Rosie Lea'. Yummy!'

I'll very soon be 61, I'd like to surprise myself with a lavish gift,
I'm a bit miffed because I can't think of one. Do you know I could
Easily waste a thousand quid on renting a high class tart and having
Some fun for the night; if my dodgy guts weren't the blight

Of my love life I might well have given it some serious consideration.

Masturbation's a much cheaper option and there's no one to nag you
After you've come too soon, moaning, 'What about me?' Like me,
You can turn over and say, 'Go and fuck yourself, it's what I have to
Do.'

When you live in a dumbed-down, 'don't offend anyone' atmosphere
Like we do, otherwise the anally retentive, politically correct posse
Will be after you to force you to learn the error of your ways,
It doesn't pay big bucks to say what you like, except on TV,
Why should those bastards get away with it and not me?
(I'm talking so-called new wave, modern comedy here.)

Patience should be a virtue, instead of placing all your misguided
Faith in luck; mine's all Mickey Mouse and Donald Duck anyway,
With a bit of Pluto thrown in; I'm only indulging myself in this
Direction to spin out this collection, and once I've started
I don't like to stop until I've filled up 2 sides of handwritten A4.

Most people live purposeless lives it's been cynically said,
I'm hemmed in by the living dead who, unlike me, seem to accept
Their limitations (living on benefits with a spot of rubbish crime
thrown in); I've always had unreachable expectations from my
Life: good fortune, a beautiful wife and a successful writing career;
My biggest fear is dying in obscurity. (It's getting closer all the time.)

One more long verse to go, I've no idea how to keep it
Light and fluffy, cute and cuddly. There's some kind of grisly gripe
Going on in my lower abdomen, as if I'd swallowed a prickly pear
With its skin on; this interspersed with copious amounts of air
Being regurgitated. At least this air doesn't smell, unlike the
Hellish stenches that come out my 'ass' ('Oh please don't offend
Our sensitivities, we're so hybridly refined our nerves [as well as our
nostrils] can't stand it.')
Well what do you think it's like for me? I've been stuck in this
Lonely limbo for 22,273 days. I'd have been better off dying on a
'Purple Haze' acid trip aged 23 from a lack of oxygen to the brain,
But then I'd never have lived long enough to write my catalogue of
Pain...would I?
(Oh no! I've just broke wind of the most sulphurous kind, at least
My mind and body feel a bit lighter now, until this noxious gas
Builds up again...and again...and again.

Phil Fletcher-Stokes, the last of my undistinguished line.

....

SYLLOGISMISTIC SOLIPSISTIC SILOLOQUY
(Try wrapping your tonsils round that lot.)   2/3/08

I spend so much time by myself, inside myself, that myself is the only known reality I can rely on. I think that anyone who enjoys wordplay and/or 'brain training' will appreciate the mental effort required to get your head round: 'Syllogismistic Solipsistic Soliloquy.' I know my own crumbling brain has been struggling with 'syllogism' (it's got 'gism' in it, heh heh heh!), earlier misspelling it as 'soggylism'. (I've added 'istic' for effect, I doubt if anal retentives would allow it, same as in 'solipsistic'.)
I came across 'syllogism' by chance in my dictionary, which quite often happens to me; I start off looking up the meaning of one particular word and end up by getting really captivated by other words that catch my eye. 'Syllogism': 'form of logical reasoning consisting of two premises and a conclusion'. 'Premise': 'statement assumed to be true and used as basis of reasoning'. I think I've fulfilled my obligation to 'syllogism' in the first two lines of this piece. I think my title knocks spots off 'Surrealistic Pillow' (title of a Jefferson Airplane LP) into a cocked hat. (I can't find a definition for 'cocked hat' in my scaled down for everyday use dictionary.)
When I say my brain is crumbling I'm not sure if I'm being serious or not; I know for a fact I put 'duel fuel' in an email to my energy supplier last Friday without even noticing it was wrong (it should have been 'dual' if that's not insulting your intelligence too much?), it, only occurred to me today, Sunday; likewise 'palindrome' and 'paradigm', I've been confusing their meanings, and even now after just looking it up I can't remember what 'paradigm' means, only 'palindrome'.
Am I over-taxing my mind or is this the thin end of the wedge on the slippery slope to Alzheimer's, the death of the brain? Or even the human version of 'mad cow disease' could be devouring my brain cells at a rate of knots?

Phil Fletcher-Stokes.

....

HOW SYCOPHANTIC CAN YOU GET?
(With a strong emphasis on the 'syc'.) 3/3/08.

Last week on 'Lily Allen & Friends' (or was it the week before?)
(BBC3, Tues, 10.35pm), this young lady confessed to having oral sex
when she was 14, ('sucking her teacher's cock' was how she put it).
Can you imagine the furore that would have ensued if a man had said
he'd had oral sex with a 14-year-old girl? I've heard no outcry from
Miss Allen's confession, and on Tuesday night's 'show', apart from
using the 'f' word quite a lot, she regaled her audience with the fact
that when she should have been doing an encore, she was stuck on a
toilet doing a massive crap; I only watch this 'modern toss' so I can
keep in touch with how young people are thinking. If you saw Lily
Allen at a do, you'd think she looked like butter wouldn't melt, but
once you got to know her a bit you'd be in for a rude
awakening…literally. I wonder if she'll ever live to regret such
intimate frankness, I know Denise van Outen did, and as for
Charlotte Church, the foul-mouthed cow…
Last night (?) I sat through 'Dawn Gets Naked', again on BBC3; I
don't know who Dawn Porter is, she looks a lot like Lily Allen, and
this was the kind of programme that would have ancient feminists
like Germain Greer hanging up her ball cutters in disgust and
despair. And as for 'Pulling'? on BBC2, this 'hot comedy' is merely
role reversal, young women behaving as obnoxiously as young men
are reputed to do, and the young men involved in this appalling
travesty of humour, behaving like chaste young ladies.
Dawn never got naked in an up-close and personal way, she dithered
about for nearly an hour, and the most that I could make out was her
flashing her 'threepenny bits' (tits) in a strip joint full of 'lessas' very
briefly. This rubbishy 'show' climaxed with an open topped busload
of females riding round London, whooping about how liberated they
were because they were exposing themselves; you'd beg most of them
to keep their clothes on, they were so awfully out of shape.
When a man gets accused of rape he's named before the case even
gets to court, in many cases the accuser's identity isn't revealed
publicly. I used to think that women are the weaker sex, weak willed

creatures without minds of their own; it's what I was brought up to believe, I suppose Marilyn Monroe films didn't help to dispel this myth until it was too late for me.

Now I know that the difference between men and women isn't that great, most women weigh a lot less than men and that's where the sexual inequality comes in. But the idea that women are going to swoon and faint away at a bit of strong language or seeing male genitals is a farce; it's just their psychology you have to be wary of. Yet the law still treats them as the weaker sex whose modesty and vulnerability has to be protected. I say BOLLOCKS! to that.

Phil Fletcher-Stokes.

....

I VOW TO FLEE MY COUNTRY (the first realistic chance I get.) 1-2/3/08.

An absent-minded man who loved reading books bought a Euro millions lotto ticket on 28th September 2007; he felt lucky, which was uncharacteristic for him. Almost as soon as he'd bought it he began to feel guilty about wasting his precious benefit money. Still, what the hell!

He scoured charity shops for books by his favourite authors, like Camus and Gerald Kersh and Emile Zola. He was building up quite a collection in his one-bedroom social housing flat; he kept them in an old bookcase he'd spotted in a second-hand shop and paid 20 quid for (including delivery.) He never paid more than £1.50p for a book, and he preferred old ex-library hardbacks. He loved the smell they gave off, like a village library smell, old and comforting and reassuring. He savoured the bookish odour most strongly when he staggered into bed after a good drink (in the house, he never went out) on a Saturday night; he hazily felt he was entering the church of the written word.

He'd become totally isolated in a hostile community, he was a man over a certain age living alone; he looked weird due to having to wear bulbous-lensed glasses because his eyesight was so weak. A perverse series of events had driven irreversible rifts between him and his relatives, and now his mother was dead he wasn't that bothered; as for friends and romance? Books were his friends, the only friends he needed or valued. He'd always loved women but they didn't love him, so he'd gradually managed to quell and quash his libido into complete submission; besides, there were romantic heroines in literature that (who?) he could love instead.

He'd just read a novel by Emile Zola called 'THE KILL', that had a really in-depth theme of a young society woman in Paris in the latter part of the 19th century, and her untimely disillusioned end.

He admired the work of Emile Zola a lot more than he did of Charles Dickens, apart from Oliver Twist, A Christmas Carol, and his Christmas tales

He sometimes pondered on how writers like Zola found the time to develop such detailed insights into human nature and behaviour, while at the same time turning out massive amounts of work, all written in longhand. He'd learned that M. Zola had died aged 62, not from exhaustion but from toxic fumes from a fire in his bedroom, due to the chimney being capped; foul play wasn't entirely ruled out. The subject of this very short story had difficulty in keeping up a daily diary, so monotonous was his existence; the entries he did make were mainly about finds he'd made in the Charity shops, or about how awful the weather was, matching that of his 'empty' life.

On the day he'd bought his Euro millions lotto ticket, he'd also bought a 'job lot' of 4 old books for a fiver; despite his debilitating sense of low self esteem he could still haggle a bargain on a good day. Like he pointed out to the volunteer assistant in the shop, 'These books have been on your shelves for months.'

There was nothing special about them, he just liked the fact they'd been published up to 80 years ago; they were aged and mellow. Unlike the brash product that was mass produced today, which in his ignored opinion hadn't the feel of longevity about it; nowadays when you picked up a copy of a new book it had no weight, literally. Hardbacks felt as light as paperbacks. Still, when you realised that execrable dross like Harry Potter was churned out by the million, it figured; there was no way he'd ever collect that kind of lightweight rubbish.

Back in his bedroom he was in his element, standing before his beloved bookcase; he was glossing through one of his purchases: 'I WAS AN UNDERTAKER'S CHIEF MOURNER FOR 50 YEARS (the one who walks in front of the funeral procession in black top hat and garb) AND HAVE LIVED TO TELL MY TALE', by a Mister Al Zimers, fascinating. He'd noted a chapter headed, 'WHEN A CORPSE SITS UP AND GROANS', and decided he'd get back to it later; he plucked a piece of paper out of his pocket and used it as a bookmark for future perusal of a topic dear to his frozen heart, death. He inserted the book into a narrowish gap on the 3rd shelf down and promptly forgot all about it.

He didn't have a TV, he thought the licence fee was extortionate and he was too scared to risk being caught by the licence people, besides, nowadays with nothing but bad news and gloom and doom everywhere, he figured that the radio was much better value and you didn't need a licence for it; he spent a lot of time in bed (saving money on the heating) listening to it on earphones with an old personal stereo radio he had, this was an invaluable piece of kit for him.

Not having a TV and not being at all clued up about' teletext', it would never have occurred to him to check his lotto numbers, even if he'd remembered buying a ticket; like hibernating animals he shut himself down mentally for the long winter ahead, 6 months of semi darkness and evil weather. He'd never know that that piece of paper he'd stuck inside that book held the key to untold wealth, namely nearly 7 million pounds!!! He'd won and didn't even know it, he never even went back into the shop where he'd bought it (just in case you were thinking along those lines), and during his winter depression he ignored his books (ha ha ha!)

The ticket expired on March 26th, 2008, 6 months after it was bought, the money went back into the 'good causes' pot, the kind of good causes that would never benefit him; what a massive CHUMP this pathetic poltroon is/was; he deserved everything he got…or didn't get as this fable has pointed out, and the moral of this fable is: never go peeping tomming without a torch.

Phil Fletcher-Stokes.

....

If it weren't for this debilitating sickness I'd take what life throws at me philosophically; knowing I'll get my reward in the end.   3/3/08.

THE FATAL VIRUSES WITH AN UNHEALTHY DEATH WISH.

This is a tough topic for me to attempt because my medical knowledge is very limited indeed. The point I'm trying to make is that when a viral disease has killed its victim host, it's trapped inside the corpse and must die with it, preferably by cremation.

Is a tumour a blind, unthinking organism? They're the most loathsome manifestation of self-destroying horror, sometimes growing to horrendous sizes on their victims' bodies, with teeth and hair inside them when they're opened up. Cancerous tumours, white blood cell eating cancer; pancreatic cancer killed my mother 22 years ago aged 62, she was a reformed heavy smoker, only giving up 12 months before she died. She used to inhale the smoke right down inside her, maybe that's how she got the killer disease? Though there's a lot of cancer on her side of the family, as well as the eye disease that I've got, 2 male cousins and a nephew suffer from it as well.

I suffer a lot from gut-wrenching depression, the abdominal pain can be agonising, like something gripping your intestines and squeezing them hard. There's also the emotional anxiety of depression; in the past I've called it 'soul cancer'. I think the poet and writer Sylvia Plath suffered from this particularly evil ailment (soul cancer). She touches on utter desolation in 'JOHNNY PANIC AND THE BIBLE OF DREAMS'; a sensation of vast mausoleums echoing with emptiness (or is that me?)

And her late poetry encapsulated a cosmic awareness of being far removed from mere mortals (no such luck for me on that one, alas.) The final injustice she's had to suffer is being stuck out in a burying field in Heptonstall, you have a bit of a job locating her burial plot, and it must literally be like the icy blasted heath in the winter time for her mortal remains to be mouldering in.

Ted Hughes on the other hand, is resting in peace down in sunny Devon, with his soul luxuriating in Heaven maybe, the miserable old goat.

Phil Fletcher-Stokes.

....

PREFACE TO THE SECOND EDITION OF THERESE RAQUIN.
By Emile Zola. 1868.

I naively thought that this novel could do without a preface. Being accustomed to speaking my mind out loud and to stress the least detail in what I write, I hoped that I might be understood and judged without having to explain myself further. It seems that I was wrong. The critics greeted this book with anger and indignation. Some virtuous folk, in no less virtuous newspapers, puckered their faces with disgust as they picked it up with the tongs to throw it in the fire. Even the little literary papers—those same literary papers that every evening report the gossip from bedrooms and private dining rooms— held their noses and spoke of stinking filth. I have no complaint to make about this reception; on the contrary, I'm charmed to discover that my colleagues have the sensitive feelings of young ladies. It is quite evident that my book belongs to my critics and that and that they might find it repulsive without giving me any cause for protest. What I do mind, however, is that not one of the prudish journalists who have blushed as they read Therese Raquin seems to me to have understood the novel. If they had understood it, perhaps they would have blushed even more, but at least I should now be enjoying the private satisfaction of seeing that they were disgusted for the right reason. Nothing is more irritating than to hear honest writers protest about depravity when one is quite certain that they make these noises without knowing what they are protesting about.

It is necessary therefore, for me to present my work to to these critics myself. I shall do so in a few lines, simply to avoid any misunderstanding in the future.

....

There is a few more pages of this in the book, but they're not as pertinent to my style of writing as the above extract, because even 140 years later we're still subject to 'moral' censorship; quite right too if you're peddling absolute filth, like a lot of the porno' industry is today; total depravity that will corrupt your soul if you expose yourself to too much of it. You could end up like Fred and Rose West if you've got a soul mate who is inclined to great evil.

I found this novel really groundbreaking for its period, I think Charles Dickens might have been one of the critics who would throw it on the fire, it was so outspoken for its time, and its subject matter was still largely taboo, unless the language was heavily couched in overblown 19th century writing; I'd recommend Therese Raquin to anyone to read, as well as every other Zola work, apart from THE DREAM, I couldn't finish that one, it was so full of the ethics that I despise in literature, because we all have to shit don't we?

Phil Fletcher-Stokes

....

I KNOW THAT I NEED TO LIVE, BUT WHY DO MY INSIDES FEEL LIKE THEY'RE TRYING TO KILL ME MOST OF THE TIME?
(Confessions of a scatology obsessed man.)   9-10/3/08.

I have a lot of 'borderline' medical complaints, not least my eyesight, which condition is more serious than borderline crap, it's really crap! Likewise my mental health complaints, over the last 50 years I've been suicidal with depression (I started off very young, aged 11)(I haven't really got the guts to 'top' myself.) I'm prone to bouts of paranoia, severe mood swings, unpleasant urges, hearing nasty voices, delusions of grandeur, (if the last symptom wasn't borderline I'd be expecting people to bow down to me and obey my every whim; I might even be worse than Caligula or Gilles de Rais.)

It's the same with my writing, even though I love to create, it takes a Herculean effort for me to turn out a few hundred words on any one topic; I have to drag it out like a tape worm, wriggling and hissing. But I'm 'not bovvered' anymore, this is meant to be the last piece in this collection, and this collection is the 6th out of 8; my life's work is done, I can rest easy now. One of my collections is winging its way to The British Library even as I pen this article (I'm writing it in longhand first.) It's called 'COPING WITH MADNESS', I'll soon be immortal.

It's my stomach complaints that have inspired the above title, I can't even begin to describe how awful it makes me feel at times; I'd need to have Emile Zola's descriptive powers to be able to do that. A lot of it can be put down to Irritable Bowel Syndrome, which has been described as unpleasant but not serious, except if you're suffering with it of course; it's the abdominal equivalent of migraine, and I've had that as well.

These complaints I've listed have ruined my life, women tend to treat me as an 'untouchable', and to be brutally honest, I don't blame them. They'd have to contend with my mental ups and downs as well as my physical highs and lows. Holistic practitioners take all aspects of your health into consideration when diagnosing you, not that it makes any difference to treating you; if you're having to endure a highly stressed existence like mine then you're going to suffer accordingly. Thank providence I haven't got a nut allergy.

I don't know what brought on a bowel crisis I had last Saturday, apart from the weather and ennui, but I went to the toilet as usual (at least I think I did) to deposit the first semi solid evacuation onto a sheet of kitchen towel (I hate the thought that the plebs in the flat underneath me might hear this rapid plopping sound.) My colon still felt heavy but I had a few errands to do and wanted to avoid the worst of the Saturday crush at the shops.

I felt the first sense of urgent need to go to the toilet again while I was waiting for a bus, luckily I was sitting down so it was easier to control the spasms. By the time I got back home the abdominal pressure was getting quite desperate, it was like the famous toilet scene out of 'DUMB AND DUMBER'. I just had time to grab a sheet of kitchen towel, drop my pants and sit down, and then SPLADOOSH!! This toxic mess shot out and hit the water, it was like a geyser blowing or a volcano erupting, AND THE STENCH! Not that I sat in it for very long, I flushed it away immediately. But it was there, going right up my nose like a mixture of pig and cow slurry; it took a good spray of Neutradol full strength to shift it I can tell you.

But this incident got me thinking, what if I'd been in this dire strait in the middle of Halifax town centre with all the shoppers milling about? This diarrhoea attack wasn't going to wait. Would I have had to squat down over a grid? (If I could have found one.) And let it go with my arse and bollocks hanging out? If I feel like a social pariah now, imagine how I would have felt after that!? I might even have been beaten to death by angry shoppers, though I think the stench might have kept them at bay.

Phil Fletcher-Stokes.

···

MAN INFESTED DESTINY ENNUI.

That's it, it's a good title to finish on don't you think? Like Jimi Hendrix said in a song whose title I can't remember: 'Can you see me'? And I think the answer is NO!

Phil Fletcher-Stokes.

···

This is my fifth and shortest collection, it's only about 18 pages in length; when I self published it in booklet form, I called it 'EXISTENTIALISM', dubbing myself 'a free agent in a meaningless universe'; I still have a lot of unsold copies, dating from 2004.

LIVING IN A SMALL TOWN.
11/4/03

Living in a small town has its ups
and downs, the less enterprising of
our young people moan that there's
nothing for them to do; so they smash
a shop window or two, maybe get into a
fight after a few cans of strong lager on
a Friday or Saturday night, and leave their
litter and graffiti all over the place.
And it's true, there's never a copper about
when you need one, today if I'd been one
I could have slapped instant fines on
two men, both old enough to know better
than to ride their bikes on the pavement.
In our local paper there's always something
to laugh about: 'STEW PAN CAUSED FIRE' made
me chuckle; I suppose the hapless stew maker
had to sample someone else's fare after his/hers
went up in smoke signals to the fire brigade?

The art of charcoal making is alive and well
here, it helps to absorb a tear or two.

....

A ONE THOUSAND POUND INCENDIARY DEVICE.
11/4/03

I'm glad I'm 56 in this day and age,
almost too old to care about the rage
that's everywhere; maybe I'll be able
to generate some old age rage when
it's time to draw my pension; "How am I
supposed to live on that!? There's not
enough there to feed the cat, let alone the wife.
I've worked all my life to end up on this pittance;
bang goes my remittance to the golf and bowling
club, I'll be lucky if I can afford to buy fly killer
for my roses."
Actually, if my dad's anything to go by,
extremely ancient O A Ps have never had it
so good. Free TV licence, virtually nothing
to pay for winter heat, heaven will find

it hard to compete. They'll have to offer him
unlimited mileage in his electric buggy to get him
to go up there, as well as free battery charging;
he's too busy 'larging' it down here.

....
....

ICE CREAM VAN MAN.   11/4/03

Hey, Mr Ice Cream Van Man, don't play your jingle
for me, its title has too many painful interpretations.
There's an ice cream van comes round our way
at roughly the same time every day, his jingle
plays: 'BOYS AND GIRLS COME OUT TO PLAY',
but nowadays we know they can be all too
easily spirited away by doing just that.
Our society's become a predatory one, we've put
innocence on the run; the perverts are having
fun at the nation's expense; and even though
the numbers of children killed or violated is rather small,
it's a deep-rooted cancer that affects us all.
Men who live on their own in particular.
I'd put child killers up against the wall
after making them dig their own grave,
let them rave about the infringements of their
human rights when they're roasting in Hell.

....
....

WHAT IF NO-ONE TURNS UP? 27/3/03

Well at least if no-one turns up I won't have to worry about whether
I'm going to bomb, or whether this, my first ever soiree, is going to
go down like the proverbial lead balloon, or the Titanic, with those
few present pushing and jostling each other to escape the
unmistakable odour of a giant egg-laying event.
But what if a decent-sized crowd does turn up for this, my first ever
hosted literary evening, what will I do? Hide behind the 'Dutch
courage' of a glass of wine or two? As long as I stop at two and don't
have any more, three or four and I'll be roaring at the first hint of a
whisper or a cough, (pregnant pause), "SHUT UP OR GET OUT!
CAN'T YOU APPRECIATE A CREATIVE ARTIST IS AT WORK
HERE?" And I'd sternly watch the culprits take the walk of shame,
muttering in order to save face that they've got a train to catch.
Three or four glasses of vino and I wouldn't want anyone else to
snatch the limelight away from me, I'd want to hog the non-existent
mic', perhaps even tell a joke or two, like the risqué pulling line,
"Have you got a mirror in your pocket?" "No why?" "It's just that I
can see myself inside your pants." If I tried using that as a chat up
line at my age I'd probably get a slap, especially from the militant
feminist crew. I'm best off sticking to an oily Lesley Philips

approach, with that long drawn out "HELLO, fancy a sh---sh---
sherbet dip? They've got liquorice straws and you can blow bubbles
out of them."

....
....

I'M WATCHING TOO MUCH REALITY TV BECAUSE NOT ENOUGH POSITIVE REALITY IS HAPPENING TO ME. 27/3/03.

Why can't it be me who's going off to France to start a new life, with
my beautiful, dutiful wife and boisterous but well adjusted and
happy flock; to take on a rock and a hard place in the shape of a run
down French farm, that has stubborn Gallic livestock to regain
control of? And the cunning and wily neighbours eat whole bulbs of
garlic for breakfast, before they come round to complain that your
stinking English mutt has peed on every stalk of grain on their land,
and keeps leaving an insulting calling card on their doorstep.
Or I could be a wheel clamper, the first in Tod', threatening to
harass and hamper every motorist who refuses to cough up when
parking charges are raised to an unacceptable level. Or Stoodley
Pike's first resident hermit recluse? Throwing rocks down on the
heads of those ramblers unwary enough to venture too near, "Clear
off, get away from here! This is my permanent retreat, the sheep are
my only friends; if you want to leave your green Wellies behind
they'll be much appreciated, heh,heh,heh!"
Yeah, I deserve my very own camera crew to monitor everything I
do. Look, that's me going in SAFEWAYS, scowling at all the other
shoppers. Woe betide you if you get in my way with your trolley, I'll
give you a look that says 'I know where you live and I'm going to pay
you a visit', unless you let me get to that last tube of money off
toothpaste before you, you over-fed trolley filling moron. And with
that cutting remark, I'm gone.
(I'm fairly certain, the two above pieces have been produced
elsewhere, but if something's good, it's worth a second showing, isn't
it?)

....
....

THE G-NOME PROJECT.
16-18/4/03

Is the G-Nome project short for 'garden-nome'? But then of course, a
gnome of the garden variety begins with a 'g' doesn't it? From what
my limited intelligence tells me, the g-nome project is the mapping of
human DNA,, totalling nearly 3 billion letters; there again I thought
there was only 26 in our alphabet.
What intrigues me is, why do we have differing levels of intelligence?
I mean, we go from the super human to what is, quite frankly, the
sub human, intelligence-wise. I think the vast majority of humanity is
somewhere in-between, neither super nor sub, 1 come under the
square peg in a round hole category, neither super nor sub, a bit of
an intellectual snob actually.
Will they ever be able to decipher what it is that controls the
personality and thought process? And why are some born beautiful
and others have to rely on their personalities to get by on? And what
about depression and loneliness, will they ever find a cure for these
quality of life affecting ills? If they do it will probably come too late
to help me, and the other victims of these two pernicious social evils.
I've had to submit to becoming a reluctant stoic, my every attempt to
break free from social isolation has been thwarted; mainly, as I see it,
no pun intended, by a lifelong visual handicap.
People are becoming more sympathetic now, but when I was young
and vulnerable I had to endure a lot of vicious comments, and
attitudes, from young women; I was 24 before one of them saw
beyond my thick glasses lenses and let me into her bed. And now, just
after I've made that statement about people becoming more
sympathetic, I find women are becoming more discriminating than
ever; even though there's a severe shortage of eligible, perfect males.
There are supposed to be two million more women than men in this
country, so why am I not being mobbed every time I go to the shops?
Is it because the 'sisterhood' instinctively knows that I haven't got
much cash to splash around, and that I don't drive, and live in an old
folks bungalow?
But I'm a writer you know, if I could write for the radio or the telly
I'd be loaded. Major respect goes out from me to those writers who
can churn out scripts for the soaps, (apart from EASTENDERS, it's

my least favourite, I never watch it), and THE BILL, and all the other electro-valium drivel that occupies a large amount of my time; me not having a social life to speak of.

And scathing 'black comedy' like 'BLACKADDER' and 'GIMME, GIMME, GIMME'!!! If I sat here for evermore I couldn't come up with anything comparable, my work seems to consist of parables for the lost and the lonely, and just like the statistical house that gets burgled every fifteen seconds in our crime infested country, I'm getting heartily sick of it; it's ruined my physical and mental health.

Even in Coronation Street, there now has to be a crisis of one sort or another every other week or so; Betty's hot-pot is having to take a permanent back seat; and how Emily Bishop survived a massive blow to the back of the head with an iron bar from Richard Hillman, sustaining only a mild concussion and a headache, is beyond me? If I was a writer for 'Corrie' I'd fix it so someone rammed a fog-horn down Fred Elliot's gob, broad end first, that might just shut him up, or reduce his volume.

....
....

'COUGH AND YOU'RE OFF' RAP.
18-19/4/03.

Who wants to be a millionaire? I do, ten times over. I think it's crap that programme; who wants to sit watching someone else get relatively rich in a very short space of time? Not me! Most of the contestants are smug fuckers; you can see their partners drooling when the camera focuses on them, positively drooling with avarice. I only like the poor mugs that go away with next to nothing; I wonder if there's a compilation video of those who go home with a thousand pounds or less? I suppose that's my embittered sadistic streak coming out.

I reckon all this 'coughing' court case business was a ploy to boost flagging viewing figures; I think the Ingrams and that other bloke should make a comedy record along the lines of the old John Macinroe 'THE BALL WAS OUT' smash hit, to pay off their court costs, and call it the 'COUGH AND YOU'RE OFF RAP.'

"Did you cough?" "No I didn't." "I think we should ask the audience, phone a friend, and take away two wrong answers. Bring on the dancers miming the chorus: "Did you cough, did you cough? OFF, OFF, OFF!!"
'My wife's got a deep, tickly, throaty cough, she gives the most amazing head ache-making bellowing reports, loud enough to wake the dead and inspire retorts like, "Cough like that behind me again, and I'll knock your block off with a single swipe, that'll wipe the smug smirk off your face. I bet your cough is laced with germs, who'll turn into tape worms once they're lodged inside my gut. If I ever win a million I'll put a safe distance between myself and anti social behaviourists like you..'

It's the same everywhere you go, some shmoe is in your face, "BIG ISSUE?" "No! Buzz off and take your drug resistant, tubercular cough with you. "Help the poor, help the needy?" SODDEM! I'd rather be greedy. Let them do the lottery like me; okay, so their kids won't get any tea because all the money's gone on tickets. If they get rickets they'll be taken into care, and get three square meals a day on round plates, and have mates who'll be just as warped as they are; twisted little fire starters in stolen cars; throwing jars of petrol on tinder-dry moor land grass, just for a laff. 'Cos' there's fuck all else to do.' Smear poo on the door handles of a public loo for girls, and cackle uproariously when you see them sniff their hands, as you stand in a huddle across the road with a load of cans of lager to demolish.

Spit and polish means nothing to the lowest echelons of the hoi polloi, there's not much street cred' in being smart, except in a street-wise way. Rat's eyes in a rat's brain inside a human frame, will have your new £340 picture imaging mobile phone away on the double in their air bubble-filled trainers; or your Rolex or customised car. Or what about the ones who burst into your homes wearing masks and wielding baseball bats, demanding cash, and threatening to bludgeon your wife and kids if you don't cough up? Ah! We're back to coughing again, bring on the dancers so they can mime the chorus: 'DID YOU COUGH? DID YOU COUGH? OFF? OFF, OFF, OFF!!!'

....
....

SOLIPSISM IS MY ONLY TRUE FRIEND.
20/4/03.

During my love/hate relationship with Channel 4's 'THE SALON',
which has just finished, and which I only sporadically watched when
I was sick of seeking out culture; I couldn't help becoming intrigued
by two young women staff members. They both decked themselves
out, using clothes, hair and makeup, like two radiant birds of
paradise; they looked cool and sophisticated. But it was all for show,
there seemed to be no real substance to them, except perhaps as eye
and arm candy.
One of them appears to have the makings of a real Welsh
homemaker, (as well as a Welsh dresser). First off, she went gaga
over a raging homosexual Salon assistant called Oliver, a young
Julian Clarey; and who'll probably end up as a drag queen if his
speech pattern is anything to go by. But she couldn't see it, she was so
dim; when he was sacked for gross inefficiency, she was distraught.
However, she didn't have to wait long before a substitute came along
in the shape of a guy called John; the type of self obsessed preener
you'd be itching to slap, after a very short space of time.
Actually, the way he piled his hair up on the top of his head, which
gave the impression that his face was being pulled up towards his
scalp, reminded me of a parakeet. But to our little fashion dresser it
was like the attraction between Olive Oyl and Popeye; even though
he was more reminiscent of Bluto. Her cork well and truly popped as
soon as he greasily smiled at her, even though a very camp Frankie
Howard hairdresser in the Salon, was convinced John is gay. The
other page three-stunner look-alike, could have a really lucrative
career in the glamour business if she's managed properly; I haven't
seen many sexier pouts in this long, voyeuristic life of mine. I'd
willingly take her in hand, tho' I think she's got 7 brothers who're all
plasterers.

At a time when we're being told that STDs are reaching epic
proportions, and teenage pregnancies aren't on the decrease, I just
don't get it; and I don't mean literally either. There's nothing in the
atmosphere of this nation of ours, riddled with fear and loathing, to
suggest there's an unprotected sexual revolution going on. Is it being
led by our new breed of 'ladettes', getting totally rat-arsed and shit-
faced? Taking on all comers and then swearing they were date raped
or drugged? Both here, and all over the Med? Great british slags
who've turned us into the degenerate nation of Europe. I mean, we

males are biologically programmed to shag anything with a pulse, or even without, providing it's still warm.

But in a recent episode of ITVs 'THE CLUB', an execrable piece of rubbish TV if ever I saw one, is anything to go by, there were 5 young British guys, one of them 'gay', who swore they'd rather be castrated than sleep with a full on 'ladette', busty barmaid from Liverpool, who propositioned all of them in the clubhouse; I'd have given her one night of wheezy, moaning and groaning passion, (from hip and backache), but she'd probably have rejected me for being an old lech' with no money. Now if I'd been Peter Stringfellow..........?

This is the end, my only friend, the end of nights I try to 'put out' in this schisoid-ridden culture of ours. Usurping my role as host of a writers group I organised, I approached a female member, (I'd had a few drinks), offering to accompany her on a nice scenic walk. When she declined, I threatened to bar her from the next meeting if she was not going to bring something to read; I went on to get completely blotto when I got home, suffering a 2-day hangover from Hell as a result; I'd opt for chemical castration as long as it wouldn't interfere with my mental powers of deduction.

....
....

COMPLETELY BORED BY LIFE.
23/4/03.
(Thank fuck it's happening to someone else and not you.)

How can you be completely bored by life at 18? I've been completely frustrated and thwarted by my life, and have strongly felt like committing suicide at times because of it; but killing yourself because you're bored has never entered into it.

I'm inspired to write this piece after reading two articles in today's 'METRO', free newspaper; an excellent product if I may say so, for nothing. I always feel a bit miffed if I can't get hold of a copy when I'm out, because those cheapskates who could easily afford to buy a daily paper have snapped them all up; quite often leaving them discarded and unread.

Anyway, the front page headline for today's issue was: 'SUICIDE PACT OVER THE NET.', very intriguing. It seems there's a web site for those people who are so disaffected by life, they're fairly determined to end it all; the site lists a hundred ways to kill yourself, according to METRO. The main story was about two mid thirty-year-old men who met up after making contact thru' suicidesanonymous.com, (that's my own name for this site). They arranged to meet at the 'IF YOU'RE GOING TO JUMP, GET TANKED UP FIRST' pub, near Beachy Head; a very popular 'last gasp' saloon for the lost and the lonely. What made me laugh, was that one of them 'bottled out' at the very last moment, just as his newfound friend dashed past him wearing only his underpants, (clean on that morning I presume?), and leapt off the 400ft high cliffs.

The unsuccessful jumper was due in court yesterday for inciting someone to commit a rash act, but he failed to appear because the silly fucker had hung himself at his home; haven't these people heard of 'PROZAC'? Or are they among the minority who've had a bad reaction to it?

The 18-year-old who was 'completely bored by life', set up his own death site before hanging himself; and given the current phenomenon of suicides among young, able bodied men, I'm tempted to ask the question, 'Why!'? But I can't come up with any likely answers, there's no excuse for them. You're going to be dead for a hell of a long time to come, so why cheat the reaper?

The picture painted of heaven seems rather dull. What are you supposed to do for all eternity, apart from feeling initially grateful that there is life after death? Sit around watching celestial daytime TV with the god-awful likes of Richard and Judy running it? It's bad enough trying to fathom out what they see in each other down here; the Peter Pan of chat show hosts and his substitute mother? And when you're bored shitless with them, (but you won't need to piss or shit in paradise, it's not nice is it?), you'll be able to doze your way through endless snooker and golf tournaments, played for free; no need for money if there's nothing to spend it on, or trophies, because they're so triumphalist aren't they?

The ultimate in passive entertainment will be cricket and tennis; Wimbledon fortnight will last for a thousand years, or so it will seem for those of us who detest it to the point where we'd gladly see it nuked down here. There'll be no chance of seeing American wrestling in ultra 'PC' heaven, you can only see it here if you subscribe to SKY TV. And I can't afford to pay a licence fee to the self indulgent BBC, with its penchant for setting up digital channels and internet sites that only a privileged elite can access, and pay their subscription rates as well.

Instead of killing themselves in droves, why don't these young, and not so young males, sign up for VSO? Or join the army, and risk dodging death from 'friendly fire' in Iraq?

Or better still, live from month to month in anticipation of VIZ adult comic landing on their door mat, if they can be arsed to take out a subscription? If not, they could drag their useless carcasses down to my, soon to be newsagent's, (if I can access loads of grant aid to get it going in a hard-to-let shop), and let me have all the profit.

....
....

I'M FEELING MORE THAN A BIT TOUCHED, (AND NOT BY THE HAND OF A BENEVOLENT DEITY EITHER.)   27/4/03.

A couple of months ago I had to renew my passport, and consequently, my passport photos as well. It was a cold, late January day when I went into the chemists in Todmorden to have this painful operation performed; for which I had to fork out 4 quid, OUCH! The first set didn't take because I'd stuck my tongue out the corner of my mouth in a nervous reflex. When I was finally given the offensive items, I was shocked and horrified by what I saw; eyesore being the right word for them. My glasses looked like car headlamps, and gravity seems to have concentrated on making my face a lot longer than it used to be, especially my chin.

I was so depressed by these horror pics, I was going to throw them away and have another go at another shop; but the only other shop in Todmorden that was suitable, was out of passport film; and besides, £4 a throw photos, doesn't come easily to me. Ten years ago I was able to have a decent semi profile set done at a shop in Hebden Bridge, but that facility has gone, along with any fleeting hope I had of a reprieve of not looking like a mass murderer on my passport; maybe I should put mass murderer as my occupation, instead of 'undiscovered literary genius'? That way, customs officials would wave me through saying, "Have a safe and pleasant trip Mr Fletcher", instead of looking at me askance.

Apart from this awfully rude awakening that time is no longer necessarily on my side, I feel the same as I've always felt; unrealistically optimistic, when the sun's out anyway. I'm still young at heart, and now I've stopped trying to destroy myself with booze and depression, and am taking regular vitamin and mineral supplements, cautiously confident that I can live to a hundred and make up for all those lost years.; (I hope they'll have to wait three days before they can screw my coffin lid down, as I lie there with a big smirk on my face...as well.)
I've developed the philosophy that the longer you live, the more you can achieve; if you can train your mind and body to resist the frenzied urge that time is of the essence in this frantic age of money and celebrity-grabbing status; it's a contagious disease; I've been infected by it time and time again, and unlike the common cold, vitamin C won't make it go away. Believe me, enough IS as good as a feast.

The list of this country's most obscenely rich is published in The Sunday Times, I heard in a snippet of news on the radio. The so-called duke of Westminster is sitting on £4.9 billion pounds worth of personal wealth in property etc; Sir 'super Paul Macca' is worth £720 mill', (if I was John Lennon's ghost, I'd be constantly haunting Macca's conscience, if he's got one, to offload most of that unwholesome wealth), and the creator of Harry Potter, (the little fictitious bastard), J.K.Rowling, is £30 million pounds better off than the queen at £280 million.
If I was the Chancellor of the Exchequer I'd be devising ways of seriously liberating most of those ill deserved assets, swingeing taxes on the super rich, enough so the howls of protest would be heard loudly across the land. What can a writer want with £280 million? You're going to lose whatever creative edge you might have had; you can afford to pay someone else enough money to discreetly do what you no longer can be bothered to do; (I know that would be the case with me, even £1 mill' and I'd be off like a shot to my dream destination, to soak up the sun and sex) because you're too bowled over by your new found wealth and celebrity. You should, out of all conscience, give most of it away to try and save the planet's dwindling resources, and to help replace all the wood that's been cut down to make zillions of copies of your books. I pride myself on not having been caught up in the Harry Potter phenomenon, and as for

'super
macca'...!!
!!!!!!!!!!!!!!!!!!!!!!!!!

....
....

SWEARING FOR EFFECT.
27/4/03.

Swearing, you either love it or you loathe it; the arbiters of taste tell
us that the 'f' word is now so commonly and widely used, it's no
longer really considered as swearing. That only leaves the 'c' word to
go, and I have heard it used in films on television, such as the first
'DEATHWISH' movie, starring Charles Bronson, made in 1974 I
think, and only recently shown; I was quite surprised to hear it, it
must have been the uncut version.
And a few weeks ago, I read a book called 'CLUB LAND' by a writer
named Kevin Sampson, where the word 'cunt' seemed to be used
every other line or so; a read I can highly recommend to anyone
who's scatologically obsessed; I'll stick with golden showers in my
fantasies thank you. I've even heard schoolgirls happily calling each
other cunts, on a bus in Hebden Bridge some time ago.
I'd gone upstairs to escape this woman openly coughing on the
downstairs back seat, I was afraid of catching a nasty cold from her
inconsiderate behaviour. I had opened a side window earlier on in
the journey from Todmorden, but this old cockney wanker came up
from behind me, slammed it shut and said, ""Do you want a poke,
cos you'll get one,", and plonked himself down in the seat in front of
me; very provocative behaviour. I had a rolled-up umbrella with me,
it being a bleak winter's morning, and this umbrella has a rather
pointed steel tip on the end. For dramatic effect I raised it above my
head with both hands, pointing it at the back of his neck in a
downwards thrusting motion, as if I was going to stab him with it;
the coughing paused momentarily and I lowered my brolly, much to
the relief of the woman sat behind me; nobody spoke a word. As he
kept looking up to make sure I hadn't sneakily opened the window
again, I said in my gruffest voice, "I opened it because of that woman
coughing her head off on the back seat mate, alright?"

This geezer got off at Hebden Bridge, so I took advantage of the bus being stationary to go and sit upstairs; the next moment this gaggle of human geese came clattering up top, I very soon got pissed off with this adolescent licence, ('So and so's a real cunt in't she', etc) and decided to get off the bus altogether, and make the 10 minute walk to the railway station, where I had to wait 20 minutes for a train to Halifax; but it was a blissful relief to be away from common humanity. ('Who does that cunt think he is?')

Only yesterday I was called a wanker by some bozo who I couldn't even see, as I passed by on the opposite side of the road to where he was pruning his privets with an electric hedge trimmer. The fact that I am an occasional, reluctant onanist, due to the absence of a suitable orifice to stick my ample dick into, is neither here nor there; I spent a good part of the rest of that day fantasising about smashing his fucking head in, if my eyesight was better than it is.

Apparently, and I'm making a general assumption here, my own personal experience of it being absolutely nil at 56, women like men talking dirty to them during, or leading up to sex. So, if I was in that fortunate situation and I said, "I'm going to shag the arse off you, you bitch," would it have the desired effect of her letting me do it to her 'doggy style'? Ramming it in from behind, with her moaning in ecstasy for me not to stop; I might have to strap a dildo on if I did…come too soon that is.

And if I said, "I'm going to lick your fanny out and make you come in my mouth", would she lie on her back with her legs and cunt lips wide open, and her clitoris on fire, and lots of love juice coming down, pulling my head down on to her; could I achieve ecstasy and still be able to slip my raging erection into her sloppy vagina after her initial orgasm, and make her come like a train? I'd be up for this sort of thing if it didn't smell like an opened can of tuna down there, and the merest odour of excreta, and I'd be off like a shot.

Traditionally, we're led to believe it's women who are offended by coarse language, or so I was brought up to observe; I've risked a fat lip and worse by asking males to mind their language on buses when I was much younger, because it might offend the delicate sensitivities of the gentler and fairer sex. Not any more! Have you seen the way they behave at women only, strip club nights? And they can swear worse than the most hardened building worker or docker. It has to be said that now, in a liberated society like ours, the two sexes are very much alike, except that females can all too easily play the rape card and go all soft and girly when it suits them; usually when they want something expensive out of a man.

....
....

DIABOLO PICASSO, THE RANDY OLD PATRIARCHAL SATYR.
1/5/03.

There was a film on TV last night called 'SURVIVING PICASSO', starring Anthony Hopkins. I'm a sexist pig and a misogynist, but I thought he (Picasso) abused his position as a patriarchal satyr; I wonder if young French women are still so submissive by nature? Self abasing and self effacing.? I suppose you react to what you can get away with, depending on your nature. If you've got people throwing themselves at your feet and there's a tyrant lurking inside you, petty or otherwise, then given its head it will out. When I hosted my first writers evening the other week, and abused some wine that was on offer, I felt a glaring superiority complex coming to the fore; I virtually dismissed the group at the end of the evening, as well as their work.
I hadn't had a drink for about 3 months prior to this event, and I certainly made up for lost time; when I got back home...alone, still with two thirds of a bottle of 'rose' wine in tow, I made the drunken decision to sit on my doorstep and celebrate the nearly full new moon with a modest-sized cigar and a guzzle; and that's the last I remember.
If I drank the wine it mustn't have touched the sides, and I've no recollection of smoking a slim panatela, maybe I ate it? I'm only glad I was here at home, because I would have been in a real alcoholic blackout if I'd been out. Nothing untoward happened, I seemed to have put myself to bed in an orderly manner; even the empty wine bottle was still there to be recycled the next day; and I was really disappointed when I came out of my drunken stupor all too early the next morning, to begin a 36-hour hangover from Hell; full of guilt, remorse and self loathing.
Now, one of the few interesting facts to emerge from the Picasso movie, was that he didn't allow any of his hair or nail clippings to 'fall into the wrong hands', to be used against him in black magic

rituals; anyone who's not had the 'evil eye' pointed at them will think this a load of tosh; myself chief amongst them if I'd not had first hand experiences of 'dark forces' reigned against me. And believe you me, they don't need physical nail or hair parings to act against you. One of three 'mind stalkers' that I'm acutely aware of, was a total alcoholic; it was as if booze had replaced his life's blood, he was so dependent on it. It's crossed my mind that my lapse of two weeks ago, was due to his influence. I've not seen or heard anything from this 'diabolical' character for a few years now, but I know he had direct psychic access to my innermost private space, along with the other two psychic perverts. Maybe he's a 'dry' alcoholic now and saw his chance, through me, to have a good drink? I certainly felt his unwelcome presence around me while I was recovering.

As with all mind stalking activity, nothing can be proven, if you tell this sort of theory to a psychiatrist, he or she will say you're delusional, possibly paranoid schizophrenic. But years ago, I heard someone say on TV that the symptoms of black magic victimisation are very similar to these psychiatric terms; and that escaping the clutches of these inhumans is virtually impossible.

My only hope is that when they stop robbing good air out of this world to suck into their asbestos lined lungs, these perpetrators are dragged back down into Hell where they rightly belong, to begin their tortures in earnest; the evil fuckers! Ha, ha, ha!!!

....
....

I'VE BEEN WELL STUFFED BY THE TURKEY NECKS.
26/5/03
(Why honking car horns can cause you to live without any sense of optimism.)

It just goes to show that everywhere I go, this blight goes with me. Having safely and exhaustedly arrived in my hotel room in Thailand, 2 days after penning the above title, I was immediately made aware of some real heavy duty horn honking; the sort you get from a klaxon, and during the whole of my ten day holiday I never discovered where it was coming from. I was 18 floors up, and the busy main road was about a hundred yards away; but every night I had to shove cotton wool in my ears to drown out the worst of the din. Human traffic was noisily active till 2 & 3 in the morning; if I get to go back there again I'll definitely upgrade to a sea view room for a good night's sleep.

Such is the exiguous nature of good fortune in my life when it comes to finding a soul mate or partner, as well as a substantial stash of cash, that I'm having to live my life in reverse. When many of my generation will be creaking gratefully towards retirement, either here or abroad, and more and more are opting for the latter, on the Costa Del Safeway; I'll be heading back to Thailand to start a new life. Where, if you've got the cash, you can get a lovely young wife and a place to live, and people don't look down on you as a dirty old perv'. It will serve this country right if I'm able to draw my pension out there, where neither the climate nor the people are begrudging.

But can I survive till I'm 65, here in the land of the evil dead? Where fat-arsed, lard-brained turkey necks rule the roost, with the power of the honking car horn; even on a quiet little road like mine. Why drag your corpulent carcass out of the driver's seat to go and knock on someone's door, when you can alert their attention by loudly impressing your fat paw on the car horn? And, at the same time, cause distress and upset to sensitive souls like me? Of course, there's the slamming car door as well, and the car alarm, and the exhaust fumes; gunning motors, road rage, and hey! You can even kill people in your car and not be called a murderer, merely a dangerous driver; and only be given a derisory prison sentence and a five-year driving ban.

I view the motor vehicle as nothing more than a useful means to an end, whereas I'm sure a lot of males regard the automobile as an extension of their manhood. I'd love to hear of some besotted stud caught with his engorged penis stuck in the exhaust pipe, pants round his ankles, car gloved hands clutching the rear bumper.

Air travel is possibly the nearest we'll come to time travel, it's great. If we could completely eradicate the risk, and fear of plane crashes, I'd happily experience turbulence at 40,000 feet. Even though I've done it quite a few times now, it still never quite rings true, watching the ground drop away from you as the plane hurtles skyward; it should be an awesome feeling, but I've become rather blasé about it. Mind you, if I was still prone to panic attacks, a plane is the last place I'd want to have one. You can't get off it can you and gulp in deep breaths of what passes for fresh air? (All those exhaust fumes and particulates going into your lungs), the best you could hope for would be a massive dose of valium pumped into your arm.

....
....

DUSTPAN AND BRUSH.
31/5/03.
(An abstruse paucity of vital energy is slowly killing me.)

Okay I'll admit it, I'm fucked physically and mentally; but it's my
physical decline that's sapping my mental strength. So what? It only
matters to me; my whole world revolves around me alone; having no
one else to care for, and having no one else to care for me.
56 isn't young, but it's not ancient or decrepit either; in my mind I
feel the same as I always have, sometimes good, at other times bad. I
believe a strong mind could far outlast its physical confinement, that
no matter how extreme the provocation, it could survive if it wanted
to; but like the body, it too can grow tired of life in acute solitary
confinement.
 Money may well be the root of all evil, due to human greed; it's also
the key factor in most opportunities reaching fruition. Socialists can
whine on all they like about equality for all, but they always forget to
take into account, the intrinsic human need to achieve and acquire;
very few of us are prepared to go through life willing to sacrifice
everything for the common good. And in my opinion the masses just
aren't worth it.
In this precarious era of over global population, when we're
outstripping Nature's ability to replace what we're destroying at a
rate of knots, random breeding and waste should be outlawed; if
that's a form of socialism then I'm all for it. There should also be a
sealing on personal wealth, to curb excessive avarice; I'd put it at no
more than £10 million, the super rich are nothing more than evil, life-
blood sucking parasites who should be eradicated; and would be if I
had my way, ('UP AGAINST THE WALL MUTHAFUCKAS!')

An interesting, fictionalised need to achieve and acquire is running in
Coronation Street at the moment, a mercenary miss, aged around 25,
is aiming to entrap a 70 year old lecher with plenty of dough; last
night's depiction of their tryst was brilliantly performed, and had me
laughing sarcastically. Of course, if such a character had no money
he'd judgmentally be thought of as a dirty old pauper; a fate I

anticipate with dread. Luckily, I've set my sights on Thailand to semi retire to when I'm 65; I only hope that in the next ten years they don't catch up with us here in the west, and end up like us, with both sexes vying for supremacy, and neither side winning outright; only engendering a heightened atmosphere of fear and loathing, and extreme sexual frustration. (Or is it only me?)

Part of my dictionary definition of 'existentialism', is 'a free agent in a meaningless universe'; I've extended this in my own case to read, 'a free agent in a meaningless universe, investigating varying levels of death, and drawing the conclusion that the death of the Spirit is the worse form of all, closely followed by the slow death of your physical health. Your actual demise can come as a blessed relief'. (I've reduced this to 'a free agent in a meaningless universe', thank fuck.) Right now, the human race is sacrificing the quality of life in favour of plague- proportion-reaching quantity, we wouldn't allow any other species to pose such a threat, and now we're beginning to reap the whirlwind. I've heard very recently that there's an increasing water shortage in Northern Italy; and record breaking temperatures of 50-degrees centigrade have allegedly killed a thousand people in India. Will scientists come up with a cure for global destruction of the environment? I hope not, not until we're ready to face harsh reality anyway; the harsh reality that we're no better than a plague swarm of locusts in our rapacity.

And thus endeth the final lesson from me to you, I've finished with writing...I hope!

Incidentally, the main title of this last piece was inspired by the fact that I had to resort to using my trusty dustpan and brush, (the two items cost me a quid), to get bits of fluff off my sorry floor coverings, after first going over them with a noisy hoover. The dustpan and brush picked up more than just surface dirt; but what irked me badly was that it took all my energy to sweep over a small area in my minuscule home. The unrelenting harshness and soul-destroying bleakness of my life in this country, have resulted in the breakdown of my physical health; the fact that I'm 56 has got nothing to do with it...ha, ha, ha! And lastly, for anyone who's not a devotee of Coronation Street, the ending of the gold-digging story was hilarious, and one that I hadn't predicted at all, pure magic, pure genius.

....
....

(Yeah, the writing hadn't finished with me then, I feel it has now though; and I'm definitely finished with it…unless there's money to be made. If I can set up my web site before I go and live in Thailand; that will be the job done and dusted.
I'll also be putting nearly 60 years of misery and frustration behind me; whatever time I've got left on this Earth will be MY time. My fate now truly lies in the hands of fate. See ya!   Phil Fletcher. 6/6/06.)

....

THAILAND, A PARADISE LOST IN A SEA OF COMMERCIAL GREED. Oct. 07

15/10/07   Well, a lot of time has passed since I was last here updating this short but dynamic collection; I moved, lock, stock, and one smoking barrel (my sex starved penis) to Thailand last December, the 6th oddly enough, if you think that 5 months to the day of writing the above statement has any significance? I thought I was going for good, I distributed all my worldly goods that I thought were resalable to charity shops, and either threw out or left behind everything else; I notified people by post who I thought it was necessary to notify, even posting the keys to my flat to the housing association, oh what a good boy am I.
I arrived at my destination in Thailand about 9pm on Thursday, 7th December '06 to start my new life at 'Majestic Condos', Jomtien, Pattaya, a complex that's so nice even Joe Walsh out of The Eagles has stayed there, and might still even be a resident for all I know when he's not touring or helping to promote The Eagles new double CD.
It was okay there at first, but I soon became aware of the traffic noise from the road that passed beneath my windows, a global problem now; and the noise I hate most in this world is harsh mechanical noise, the type that cars, juggernauts, and motorbikes make; I've now got 'tinnitus' quite badly in my left ear.
I should have been happy there but it didn't take long before I realised I wasn't, I began to feel like a ghost haunting the place. I blame my lousy low vision eyesight for most of my problems, well all of my problems to be exact; this major disability has always held me back from successfully achieving what I want to be, like a successful writer for instance.

Not being able to ride a motorbike (when you're on one with a helmet on you can't really hear the racket you're making) was a big handicap, I felt conspicuous every time I had to walk along the road into the town, and I resented paying inflated baht taxi bus prices to go a short distance; it was one price for us 'farangs' and another one for the locals, a lot lower one for the locals actually. I did like the hot sun burning into my back though when I was making this fairly short journey to get groceries, etc.

Once I discovered there was a big TESCO LOTUS superstore within walking distance (about 40-45 minutes on a good day) I was hooked. The same journey by motorbike would have taken about 10 minutes.... I used to get back from my shopping expeditions soaked in sweat, and sometimes when I got to the store I looked as if I'd had a bucket of water thrown over me; eventually I opted to wear only black T-shirts on these trips (as well as pants of course), but I always felt daunted at the prospect of making these vital forays for food by the sheer physical effort of getting there; as well as being a bit wary of viciously barking dogs who seemed more anti foreign than the Thais themselves, maybe they'd trained them to be anti social to 'farangs'? I don't know; thankfully I was never bitten, but my nerves were jarred up on several occasions.

Quite accidentally I found out there was a beach road bus service, I found this out by reading an article in the local paper; the same paper that printed 7 of my letters over a seven month period.

Anyway to cut a long boring story short, I noticed a big bus stop on the beach road that I'd walked past loads of times without seeing it, it was red, and the lovely little beach road bus was red on most days, though sometimes it was yellow or green.

The first time I flagged it down I didn't have a clue where it or I was going, I said, 'TESCO'? to the driver and he nodded, the bus price was only a fraction of what it would have cost by baht bus or motorbike taxi, and a lot safer. We went through Pattaya city and just kept going, I began to feel despair setting in, where the hell were we!? Another fluke saved me from total panic, there was a big store called the BIG C, which I knew wasn't that far from Jomtien and it had a distinctive sign which just happened to materialise opposite the bus window I was frantically staring out of. I thought, 'Well at least I'm not that far from home,' and it was a nice sunny day to be lost in. And a bit further on, on the same side as the big sign, I spotted the big TESCO Lotus sign; I was able to get off the bus right opposite the superstore, all I had to do then was climb the 3 flights of steps up to the walkway over the constantly busy Thepprasit Road and back down the other side. The journey had taken over an hour.

I eventually learned that the beach road bus only went one way, a long circuitous route from Jomtien and back again, covering Pattaya and Naklua; what confused me for quite some time was, there were bus stops on both sides of the route, not all the way but for quite long stretches of it; the trip back home from TESCO took about 10 minutes, though you could be waiting half an hour for your red, green, or yellow bus to turn up among the heavy traffic of baht buses, totally insane bigger blue and white buses that barely stopped long enough for people to get on, and motorbikes coming along the road the wrong way against the traffic and happily coming onto the pavement; how I never got splattered is a mystery far beyond my understanding; am I being kept alive so I can suffer more, or is fate just totally indifferent to me? I ask myself this question now as I tremblingly wait to hear the outcome of a rash act I've committed very recently.

I've dared to challenge the might of my paymasters: The Department of Work and Pensions (or the DSS, I'm not really sure) by refusing to fill in a horrendously long and complicated form they sent me; I sent it back last Friday saying 'You people have plagued me all my adult life and I've had enough, my doctor's given me a sick note because of my visual handicap: 'until further notice,' and if that's not enough for you I'll sign off and go onto full Pension Credit...so there!' (Or words to that effect.) Pension Credit is a benefit payment paid to people over 60 who have no, or only a low weekly income; I'm only staying on combined Incapacity benefit and pension credit so I can get enough national insurance credits to qualify for a full state pension when I'm 65. You don't get NI credits if you're only on PC, so ha ha ha!, hee hee hee!, I wonder what the outcome will be? Watch this space, I've done enough for today, I never intended doing this journal anyway, I was only going to put some new work on this collection to flesh it out.

Like I said, I used to feel like a ghost haunting the Majestic Condos. My severely impaired eyesight makes it difficult for me to recognise people easily in anything other than a strong light; so I have to peer about or listen out for voices I recognise, the peering about can make life depressing and embarrassing at times. I can see the sky without any problems and distant landscapes, but making out details of buildings and people is beyond my visual capability; plus I can only use my left eye for seeing, the right one's virtually useless. I missed out on a free Christmas, open air party there because of this handicap; I felt alone and insecure and unable to identify what the buffet consisted of in the evening gloom, though there were plenty of coloured lights strung up from trees around the pool area. I couldn't make anyone out who I might have known and the party seemed to be being enjoyed by family groups, lots of nippers scurrying about; I beat a dismal retreat back to my room to watch TV…AGAIN!

Apart from the traffic noise I began to notice a loud swishing noise coming from the room above me, usually after midnight when the road was quieting down; apart from it being really annoying, it was a mystery. It eventually dawned on me that it was a mosquito net in a frame, set in the grooves of the windows, if that makes any sense? The condo that I used to own there had one; if you wanted to leave your sliding windows half open you could do so by pulling the insect repelling frame across. There wasn't one of these in the room I now occupied, and quite often I'd be kept awake by my 'pet' mosquito flying up close and too personal, like into my ear for instance, usually just when I was dropping off to sleep. This swishing noise eventually got to me more than the traffic noise, nearly driving me insane in fact. I never saw the occupant of the room either, I couldn't bring myself to go up and complain: 'Listen mate, do you mind keeping your swishing noise down a bit, only it's driving me mad.' I might have been met with a blank stare and, 'Solly, I no unnerstan.'

So after 3 months I was more than ready to move, my landlord wasn't very happy because I'd paid 6 months rent in advance and I now wanted half of it back; he was my friend as well which didn't make things easier. He's also Dutch, and despite having a really good grasp of English there are times when the meaning of what you say to him are lost in his mental translation facility. I tried to explain that my desire to leave was due to several contributing factors: the walk into Jomtien and my unhappiness at staying there were the 2 leading problems; I don't know if he understood about my feeling isolated and lonely? As an active able-bodied man I don't suppose he did. I'd lined up somewhere else to go, a room above an Internet café on a street or 'Soi' that again, due to my lousy eyesight, I hadn't noticed existed until it was pointed out to me.

It was an attractive young woman who ran the place, I had visions of us getting together…how wrong could I be. The deal was that I'd rent a room initially for 2 months at a discounted rate, the room itself wasn't very big but it did have a big outside balcony area and its own toilet and shower; I moved in, it was mid-February this year.

The first couple of days I was there were okay, I didn't notice the air con generator planted right next to my living room windows, but once its loud fan whirring noise kicked in that was the beginning of the end of the brief honeymoon period. There was also an electrical humming noise that used to make itself known to me late at night, coming through a wall opposite my bed; it became necessary for me to lie across the bed at an angle to find a spot where this sleep denying noise wasn't so intrusive, quite often I'd still be awake at 4 am. Add to this misery the young lady's constantly yapping dogs, doors banging at all hours of the night, and the traffic noise from the street outside and you've got some idea of the hell I was in.

My 60th birthday was due on 5th March, I didn't think I had much to celebrate given my current circumstances; my bid to start a new life had gone shit shaped, I'd substituted my lifestyle from England to a similar one in Thailand: stuck in a room most of the time watching TV, when I wasn't out shopping or messing about in the Internet café (the light in their Internet Cafes was appallingly dim, I'm surprised I can still see anything, I used to strain my eye so much to see the keyboard in them.) On Sunday 4th March I'd reached an absolute nadir of mental distress, I was physically catatonic (I couldn't get off my bed) but my mind was trying to kill me; if I'd had a syringeful of liquid Nembutal, (the favourite choice of euthanasiacs in Australia apparently, where they can buy it over the net I think) I might have been sorely tempted to use it, thus passing into a golden state of warmth and tranquillity before 'breaking on through' to the other side maybe, if there is another side...

T he actual physical effects of the depression were horrendous, a spasmodic gut wrenching, like being disembowelled while you're still conscious, or having a tooth pulled without anaesthetic. The usual hubbub was continuing around me and the heat was sweltering.

At 5pm I was able to drag myself off my bed of pain and go to the nearest minmart to buy something; there was a Welsh guy there who I knew from the Majestic having a drink. You could do that out there, not like here. For some reason he couldn't see the misery staring out of my face and depressing everybody (or so I thought.) around me, but he was drunk most of the time, until he decided to go 'cold turkey' a couple of months later; and the last I heard he'd gone back to Wales for a visit.

Anyway, I had 3 beers with him, one at the shop above which I was eventually to make my home and 2 at a bar nearby, but I was in no mood to socialise and took the first opportunity to slink off back to my room; maybe I should have opted for a policy of staying drunk all the time? Though that option can soon become a worse fate than death beyond a certain age. Jack Kerouac drank himself to death because he couldn't cope with the fame of success, aged 47. He died leaving a mere 91 dollars; now his posthumous estate's worth $20 million, all due to 'ON THE ROAD', the rest of his output is largely ignored. I know I've never been able to finish any of the other books of his I've tried to read.

Maybe I could have got so drunk one night I could have waded into the sea, just across the beach road. I can't swim and I suppose as soon as my feet wouldn't have felt sand beneath them without my head dipping below the surface, I'd have started to panic. Hopefully my specs would have come off in the water and I wouldn't be able to see which way the shore was, and very quickly got too tired to do anything other than drown. I did see some footage of a drowned man on a local TV channel; like I put in my diary, he didn't look that bothered to be dead, and once you've got over the instinctive desire to resist death for as long as possible and slipped into a black void, like a general anaesthetic for instance, I'm fairly certain I'd feel the same.

But being an abject coward I've opted to stick this existence out to the bitter end, and it will be bitter, I feel assured of that. My 60th birthday passed without any fanfare whatsoever, zilch, nada, I should have gone out and got myself a paid shag but my whole metabolism was strained to the limit; like that song by FAITHLESS went: 'I can't get no sleep…' By Friday 9th March, my brain was in shreds, I knew I had to get away from the Internet café but where would I go? There was a big hotel on the front not far away so I went there to enquire, thinking there'd be plenty of rooms at reasonable rates, I was wrong on both counts. There was a posh looking place not very far from where I was staying, I enquired there, prohibitively expensive. And next, to prove that '3rd time lucky' does have some basis in fact, I spotted a sign that said 'ROOMS'. On enquiring I found that the daily rate wasn't too exorbitant and I even managed to secure a discount for a 'long term stay' (one month.) This inn was just round the corner from the Internet café.

It was still only early when I told my landlady I was moving out, I'd already packed up a lot of my stuff, she wasn't very happy at the prospect of having to give me some money back; I did point out to her that she could charge me the more expensive daily rate for the 2.5 weeks I'd stayed there instead of the rate we'd agreed for the 2 months, but she couldn't take this on board straightaway and phoned the police!

Reaching 60 (the new 40 if you're still in any kind of fit state) has hit me like a ton of bricks and had a very harmful effect on me, given the lifetime of disappointments I've amassed; it's no wonder I suffered those gut-wrenching depressions leading up to my 60th birthday. People kill themselves for a lot less reasons than I'd have to, but I figure I'm going to be dead for a long time anyway so why cheat the reaper? And also at 60, by the sheer laws of nature, you're on your way out anyway, to add to all your other miseries. I might spend a lot of time feeling sick and tired of my life but I'm not sick and tired of life itself; like Ken Kesey wrote, it's: 'SOMETIMES A GREAT NOTION.'

I'd actually got quite a bit of stuff to move, quite a few holdalls full, and my new hosts weren't fussy about entering another Thai person's premises to help me move it round to their place. My ex landlady had had no luck with the police in getting me arrested for breaking a verbal contract and resentfully gave me the money I was owed; she didn't lose out by the deal but relations between us were permanently soured, I never went back into her Internet café, luckily I didn't need to because there was another one next door with equally dim lighting.

So now I had a month to spend in the SMILE INN, I was due to move into a permanent room above the mini mart I mentioned earlier in mid April after it had been tidied up and repainted. There was a lot of renovating building work going on in the four storey property next door to the store, I had been bothered by it while I was staying over the Internet café 50 metres away up the street, and which was to make my life an even more painful hell when I took up residence there.

Once again, new surroundings, it was a nice room I'd been allocated; I was exhausted so I spent the afternoon in bed. I did hear a few bass booms but nothing to warn me of what was to come. The street had a lot of bars in it, it came alive after dark, whereas I tended to wind down for the evening, preferring to stay in and watch crap TV rather than risk going out and being fleeced of my carefully controlled living allowance; all in all my life was pretty dull. I watched a lot of French films in the time I stayed at THE SMILE INN, the subtitles were big enough so I could follow them quickly enough to keep up with the film's plot, the reception wasn't always that good though.

I used to guiltily buy food to eat in my room though I was on a room only basis; and by food I don't mean food I'd ordered from a rival eating establishment to have brought to me, I mean food that I either bought from Tesco or the local mini marts, I was very self contained and very lonely most of the time. To hire a girl's services for the night cost about 1300 baht, plus you might buy her drinks and a meal, bringing it up to maybe 2000 baht; that was for a Thai girl, if you wanted a white woman you'd be paying 2000 baht for a short time. I did get my fingers burnt a few times when looking for comfort; I ended up feeling really grateful for any attention even if I was paying for it.

Ideally when I retire there in my 65th year, I want to meet a nice Thai lady either at a marriage bureau or introduction agency, I'm definitely not going to get stuck with a bar girl. Also out there, major age gaps are no big deal, at 65 I could be living with a 25-year-old lady and provided I had plenty of cash to support her, no one would go round saying, 'Look at that dirty old fucker living with her,' not like here; I'd never bring a young Thai woman to this country for obvious reasons, apart from the climate.

Once more I think it took a couple of nights for the new noise nuisance to really kick in, namely the 'BOOM, BOOM!' of the sub woofer bass from the bar opposite me; but once I did become glaringly aware of it that was it, the nightly torture had begun. It usually got bad about 10.30pm and carried on fairly non-stop till well after 1.30am, sometimes later. It was an open-air bar and the noise would come right out at you. On a few nights someone would be celebrating a birthday and all the balloons that had been tied up in bunches around the bar would be burst to the accompaniment of 'Happy birthday to you,' it sounded like a load of fire crackers was being set off.

After 12 nights of this Thai version of the Chinese water torture I was at my wits end; I managed to make myself understood enough to convey to the management that a move to the other side of the inn was urgently in order, the ladies moved all my stuff to its identical place in a nearly identical room opposite the noisy one; it was de ja vu for a while, but it was now heavenly quiet...for a week or so. Also I had some greenery outside my windows, a few trees harbouring a few birds; at times I could almost imagine I had an English garden at the back of me.

The Thai language, like most foreign languages, is totally inscrutable to me, I don't even like using their universal greeting for hello because it makes me feel embarrassed; to my shame I became very dismissive of my host country's language and expected everybody to understand me, a typical Brit abroad who should have won a pretentious twit award.

Yes it was lovely at first on the sunny, quiet side of the SMILE INN, apart from the kitchen smells, I now anticipated spending a relaxing time waiting till I could move permanently above the mini mart. A place run by a very moody New Zealander who I grew to hate with a vengeance once I'd lived there for a while; I ended up calling him 'mad dog' (but not to his ugly mug.) I still had the crippling morning depressions to cope with, I was usually kept pinned down in my bed, curled up in a pre natal ball, heavily sighing and wishing I were dead. Things tended to improve mood-wise once I'd managed to turn my radio on to one of the few English-speaking radio stations. I say English-speaking, quite often the DJ would go off into a whole rigmarole of Thai, so I had to try flicking round for another channel. Their airways were really cluttered up with replication stations, pumping out gushing love ballads or, what was far worse for me, traditional Thai music, it was like listening to cats being degutted without any anaesthetic.

People were heavily into slamming room doors as well, I don't know what it is about hotels and guest houses that seems to bring out the worst or most boisterous in people who stay in them. They adopt a policy of, 'Why close a door if you can slam it shut'? Just like where I live now in Halifax, England; though the excuse they have here is that...THEY'RE AS THICK AS PIG SHIT!!! And just as smelly.

....
....

I've decided that I can't go on with this account anymore because I'm bored with it and it's depressing me as well as quite possibly depressing you, my non existent readership. I'm a lot happier putting shorter pieces of work I've created to round this collection off.
26/10/07

....

30/10/07. It's amazing how many unscrupulous operators there are out there in cyber space, hoping to reel in gullible writers...quite possibly like me. Recently I checked out 'createspace.com' because they offered a 'print on demand' service for your books. Through them I was forwarded onto 'booksurge.com' who supposedly offered a $99 adobe pdf file deal for print on demand. With the help of a young library assistant I was able to create the required files for 'COPING WITH MADNESS', I e-posted these to them.

There then ensued a whole load of flim-flam about my pdf files not being compatible with their technology and I'd need to spend a lot more than $99 to bring my project up to speed; a figure of $899 was mentioned. I've hotly contested this exorbitant amount, I've not heard from them since last Friday...

And there's my old friend 'helium.com', the site that reckons you can earn real money by writing articles and rating other people's efforts; I'd like to meet someone who's actually made any money out of them. I rejoined Helium last week and I wrote one tongue-in-cheek piece about elderly people...like myself for instance. While I was there I spotted 'poetry.com'. It turns out they're another aspect of the 'Internation Library of Poetry', a vanity publisher who I've crossed swords with in the past.

I've created a 'poem' for one of poetry.com's poetry contest which I'll reproduce here shortly; I doubt very much if it will win a monetary prize, it's already buried in a mass of other hopeful's work on their web site. The one aspect of their site that I like is the area where you can rate other poets' work, I like marking down the female efforts, mostly because, in my estimation, they're not very good; I've read one woman's work that impressed me, I wish I could remember her name.

....

This is the piece I created in one go for the virtual poetry contest for poetry.com

MY MIND'S EYE IS GOING BLIND.   22/10/07.

I've always had low vision,
But I always thought like a visionary,
I wanted to put the world to rights around me;
Now I couldn't care less, the planet seems to be
In a terminal mess, or so we're told daily.
Where are the superheroes when we really need them,
Off saving other worlds?

I used to be able to rely on my imagination to take me
On transports of delight, now my mind's eye's
Developed a blight, I think it's a cataract, everything's
Blurred and grey. I can't find a way forward, I need

Psychic laser surgery to remove it.

If I can ever improve it by constant internal blinking,
I'll try rethinking the state I'm in, and walk round wearing
An idiot grin (can you still say 'idiot' in this word sensitive age
We're nervously living in?) of happiness even if I don't mean it,
Rather than a discontented lump of misery on my back. (You
Definitely can't say 'hump' as in hump-backed.)

Phil Fletcher.

....

`This is what I've written at the head of this piece on the original
hand written sheet:

My father's been dead one year to this day (13/10/07), maybe he's
one of them?

THE FEEDER off my emotions and vital energies; a perverted
telepath or telepaths skilled in the art of ESP. Mind hackers and
stalkers.   13/10.07.

The pursuit of happiness through quietness from other people's
Unwanted and hated noise eludes me as much as ever. Apart from
The lovely sound of music and laughter and the spoken word,
The human race has got nothing to offer me; the 'crown' of
Creation is a stinking 'turd.'
The human race goes back a long way, maybe 3 million years or so,
Time enough to grow more harmonious with Nature, or so you'd
think;
But in the blink of an eye the chimp can come screaming and raging
out
Of people's faces, and their bloodlust is up and they want to tear you
Apart.

The heart of mankind is really a dark place, except for those in love
With true art, not what passes for art today; I think the Id is playing
Games along the lines of: 'The Emperor's New Clothes'. When will
People wise up to the modernists and find them naked of any real or
Lasting talent? A Bonobo ape could do much better, and with more
Genuine emotion too.

And so where does telepathy and ESP come in? You tell me, you're
The one doing it to me. I don't even know how it's humanly possible
To do it? Maybe it dates back to primordial times when the Liplaurodon
(allegedly the largest creature ever to inhabit our planet, weighing up to
150 tons, and truly the stuff of nightmares) ruled the ancient oceans and
hoovered everything up that couldn't get out of their way fast enough.

It's a form of evil slimey predation, allowing the sensory predator to get
Right inside its victim's head; I don't know if it can pull out in time
Before it's killed its fixation dead? Like an aggressive cancer tumour
Rotting in the ground along with its no longer living host; or else bubbling
And boiling in the cremation chamber.

My mind stalker or hacker's led me a fruitless chase, I still can't put a name
To the face of who I think it might be; it's some devil spawn that's for sure.
It's got a psychic eye set in its frontal lobe, its own mind cam' constantly
Trained on me. It can probe deep inside my thought processes and attempt
To censor me, it hates me being free.

But when I've finished writing this that's exactly what I'll be; I'm going
To watch a WWE DVD on my TV. And if I had loads of money I'd be
Drinking honey from the furry cup inbetween coming up for air.
And it wouldn't be any old drug addicted, disease raddled street hag for me,
Only the best would do; the type who've blown me off (as in dismissed me as
Being substandard) all my life. I'm not looking for a life-time partner, I might
Not have too much of this precious commodity left. A few decent lovers

Would do, but they've got to be beautiful. I think ugliness is a sin and a possible
Punishment for being an evil monster in a previous life.

I might not always have the last laugh but I will have the last word…and this is it!!!

Phil Fletcher-Stokes.

…………………………………………………………………..

I usually think I've written my last word after every piece I write, along the lines of, 'And 'SATURN' said it is good,' but enough is never enuf for me, so here goes my latest creation:

3-4/11/07. 'A world without me in it? I can't conceive of it!!!'
(This one ends on a funny note, believe me.)

I CREATE ME, I DON'T IMITATE.   3-4/11/07.

I send work out into cyberspace where it hibernates,
Waiting for a time when my creative genius will be recognised;
I only hope that recognition won't come too late.

There's a 35-year old 'black hole' in my life, the last 35 years
Of waking up alone on Christmas Day with no one beside me
To chase my blues away. A black hole full of the freezing black
Horror of loneliness and isolation, of being unloved and rejected
On numerous occasions due to disability; and the ultimate
Horror of knowing that on top of all this I've still got
Death to face, the greatest black hole of them all.

I try to live in the 'here and now', but every so often the
'dead and gone' will find a chink in my armour and attempt
to pierce me to the quick, leaving a sick feeling in my head, guts,
and heart. Y ou can't have endured a life like mine without
being physically and emotionally torn apart; my biggest fear
now is that my physical health will collapse completely, long
before my mental resolve to win this battle against adversity

at all costs.

And now aged 60, my body does feel worn out, and I know the
Reason why, it comes under the loose heading of 'wear and tear';
The kind of wear and tear that being forced to live a life alone
Can inflict. Also harbouring 'unrealistic expectations from life'
In a cold climate, when you're born less than beautiful and severely
visually handicapped.

Traditionally, the English don't like overt displays of self pity,
The ones who aren't suffering believe you should suffer in silence
And grittily soldier on and not embarrass or depress people around
You; and if you can't do that then you should go and disp ose of
Yourself discreetly and politely.

A glaring example of someone exposing their feelings in public
This week and getting a harsh backlash for it. Has been
Heather Mills-McCartney, the lady who married a Beatle and
Who's now paying a high price of vilification for daring to
Divorce him. She broke down on daytime TV, saying she's had
Worse press than a murderer or a paedophile, and all she's
Ever done is work for charity.

Maybe when it's all over she could marry me? Her one whole leg
Being more than an adequate match for my one partially sighted
Eye? She's still a bonny-looking lass at 39, and I'm like a sour old
Wine aged in the wood. Money wouldn't be a worry for me,
I'd happily live off what she got out of 'Macca'; it's said she could
Walk away with up to 200 million quid…Maybe he'll pen another
'Yesterday' to recoup his losses…? 'Yesterday I had 800,000,000 to
play with, now she's taken 25% away, oh how I long for the day
before yesterday.'

Phil Fletcher-Stokes.

And that should be it, it's no joke slaving away with a notepad and
pen, hoping that one day you might make a few bob out of your
efforts; nothing like the execrable 'Macca' of course, but enough so
you could go and live out the rest of your days in comparative luxury
away from here where it's dark and cold 9 months of the year.
5/11/07. This would have been Guy Fawkes 402nd birthday if he
hadn't met such a terrible fate, I know I wouldn't like to be hung,
drawn and quartered…mate.

....

The word 'black' features quite strongly in the next couple of items;
firstly I have sent work to BLACK SPARROW BOOKS this year,
the press that was originally set up to publish Charles Bukowski, and
if you haven't heard of him then tough shit. Can you imagine
someone having so much faith in you they'd set up a publishing
house to promote you? Both the publisher and the author are dead
now, and times and attitudes have moved on, I had no response
whatsoever from the new Black Sparrow Books people. Luckily for
me I've got so much faith in my own abilities that I've set up my own
'press' thanks to the Internet; I am now THE BLACK SUN ePRESS,
I have a blog site at blogger.com, user name errolfinn, and I'm
registered with Lulu ePublishing and Publishers Portal. That's all I
can do right now, I can't promote my career any more; but I would if
I could. 6/11/07.

....

'BLACK' JACK KEROUAC, he's no relation to 'BLACK JACK
SHELLAC. 11/10/07.

Jack Kerouac's turned black, his body's mouldering in its grave;
He gave his life for his art and died of a broken heart, spurred on by
Alcoholism. Dead and broke aged 47 (he only had $91 when he died),
And now his 'estate' from 'ON THE ROAD' is worth $20 million;
I wonder whose earthly life has been turned into a no-money-worries
Heaven thanks to that cruel twist of fate.

I read 'ON THE ROAD' 37 years ago, I don't think it affected me
As much 'THE TICKET THAT EXPLODED' or 'THE ELECTRIC
KOOLADE ACID TEST', or even the masterly 'ONE FLEW OVER
THE CUCKOO'S NEST.' Jack's ultimate creation encapsulated
The vibe of the beat generation, the school of cool and literary
onanism.

It became a pest to him once it took off, like a TB sufferer's cough;

Written in 1947, the blighted year I was born; it was booted out
Publishers offices for the next 6 years (that fact warms the cockles of
my
Atrophied heart), and by the time it reached its zenith Jack was
already
In his creative nadir.

I've never been able to finish any of his other books, I found them
just
Too boring; that's the problem with an alluring best seller, like 'THE
GREAT GATSBY' for instance, or 'BABYLON' by David Grey, or
'YOU'RE BEAUTIFUL' by James Blunt; everything else you do
Fades into pale insignificance by comparison.

....

MY SOLILOQUY.

I wonder how Mr Kerouac would fare in the UK today (I don't know
What it's like in the USA), where you can't say what you think, not
unless
You've got a good drink inside you and when you sober up there'll be
all
Hell to pay; you'll have to hide away from the baying mob and lose
Your job.
Now for instance, if I
said..
I'd be socially dead and buried in the blink of an affronted eye; I
wouldn't
Need to die from encephalitis or spondylitis or even aggravated
arthritis,
The politically correct lobby would hang me out to dry before
hanging me
High on their gallows of moral indignation.
I'm a stranger in my own nation now, I don't know what makes it
tick
Anymore, I get by on the good old days of '60s nostalgia when I was
young
And free; I did (not intentionally for the most part) try drinking
myself to
Death, mixed in with other toxic substances as well. But apart from

Suffering a physical and mental hell I seem to have been spared.
Spared to live on alone in this solipsistic age, to rage against the injustice of
My life; no wife or offspring to love me, no self worth to speak of, merely
A desire to hold out for as long as possible before my immune and nervous
Systems completely cave in. I want to taste success after the mess of blues
That's been my lot so far, I'd rather have a beautiful lady to drive my car
Than the car itself.
I hope I live long enough to be the sexagenarian and septuagenarian
Version of Russell Brand and worth a million grand.

Phil Fletcher-Stokes. (Stokes was my mother's maiden name and what ever creative energy I've got must come from her, she's been dead for the last 21 years; I certainly didn't get it from my late father (dead 1 year), he gave up the creative ghost long before he gave up on his life; tho' he was a very talented man...maybe my mother killed his spirit years ago, they were always having blazing and destructive rows, turning the family home into a battleground, me and my sisters all had nervous ticks. 6/11/07.

....

MY 'FRIEND' JACK SHOULD EAT SUGAR LUMPS COATED IN CYANIDE.
(I know I can't say that and hope to get away with it, but right now no one's reading me so I can say what I want. 6/11/07.)

Any English person will have heard of Jack Straw, he's a politician who's been around for far too long, and he's held various posts in the current Labour administration; right now he's the Justice minister. A few weeks ago I heard him say on the radio that he wants to make it a crime to incite hatred against homosexuals; I was incensed. I wrote to him saying, 'Why don't you make it a crime to be heterosexual except for procreative purposes?' I also pointed out that there was nothing natural or normal about homosexuals wanting to insert foreign bodies into each others anuses;; I'm certain that anal sex is bad for both sexes, now a little rimming maybe, even though it's a very rude practice.

I also said that in any other profession than politics he'd have been booted out years ago, the man whose catchphrase is: 'Hang on!' I rounded off my blistering tirade by saying he's a useless waste of space and I was omitting my address because I didn't want a communication from him on any level.

For all I know, MI5 could be watching my every move right now……..?

....

The title of this collection is: EXISTENTIALISM (A FREE AGENT IN A MEANINGLESS UNIVERSE.). The next piece emphasises the fact that I believe in freedom of expression even, if at times, this is quite unpalatable; I always put a disclaimer on the covers of my collections, and I do exercise a certain level of self-censorship.

OMNIPOTENT, OMNIPRESENT, OMNISCIENT OMNIVORE THAT'S ME…ONLY JOKING, I'M A MEGALOMANIAC REALLY. 4-7/11/07.
(A desultory chat with myself.)

On a level of tedium I equate the necessary, from time to time, the chore of giving myself a pedicure (scraping off the hard dead skin and giving the nails a trim) on a par with defrosting the fridge; a job I always put off till I can no longer get into the freezer compartment for accumulated ice.

I feel constantly that my freedom is under threat from totalitarian fascists, climate change, global warming, potential famine thru' drought or flood, and government gagging orders on freedom of expression, like Jack Straw wanting to make it a crime to incite homophobic hatred. If 'gay' people (mainly men) accepted the fact that what they do is unnatural and depraved, and were prepared to keep a low profile in public instead of flaunting their activities as 'normal', such as fostering and adopting children (for sexual grooming purposes I suspect) and 'civil partnerships.'…These people are deviants, make no bones about it.

336

There's an American writer called Denis Cooper, one of the few writers I find really disturbing to read; in fact the last book of his I got out of the library to read, I couldn't face it; one line from it that's stuck in my memory is: 'Carl knew how to access the evil in me', and we all know where that kind of diabolical teamwork can lead, take this English girl who's just been murdered in Italy for instance, it's been done through an unholy alliance... He writes about the dark, dehumanised side of human nature, like necrophilia and child rape by a homosexual parent.

Another writer from the 19th century, JK Huysmans (the only other writer I know with the initials 'JK' is JK Rowling, and I'd say she's in league with the devil over her accrued wealth through the abominable Harry Potter phenomenon), he wrote a book about Gilles de Rais, reputedly the most evil man in the history of France; he was a former field marshal of France and fought with Joan of Arc. He conducted a medieval reign of terror of terror against the French peasantry, murdering about 800 women and children for sexual pleasure in the name of alchemy? (It's a long time since I read the book.)

On Monday night on C5 at 10pm I watched half of an hour long documentary about a German cannibal who's currently serving time for murder. Fate made it possible for him to link up with a man who had an overwhelming desire to be eaten alive. When they met up they had 'gay' sex, which the 'victim' didn't like very much. The next step, by mutual consent, was for the cannibal to cut the man's penis off and cook it for their consumption. The cannibal said the man let out a piercing scream for about 30 seconds after it was done but then he said it no longer hurt, the blood gushed out. The severed penis proved to be a gastronomic letdown when it was cooked, it was so fresh it shrivelled up;. The cannibal eventually finished his willing victim off by cutting his throat, he cut the body up and kept the choice cuts in his freezer for his own consumption.

Before he was tracked down and arrested, this particular cannibal had eaten about 40lbs of human flesh, he said it tasted like pork but with a richer flavour (putting Hannibal Lecter in the shade I presume.) It's human monsters like this, totally devoid of ordinary human emotions, and completely dehumanised, who quite often get jobs as 'state torturers' or even killers because they're impervious to feelings of pity or shame.

Last night (6/11/07) Gunther von Hagens was back on C4's AUTOPSY: EMERGENCY ROOM, 11pm. What disturbed me more than the dissections (one frozen corpse was cut in two from head to genitals with an electric saw, it was a bit gruesome when the two halves fell apart; but this cadaver was frozen stiff so there was no blood or guts) was the use of a naked male model, a live one. I didn't want to look at his cock all the time, there was no need for it; especially when he lay on the floor on his back and parted his legs slightly so a paramedic could demonstrate doing mouth to mouth resuscitation on him and he gained an erection. (The erection bit isn't true.)

Last Sunday night I stayed up late to watch THE SKY AT NIGHT on BBC1, it's a long time since I've seen Sir Patrick Moore, he must be about 90 now and he's one of those national fixtures, like the queen; god help us when she snuffs it, we'll have to endure weeks of official mourning I suppose.
Anyway the topic was galaxies colliding, it seems that the Andromeda galaxy which is over 2 million light years away from us, is heading on a collision course with the Milky Way galaxy at some unspecified date in the future, billions of years away actually. A thought that intrigued me was, is there the remotest possibility that the human race could survive for a billion years? It's about 2.5 million years since homo sapiens first stood upright, quite possibly gazing up at the Andromeda galaxy, and look at us now, on the brink of destroying this planet's whole ecology through over-breeding and self centredness
I also thought after watching the autopsies, where one corpse lay on the dissecting trolley with his mouth permanently open while his chest was cut open; if the human soul doesn't leave the body at the point of death then the whole concept of immortality is just a myth to protect ourselves against the horror of dying. When I was younger I'd have been crying at the thought of such a dreadful prospect of total annihilation after death, now I'm too disillusioned with life to care very much.

Phil Fletcher-Stokes.

....

THE FATE CONTROLLER   9/11/07.
9Definitely my last creative piece for the foreseeable future.)

You can't hear it, see it or smell it, but you know it's there,

338

The fate controller.

Days when you wake up in a really shitty frame of mind,
You're wound up tighter than a fishes behind, you're going to find
It hard to have a kind thought towards anyone or anything.

Be afraid of a fate that hates you,
To be pursued by something that's truly evil and inhuman
That revels in your empty nights and delights in your every
misfortune;
But keeps you alive when all around you people who have a much
better
Reason to live, are dying horribly (Meredith Kercher is the latest
example
Of a young promising life being snuffed out in a random act of evil.)

Apart from my mother (and she had a funny way of showing it), I've
been
Unloved all my life; imagine my chagrin when I saw on TV the other
night,
The plight of a woman whose husband's been given 7 life sentences
For rape; his youngest was aged only 10, then 13 and 14, his oldest
was 52.
She's managed to forgive him in her mind and is determined to wait
for him
Despite the fact he was only using her as a front, and would have had
sex
With her teenage daughter, his step daughter, if she'd been willing.

My fate controller has decreed that every time I get close to a woman,
Something will go wrong to fuck it up; a pattern that's unceasingly
Never erred, but I would never have dared to turn into a homicidal
Misogynist. It takes a lot of physical effort to bump someone off
unless
You shoot them; and then you've got to get rid of the body and try
And avoid detection.

I don't get an erection at the sight of blood, I'm a romantic by nature
And a good person. But I think it helps in this day and age not to let
Yourself be upstaged in the shockability stakes; I'll absorb whatever
It takes to show me just how horrific and depraved the human race
Can be.

Ideally I'd like to have used my life to have had a wife and kids, procreations
Why we're born, but my sense of eugenics and aesthetic appreciation has
Made me realise that I couldn't countenance siring ugly children even if
They had mellifluous voices and inquiring minds.
In my mind's eye I fantasise about being 23 for an eternity, to be free to drink
And smoke and screw like a late '60s hippy would do; a beautiful person
In body and soul, like Jim Morrison before he got bloated and fat. I wouldn't
Want to die a bohemian death unless it came with a phoenix-like rebirth.
I would like to be on an earth like I've described in 'MY HIPPY HEAVEN',
Your job now is to find it in this (for some) godless world.

Phil Fletcher-Stokes.

....

I submitted this leter for THE HALIFAX COURIER by email, asking that my name and address be omitted for personal safety fears, knowing how malicious motorists can be; but they said they couldn't or wouldn't print it without some form of id' on the letters page:

yoursay@halifaxcourier.co.uk

I think the most ignored vehicle regulation of all has to be: 'A motorist must not make more noise than could be avoided by using due care and attention,' especially if the roaring of engines and hissing and squealing of air brakes from the buses (both large and small) constantly moving along Market Street is anything to go by. The resulting stress and strain to the ears and nervous system from this near permanent noise pollution is horrendous, and most of the time these buses are riding round almost empty.
All drivers, it appears to me, think its their natural right to cause as much nuisance as they like through noise and air pollution, especially

on busy roads and even on otherwise quiet streets; the biggest culprits are motorbikes and sportscars, police and ambulance sirens, which I liken to wailing banshees.

Whether you're aware of this pollution or not, it's still undermining your immune and nervous systems. I have to endure a constant vehicular din from Skircoat Road, and in the street where I live there's a culture of: 'Why close a car door if you can slam it shut?' The effect that this mindless, aggressive attitude from motorists has on me is, I find it difficult to concentrate, I get ringing in my ears and a band of pain round my scalp which is probably migraine. I think a serious national debate about this level of noise pollution is long overdue; the legislation needs to be updated or enforced more rigorously.

Phil Fletcher-Stokes.

....

DOUBLY DEAD. 14/10/07.

Kurt Cobain made sure he was doubly dead when he decided
To blow a hole in his head; he filled an arm with liquid lead
Poisoning at the same time. It was a family tradition to make
Sure you killed yourself twice, to ice your body and your soul;
So that when you re-submerge, you turn up in the deepest hole in
Hell as a mindless zombie (like a typical supporter of the politically
Correct party), where you'll stay for eternity with your mouth
Hanging open.

Phil Fletcher-Stokes.

....

SOPHISTICATED SOPORIFICS. 14/10/07.

Richard Hawley might have the edge on Katie Melua when it comes
To sleep inducing relaxation music, but I know which one of them
I'd rather make love to. (Do you?)
What would it take for me to get into Katie's head enough to get her

Into bed? She's an alpha female and I'm a z-list nobody whose
Life race against death is 3 parts run. Even one night with Katie
would
Make up for the decades of 'no fun' I've had to endure;; one night
with
Katie would make up for the last 35 Christmas mornings I've woken
Up alone, with only a spot of onanism to look forward to as the day
Wears on.

Phil Fletcher-Stokes.

....

This next piece has appeared at the end of COPING WITH
MADNESS, but I'm now in the process of rounding everything off, so
it's appearing here as well.

STRANGLEHOLD. 29/9/07

The difference between sexual biology and psychology is sensitivity,
And an over sensitive male does not make the ladies hot; recreational
Sex is the best outlet for stress that we've got. I only ever hit the G-
spot
Once in my prime, and now that I've got lots of time to think about
sex
I've got a hex on my libido.

I'm lying in bed listening to music inside my head, courtesy of my
Faithful old personal stereo radio cassette player earphones. I feel
Sorry for people who've never discovered the delights of radio;
Other than Radio 1, the 'yoof' station to which my listening days
Have long since gone; tho' I'm still partial to a spot of Judge Jules
Or Pete Tong.

Before 'Dance' and/or 'House' music came along my interest in
Pop music had virtually gone, I was stuck in a time warp around
Al Stewart's 'YEAR OF THE CAT'; music took on a much harsher
Tone after that with the advent of 'punk' and much worse still to
come,
The 'thrash' and 'death metal' scum for instance, as well as the 'new'
Romantics.

Generationally speaking, I'm far too old to supposedly
Enjoy 'Dance music'. I'd look like a really sad old git
If I tried 'larging it' in Ibiza or Falaraki, but this new
Psychedelic sound with its pumping, thumping rhythms,
Really does it for me; and I envy the care-free young who
Can party all nite long and get away with it.

I think euthanasia should be a routine tool in the fight
Against senility; once you've become incontinent and
Insane you should be put out of your misery humanely,,
Not kept 'alive' because society doesn't want to be seen
As harsh or judgemental. Pity the poor carer of an
Advanced case of Alzheimer's disease say I, I'm sure
There are times when they want to die as much as the
Actual sufferer.

It should be the quality and not the quantity of human life
That counts, but we're living in an age where extremism
Rather than enlightenment dominates, the politics of fear
And hate are driven by a determined few; oppressive regimes
Could be removed by a million pairs of angry feet on the street
Chanting, 'PEOPLE POWER, PEOPLE POWER!' Military
Dictatorships can't hold out against a sheer weight of numbers,
This is a historical fact.

Aged 60, I'm now concentrating on my own personal paradise,
My version of the after life might differ greatly from yours.
It'll be just me aged 23, and a whole harem of beautiful women
Living miles apart in an idyllic green and lush setting, letting me
Play lord and master whenever I deigned to pay them a visit.
There'll be no mechanical noise of any kind, just magical colours
And the best music I can find in my youthful eternity.

Phil Fletcher-Stokes.

....

THE FEAR OF IMPENDING DEATH, AN OBSTACLE TO MY
MATERIAL HAPPINESS. 18/9/07

I've 'dissed' you so in order to make me pay you're going to have to spray my splattered brains around my shattered skull with a few well aimed wallops with/from a baseball bat, you educationally subnormal twat…unless I get you first!

At worst I could only come off second best, done in by a pestilential threat to society; the only thought you ever had was, 'If I act head enuf they'll be shit-scared o' me,' which is patently true. Who, in their right mind, wouldn't be terrified of a 'knuckle dragger along the pavement' like you?

....

(Anal sex and double penetration are Britain's most popular porn' right now, apparently.)

A LIMERICK TOO FAR (MOST LIKELY) IN THIS ANALLY RETENTIVE AGE OF FALSE MORALITY. 17/9/07

There was a young lady from Kent, who knew what
Reggie meant when he asked for a bit of what she'd vowed
To give up for Lent.

He said he'd spent a fair amount on scent (from the 99p shop naturally),
Which he wanted her to spray around her fundament, so he could
Stick his tongue where a tongue doesn't naturally belong; but she said
'No!' so he went before he came.

Determined to seek pleasure wherever he could, he got 'wood' just by
Looking at scantily clad models in a shop window display; he ended up
Pulling his pud just before daybreak in front of the erotically garbed
Manikin of his choice, panickin' lest a cop car went cruisin' past.
He was pumpin' hard and fast in the pre dawn light, fighting the good
Fight against flaccidity at the futility of his wrist action.

There was no real interaction between himself and this stoney-faced
Wench, she continued to stare blindly out in front of her; not seeing
His features blur momentarily in an orgasmic wrench.

A really discerning eye would have caught her smirking slyly as he
Bent to pull back up his hastily dropped pants.

Phil Fletcher-Stokes.

....

24/9/07.   I watched a programme on Tuesday night called 'TRIBE'
(BBC2). This guy called Bruce Parry goes to remote parts of the
world where tribes of people still live Spartan lives compared to ours.
I think he's mad for the most part, as are the people he goes and
stays with, with their bizarre and macabre customs; the worst thing
I've seen him do is drink warm blood drained from a cow's neck, the
thought of it makes me want to gag. Last week he ate a piece of still
steaming liver from a freshly slain Kudu deer, gruesomeOn Tuesday
night he was up in the mountains in Tibet where for once he was able
to keep his clothes on. He stayed with some pleasant tribes people
who are Buddhists, and one of them said that if you've behaved
really badly in a past life, you will return to this one either as an
animal, a demon, or a hungry ghost; I've been a hungry (for love)
ghost most of my life. The Buddhist 'monk' also said that the main
teaching of the Buddha was/is: 'The root of all our suffering is
desire.' Bruce took this on board after he failed to make it over a
snowed up mountain pass to his next village destination. He and his
team tried for about 5 days but had to give up when his yaks refused
to go any further; he adopted a philosophical viewpoint from then on
and contented himself with spending more time back at his first
village.
I reckon that the root of all my suffering is down to UNFULFILLED
desire, 'It's a killer, man.' (I'm experiencing some unfulfillable desire
right now in the form of a young library assistant sitting not very far
away from me.)

THE NEW GODS.

The new gods interests are at odds with the welfare
Of the planet, they're siphoning off its life blood, no good
Can come of it. What will be the good of personal wealth
When the health of the world is beyond repair?

They're in league with the devil, these new gods;
If they ever had souls they've sold them long since.

The only quest for a 'golden fleece' today is the so-called
'golden handshake' for taking as much out of the communal
pot as you can, while putting nothing back in but a belch and a
fart of fetid air.

I'm not making a moral statement here, I'm no Buddha-like
Saint, I'm tainted with as much greed lust as the next wannabe
Capitalist.

Phil Fletcher-Stokes.

....

IF YOU CAN READ MY MIND, HOW COME I CAN'T READ YOURS? 4/9/07.

I don't know how this one's going to flow, I only know that with a
title as good
As this, I can't let it go. I know what I'll do, I'll show you how
psychic everyone
Is bar/but me, even tho' realistically don't know how to do this. I've
had telepathy,
Esp, and black magic aimed at me, it's known as being under psychic
attack.

I am now paranoid to the Nth degree, who wouldn't be when they've
had to fight
Like an American Pitt Bull Terrier for every inch of ground they
occupy?
Sink or swim, live or die, and no one giving a damn whether you float
or lie
At the bottom of the ocean.

I't's been like a slow unstoppable descent into Hell, with constant
recurrences of
De ja poo wherever I go on the way down.
I even moved 6000 miles away to try and find some peace of mind,
but the same
Kind of harassment followed me from move to move; I moved 4 times
in 7 months
To escape other people's noise; ranging from the traffic's roar to
loud bass late at

Night, and worst of all, prolonged building work in the premises next door to
Where I finally chose to live. There was no give and take, it was all take and no
Give.

Eventually it got so bad for my health that I couldn't stand being there any more,
So I flew back here to the UK, I had no home to come back to. Luckily as I was
Getting off the train at Halifax station, I remembered someone who might be able
To help me out of my sticky situation.
And now I'm living on Psycho Street where the creatures eyes meet warily before
Backing off, like the primal Komodo Dragon, and their primal urge to splurge
Gives free rein to its appetite for causing neurological pain by never closing a door
If you can slam it, house or car. Never drive a vehicle in a reasonable manner if you
Can make it grunt, growl or roar, and let your rat brats kick the loudest football
You've ever heard up against their neighbours house door or car.

I might have strayed a bit far from defining the title of this piece, but I know
There are dark forces at work against me; even as I've been writing I've had
One sliver of hate infiltrated into my left ear, it would have drawn blood if it
Could (left for hate, right for love), and the neverending pattern of my not
Being able to find any real tranquillity wherever I go, continues to stalk me.
Of course if I had money I could at least take care of this aspect of my life;
I'd find a private house and garden where I could follow the changing
Seasons with my soul. But I seem destined to spend the whole of my existence
On earth on my own and with a serious shortfall of cash; people have dashed

Their brains out for a lot less provocation. Maybe I'll get an explanation
From God when I go back to Heaven and sit at his right hand…and I'm not even a believer.

Phil Fletcher-Stokes.

....

THE UNKNOWN POETS (SOSIGHATEAR) SOCIETY. 1/9/07.

I love it when I see that such and such a poetry magazine has 'ceased publication'; it reassures me to know that setting up a poetry mag' is still a risky and precarious business.
You won't have any shortage of contributors, it's subscribers you might find hard to enlist, most poets are hard up egotists; they're not willing to pay for stuff that isn't of their own creating, or is it me merely prating on and underestimating the potential target market out there?
Last night I heard Radio 4's first poetry 'slam', a decade after this phenomenon first began; I'd like to say that the standard was egregious (outstandingly bad) but that would only make me a sad liar. If anything it should have reassured me that I'm not alone, that there are other aspirants to the throne of the muse out there; but I hate all other rhymers, I hope they all get Alzheimer's and leave the coast clear for me.
That's not very nice of me is it? I've learned the hard way that being nice and trusting only gets you dumped on from a great height; and when you're left all brown and smelly, you won't have a literary friend left in sight; not that they ever were really your friends to start with.
It's the devil take the hindmost 'dear boy', the only thing losers take first prize in is humiliation and pain, and a constant nagging doubt in their brain: 'Should I have chosen another profession instead? Like cleaning up after the dead who've messily destroyed themselves for instance?'

Phil Fletcher-Stokes

....

HI TECH WRECK.   28/8/07.

When all your hopes and aspirations have gone, like lambs to the slaughter, their bloody corpses still lying tits and bloated belly up in the water, and suicide is the only decent option left open for yer to choose, you can still stick two fingers up to your evil fate thru' deriving some pleasure from eating, drinking and shagging...even if the latter can only be achieved by using hand relief; I know I do.

Phil Fletcher-Stokes.

....

I wrote the above piece while lying in bed, (obviously I sat up to apply pen to paper), with my trusty earphones in, listening to my personal stereo radio tuned in to Radio 3's 'IN TUNE', where the fabulous John Williams was playing live; you know, the world famous classical guitarist?
Earlier on I'd been terrorised by two thuggish 'neighbours'; the type of cretins who've learned how to terrify their neighbours and depress people. The first incident happened in the street from the rooming house opposite; he used his car as a loaded weapon, gunning the engine while at the same time pumping out loud and aggressive 'drum and bass', total anathema to my ears.
The other anti social nuisance occupies the room across from me (he's been there about 3 years, I've lived in this seedy 'guesthouse' for 8 weeks.) He announces his return to the house by slamming the heavy communal front door to the property, which causes both a shock reaction through my room and through myself.
I'm not sure if either of these unpleasant individuals is vieing for position of 'King Rat' over me? They're certainly twat-brained enough to qualify...it looks as though I might have to move again.

Errol Finn, the man who left all hope behind when into this world he did enter.

PS. I have moved, I have a lovely flat, but I'm still feeling vaguely terrorised by this breed of subhuman scum whose existences serve no purpose whatsoever; they're parasites living off the misguided softness of their betters; I'd like to see them destroyed like the vermin they are. 4/12/07

....

CADAVER PHUN UNDONE. 16-17/8/07.
(The human race as it is today isn't worth the destruction of the planet's eco systems.)

When you're dead you can lie in bed and never get warm under the duvet; eventually your head will rot away and day after day will come and go with varying degrees of light and shade, in a rundown shack in an overgrown green glade, and no one will ever come and look for you.

In my afterlife fantasy will reign supreme, and my mind's eye shall live the dream.

And once safely passed over to the other side I might spend a short eternity pondering on what happened to me before I died. Why it was decreed by a callous fate who thought so little of me, it allowed me to go on living alone for the whole of my earthly existence? Putting nothing but harmful temptations in my way, some of which I almost fatally succumbed to, like drink, tobacco, hallucinogenic and prescription drugs, and tainted sex partners.

Only music and the written and performed word saved me from a deeper living hell, as well as a belief in a higher level of spiritual attainment; a sorely tried longing for the magic of love which was always kept tantalisingly out of reach, except for the beach of Nico's 'Desert Shore'.

And if I'd died of a broken heart from lack of recognition of my
artistic merits, like Bizet for instance, instead of living on in a trance
of disillusion and confusion; Id be in the good company of the great
losers throughout history.

Even the dreaded Alzheimer's (the brain dying) can't be that bad
after a while, for the sufferer at least; you simply forget you've got it
or who you are or ever were, or what your bladder and bowels are
for before you sink into oblivion forever more...a zombie in paradise.

And even the dreaded Alzheimer's... Hey! Hang on! Didn't I already
write that I'd gone out to lunch in a previous life with a wife named
Polly Phemus, a one-eyed lady with a Venus mound to die for?

Actually I think I died from boredom, ennui, mood indigo, lassitude,
living the same old show too many times for any one person to bear;
even writing this puts me in despair of ever finding peace of mind.

If only with hindsight at the point of birth I'd seen what was in store
for me, I'd have cosen to be anything other than what I've become.
I'd have worked hard at being a disabled victim, grovelling for
sympathy on any female breast I could suck on.
Phil Fletcher-Stokes

THE BACK STREETS OF HALIFAX.   13/8/07
(Mentonymy, [when different words have a similar meaning] 'Are
you calling me a cunt? 'No, I'm calling you a twat!')

I'm not here because I want to be, I'm here because I have to be;
Fame and fortune elude me. I could enjoy living here if there wasn't
An atmosphere of thinly veiled hostility around me.

If you don't have a violent nature but are forced to eke out your
Existence among those who view violence as a viable option to
Sort things out, including you, what can you do except tread
Rather carefully?

It wouldn't bother me too much if I could see well enough to
Defend myself, I've got killer fists and a pretty hard head; I just
Don't want to end up dead at the hands of some pointless psychos',
Like what happened to Christopher Marlowe. Shadowy figures
Coming out of their own darkness to beat you to death without

Exhaling a breath of remorse afterwards.

A typical example of raw testosterone over soothing seratonin
Is the wife-murdering psychopath Billy Dunlop. She laughed at him
One drunken night so he killed her like Bill Sykes slaughtering
Nancy (in Oliver Twist.)
Dunlop hid his young wife's body under the bath in their house, of
All places, where it lay undiscovered for 3 months despite intensive
Police searches; the body was finally detected by the dead young
Woman's mother investigating an awful smell around the bath.
Dunlop also nearly murdered a man who'd crossed him, presumably
For not showing him enough 'respect.'

'Respect' in the eyes and minds of 'men' like Dunlop, amounts to
Fear and submission. They view violence and intimidation as a
Means of gaining 'respect'. Their brute ignorant stupidity might
Terrify me but intellectually they don't frighten me; I would
Like to show them zero tolerance as a breed and if necessary,
Use other trained psychopaths to control them.

Of course, if I had plenty of cash (like a much longed for win on
The lottery for instance) I'd be out of here in a flash, putting a safe
Distance between myself and this paranoid environment, making the
Most of whatever time I have left on this tortured earth.

It's already too late for my physical health, it's only my willpower
That keeps me going; the wear and tear of my daily stress is showing
Thru' every pore. I've had more emotional overdoses than Kurt
Cobain
Had heroin Ods. I've been on my knees praying for death to release
me
From my life-long sufferings. The day before my 60th birthday was
one of
The worst I've ever had, if I'd had a syringe full of liquid Nembutal
I'd
Have gladly used it to stop myself from feeling utterly sad.

Phil Fletcher-Stokes.

....

6/12/07. I did send out 4 copies of this letter and poem to 4 different newspapers, 2 here in the UK, The Times and the Daily Mail, and 2 in America, The New York Times and The Washington Post, as well as one copy to the new PM, Gordon Brown; I had an official letter back from 10 Downing St, and a post card from the Daily Mail saying they couldn't use it, so the other 3 can fuck off.

It's also 12 months ago today that I set off for my new life in Thailand, I lasted 7 months of mainly misery, which I've tried to relate earlier in this collection. I'm now in a new flat but still with the attendant undercurrent of impending doom, thanks to the proles who I have to share a common space with. I've got an ample amount of money to live on, I'm not over-bothered about Xmas, this one will be the 36th I've 'celebrated' on my own; I've got 2 long weekends booked for the Scottish highlands early next year, and I've already booked a flight for Thailand next June; no one can call me a sad old loser with any justification now…can they?

Dear Mr Gordon Brown, PM/MP,

I would like the enclosed piece to be used as propaganda in the war against terror, both at home and abroad.

As a person with disabilities who's been classified as 'unrealistically fit for work' for a long time now, I would like to contribute to the needs of society in any way I can. I do believe that Alqaida and the Taliban, left unchecked, would be as big a force for global evil as Hitler's 3rd reich was. It pains me when otherwise intelligent people mock George Bush; how would they react if the Houses of Parliament and Buckingham Palace were bombed by hijacked planes? Would they sneeringly laugh that off and see it from the terrorists point of view?

Was the insurgency in Iraq just waiting to happen as soon as Saddam Hussein was removed? I'm shocked and grieved by the number of American troops who are dying there, their deaths have to mean something for the cynical free world don't they?

I think the other two greatest evils in the world today are 1/ random breeding among the most hopelessly poor globally, and 2/ the excesses of the super rich. We can't possibly hope to bring global warming under control until global over-population is reduced dramatically, tho' it looks like Nature's starting to do the job for us which serves us right; we're destroying everything else to fulfil our own greedy needs.

Being poor in the UK has its advantages, we don't squander as much as the rich.

Phil Fletcher-Stokes.

....

(The enclosed 'poem'.)

I'M EARNING MY STATE BENEFIT MONEY, ME. Or THE TWIN POWERS OF EVIL.
(Nowadays it's hard enough to love your fellow man, let alone the rest of humanity.)

People are dying and being horribly injured so that I can be free,
The politics of evil and terror mystify me, almost as much as the
Attitudes of cynical appeasement amongst the intelligentsia
Here in the West. Do they think that by burying their heads up
Their own fundaments, the cancer of evil and terror will go away?

Do they believe that a force capable of 9/11, Madrid, Mumbai
And 7/7 will go away if we continue to largely ignore it and mock
Those politicians both here and abroad who are prepared to be vilified
For opposing this new evil in the world, just as deadly as Hitler's 3rd Reich?

How would these appeasers fare under Alqaida and the Taliban?
They wouldn't be allowed to belittle Osamar, they'd be too busy
Trying to avoid his death squads; the ladies huddled inside their burkahs
Waiting to be painfully circumcised and de-educated; the men busily
Trying to grow beards and an ascetic and austere attitude to existence.

Seeing the state of things in our own death wish culture among the
Disaffected young, I sometimes wonder if our values of individual
Freedom are worth defending, and if a spell of austerity wouldn't do us
Good in a world soaked in blood?

Phil Fletcher-Stokes, the elder statesman of cock manipulation

....
....

PISSING IN A BOTTLE. (Different definitions of reality.)

Black Mamba Samba, when that snake comes looking for you, you'd better to be able to outrun it in a Latin American rhythmic styley.

Hip-Hop is pig slop and 'rap' is pernicious crap.

18/7/07. I'd been living on a diet of raw squid for a week in order to generate some urine with a really high ammonia content (PLF, this is pure speculation on my part, I've no idea if such a diet would produce this end result), the kind that makes your eyes water and your nose and throat smart.
The reason being, I wanted to fill a Chablis bottle with this foul-smelling piss, re-cork it and place it in a case of 12 bottles to be sent to that pretentious arsehole Sting and his delusional partner; celebs love freebies.. My hope was that they'd uncork this 'chablis' to enjoy before and during tantric sex, only to be deterred from this apparently pleasurable anticipation bby the horrid realisation that what was swirling round in their golden goblets wasn't a product of the grape but the end result of a life lived in the cold dark depths of the fathomless deep.

19/7/07. BASEBALL BAT THE TWAT. There isn't much that brings out the killer instinct more strongly in me than some fucker pissing on my head! Not literally of course but in the toilet directly above mine in a rooming house. With unerring regularity wherever I go there's always some insecure arsehole who thinks that by pitting itself against me, it will feel more manly; sometimes I don't even get to see the identity of these 'opponents', they remain an invisible, ominous threat to my sense of wellbeing. And I don't like violence or violent people, unless I'm watching WWE on TV.

19/20/7/07. A STIFFY IN A JIFFY. (I'm a Bonobo ape man, me.)

Contrary to popular myth and belief, there's nothing constant about the male sex drive, or is it just mine? We now know that certain women can take on a whole regiment (how many men are there in a regiment?) in one sex session. I f a guy can manage 4 or 5 times a night he's considered to be a real stud. Not too long ago I read about a 66-year-old man who married a 23-year-old woman and made love to her 23 times in one week; he's since had a mild stoke which has slowed him down a bit.

Recently while living in Thailand I fell for a 20-year-old Thai girl escort/waitress; I'm fairly certain that if I could have afforded to have her as my regular girlfriend I could have been lining myself up for a stroke, but like all my encounters with women it ended badly. I did have another bar girlfriend but I never felt about her the way I felt about the first one; I didn't fancy girlfriend number 2 for sex (she was a bit fat and short and lost her 'glow' as soon as she left the security of the bar) but I liked her feisty nature and intelligence. I was also grateful for her company (even tho' I was paying for it), life could get very lonely out there due to the language barrier and living on a low income…just like here!

Back here in Halifax where I'm a fairly insignificant and invisible elderly male with silvery white hair, I'm lusting after young women all the time. I'm in danger of being seen as an 'old lech'', but inwardly I don't care, I fantasise a lot about having sex with young women; rude and raunchy sex, and my long-suffering penis will happily swell with male pride. And on these occasions I almost invariably end up 'pleasuring' myself. If any young people ever read this they might find it disgusting that a 60-year-old man still masturbates; I still have wet dreams too unfortunately.

………………………………………………………………………………
…………………….

MIGRAINE ALL IN MY BRAIN, CAUSING A PURPLE DAZE OF GNAWING PAIN.   12/8/07.
(Where there's no sense there's no feeling.)

The roaring of the brute beast on the highways and byways of our once
Green and pleasant land, the Satanists have got the upper hand, terrifying
Noise levels at their command.

And no one seems willing to lift a finger against them, these evil minded 'men'
Who think that creating extreme noise terror is just having a laff.
And when

356

They're not bellowing up and down the streets they're slamming
metal doors
Outside yours, or making the mating call of the honking car horn,
leaving
You wishing you'd never been born.

Maybe it's only me being over-sensitive to mindless, over-aggressive
behaviour
Which isn't necessarily confined to those with the lowest Iqs in our
warped society?
It seems to be a unisex macho way of reacting to overcrowding and
stress; 'The
World's in a fucked-up mess and no one's gonna mess with me unless
they're
Bigger and harder.'

I'm not into all that machismo crap, like 'hip hop' and 'rap' artists
are, another
Dischordant rant and roar signifying nothing 'y'all know wot I'm
sayin'?' Huh!
Personally, I'm praying for deafness or destruction to get sum relief
from this
Constant grief.

Phil Fletcher-Stokes.

(I'm going to e-mail a copy of this piece to 'POETRY PLEASE' on
Radio 4, a prestigious outlet that's a bit of a bore at times, it's hardly
'cutting edge'; it's the kind of English radio programme you can lie
in bed to on dark winter's early evenings and if you're not careful,
snore thru'.
I'd be terrified to hear a piece of mine read out on air, my over-
sensitive nature would tear me to shreds, claiming it was substandard
and poorly formed; yet the urge to share my genius with someone
else is overwhelming.
Perhaps if I claim to be Roger MaGough's love child from a former
life they'll read my poem out? I can hear my alter ego: Errol Finn
shout, 'Go on, give him a go, he's cutting edge you know; he deserves
a show all to himself as well as the glittering prizes that come with
recognition. Tradition move over and let Phil Fletcher-Stokes take
over

(There's another Jimi Hendrix-influenced line there, but I can't place in my deteriorating brain which of his songs it comes fom. No doubt my biographer will track it down, I think it's on his first LP.)

PF-S.

....

PROLE FOOD.   20/11/07.

Prole food isn't soul food or even wholefood, but it's cheap and filling,
Maybe that's why proles consume it in large quantities and have lots of
Health disorders; my desire to eat it borders on the miserly. And really,
If you have a strong constitution you won't find any better way of feeding
Your face. I consider it a personal disgrace that my stomach balks at
Nearly everything I eat; I've virtually cut out meat but even wheat based
Products cause me pain. But my guts will just have to continue to take the
Strain, there's no way I'm going to go on a diet of crispbread and water.

PF-S.

....

TWO HEADS AREN'T ALWAYS BETTER THAN ONE,
WHEREAS TWO EYES ARE.   29/11/07.

A couple of weeks ago I saw a reality TV 'show' about conjoined twins, the Hensel 'sisters'. I didn't catch the start of this remarkable programme, I wasn't even going to watch it, it was just that there wasn't much else on worth watching; it was on C5, still regarded as the poor relation to the other four terrestrial TV channels here in the UK, even tho' it's been around for at least 10 years now, maybe longer.

358

The Hensel 'sisters' are now 16, and they do have sweet faces on two heads on one body; classic fodder for a freak show, not that there are freak shows anymore, that would be much too un-PC thankfully. When I first saw this two-headed phenomenon my stomach turned over with shock and horror, if I'd seen these two 'girls' in the flesh it might well have unhinged me for a time, you just don't ever expect to see such a strange deformity outside of fantasy. The Hensel sisters have one body with two hearts and two sets of lungs and two different personalities; two halves of the same whole as far as I'm concerned; one head with an outgoing personality, the other one less so.

They are American and lead as normal a life as possible in a small town. They attend a normal school and have even been allowed to pass their driving test, which I think is wrong because in my opinion such a sight as a two-headed driver on the highway could prove to be a serious distraction to other motorists and cause accidents.

I've only got limited sight, I've also only got little 'piggy' squinty eyes, and for the first 47 years of my life my eyes were markedly crossed; even now this stigma hasn't been fully corrected and anyone who wanted to be cruel could still call me 'cross eyed'...and get a smack in the mouth...if I had a violent nature; and physical violence is very tiring as your body gets older, better to stab or shoot them.

When I was an overweight, oversensitive boy there was no such thing as 'political correctness', straight talking was the norm and I was quite often on the receiving end of it (even my own mother called me an 'ugly pig' once when I was about 11.) This was my choice, I never wanted to go to a 'special' school for the visually impaired, I wanted to be normal; I also had an introvert and an extrovert nature, and when I wasn't feeling sorry for myself I was out there and up for it. I broke a few pairs of specs' playing football and I was 'accepted' by a group of mates during my teenage years, though with reservations that I only slowly learned about.

My first love had always been girls, I adored the pretty and beautiful ones; my teenage years were made hellishly miserable because I never had a girlfriend, I was too ugly (presumably) to be seen out with. Also, a sadistic older sister had done a superb job of destroying what little confidence I might have had (I inflicted a similar humiliation on a much younger sister [much to my discredit], I have no contact with the remaining members of my family now.) I was 24 before I was allowed to 'sleep' with a not-over-glamorous, overweight lady; I've spent the whole of my adult life looking for love and a meaningful relationship...and I'm 60 years of age now, and all I've ever inspired is the losing end of an eternal triangle.

For a long time now I've had body dysmorphia regarding my face because of accumulated rejections over the years and I only see thru' one eye, my left (although there's some residual sight in my right), and I've become a virtual recluse because of it

My point is, how long will it be before these 16-year-old conjoined twins realise they can only ever be treated (outside of their family and friends) like freaks? They can never be separated physically and they can never live a normal life. My heart bleeds for them, maybe we could get together, heh heh heh!?

This might sound like an outlandish statement to make, a 60-year-old man leering after 16-year-old twin-headed girls, but I thought the DJ Chris Evans was out of line the other week when he said to an innocent 12-year-old girl who'd phoned in for a request on his early evening 'DRIVE TIME' show on Radio2: 'You're 12, I'm 41, where's that going to I wonder?' Was I the only one who heard him? I thought he should have been reprimanded for that remark, if not pulled off the air completely (I've never liked the ginger-haired [now almost white] bastard anyway.) Okay, he had Billie Piper when she was 18 or thereabouts, but a 12-year-old girl in his sights? That's going too far.

(I'm not moralising, just disapproving.)

PF-S

....
....

'SUNNY' TODMORDEN.   24/11/07.

'Sunny' Todmorden is a depressing dump, for the 9 years that I 'lived' there
I permanently had the hump.
But if it's any consolation, Mytholmroyd is the root of all desolation; as for
Sowerby Bridge, I'd rather live in a fridge.
Luddenden Foot? I'd be a complete nut job if I'd ever tried to eke out my
Miserable sojourn there.
Hebden Bridge and Midgely are where the diddly squat, piddly pot, pseudo,
Neuveau riche hang out their colours on the pantheon of new age bullshit

Science and quackery.
Which only leaves Halifax, everyone's council tax has been well spent in
Making it a pleasant environment for me to vegetate in; apart from the din
And bustle and the HELL that is other people. If it gets too bad I'll impale
Myself on the steeple above the town hall clock.
Oh, I forgot to mention Haworth and Heptonstall, the two most enigmatic
Places in this part of West Yorkshire, they combine everything villages
Should be, an air of mystery and history, (Sylvia Plath's buried out in a bare field in Heptonstall, I bet she's spinning in her cosmically aware grave at the injustice of it), Tho' nowadays these two historic havens are merely hollow shams, retaining
Very little authenticity; (especially Heptonstall, have you seen what the average rent is for a stone-built terraced 'weaver's' cottageYou'd have to weave round the clock 24-7, and even then you wouldn't be able to afford it.)

PF-S.

....
....
From the Halifax Evening Courier, Sat, 1/12/07.

REPORT EVERY SEXIST JIBE, SCHOOLS TOLD. By Colin Drury.

Schools will have to report all incidents of sexist, homophobic, disability and faith- related, and racist behaviour under a new equality scheme to be unveiled by Calderdale Council.
And schools that report fewer incidents than average may be investigated to see if they are compiling the data right or have effective equality policies in place.
Teachers and staff will be expected to record any behaviour that may fall into any of the categories so reports can be made to councillors at the end of each school year.
The new Calderdale Equality And Diversity Scheme will be piloted in the New Year and rolled out in full for the summer term to meet government guidelines set out in the Education and Inspections Act 2006.

It is hoped the initiative will help clamp down on bullying in schools and create a greater understanding of equality and community cohesion among young people.

Councillor Conrad Winterburn (Lib Dem, Greetland and Stainland) speaking at the council's Children and Young People Scrutiny Panel said: 'We need to make sure bureaucracy doesn't weigh too heavily on teachers. But as we've just had anti bullying week, this seems a positive step.'

....

This is my reply to the above, sent to <u>mailbag@halifaxcourier.co.uk</u>, but they don't print letters that don't come with an address and as I was posting this on to my blog at the same time, I didn't want to include it, so it might well have not appeared in the paper...which I only buy on a Saturday if at all for the 7-day TV listings:

I thought things were taking a sinister turn for the worse when 'FOX HUNTER' British fortified wine disappeared off the shelf at Netto and could only be purchased at the checkout; were they afraid the anti-hunting lobby was going to picket the store?

But this draconian action against Great British freedom to choose a very acceptable tipple openly, pales into nothing when compared to the latest government exercise in spreading total paranoia and intimidation, begun by David Blunkett and now being ably carried on by the 'justice' minister: Jack Straw. Straw already wants to make it a crime to incite homophobic hatred; like I said in a letter to him on this topic, 'Why don't you make it a crime to be heterosexual except for procreative purposes?'

The kind of measures proposed for schools in Calderdale read as close to George Orwell's nightmare vision of the future in 1984 as I've ever come across in this country, the home of free speech, or so I thought.

These proposals sound like a cross between witch-hunting and Big Brother, no one will be safe from being spied on in school; a complete atmosphere of fear and loathing will build up between teachers and pupils (if it doesn't already exist). 'Babes' will have to be vigilant about what comes out of their mouths, self censorship will become compulsory at the age of 5; and really dysfunctional 'brats' will have the added task of re-educating their totally unreconstructed parents. All this type of politically correct legislation does is to drive bullying, racism and homophobia underground, it doesn't eradicate it and is another nail in the already well screwed down coffin of freedom of expression. There might come a time in the not-too-distant future when letters to the Courier with the headline: 'THESE ROYAL HYPOCRITES' by Clarrie Shaw (nice one Clarrie) could be banned as inflammatory and liable to cause offence…to the royals, the over-privileged, over-wealthy wastes of space.

Make England a republic say I, with me as its first megalomaniac president; I'd bring back hanging and flogging for certain offences against society.

PF-S.

....

BRIGIT JOAN'S VERBAL DIARRHOEA.   6/12/07.
(The root cause of all my emotional nausea.)

A young lady worked so hard next to me in the library's Access room
For people with disabilities, doing something to library books, stamping
Them and ripping pages out, that I thought my head was going to
Spontaneously combust with her human dynamo-like efforts.

She made me feel really self conscious about my 2-fingered typing skills
And all the mistakes I kept on making; thank providence for the back space
Key or I'd have spent half my time there using Tipex, me, rubbing holes
In the paper on my portable 'typer' as used to be.

She's hyperactive and not entirely unattractive, if I could see better I'd be
Able to describe her features more accurately; but even at 60 I don't
Like to squint too obviously in order to get a good look, so I kept trying
To get a word in edgeways inbetween her frantic ripping and stamping while
I was working on my 'book': EXISTENTIALISM, my interpretation: a free
Agent in a meaningless universe.

It transpires she's into the film-making business after wasting 3 years at Uni'
Doing French, she's working part time in the Access room to help pay her
Rent. But it's only a stopgap situation, she will be moving on. 'Am I bovvered?'
I don't think so; I've only just fallen out of love with a black haired beauty who's
Worked in there a few times and really blew my mind. She should have been 'The
Woman I'm going to marry,' but she already is even tho' she doesn't
Wear her wedding ring at work. She's a writer too, initially I said the
Poem she let me read was good, but now there's no chance I'm going
To get her out of her pants I'm not so sure, I can't remember it
Anymore anyway.

She (the black-haired beauty) has aspirations of upward mobility,
I wonder what her hubby's like? I hope he's not the red-faced ginger
Minger computer tech' I've spoken to a few times in the past 4 years?
Women of her ilk with mannish personalities don't always judge
Their partner's worth by the cover; let's face it, if I could have
Coerced her into becoming my lover, this would have been a classic
Case in point.

I've already had brain sex about her with the hairy palm of my hand
Twice, (women hate that, they think it's not very nice), but when your
Cock's crowing in the dead of night and it won't go down until you've
Choked it by the neck, or else made yourself a nervous wreck by lying
There all hot and bothered, unable to sleep, having brain sex with her
Sure beats counting sheep. I've done things to her in my head that
Are barely legal, indeed weren't until a few years ago.
(Sex mafia 'snuff' and hardcore 'muff' junkies, don't get your hopes up,
I only wrote the above two lines for effect.)

The saddest part of this lament is that before my brain sex session
Can be spent, I've got to get out of my nice warm bed to find a hanky,

Because the end result of my cerebral hanky-panky's got to be wiped off
On something; I don't want that cold gloop on my Egyptian cotton sheet
When I'm glowing from my head to my feet from post coital warmth.
Now where was I………………..

PF-S?

………………………………………………………………

And now only two pieces left to go before this reworked collection is finished, thank fuck; I'm sick to death of typing. The next short item is a music review I've now got posted on play.com.. I think that's what I want to focus on from now on, posting stuff to get my name known.

Amos Milburn: BOOZE BABES BLUES & BOOGIE.

'I've just had my best rockin' boogie piano and sax' experience ever, and believe me I've had plenty of good rockin' piano and sax' in my time; not much sex but the effects of good music usually lasts a lot longer anyway.
If 'My Baby's Boogying' doesn't have you floating round your room in a paroxysm of cerebral orgasmic delite then I'm afraid you're emotionally frigid.
I like all the upbeat tracks the best: 'Down The Road Apiece', 'Chicken Shack Boogie' etc; the slower bluesier cuts are like post coital rockin' boogie piano and sax', depressing.   'rockin'plf3' (that's my tag.)

………………………………………………………………………………
…………………..

And of course I couldn't end on a cheerful note; I've very recently reread an old diary entry from 38 years ago when I was 22 in 1969. I wasn't happy then, but there are glaring extenuating circumstances to account for this depressing state of affairs: I was treated like a freakish pariah by women, my father was a raging psychopath who kept our home in a constant state of miserable tension, and then as now, I was waking up on Xmas morning on my own; this entry was my first attempt at a will. I've just rewritten my latest will on the back of a sheet of A4 paper at home, I'm leaving everything to WSPA, even the copyright of my work if they want it.

'I, John of Gaunt do hereby make my last will and testament, being in sound, vision, and working order.
1/ To those who are interested, I leave myself, to those who are not I leave heartache.
2/ To indifference towards me by people I leave sorrow; to my soul I leave hope of a better life elsewhere.
3/ To my long suffering penis and face, I leave an apology.
4/ To my mind I leave a crossroads with a clear definition of direction eventually.
5/ To all those I've wronged by judging them before knowing them (chance would be a fine thing), I leave a pile of stones with me underneath them.
6/ To myself as a person I leave all the unused love I had to give.
The void is bed and darkness and silence. (No change there then.)

EUREKA! I'VE FUCKIN' FINISHED!